MUSIC OF THE TWENTIETH CENTURY
STYLE AND STRUCTURE

BRYAN R. SIMMS

University of Southern California

SCHIRMER BOOKS
A Division of Macmillan, Inc.
NEW YORK

Collier Macmillan Publishers
LONDON

Schirmer Books
A Division of Macmillan, Inc.
866 Third Avenue, New York, N. Y. 10022

Collier Macmillan Canada, Inc.

Library of Congress Catalog Card Number: 85-27652

Printed in the United States of America

printing number
1   2   3   4   5   6   7   8   9   10

Acknowledgment is gratefully made to the following sources for the portraits of
composers appearing within the text:

The Bettmann Archive: Béla Bartók, Pierre Boulez, Benjamin Britten,
   Elliott Carter, Aaron Copland, Claude Debussy, Paul Hindemith,
   Charles E. Ives, Sergei Prokofiev, Igor Stravinsky

Malcolm Crowthers: Olivier Messiaen, © 1982 Malcolm Crowthers

Music Division, The New York Public Library at Lincoln Center, Astor,
   Lenox and Tilden Foundations: John Cage, Manuel de Falla,
   Gustav Mahler, Darius Milhaud, Francis Poulenc, Maurice Ravel,
   Erik Satie, Alexander Scriabin, Jean Sibelius, Karlheinz
   Stockhausen, Richard Strauss, Edgard Varèse, Ralph Vaughan Williams

New York Public Library Picture Collection: Ferruccio Busoni,
   Max Reger

G. Schirmer, Inc.: Arthur Honegger, Dimitri Shostakovich

Arnold Schoenberg Institute: Alban Berg, Arnold Schoenberg,
   Anton Webern

Library of Congress Cataloging-in-Publication Data

Simms, Bryan R.
   Music of the twentieth century.

   1. Musical analysis.   2. Music appreciation.
3. Music—20th century—History and criticism.
I. Title.   II. Title: Music of the 20th century.
MT6.S534M9   1986   780'.904   85-27652
ISBN 0-02-872580-8

To Shelley

CONTENTS

v

Vaughan Williams and Holst. Spain:
Manuel de Falla. The New World:
Copland and Other Composers in
the Americas. Popular Music of the
New World and the European
Composer. Bibliography.

PART THREE   MUSIC FROM 1945 TO
THE PRESENT

REPERTORY

The following are the musical works that receive primary attention in this book.

Chapter 1

Chopin, Prelude in A minor, op. 28, no. 2
Liszt, "Nuages gris"
Schoenberg, "Lockung," op. 6, no. 7
Schubert, "Kennst du das Land"
Wagner, Prelude to Act 3 from *Parsifal*

Chapter 2

Schoenberg, Piano Piece, op. 23, no. 4

Chapter 4

Boulez, *Structures Ia*
Schoenberg, String Quartet no. 4, op. 37.

Chapter 5

Berg, Monoritmica from *Lulu*, Act 1
Stravinsky, Sacrificial Dance from *The Rite of Spring*

Chapter 6

Bach, Ricercar from *The Musical Offering*, arranged by
  Anton Webern
Schoenberg, Orchestral Piece, op. 16, no. 3

Chapter 7

Berg, Four Songs, op. 2
Berg, "Lied der Lulu" from *Lulu*, Act 2
Busoni, *Sonatina secunda*
Mahler, Symphony no. 10, Adagio
Reger, String Quartet no. 5, first movement

Chapter 14

Berio, *Visage*
Druckman, *Animus III*
Pierre Schaeffer, "Étude aux chemins de fer"
Stockhausen, *Gesang der Jünglinge*
Varèse, *Poème électronique*

Chapter 15

Berio, "Black Is the Color" from *Folk Songs*
Berio, *Sinfonia*
Crumb, *Black Angels*
Peter Maxwell Davies, *Eight Songs for a Mad King*
Messiaen, *Couleurs de la cité céleste*
Rochberg, String Quartet no. 6

Chapter 16

John Adams, *China Gates*
Del Tredici, *Final Alice*
Del Tredici, *In Memory of a Summer Day*
Glass, *1 + 1*
Glass, *Einstein on the Beach*
Reich, *Clapping Music*
Riley, *In C*

INTRODUCTION

This book is a study of musical culture in the twentieth century presented through the examination of its outstanding works. No period in history exceeds our own in the diversity of its music: in it we will find much that is both sublime and shocking. We will be invited to hear in new ways and sometimes even required to redefine our notions of the function and limitations of music. But, in whatever may present itself as controversial in modern musical thought, we will look to the music itself as our true guide.

The discussion of music in this book will emphasize style and structure and the ways in which these two are related. What are style and structure? The totality of distinguishing features of a musical work or of a group of works constitutes its style. Style calls our attention to the differences among pieces of music; it brings into view the uniqueness of a language and the thumbprints that great composers leave within their works.

Structures, on the contrary, tend to be common property. They are often shared by many composers—even those living in different historical eras—and the same structures recur time and again in large musical repertories. A musical structure embodies a principle of expansion—that is, an underlying rationale for how and why the parts of a composition belong together. Structure in music is often perceived as an alternation of contrasting or similar parts. If we observe that a piece has the form A B A, we make just such a perception about similarity and contrast among its principal sections. But other compositional elements also act as structural components of a less schematic sort. Conventional harmonic progressions, tonal plans, and techniques of counterpoint and fugue, for example, provide structural frameworks in which pieces can be expanded.

Major changes in musical style during the twentieth century have been provoked by a series of "emancipations"—a term used by Arnold Schoenberg to describe his treatment of dissonance—by which new musical materials became available to the composer. The first of these seminal emancipations was of dissonance and key, followed by similar revolutions in rhythm, sound, and texture. Each of these liberations necessitated new structural principles which can be revealed by a careful examination of outstanding musical works.

This book will be divided into three parts: the first is a survey of compositional materials and current analytic principles by which structures of twentieth-century music can be perceived; the second and third parts examine the activities of major composers and masterpieces of their music in approximately chronological order. The theoretical part can function either as a preliminary to the later chapters or in coordination with them. The musical survey emphasizes original developments in style. Discussion concentrates on a few exemplary works of major composers; the analyses are intended to provide only a starting point for more detailed investigations. Sketches of the life and works of major composers are set apart from the text for easy reference.

It is strongly advised that readers of this book be provided with excerpts from the scores of works which are discussed. A representative sample of these will be found in the Anthology which accompanies this volume. It is also recommended that the text be supplemented by readings from essays by major composers. A brief sketch of literature (emphasizing sources in English) will be found at the conclusion of each chapter. The writings of some composers—among them Bartók, Cage, Carter, Copland, Hindemith, Messiaen, and Schoenberg—are especially valuable to a better understanding of their music and of the issues that have motivated them.

A single date given in parenthesis after the title of a composition is its date of completion. Works that underwent an unusually long period of composition will be identified by the dates when work on them was begun and ended.

The author is deeply grateful for the advice and support of several colleagues who have read and commented upon the manuscript. Special thanks go to my wife Charlotte Erwin, who read the entire manuscript and made invaluable suggestions, and to Donald Crockett, Janet Schmalfeldt, William Robinson, and Dean Suzuki.

◆

Structural Principles and Compositional Materials of Twentieth-Century Music

◆

◆ 1 ◆

TONALITY IN TRANSITION

Music in the first decade of the twentieth century experienced a profound upheaval which has proved to be one of the most momentous in the entire history of music. It was an eruption that soon reshaped the external physiognomy of music and established new principles for its internal organization. This transformation was felt throughout the world; it was precipitated by such diverse figures as Arnold Schoenberg in Vienna, Charles Ives in America, Alexander Scriabin in Russia, and Béla Bartók in Hungary. In the chapters that follow, we shall trace the contribution of these pioneers and the legacy of their innovations.

We can appreciate the profound newness of the musical world that they helped to create by comparing two works of the same genre and country of origin from before and after this stylistic change: Gustav Mahler's Symphony no. 8 (1906–1907)—called *Symphony of a Thousand*—and Anton Webern's Symphony, op. 21 (1928). The differences are pronounced. Mahler's symphony is gigantic in medium and length, its texts address no less an issue than the destiny of human spirit, and its musical argument is affirmative both in its purely musical sense of triumph and in its implicit statement about mankind. Webern's symphony, on the contrary, is by comparison diminutive of proportion, understated in content, and linked overtly to no subject outside of itself. Mahler's work breathes the air of romanti-

3

cism in its celebration of the heroic; Webern's work inhabits an intensely introspective musical world far removed from Mahler's grandiloquence.

These outward distinctions in style reflect many technical differences separating Mahler's musical language from Webern's. None is more striking than the use of *tonality* or *key* in the former and its absence in the latter. Mahler's work is in the key of E♭, a tonal focus that lends comprehensibility and unity to its diverse musical elaborations. Webern's symphony has no key and it relies for its understanding on other compositional principles. We turn our attention in this first chapter to the matter of key and its progressive reinterpretation by composers of the nineteenth and early twentieth centuries.

Common-Practice Tonality

Tonality in the common-practice period (roughly, the eighteenth and nineteenth centuries) was a system that guided and coordinated harmony and melody and that was influential as well upon rhythm, meter, form, and other elements of a composition. It was a common system to which virtually all major composers of this time subscribed, despite their differences in style. The central elements of a tonality are a fundamental tone (which identifies the key), the major or minor triad built upon this fundamental, and other notes of the major or minor scale having it as tonic. Via generally accepted compositional principles, these focal elements organize the major features of a harmonic and melodic argument and provide composers with a widely understood syntax for their musical speech.

Let us first examine a piece in which principles of tonality are normative and clearly in evidence. Schubert's song "Kennst du das Land" is one of many settings by composers of the romantic period of this text by Goethe. Its three stanzas are set to music by Schubert in a nearly strophic manner; the identical first two stanzas are shown in Example 1-1.

This song expresses the key of A by its harmonic and melodic components. We shall focus first upon harmony.

The basic chords of the work are triads drawn from scales of A major or minor (the parallel modes are used interchangeably by Schubert). These are organized on a large scale by the occurrence of the tonic triad at the beginning, the dominant triad toward the middle (measures 18 and following), and the tonic triad in the final two measures. Tonic and dominant harmonies are primary elements in the expression of key, and the large progression from I to V to I creates a harmonic superstructure that organizes and directs all of the other harmonic motions. This "tonic–dominant axis," as we shall call it, is a fundamental expression of tonality in any piece of music.

The space between these pillars of the superstructure is filled with other chords or temporary tonics. Between measures 1 and 18, for example, these intermediary chords guide our attention toward the dominant by a combination of melodic and harmonic processes. The harmonies that we encounter consist primarily of the flatted submediant F major (measures 12–15), prefixed by its dominant C major (measures 8–11). Both of these are drawn from the parallel minor, which prepares the listener for an overt turn to A minor at the beginning of the third stanza. Although we may consider the arrival in F major in measure 12 to be a modulation to a new key, the home tonality of A is still in effect at a higher level of organization. F major, although a temporary tonic, owes its harmonic meaning to the key of A, in which it functions as a preparation of the dominant.

The large-scale harmonic syntax that organizes the first half of the stanza is also reproduced on a smaller scale. Harmonies supporting the antecedent phrase of the opening period (measures 1–4), for example, progress from tonic (measure 1) to dominant (measure 4), which marks off a space filled by other triads that function as dominant preparations. The dominant chord in measure 4 has a different structural role from the dominant in measure 18: the first is a local point of arrival while the second is a major structural juncture, indeed, the overriding harmonic goal of the entire first half of the stanza.

Melodic motion reinforces harmonic progressions by outlining supporting chords. But the melody also undergoes a large-scale stepwise descent which helps to express the key in a more fundamental way. This motion is from scale degree 3 (C♯), which occurs as the first melodic tone

Example 1-1.   Schubert, "Kennst du das Land," stanzas 1 and 2.

Etwas geschwinder. 20

Da _ hin,   da _ hin!_____ da _
Da _ hin,   da _ hin!_____ da _

25

hin möcht' ich mit   dir,   o   mein Ge_lieb_ter, ziehn;   da _
hin möcht' ich mit   dir,   o   mein Beschü_zer, ziehn;   da _

30

hin,_____   da _ hin, da _ hin!   da _ hin möcht' ich mit
hin,_____   da _ hin, da _ hin!   da _ hin möcht' ich mit

35

dir,   o   mein Ge_lieb_ter, ziehn,   da _ hin,   da _
dir,   o   mein Be_schüt_zer, ziehn,   da _ hin,   da _

40

hin,   da _ hin,_____ da _ hin!_____
hin,   da _ hin,_____ da _ hin!_____

in measure 1, down to scale degree 2 (measure 18), and finally to the tonic scale degree at the end. At this point of conclusion, Schubert thrusts the vocal melody into a higher register to underscore the child-like eagerness of the speaker of the poem. This fundamental melodic path and its supporting harmonic progression I–V–I create the most basic expression of the key of A as it extends through the entire work. (Example 1-2 represents this structure in musical symbols.) Similar patterns were discovered at basic levels of structure in a variety of tonal works by the Viennese theorist Heinrich Schenker (1868–1935), who called them *Ursätze* ("fundamental structures").

The form of the work is clearly articulated by harmonic components of the key. The stanza begins with an expository period (measures 1–8), which concludes at the arrival of C major. The next phrase (measures 9–11) ends with a half cadence in the home key of A, which then moves quickly to F major and to the structural dominant at measure 18.

The relation of consonance and dissonance in this example is also a basic element of common-practice tonality. Consonant chords are those that contain consonant intervals; these harmonies are thus limited to major and minor triads in root position and first inversion. They are the building blocks of tonal harmony. All other chords are dissonant, which adds to music a rich variety of sound and an increased sense of propulsion through time.

In tonal music, dissonant chords serve the function of prolonging or connecting other chords. A typical example is the dissonant French augmented sixth in measure 17. The function of this chord is to connect the flatted submediant harmony that precedes it to the dominant harmony

scale
degrees: 3   2   1

A: I   V   I
meas.   1   18   39

Example 1-2.   Fundamental harmonic and melodic motion in Schubert's "Kennst du das Land."

meas.   12-15   16   17   18

(French 6th)

A: ♭VI ————————————————————————→ V

Example 1-3. Harmonic reduction of measures 12–18 of Schubert's "Kennst du das Land."

which is the goal of the progression. This role is fulfilled by stepwise voice leading in all parts. The sketch in Example 1-3, which simplifies rhythm and register, will clarify the way in which the French sixth arises. Between measures 15 and 18 there is a chromatic ascent in an inner part from C to E. This linear motion is supported in measure 17 by the familiar French sixth, which intensifies movement to the dominant, making it more urgent, just as the speaker of the poem at this point impatiently inquires, "Do you truly know it?"

In summary, then, let us bear in mind that traditional expression of key is accomplished by a number of coordinated events. Among the most fundamental is a large-scale harmonic progression from tonic to dominant, then back to the tonic. Cadential progressions in the smaller scale reinforce local elements of the key. Dissonant chords are a motoric force in music which serve primarily to connect diatonic, consonant triads. We turn now to ways in which composers of the nineteenth and early twentieth centuries reintrepreted these general principles of tonality.

[handwritten margin note: traditional tonality]

Disruptions of the Tonic–Dominant Axis

The tonic–dominant axis, which we observed in Schubert's "Kennst du das Land," is a means by which a single key exerts an influence throughout a piece or movement of a larger work. This typical unity of key may also be observed beyond a single movement in multimovement instrumental genres. In symphonies, string quartets, sonatas, and similar genres of the classical era, for example, entire works revolve about a home key. First and last movements are invariably in this tonality, and interior movements are either in the home key or in a closely related one such as the subdominant.

In the instrumental music of Beethoven and in a few works of his predecessors in the classical era, there is often a change of mode in the finale. Beethoven's Fifth Symphony, for example, moves from a first movement in C minor to a finale in C major, a transition that conveys a sense of triumph over adversity. The Ninth Symphony moves from D minor to D major, with the suggestion of triumph made explicit by the text from Schiller's "Ode to Joy." These alterations of mode were expanded in the symphonies of Gustav Mahler into outright changes of key. In Mahler's Second Symphony (1894) there is a progression from C minor at the opening to its relative major E♭ at the end. As is the case with Beethoven's symphonies, this change has a clear connection to the program of the work, which traces man's conversion from pessimism to triumphant confidence in God's love. In later symphonies, Mahler makes the progression of keys more remote. The Ninth Symphony (1908-10) begins in D major, moves to C major in the second movement, to A minor in the third, and, finally, to D♭ major in the finale. This work, furthermore, does not have overt programmatic associations which earlier supplied a rationale for nonconcentric tonal plans.

Single movements composed in the nineteenth century also underwent disruptions in the unity of key associated with the tonic–dominant axis. This new tonal diversity was prefigured by remote modulations in classical developmental or transitional passages as well as by nontonic introductions often encountered in the first movements of works by Haydn and Beethoven. Harmonic motion in the typical classical introduction prepares or prolongs the dominant, giving the initial tonic a dramatic arrival. These introductions do not in themselves disrupt the tonic–dominant axis—they solely act as a prefix to the initial statement of the tonic.

Later in the nineteenth century, however, the nontonic introduction was often extended and made more remote to the central tonality, thus creating intentional ambiguity of key. By this time the opening or introduction of a work rivaled the development as the area where a break with conventional tonality is most likely to occur.

The opening of Debussy's Prelude to *The Afternoon of a Faun* (1894) is magically remote from the primary tonality of E major, which is hinted at in the opening measures but confirmed only later. The opening flute melody outlines the tritone—an interval as ambiguous in its tonality as are the nymphs in the mind of the faun as he awakens from his dream (see Chapter 7).

hint of tonal key center

The opening of Mahler's Tenth Symphony (1910) creates tonal ambiguity by its emphasis on chromatic embellishing tones. This fifteen-measure introduction in the violas (Example 1-4) leads the ear away from the underlying F♯ harmony by elongating its neighboring tones and placing them on strong parts of the measure. We are at first invited to hear the opening as a preparation of the dominant of B♭ minor, begun by its submediant harmony G major and then moving to the dominant F major. But when the first theme enters in F♯ major at measure 16, we must reevaluate the passage and hear the first fifteen measures as an adumbration of an F♯-major triad. In the first half, the composer emphasizes the upper chromatic neighboring tones of this triad and, in the second half, the lower chromatic neighbors. We shall see later in this chapter that Mahler's emphasis on embellishing tones is carried throughout this movement and becomes an important means by which key is obscured.

Example 1-4. Mahler, Symphony no. 10, Adagio, measures 1-15. UN: upper neighbor; LN: lower neighbor. Copyright 1951 by Associated Music Publishers, Inc. Reprinted by permission.

Another means by which the tonic–dominant axis could be disrupted is the *truncation of one or more of its* elements. An example of such an incomplete structure is Chopin's Prelude in A minor, op. 28, no. 2 (1838; Example 1-5). This work is unusual, especially with respect to tonal plan, voice leading, and treatment of dissonance. The key of A is not apparent until it is suggested by the cadential six–four chord in measure 15, which leads to the first statement of the tonic chord in the very last measure. The first fourteen measures can be interpreted as a long extension of the dominant triad, first heard as an E-minor chord in measures 1–4 and then prolonged by an involved process of bass arpeggiations until it arrives at the cadential progression of the last nine measures. The entire piece is thus in the key of A minor, but the expected statement of a tonic at or near the beginning is omitted.

A more complex disruption of axis tonality is found in Schoenberg's song "Lockung" ("Lure," 1905), op. 6, no. 7. The composer refers to this work in both his *Theory of Harmony* and *Structural Functions of Harmony* as an example of extended and suspended tonality. He defines the former as an idiom in which nondiatonic chords and progressions may still be considered to be within one prevailing key. "They function chiefly as enrichments of the harmony," he wrote in *Structural Functions*, "and, accordingly, often appear in a very small space, even in a single measure. . . . Their functional effect is, in many cases, only passing and temporary." Suspended tonality occurs when a tonic chord is nowhere clearly stated. Schoenberg's analysis of "Lockung" in *Structural Functions* shows that he considered two tonalities to be in effect simultaneously for most of the song: E♭ (the principal key) and C (its submediant).

Both of these keys are represented almost solely by their dominants; the tonic triad of E♭, for example, occurs only in passing, but its dominant B♭ extends through long spans. Typical of the Wagnerian harmonic style, these dominants often do not progress to tonics; rather than setting up complete progressions that firmly establish a key, they are broken off abruptly or lead to deceptive continuations. An example is the juncture of the opening section with the contrasting passage beginning at measure 32 (Example 1-6). The B♭ dominant of measure 31 leads directly to a tonicization of B major (or C♭, equivalent to

Example 1-5.　Chopin, Prelude in A minor, op. 28, no. 2.

Example 1-6. Schoenberg, "Lockung," op. 6, no. 7, measures 11–39.

♭VI). This passage then leads to its dominant F♯ (measures 39–41), which is again left unresolved, leading to a section in D♭.

"Lockung" in fact transforms the tonic–dominant axis almost beyond recognition. The tonal regions of C♭, C, and D♭ are reminiscent of dominant preparations, the dominant of E♭ is much in evidence, and the tonic is sometimes touched upon, but their proportions and syntax are so distorted and the chords themselves so interpenetrated by nondiatonic tones that traditional key is scarcely—if at all—perceptible.

Harmonic *sequences* were also used in new ways to diminish the strength of a prevailing key. Harmonic sequences are repeated patterns consisting of recurrent bass figures and chordal successions. In classical instrumental music they are most often encountered in developmental or transitional passages; there they prolong a diatonic chord or connect two basic harmonies within a larger tonal plan. The boundary points of the sequence normally clarify its harmonic meaning within a prevailing key.

In the later nineteenth century, especially in the music of Richard Wagner, the occurrence of sequence was more widespread, and its role in the expression of a key was diminished or eliminated. This phenomenon can be observed in the Prelude to Act 3 of *Parsifal* (1877–82, Example 1-7). Let us first examine the section from measures 12–16, in which sequence is clearly evident. Both the upper and lower parts elaborate a diminished seventh chord, which moves upward sequentially from the bass note G in measure 12 to B♭ in measure 16, where the pattern is broken. This interval does not reinforce or link any diatonic triads nor does it depart from, or arrive at, diatonic harmonies.

A more covert harmonic sequence may be observed in the introductory passage of measures 1–11. The first four measures contain an incomplete progression in B♭ minor from I to V^7, which then dissolves into a diminished seventh chord. This pattern of dominant seventh followed by diminished seventh is repeated a semitone higher in measures 6–7 and another semitone higher in measures 9–11. Again, the boundary points of the sequence have no function in any prevailing key; the logic of the passage relies instead upon the ascending chromatic pattern itself. The

Example 1-7.   Wagner, Prelude to Act 3 of *Parsifal.*

suspension of key that Wagner accomplishes in this prelude by the use of chromatic sequences and diminished
chords serves an important dramatic role in the opera, as it
portrays the aimless wanderings of Parsifal prior to his
return to the Kingdom of the Grail in Act 3.

Irregular Treatment of Embellishing Tones and the Freeing of Dissonance

Embellishing tones are melodic notes, or tones arising from voice leading, that are not part of a supporting harmony. These result primarily from rhythmic displacements such as suspensions, passing or neighboring motion, and appoggiaturas. Their preparation and resolution in music of the common-practice period was strictly regulated. In the nineteenth and early twentieth centuries, however, composers greatly expanded the ways in which such tones were used. Sometimes their resolutions were delayed, ornamented, or simply omitted, and the dissonant chords produced by the embellishing motion were sustained to the point where their diatonic source was obscured. It was in this way that dissonance took its boldest strides toward "emancipation," a phenomenon that will be addressed further in Chapter 2.

Arnold Schoenberg articulates this new emphasis on dissonant chords in his *Theory of Harmony*, where he insists that chords containing nonharmonic tones must be incorporated into harmonic theory and recognized as valid musical materials. "Non-harmonic tones," he wrote, "form chords, hence they are not non-harmonic; the musical phenomena they help to create are harmonies, as is everything that sounds simultaneously."

The music of Gustav Mahler contains numerous examples of irregular treatment of embellishing tones. Example 1-8 is a reduction of the main theme of the Adagio of his Tenth Symphony (measures 16–23) showing the principal melody in the first violin and its underlying harmonies. The harmonic progression reflects the tonic–dominant axis of F♯ major as it moves from tonic (measures 16–18) to dominant (measures 22–23) and then returns to the tonic in measure 24 as the next musical unit begins. But the melody is highly irregular. Not only does it contain drastic disruptions in register, but its embellishing tones are handled with great freedom. On the downbeat of measure 19, for example, the melodic tone E♯ is an incomplete neighbor to the underlying F♯ in the B-minor chord. The E♯ is neither prepared nor resolved. The chord thus formed

Example 1-8.   Mahler, Symphony no. 10, Adagio, measures 16–24. Copyright 1951 by Associated Music Publishers, Inc. Reprinted by permission.

is one of the "triadic tetrachords" (to be discussed in Chapter 3) which was favored by early atonal composers. Here it maintains a diatonic function, however tenuous. On the third beat of measure 21, the melodic tone E♭ displaces the implicit chordal tone D. Its resolution is delayed well into the following bar, after the harmony has changed. The chord that is formed with the E♭ in measure 21 is a subset of the whole-tone scale, one of a family of chords much in currency among the early atonalists.

In Schoenberg's early songs, irregular embellishing tones are found simultaneously in several strands of voice leading. Let us return to "Lockung" (Example 1-6) and examine the first vocal phrase in measures 11–15. The underlying harmony of the entire passage is a dominant ninth in the key of E♭. It is typical of this song, however, that the dominant chord does not progress to any diatonic goal in this key. The notes F♯ and C♯ in measure 11 are upper neighbors to the chordal tones F and C♭ (B), respectively. The chord thus formed is another triadic tetrachord (see Chapter 3) much favored by Schoenberg in his atonal period.

Experimental Harmony and Tonality

In the later nineteenth century, harmonic experimentation characterized the works of several major composers. A group of musicians in St. Petersburg called "The Five" (see Chapter 8) began to adapt nondiatonic scales and a remarkably free use of dissonance to their works. Among Western composers, the innovations in harmony and tonality of Franz Liszt (1811–86) strikingly prefigure twentieth-century developments. Liszt's harmonic innovations are evident throughout his career as a composer, but they became pronounced in a series of compositions for piano and for chorus after about 1870. The late piano works are especially innovative and markedly different from his earlier virtuosic music for that instrument. They are usually short and spare in texture, and they apply a repertory of harmonies not normally part of tonal music. In these works major and minor triads are often outweighed by diminished chords, augmented triads and other whole-tone configurations, octatonic sets (see Chapter 2), bitriadic chords, and pentatonic figures. Axis tonality and the customary relationship of consonance and dissonance are little in evidence.

Throughout his life Liszt maintained a keen interest in ways by which traditional tonality could be expanded or reinterpreted. His imagination was fired by lectures given in Paris in 1832 by the Belgian theoretician François-Joseph Fétis (1784–1871), who spoke of a forthcoming "omnitonic" era in music history. A work of this period, Fétis theorized, would not be governed by a single key; tonality would instead fluctuate freely among keys linked by diminished chords. At some unknown date, Liszt composed a "Prélude

Example 1-9.   Liszt, *Nuages gris*, measures 1–20. From the *Late Piano Works*, vol. 1. Copyright © 1952 Schott & Co Ltd., London. All rights reserved. Used by permission of European American Music Distributors Corporation, sole U.S. agents for B. Schott's Soehne.

omnitonique" which may have applied Fétis's ideas, but this work is now presumed lost. In 1885 he sketched an incomplete "Bagatelle Without Tonality": a highly simplified and repetitive work which mingles whole-tone, diminished, and octatonic configurations of pitches.

"Nuages gris" ("Grey Clouds," 1881; Example 1-9) is a more artistic example of Liszt's experimental style. This starkly abstract work makes no use of a traditional key, despite its key signature and emphasis on the notes of a G-minor triad. These three pitches—G, B♭, and D—are boundary points for the melodic lines, as in the opening figure in measures 1–2. But the G triad asserts its centricity no more than do the augmented triads that saturate measures 11–20 or the four-note dissonant figure that opens the work: D G C♯ (D) B♭ (G). The principles of harmonic organization of "Nuages gris" are not referable to those of common-practice tonality; they rely instead upon new methods of association to which we turn in the next chapter.

Bibliography

Principles of tonal harmony are addressed in numerous textbooks on this subject, among which those by William Mitchell, Allen Forte, and Edward Aldwell and Carl Schachter are especially recommended. The Schenkerian view of tonality is outlined in Oswald Jonas's *Introduction to the Theory of Heinrich Schenker*, trans. and ed. John Rothgeb (New York and London, 1982) and in Adele Katz's *Challenge to Musical Tradition* (New York, 1945). Detailed guidelines for Schenkerian analyses are given in *Introduction to Schenkerian Analysis* by Allen Forte and Steven E. Gilbert (New York, 1982).

Schoenberg's two textbooks on harmony—*Theory of Harmony*, trans. Roy E. Carter (Berkeley and Los Angeles, 1978) and *Structural Functions of Harmony*, rev. ed. (New York, 1969)—deal primarily with tonal principles. The first of these is especially valuable for its exercises and examples of harmonic successions in the post-Wagnerian style.

The extent to which Schenker's unified conception of tonality is operative in works of the twentieth century is a matter of debate. Aspects of his analytic method are applied to post-tonal music by Felix Salzer in *Structural Hearing: Tonal Coherence in Music*, 2 vols. (New York, 1952) and by Robert Morgan in his article "Dissonant Prolongations: Theoretical and Compositional Precedents," *Journal of Music Theory*, 20 (1976). Also see James M. Baker, "Schenkerian Analysis and Post-Tonal Music" in *Aspects of Schenkerian Theory*, ed. David Beach (New Haven and London, 1983). Harald Krebs discusses nineteenth-century works that do not appear to be governed by a single tonic–dominant axis in his article "Alternatives to Monotonality in Early Nineteenth-Century Music," *Journal of Music Theory*, 25 (1981).

There is no completely satisfying analytic study of the transition of music from tonality to atonality. Jim Samson's *Music in Transition: A Study of Tonal Expansion and Atonality, 1900–1920* (New York, 1977) is a valuable pioneering work on this subject, which takes into account a very broad segment of the musical literature.

♦ 2 ♦

HARMONIC AND MOTIVIC ASSOCIATIONS AND THE "EMANCIPATION OF DISSONANCE"

Works discussed in the previous chapter show the gradual change in the role of dissonance during the second half of the nineteenth century. Its traditional function of prolonging or connecting consonant chords began to give way to a style in which dissonances were the central and referential units. This change contributed to the elimination of key and with it the chief unifying element in music of the preceding 200 years.

Prominent composers early in the twentieth century had a keen awareness of their place in the establishment of a new compositional order, and they also perceived that a new treatment of dissonance was the fulcrum by which the old order was to be toppled. In his Norton Lectures at Harvard University (1939–40), Igor Stravinsky called attention to this expanded role of dissonance:

For over a century music has provided repeated examples of a style in which dissonance has emancipated itself. It is no longer tied down to its former function. Having become an entity in itself, it frequently happens that dissonance neither prepares nor anticipates anything. Dissonance is thus no more an agent of disorder than consonance is a guarantee of security. The music of yesterday and of today unhesitatingly unites parallel dissonant chords that thereby lose their functional value, and our ear quite naturally accepts their juxtaposition. [From *The Poetics of Music*. See the Bibliography to Chapter 8 regarding the authenticity of this work.]

Arnold Schoenberg asserted the "comprehensibility" of dissonance in his lecture "Composition with Twelve Tones" (1941): "The term *emancipation of the dissonance* refers to its [dissonance's] comprehensibility, which is considered equivalent to the consonance's comprehensibility. A style based on this premise treats dissonances like consonances and renounces a tonal center."

In this chapter we shall survey aspects of structural unity in music where dissonance is "emancipated" and in which traditional key is absent. We shall first examine an atonal work by Schoenberg, but the analytic techniques that will be developed are general enough to apply to a broader geographical and chronological spectrum of modern music.

The Role of the Motive

Schoenberg, despite his extensive theoretical writings, did not make detailed or systematic explanations of the techniques of harmonic unity in his works characterized by the emancipation of dissonance. He was inclined instead to emphasize only one aspect of their construction, recurrent motivic variation, which was a feature they shared with earlier tonal composition. Schoenberg discusses the nature and use of motives in tonal music in his textbook *Fundamentals of Musical Composition*; these remarks serve equally well to describe his use of the motive in atonal music.

> The (motive) generally appears in a characteristic and impressive manner at the beginning of a piece. The features of a motive are intervals and rhythms, combined to produce a memorable shape or contour which usually implies an inherent harmony. Inasmuch as almost every figure within a piece reveals some relationship to it, the basic motive is often considered the "germ" of the idea. Since it includes elements, at least, of every subsequent musical figure, one could consider it the "smallest common multiple." And since it is included in every subsequent figure, it could be considered the "greatest common factor."
>
> However, everything depends on its use. Whether a motive be simple or complex, whether it consists of few or many features, the final impression of the piece is not determined by its primary form. Everything depends on its treatment and development.
>
> A motive appears constantly throughout a piece: _it is repeated_. [But] repetition alone often gives rise to _monotony_. Monotony can only be overcome by _variation_.

The main motives in a piece by Schoenberg are in themselves unstable: they demand, as it were, to be varied and to spawn a network of interrelated forms such that any one occurrence will be a variant of its preceding versions. A web of organically connected statements of the basic

Example 2–1.   Schoenberg, Piano Piece, op. 23, no. 4. © 1923, renewed 1951, by Edition Wilhelm Hansen, Copenhagen. Reprinted by permission.

Example 2-2. Schoenberg, Piano Piece, op. 23, no. 4. © 1923, renewed 1951 by Edition Wilhelm Hansen, Copenhagen. Reprinted by permission.

motives is spun in a manner that Schoenberg elsewhere termed "developing variations."

Schoenberg's Piano Piece, op. 23, no. 4 (1920–23; Anthology no. 6) will provide examples of his use of the motive in atonal composition. Three principal motives are found in the first measure, of which the right-hand figure is most important. This central idea returns in a series of exceedingly remote forms, of which one of the most straightforward is in measures 12–13. Its relationship to the original, illustrated by the juxtaposition of the two figures in Example 2-1, is through its similar intervals, contour, and rhythm. The right-hand motive of measure 2 is a varied recurrence of the opening left-hand motive of measure 1, since they share similar intervals and rhythms (Example 2-2). The succession of three pairs of thirds which characterizes the second left-hand motive of the first measure recurs in many varied forms, for example, the left-hand part in measures 2–3, where the major thirds of measure 1 are contracted to minor thirds or their inversion (Example 2-3).

Example 2-3. Schoenberg, Piano Piece, op. 23, no. 4. © 1923, renewed 1951, by Edition Wilhelm Hansen, Copenhagen. Reprinted by permission.

Harmonic Relationships

The harmonic logic of this work is more difficult to perceive, partly because the composer did not leave specific guidelines for its understanding and because there was no widely accepted harmonic practice at this time. Indeed, our first impression of the Piano Piece may well be that its pitches were chosen randomly or that the composer was guided solely by his desire to avoid conventional chords. There are no prominent triads or seventh chords in the entire work, and only fleetingly do we hear other dissonant combinations familiar from music of the past. The difficulty of comprehending harmonic relationships is made more acute by the dense and complicated texture, a rhythmic style that does not project a firm sense of pulse or stable metric organization, and the lack of clear sectional repetitions.

Nevertheless, Schoenberg frequently alluded to the presence of harmonic logic in his atonal works, although he was inclined to see this dimension as the product of an "unconscious" intuition rather than a methodic technique. He wrote of his nontonal musical style in his *Theory of Harmony*: "Every chord I put down corresponds to a necessity, to a necessity of my urge to expression; perhaps, however, also to the necessity of an inexorable but unconscious logic in the harmonic structure. I am firmly convinced that logic is present here too, at least as much so as in the previously cultivated fields of harmony."

In order to understand Schoenberg's harmonic language, we must first expand our idea of a "harmony" beyond its conventional meaning in the analysis of earlier music. Rather than a chord that can be arranged in superimposed thirds, a harmony (or *set*) will refer here to a collection of pitches that are associated by *adjacency* in some musical context—normally adjacent pitches found in a melodic idea or motive, a vertical chord, or a combination of the two.

This integration of vertical and linear structures is found in tonal music as well, but it is made more explicit in works of the post-tonal era. In his article "My Evolution," Schoenberg wrote, "A melodic line, a voice part, or even a

melody derives from horizontal projections of tonal relations. A chord results similarly from projections in the vertical direction. . . . The main difference between harmony
and melodic line is that harmony requires faster analysis,
because the tones appear simultaneously, while in a
melodic line more time is granted to synthesis, because the
tones appear successively, thus becoming more readily
graspable by the intellect."

harmonic horizontal vs. vertical

Let us return to the principal motive of the right hand
in measure 1 of Schoenberg's Piano Piece, op. 23, no. 4. In
addition to presenting the potential for motivic development by virtue of its distinctive rhythm, meter, and contour, this linear element also represents a harmonic entity,
which is characterized solely by its content of pitches and
which will contribute to the intervallic unity of the piece
by its recurrence in varied forms.

Recurrence of Harmonies: Restatement, Transposition, Reordering, Inversion

The simplest form in which this harmony recurs is a
restatement. In Example 2-4 we can compare the restatement in measures 33–34 to the original in measure 1. The
pitches of both are identical, with the exception of the
final E and G in measure 34, which appear an octave lower
than before. Changes of register of this type produce at
most a disruption in the motivic contour; they do not alter
the underlying harmony. So we shall consider all notes an
octave apart to be structurally equivalent and introduce
the term *pitch class* to refer to a representation of all notes
of the same or enharmonically equivalent spelling.

1. restatement

m. 1

mm. 33-34

Example 2-4. Schoenberg, Piano Piece, op. 23, no. 4. © 1923, renewed
1951, by Edition Wilhelm Hansen, Copenhagen. Re-
printed by permission.

We may now define the harmony of our basic motive by its six pitch classes: D♯ B B♭ D E G. Any set of six different pitch classes will be called a *hexachord*; a set of four, a *tetrachord*, and so forth. An atonal harmony is an abstraction since it has no musical contour or rhythmic shape. It takes on these features, however, when it is brought to life as a motive.

A second means of varying the harmony is by *transposition*. Let us return to Example 2-1 in which we will see a recurrence in measures 12–13 of the principal set transposed up two semitones. This new version of the harmony is also assigned a musical configuration that strongly resembles the original motive in rhythm and contour.

A third and more remote method of variation of the basic harmony is accomplished by *reordering* its notes. In Example 2-5 we see the notes of the main set reordered in the right-hand figure in measure 24. One of the main compositional and structural changes in music by Schoenberg and others after about 1921 was the preservation of a fixed order within the linear presentation of a harmonic unit. Music of this type is said to be *serialized*, and it will be discussed in Chapter 4. But in the post-tonal idiom prior to 1921 and in nonserialized music after that time, reordering is a basic means of achieving variety.

The fourth principal means of harmonic variation is *inversion*, which will refer to a symmetric intervallic rotation about a fixed pitch within a set. An inversion of the basic harmony D♯ B B♭ D E G can be obtained, for example, by allowing the note D♯ to remain fixed and rotating the other elements around it symmetrically. Thus D♯ remains constant, B (four semitones below D♯) now becomes G (four semitones above D♯); B♭ (five semitones below D♯) becomes

Example 2–5.   Schoenberg, Piano Piece, op. 23, no. 4. © 1923, renewed 1951, by Edition Wilhelm Hansen, Copenhagen. Reprinted by permission.

Example 2-6.   Schoenberg, Piano Piece, op. 23, no. 4. © 1923, renewed
1951, by Edition Wilhelm Hansen, Copenhagen. Re-
printed by permission.

Ab (five semitones above D♯), and so forth:

Basic Harmony

B D E Ab G D♯ B Bb D E G

Inversion

Schoenberg makes little significant use of inversions of the
basic harmony in the Piano Piece, but for purposes of illustration let us observe a group of pitches found in measures
4–5 (Example 2-6). The six pitch classes of this adjacency,
with reordering for easier comparison, are B D E Ab G D♯,
thus the inversion of the basic harmony shown above.

These four operations upon basic collections of
pitches—restatement, transposition, reordering, and inversion—are manifested time and again not only in the music
of Schoenberg, but also in works by Bartók, Scriabin, Stravinsky, and other masters of the atonal language. In fact,
they are so commonly encountered that we may postulate
that two collections of notes will be harmonically *equivalent* if the pitches of one collection can be made identical
to those of the other collection by transposition, reordering, inversion, or a combination of these. (The identity of
sets related by restatement is obvious.) This postulate of
equivalence greatly simplifies the task of the analyst who
seeks principles of harmonic unity in atonal music, since it
reduces the number of families of equivalent sets to
approximately 220—a sufficiently small number to allow
their recurrence and interaction to be observed and
interpreted.

Example 2-7.   Schoenberg, Piano Piece, op. 23, no. 4. © 1923, renewed 1951, by Edition Wilhelm Hansen, Copenhagen. Reprinted by permission.

Additional Harmonic Relationships: Complementation, Inclusion, and Similarity

Schoenberg's Piano Piece provides excellent examples of relationships that can exist among nonequivalent harmonies. One of the strongest such relationships is _complementation_. Two sets are complementary if they have no pitch classes in common, but together encompass the entire chromatic set. The complement of the basic harmony D♯ B B♭ D E G will be the hexachord C G♯ F♯ C♯ A F, since these pitches are precisely those six not found in the original set. Schoenberg clearly exploits the complement of the basic harmony near the beginning of the piece, in the right hand of measure 3 (Example 2-7).

An important relation that may obtain between sets of different sizes is _inclusion_. If the pitches of a smaller set are contained among those of a larger one, forming a _subset_ of the larger collection, then the two are related in this way. The left-hand figure in measure 13 consists of the four notes B♭ G♭ A F. This tetrachord is contained in an

Inclusion
Subset

Example 2-8.   Schoenberg, Piano Piece, op. 23, no. 4. © 1923, renewed 1951, by Edition Wilhelm Hansen, Copenhagen. Reprinted by permission.

A   D♯ B B♭ D E G

B   D B♭ A C F D♭

C   A♭ C G♭ B♭ A F

Example 2–9.   Schoenberg, Piano Piece, op. 23, no. 4. © 1923, renewed 1951, by Edition Wilhelm Hansen, Copenhagen. Reprinted by permission.

accompanimental figure from measure 1, as is shown in Example 2-8.

    Nonequivalent harmonies may also be *similar* if they share common or equivalent subsets. In Schoenberg's Piano Piece, the three hexachords that underlie the three basic motives of measure 1 are similar in this way. In Example 2-9 these sets and their motives are labeled A, B, and C. The first four notes of motive A, the lowest four notes of motive B, and the last four notes of C are all transpositionally equivalent, which can readily be seen by comparing them in the reorderings that follow:

> B♭ B D D♯ (from A)
> A B♭ D♭ D (from B)
> F G♭ A B♭ (from C).

This family of equivalent tetrachords plays a central role in the Piano Piece, sometimes drawing more attention to itself than to the parent hexachords from which it emanates.

    Schoenberg's Piano Piece is a remarkable example of the penetration of a few harmonies throughout an entire atonal composition. Virtually all pitches of the work can be divided into segments that are equivalent to hexachords A, B, C, or their complements. The recurrences of these sets within a complete section of the work—the coda-like passage in measures 29–35—are shown in Example 2-10. A

Example 2-10.   Schoenberg, Piano Piece, op. 23, no. 4. Sets that are
transposed relative to their first occurrence (see Example 2-9) are indicated by *t*, followed by the number of
semitones above this first occurrence. © 1923, renewed
1951, by Edition Wilhelm Hansen, Copenhagen. Reprinted by permission.

few notes that would complicate the appearance of this
example are not analytically interpreted, but these as well
as all other pitches in this section are constituents of sets
that are varied forms of A, B, or C. This coda contains a
preponderance of sets that are identical in their content of
pitches to measure 1, perhaps as an analogy to a tonal
piece that returns at the end to its original tonic key.

Arnold Schoenberg, autograph sketches to the Piano Piece, op. 23, no. 4. Schoenberg's analytic annotations are of special interest. (Courtesy of Lawrence Schoenberg and the Arnold Schoenberg Institute.)

Types of Harmonies

The harmonic languages of major atonal composers each contain distinctive and favored vocabularies of sets. Some of these musicians, including Hindemith, Stravinsky, and Britten, maintained triads and other conventional chords in their parlance. We shall return to these composers and their harmonic practice in Chapter 3.

We focus now on atonal works which rely upon harmonies that do not have a prominent place in tonal music. Probably more than any major composer of the first half of the century, Schoenberg took an extreme position in his avoidance of triadic sonorities. In his *Theory of Harmony* he describes his reluctance to use traditional chords in his post-tonal music, and he also betrays his excitement in the sheer number and diversity of harmonies newly available to the modern composer:

> There is perhaps also an instinctive (possibly exaggerated) aversion to recalling even remotely the traditional chords. For the same reason, apparently, the simple chords of the earlier harmony do not appear successfully in this environment. I believe, however, that there is another reason for their absence here. I believe they would sound too cold, too dry, expressionless. Or perhaps, what I mentioned on an earlier occasion applies here. Namely, that these simple chords, which are imperfect imitations of nature, seem to us too primitive. That they lack something, which, for example, Japanese painting lacks when compared with ours: perspective, depth. Perspective and depth of sound could be what we find wanting in the simple three and four-part harmonies. And as in a picture one section can hardly show regard for perspective while another disregards it, without impairing the effect, so perhaps, analogously, these somewhat empty sounds cannot appear alongside those full, sumptuous sounds; whereas the exclusive use of the one *or* the other assures coherence, hence the right effect.

The survey of harmonies that follows is limited to the most distinctive and easily recognizable types. As such, it omits many of the favored harmonies of composers like Schoenberg who avoided musical materials that might seem commonplace. One of Schoenberg's most characteristic sets, for example, is the principal harmony of the Piano Piece, op. 23, no. 4 (D♯ B B♭ D E G). His emphasis on this and its equivalent sets may derive in part from the musical letters of his name: *S c h ö n b e r g* outlines the German pitch names Es C H B E G, that is, E♭ C B B♭ E G. These notes are equivalent by inversion and transposition to the principal set of op. 23, no. 4.

Symmetric and Quasi-Symmetric Sets: Whole-Tone and "Nearly-Whole-Tone" Hexachords, Octatonic Scales, and the Major/Minor Tetrachord

Among the various categories of dissonant harmonies that characterize atonal music, symmetric sets are some of the most important. A symmetric harmony is one whose pitches can be ordered so that they create the same succession of intervals read from either left or right. Although some such collections of notes (such as the diminished seventh chord) have use in tonal music, diatonic scales and most tonal harmonies are asymmetric in their intervallic makeup.

Most symmetric sets present the composer with restrictive harmonic resources. Some intervals may be entirely lacking in them and others all the more strongly represented. The augmented triad—a widely used symmetric set—illustrates this point. As shown in Example 2-11, the intervals of an augmented triad consist solely of major thirds or their inversions, minor sixths. The whole-tone scale, another familiar symmetric structure, contains only major seconds, major thirds, tritones, and their inversions, but no minor seconds, minor thirds, or perfect fourths. Thus any motive made up of notes from a whole-

Example 2-11.   Intervallic content of the augmented triad.

tone scale will be decidedly limited in the intervals available to it and all the more distinctive in its sound.

limited in trans.

Symmetric sets are also more limited in their transpositional resources than diatonic collections. They are comparable to what Olivier Messiaen has called "modes of limited transposition," which are seven symmetric sets discussed further in Chapter 15. Each can be transposed to alternative pitch levels only a few times before the set repeats itself. The whole-tone scale, Messiaen's first mode of limited transposition, is a simple example: it can be transposed up one semitone and render a new set of six pitches, as shown below. But if it is transposed up two (or any even number) of semitones, it will produce the same collection of pitches as the original:

Whole-tone scale:	C	D	E	F♯	G♯	A♯	(C)
Transposition up one semitone:	C♯	D♯	F	G	A	B	(C♯)
Transposition up two semitones:	D	E	F♯	G♯	A♯	C	(D)

Each of the diatonic scales, on the contrary, can be transposed to all twelve pitch levels without replicating itself completely.

inversion

Symmetric sets, finally, do not produce distinct inversional forms; that is, any inversion of a symmetric set can also be generated by transposition. These restrictions on intervallic content, transposition, and inversion contribute to the relatively unvaried or static harmonic quality of music in which symmetric collections are central. But as the principal harmonic elements in a composition, these sets are powerful means by which the traditional expression of a key and the harmonic idiom of tonal music can be eliminated.

Composers of atonal music have used many different symmetric collections. We shall focus only on the most important and widespread of these—whole-tone and related sets, octatonic sets, and the major/minor tetrachord. We shall also describe subsets of these formations as parts of the same family of chords, although these subsets will not themselves always be symmetrical. The reader may be surprised to find the chromatic scale—a familiar symmetric formation—missing from this group. The chromatic scale or its contiguous segments have relatively little use as central elements in atonal music. The chromatic scale is too unrestrictive in its intervallic contents, since all intervals are contained in it at the maximum possible frequency. It has central importance only in experimental music such as tone-cluster compositions or in idioms where the harmonic principles outlined so far in this chapter are not operative. Chromatic clusters, however small, are rarely basic to the harmonic structure of an atonal composition: instead, they usually function as motivic details that often hide the more fundamental units.

The whole-tone scale and its subsets were increasingly in evidence in tonal music of the nineteenth century. The whole-tone set is encountered in this literature mainly through two of its subsets—the augmented triad and French augmented sixth chord. These two chords continued to be used outside of a tonal context by early atonal composers. These and other whole-tone formations are seen as extensions of diatonic progressions in music by Russian composers of the nineteenth century (see Chapter 8) and by Western European composers, including Debussy, Dukas, Liszt, Strauss, Schoenberg, Mahler, and Berg.

Whole-tone sets continued to enjoy primacy in early atonal compositions. Berg, for example, uses the whole-tone scale as a means of unifying an entire piece in his song "Schlafend trägt man mich in mein Heimatland," op. 2, no. 2 (ca. 1908–10). An excerpt from the beginning is shown in Example 2-12. Three- and four-note subsets of the whole-tone scale constitute every vertical chord. Occasionally, these dissonant chords will take on a decidedly familiar sound, as in the last measure of the song, where the bass note E♭ supports a sonority identical to a dominant seventh without its fifth. Berg, unlike his teacher Schoenberg, did not reject the use of familiar triadic harmonies in his atonal music; such chords, however, have no traditional tonal function. They are integrated with other chords in the song by the operations of reordering and transposition, and, by the inclusion relationship, they derive their meaning from the master whole-tone set that dominates the entire harmonic dimension of the work.

Related to the whole-tone scale is a hexachord com-

Example 2-12.   Berg, "Schlafend trägt man mich in mein Heimatland," op. 2, no. 2, from *Vier Lieder für eine Singstimme mit Klavier.* Reprinted by permission of Robert Lienau, Berlin.

monly used by composers of the modern French and Russian school as well as by the Viennese avant-garde. For lack of a better term, it will be called the "nearly-whole-tone hexachord." It is derived from a whole-tone scale by raising or lowering any one pitch. Its relationship to a whole-tone scale is shown in Example 2-13.

This collection is one of the harmonic trademarks of the music of Alexander Scriabin composed after about 1908. Its use in his symphony *Prometheus* (1910) has led to its being dubbed the *Prometheus* or "mystic" chord. The collection is sometimes described as a series of superimposed fourths, a conception that is doubtful since the fourth is not at all strongly represented in its total intervallic content and is far outweighed by whole-tone intervals of the major second, major third, and their inversions.

Scriabin's Piano Sonata no. 10 (1913) is based upon subsets of this harmony or of other sets similar to it. The principal theme of the work is heard in measures 1–8: at its midpoint (Example 2-14) a five-note figure is presented, which lacks only B♭ to make up an inversion of the "mystic" chord. The B♭ is then added at the cadence of this

Example 2-13.   Derivation of the "nearly-whole-tone" hexachord.

mm. 3-4

F♯ A♭ [B♭] C D E♭*

Example 2-14.   Scriabin, Piano Sonata no. 10. *Henceforth, sets will be stated in their *normal order*, which is a scalewise representation covering the smallest possible total span. Used by permission of the original publisher Rob. Forberg-P. Jurgenson Musikverlag, Bonn.

phrase in measures 7–8 (Example 2-15), making the central hexachord explicit.

The nearly-whole-tone hexachord also plays a central role in Berg's opera *Wozzeck*. Acts 1 and 3 are ended by the sonority F G A B C♯D, which is a form of this hexachord (compare it to the set in Example 2-15 transposed down one semitone). In a lecture on *Wozzeck*, Berg likened this chord to a cadential or tonic point of rest in a tonal composition. It functions in this way not only in the absolute musical sense, but also as a dramatic-musical summation of the story of the opera. The harmony is used elsewhere as an associative reference to the character Wozzeck, and its component pitch classes and intervals are referentially linked to the main events of Wozzeck's downfall.

The *octatonic* set may be viewed as a scalewise alternation of half and whole steps; one such form of this collection is illustrated in Example 2-16. The octatonic scale

mm. 7-8

F♯ A♭ B♭ C D E♭

Example 2-15.   Scriabin, Piano Sonata no. 10. Used by permission of the original publisher Rob. Forberg-P. Jurgenson Musikverlag. Bonn

Example 2–16.   The octatonic scale.

has many distinctive properties. It contains, for example, all of the intervals, although the minor third and its inversion are most frequently represented. It also contains a large inventory of subsets, including familiar diatonic chords (major, minor, and diminished triads; dominant, diminished, half-diminished, and minor sevenths).

The more distinctive octatonic subsets were used by several nineteenth-century composers, notably Liszt and Russians such as Glinka and Rimski-Korsakov. Octatonic

Example 2–17.   Bartók, Suite, op. 14, third movement. Copyright 1918 by Universal-Edition. Renewed 1945. Copyright and renewal assigned to Boosey & Hawkes, Inc. Reprinted by permission.

Example 2-18.   Octatonic source of triads in Bartók's Suite, op. 14, third movement.

sets became central to the harmonic organization of music by numerous early atonal composers, for example, Stravinsky and Scriabin, and they were also prominent in atonal works by Busoni, Bartók, Debussy, and Ravel. Among later figures, Messiaen has emphasized the octatonic collection, which he calls the second mode of limited transposition. It has also been adopted by modern jazz musicians, who sometimes refer to it as a "diminished" scale. It has very little use, on the other hand, in the music of Schoenberg or his followers.

An example of a work based upon predominantly octatonic structures is Bartók's Piano Suite, op. 14, third movement (1916). This fiery perpetuum mobile opens with fragments of two octatonic collections in counterpoint (Example 2-17); these lines subsequently flesh out more of their underlying scales. The contrasting middle section (measures 60–84) is introduced by a passage in measures 50–59 with a ringing succession of F♯-, A-, and C-minor triads. These arise as subsets of a transposition of the octatonic set shown in Example 2-18. This transposition accounts for virtually every note of the middle section until measure 80.

The octatonic scale contains a four-note subset that is often encountered in atonal music, either in the context of this larger set or independent of it. This harmony will be called the *major/minor tetrachord*, since it may be viewed as a statement of both major and minor forms of a single triad (Example 2-19). One attraction of this collection for the early atonal composers was its strong aural relation to

Example 2-19.   The major/minor tetrachord.

Example 2-20.   Stravinsky, *Le roi des étoiles.* Used by permission of the original publisher, Rob. Forberg-P. Jurgenson Musikverlag, Bonn.

the triad. It is used prominently by Igor Stravinsky in his cantata *Zvezdoliki* (1912). The piece begins with a motto-like succession of three chords setting the word "Zvezdoliki" ("the starry-eyed one") (Example 2-20). The first of these chords is the major/minor tetrachord, which subsequently recurs with its pungent sonority at the end of the first line of text (measure 7) and repeatedly among the powerfully scored verticalities accompanying the prophecies of this "king of the stars" (measures 27–33).

All-Interval Tetrachords, Fourth Chords, and Pentatonic Scales

All-interval tetrachords have proved to be among the most favored harmonies of atonal composers from early in the century to the present day. These collections derive their name from the fact that they contain each of the six basic intervals (minor second, major second, minor third, major third, perfect fourth, and tritone) or their inversions. All-interval tetrachords may be reduced in number to only

Example 2-21.   The all-interval tetrachords.

two nonequivalent types, which are shown in Example 2-21. Let us focus on type A to illustrate how this set contains all of the basic intervals. If we pair off each of its notes with each other note, we will see these six interval "classes":

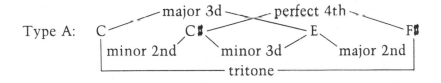

Both types of all-interval tetrachords have been frequently employed by the contemporary American composer Elliott Carter. His First String Quartet (1951) in fact uses these sets as elements of focus throughout the entire work. Their occurrence in the opening measures is illustrated in Example 2-22.

In "Shop Talk by an American Composer," Carter describes his application of an all-interval tetrachord in this

Example 2-22.   Carter, First String Quartet, first movement, measures 1–12 (cello), rhythm omitted.

work, although it is curious that he recognizes the use of only one of the two types in a piece where both are much in evidence:

> In my First String Quartet, I did use a "key" four-note chord, one of the two four-note groups, that joins all the two-note intervals into pairs, thus allowing for the total range of interval qualities that still can be referred back to a basic chord-sound. This chord is not used at every moment in the work but occurs frequently enough, especially in important places, to function, I hope, as a formative factor.

A family of sets that had particular importance to early atonal composers consists of those that can be stated as a succession or simultaneity of perfect fourths. Chords of this latter type may be termed *quartal* or *fourth chords.* It should be observed, however, that chords in which perfect fifths are superimposed are inversional forms of chords in fourths and that these sets may also be encountered in motives that move through intervals other than fourths. Quartal harmonies had a broad currency among transitional composers to the atonal idiom and among neoclassicists in Europe and America in the period between the world wars. They are occasionally found in tonal music, where they displace triads. A memorable example of the latter is the introduction to the finale of Beethoven's *Pastoral* Symphony (measures 5–8) where the superimposed fifths in the cello, viola, and horn are created by suspension between a dominant and a tonic harmony.

If the interval class of the fourth is compounded, it

Example 2-23.   Quartal harmonies.

Example 2-24.   Hindemith, *1922: Suite für Klavier.* © B. Schott's Soehne, Mainz, 1922; © renewed Schott & Co, Ltd., London, 1950. Used by permission of European American Music Distributors Corp., sole U.S. agent for B. Schott's Soehne.

will duplicate the entire chromatic set before repeating any pitches. For practical reasons, we will limit our discussion to three-, four-, and five-note quartal harmonies, which are those most frequently encountered. These are shown in Example 2-23. The first two measures of Paul Hindemith's "Ragtime" from his Suite "1922" are made up from fourth chords of the three-note type or its subset, the minor seventh (Example 2-24). This trichord is heard throughout the piece, although Hindemith also exploits whole-tone sets, bitriadic chords (see Chapter 3), and diatonic harmonies in this work.

The *pentatonic scale* consists, as its name suggests, of five notes (Example 2-25), its intervals may be easily recalled since an equivalent set is created by any five adjacent black keys on the piano. It is also a subset of both the major and minor scales.

The pentatonic scale is prominent in the folk music of many cultures, including those of China, Africa, Russia, Scotland, and the American Indian. It colors many well-known melodies of Western music, often lending them the flavor of folk song. The pentatonic scale and its subsets became a great harmonic and melodic resource in music of the twentieth century by Bartók, Debussy, and Ravel. For Bartók it established a link between his own work and peasant songs of Eastern Europe, in which this scale was very common. The pentatonic element in Debussy and Ravel

Example 2-25.   Pentatonic scale.

may reflect their interest in Russian and other exotic folk cultures.

The pentatonic set is related to diatonic harmony since it is a subset of diatonic scales. It is also closely allied to quartal harmony, since the five-note fourth chord (see Example 2-23) is a pentatonic collection. These relationships were exploited by several major composers of the twentieth century, for example, by having a pentatonic melody accompanied by a succession of fourth chords. The opening of the middle section of Debussy's Saraband from *Pour le piano* (Anthology no. 2, measures 23–26) contains a straightforward example.

Not all major composers of the twentieth century have shared Schoenberg's enthusiasm for the resources and richness of dissonant harmony. Others have maintained the necessity of preserving the triad as the harmonic basis for music in this century. On this matter Paul Hindemith wrote in his *Craft of Musical Composition*, volume 1:

> Music, as long as it exists, will always take its departure from the major triad and return to it. The musician cannot escape it any more than the painter his primary colors or the architect his three dimensions. In composition, the triad or its direct extensions can never be avoided for more than a short time without completely confusing the listener.

Thus we turn in Chapter 3 to the subject of triadic harmony and tonality.

Bibliography

The conception of harmonic relationships described in this chapter is largely derived from Allen Forte's *Structure of Atonal Music* (New Haven, 1973). Numerous applications of this approach to twentieth-century music may be found in periodicals such as the *Journal of Music Theory, Music Theory Spectrum, Music Analysis, Perspectives of*

New Music, and *Musical Quarterly.* Forte's article "Schoenberg's Creative Evolution: The Path to Atonality," *Musical Quarterly,* 64 (1978), is especially recommended, as is Janet Schmalfeldt's chapter "Pitch-Class Set Theory: Historical Perspective" from her book *Berg's Wozzeck* (New Haven and London, 1983).

Schoenberg's observations on the structure of his atonal works are found in various essays and lectures in *Style and Idea,* ed. Leonard Stein (London, 1975) and in *Arnold Schönberg Gesammelte Schriften,* vol. 1, ed. Ivan Vojtech (n.p., Fischer, 1976). Schoenberg's analysis of his Orchestral Songs, op. 22, is typical of his approach to the discussion of his post-tonal works; an English translation by Claudio Spies is found in *Perspectives of New Music,* 3 (1965). Schoenberg's *Fundamentals of Musical Composition* (New York, 1967) deals with tonal composition, but it is also a valuable guide to post-tonal musical form. His article "My Evolution" appears in *Musical Quarterly,* 38 (1952), and the concluding chapters to his *Theory of Harmony* touch upon aspects of early atonal composition.

Major writings by the following composers on their own music are cited in bibliographies to these chapters: Stravinsky (Chapter 8); Bartók (Chapter 9); Messiaen (Chapter 15); Carter (Chapter 12). Alban Berg's lecture on *Wozzeck* is found in Hans F. Redlich, *Alban Berg: The Man and his Music* (London, 1957).

◆ 3 ◆

TRIADIC HARMONY, DIATONIC COLLECTIONS, AND TONALITY

Schoenberg's rejection of triads, familiar seventh chords, and diatonic scales proved the exception rather than the rule in the twentieth century. By far the majority of composers have maintained familiar chords in their harmonic vocabulary, even though their customary diatonic functions have often been ignored or reinterpreted.

In the work of composers who continue to write tonal music in the twentieth century, triads and seventh chords are to be expected. But the triad and its extensions are also found repeatedly in music of this century that uses dissonance in a liberated manner and that bypasses the tonic–dominant axis and other trappings of common-practice tonality. We focus first upon the use of these harmonies in music where they do not primarily express key.

Triads and Triadic Extensions

Triads are especially prevalent in works by transitional composers such as Debussy or figures such as Hindemith, Stravinsky, Satie, or Prokofiev, whose music maintains contact with traditional tonality and form. They may also be found as central harmonies in music that is entirely atonal. A common function of the triad in such works is to mark the beginning or end of major sections of a piece. The familiar sound of the triad thus articulates the structure of a work much as perfect consonances did in early polyphony.

A striking example of a triad signaling the end of an entire atonal composition is the conclusion of Scriabin's symphonic poem *Prometheus*. This esoterically programmatic work emphasizes the nearly-whole-tone hexachord mentioned in the previous chapter, a harmony commonly known as the *Prometheus* or "mystic" chord after its appearance in this work. Example 3-1 shows the string parts at the end of this symphony. At rehearsal 63 we hear the nearly-whole-tone set (F G♭ A♭ B♭ C D), which moves by the end to an F♯-major triad. This is the first occurrence in the entire piece of a major or minor triad, which—by its uniqueness—emphatically marks the end of the work.

All forms of *seventh chords* continue to play an important part in music of this century. Five types of diatonic seventh chords were inherited from common-practice music: the dominant seventh (for example, C E G B♭), minor seventh (C E♭ G B♭), major seventh (C E G B), diminished seventh (C E♭ G♭ B♭♭), and half-diminished seventh (C E♭ G♭ B♭). In atonal harmonic theory there are only four distinct types, since the dominant seventh is an inversion of the half-diminished seventh, hence its equivalent (Example 3-2). This relationship of equivalence has no analogy in tonal harmony, since these chords have entirely different functions in the expression of a key.

Of the five types of seventh chords, the dominant and diminished sevenths are least often encountered in atonal twentieth-century music, probably because of the directness by which they may define a key. Chains of parallel dominant sevenths are nevertheless common in the music

Example 3-1. Scriabin, *Prometheus*, conclusion.

dominant
seventh   inversion:
                   half-diminished
                      seventh

Example 3-2. Inversional relationship of dominant and half-diminished seventh chords.

of Debussy, where they usually serve to enhance a melodic line.

The half-diminished seventh was exceedingly prominent in music around the turn of the century, both in late romantic music and early or transitional atonal works. This chord is one of the mainstays of Wagner's harmonic language; perhaps its best-known occurrence in his work is the so-called *Tristan* chord, from the Prelude to Act 1 of *Tristan und Isolde* (1857–59). The *Tristan* chord is enharmonically equivalent to the half-diminished seventh (Example 3-3). Its memorable sound and well-known association with the dramatic basis of the opera—the yearning for fulfillment of love—made it and its like-sounding seventh chord fundamental to music of the generation after Wagner.

The half-diminished seventh plays a leading role in tonal music of the early years of the twentieth century. Yet only rarely does it fulfill its normative diatonic function as a seventh chord on the second scale degree in minor, preparing the dominant. Instead, it is most often encountered as a harmony produced by stepwise or common-tone connection within parts which prolong an earlier diatonic chord. In measure 6 of Fauré's song "Dans la forêt de septembre" (Anthology no. 10), the half-diminished seventh (ϕ7) serves to prolong the dominant harmony as the bass moves down by step in parallel tenths with an inner voice (Example 3-4).

"Tristan"
chord

compare:

half-diminished
seventh

Example 3-3. *Tristan* chord and half-diminished seventh.

Example 3-4.   Fauré, *Dans la forêt de septembre*, measures 6–8.

A work in the post-Wagnerian idiom which makes even more extensive use of the half-diminished seventh is Schoenberg's "Song of the Wood Dove" from *Gurrelieder* (1900–11). This chord harmonizes the motive of Tove's death (Example 3-5), which recurs throughout the song in rondo fashion amid stretches that freely express a succession of keys. The chord is only weakly related to any diatonic function. It serves instead as an independent motto or "emancipated" dissonance and may thus be considered an atonal set.

The minor seventh chord is often encountered outside of a tonal context in music using pentatonic melodies or harmonies, since it is a subset of the pentatonic scale. A

Example 3-5.   Schoenberg, "Song of the Wood Dove," from *Gurre-Lieder*, part 1. Copyright 1912 by Universal Edition for world excluding U.S.A. Copyright renewed 1940. All rights reserved. Used by permission of European American Music Distributors Corporation, sole U.S. agent for Universal Edition. Used by permission of Belmont Music Publishers, Los Angeles (U.S.A.).

Example 3-6.   Debussy, "The Girl with the Flaxen Hair," from *Préludes,* book 1, measures 1–3.

typical occurrence in early twentieth-century French music is in Debussy's piano prelude "La fille aux cheveux de lin" ("The Girl with the Flaxen Hair"). A minor seventh chord is spelled out melodically as the initial motive of the main theme (Example 3-6). But this chord has no traditional tonal function as a seventh chord. Instead it represents a conflation of triads of the two primary tonal centers of the piece, G♭ and E♭. It also creates a four-note subset of the pentatonic scale, which would be completed by adding to it the note A♭. The pentatonic scale and its subsets subsequently underlie all melodic material (and much of the harmony) of the entire piece.

The major seventh chord has great prominence in the music of Igor Stravinsky. In the Credo from his Mass (1944–48, Anthology no. 23), virtually all cadences of the middle section (rehearsal 27–32) settle on this harmony in the form D F♯ A C♯.

Seventh chords are only some of the more familiar four-note extensions of the triad. Other tetrachords that contain a triad are also commonly found among composers of atonal music who wished to maintain sonorous contact with consonant harmony. The diagram in Example 3-7 illustrates all of the possible tetrachords that contain a major or minor triad. All are given in relation to a triad on C—shown in open noteheads—with the fourth pitch entered as a black notehead. A different tetrachord is formed when any pitch class not part of the root triad is added, so there are a total of nine such sets. After each extension of the major triad, its inversion is shown. In each case, the major-triadic component inverts to a minor triad. This relationship can be visualized by imagining the major third and fifth of the C-major triad inverted about the root pitch C, thus producing an F-minor chord. In Example 3-7

Example 3-7. The nine triadic tetrachords.

all such minor triads are transposed so as to appear as C-minor harmonies.

Tetrachords 1, 2, and 3 are familiar seventh chords which were just discussed. A few other tetrachords with triadic subsets were mentioned in the previous chapter: tetrachord 5 and its inversion (abbreviated 5i) are forms of type B of the all-interval tetrachord; tetrachord 7 is the major/minor tetrachord (which—like tetrachord 3—is equivalent to its inversion since it is a symmetrical formation); and tetrachords 3 and 8 are subsets of the pentatonic scale.

Only those tetrachords that are synonymous with familiar seventh chords—tetrachords 1, 2, and 3 and their inversions—played an important role in tonal music of the classical period. But in the later nineteenth century a freer use of melodic embellishing tones brought the other triadic tetrachords to greater prominence. The opening of Mahler's Symphony no. 3 (1895–96) contains a revealing example of the ways in which embellishing tones—an appoggiatura in this case—can create triadic tetrachords that call attention to themselves as quasi-independent harmonies. A reveille motive first heard at rehearsal 4 pits a C♯ in the trumpets against an underlying tonic D-minor chord (Example 3-8). The appoggiatura is extended a full two-and-one-half measures before resolving to D, and the chord created by the appoggiatura is triadic tetrachord 4i. When this motive

Example 3-8.   Mahler, Symphony no. 3, first movement.

recurs, it is harmonized in constantly changing ways, for example, as triadic tetrachord 5 (fifth measure of rehearsal 7), as 7 (rehearsal 9), and as 9 (third measure of rehearsal 17).

Among early atonal composers, these same harmonies continued to be employed, but usually without resolution to underlying diatonic triads. An atonal work almost totally dominated by triadic tetrachords is Scriabin's Piano Prelude, op. 74, no. 4 (1914). The first four measures (Example 3-9) show the variety of such chords: virtually every

Example 3-9.   Scriabin, Prelude, op. 74, no. 4, measures 1–4.

verticality is one of the triadic tetrachords, and no fewer than five different types are used in this opening phrase. The Prelude exhibits an extraordinary exploitation of similarity among chords based upon recurrence of the triadic subset. Tetrachord 7 (the major/minor tetrachord) plays a central articulative role, as it is heard at the beginning and end of this first phrase and also at the end of the piece. The middle section (measures 11–17) is dominated by tetrachord 4 and its inversion, which then leads to a return at measure 18 of the opening music.

Triadic tetrachords are also basic to the harmonic vocabulary of composers such as Berg and Hindemith, who maintained a strong allegiance to the triad. They are among the most prominent harmonies described in Hindemith's *Craft of Musical Composition*, volume 1, in which the author attempts to devise a unified conception of harmony that includes both traditional chords and the expanded harmonic resources of the twentieth century. Hindemith derived six groups of chords with varying degrees of "harmonic tension." Five triadic tetrachords appear in his Group III, which plays an especially large role in his music.

Bitriadic harmonies create another family of atonal sets based upon the triad. A bitriadic harmony is one in which two triads (or seventh chords) are heard simultaneously or in association, these triads made distinct by separation of register or difference in timbre. Such chords held a great attraction for atonal composers who wished to keep the triad as a sonorous reference. They are prominently used in the early ballets of Stravinsky. The *Petrushka* chord, for example, combines major triads on C and F♯, and the "Augurs of Spring" chord from *The Rite of Spring* joins an F♭ triad in the lower register to an E♭ dominant seventh in a higher register. Stravinsky's use of these two chords will be discussed further in Chapter 8. Just as the appearance of a triad does not in itself establish a tonality, the occurrence of bitriadic chords does not alone posit "bitonality," a phenomenon to be discussed shortly.

Charles Ives's song "From *Paracelsus*" (Anthology no. 12) uses a bitriadic harmony as a means of transition. This song begins with densely scored dissonances, which give way in the middle to a progression in G major. The linking of these two sections in measure 15 is facilitated by a chord made up of C- and D-minor triads (Example 3-10).

Example 3-10. Ives, "From *Paracelsus*." © 1935 by Merion Music Inc. Used by permission of the publisher.

Example 3-11. Harmonic equivalences in Ives's "From *Paracelsus*." © 1935 by Merion Music, Inc. Used by permission of the publisher.

This transitional passage includes two other chords which are harmonically equivalent to the bitriadic formation of measure 15. These are heard on the words "blind" (measure 13) and on "shun" (measure 14). The diagram in Example 3-11 shows the relationship of the three chords, which are equivalent by transposition or inversion. Ives's presentation of them helps to accomplish an orderly transition from the dissonance of the opening to the triadic middle section. The first appearance of the chord (measure 13) is ordered in such a way that its triadic subsets are not readily audible. In its second appearance in measure 14, we find its two triads separated in register but still closely positioned. By measure 15, the equivalent chord is stated as a true bitriadic configuration, with its constituent triads clearly audible as separate units.

Modality

In twentieth-century composition, *modality* refers to the occurrence of a set of pitches of which one is asserted as central or "tonic." *Modes* are synonymous with the collection of pitches in effect, provided that one note is shown (often as the first note in a scalar arrangement) as central. Modes thus join two independent structural principles of modern music: the pitch-class set and pitch centricity. This latter phenomenon will be discussed shortly under the rubric of "tonality."

Any set can be treated modally by consistently emphasizing one of its pitch classes. The pentatonic set in music by Zoltán Kodály, for example, is often encountered in a musical context where one of its pitch classes is emphasized. This note is usually the one falling a minor third below the cluster of two whole steps found in all pentatonic sets (Example 3-12). Kodály's use of this pentatonic mode reflects his study of Hungarian peasant music, in which repertory it underlies the oldest melodies.

But modality in the twentieth century is most important among diatonic sets, that is, among collections of seven pitch classes equivalent to the notes of a major scale. Since there are seven pitch classes in the diatonic set, there can be seven modes created from it by asserting each of its elements as tonic.

These seven modes are often called the "church modes" because of their similarities to the modes of medieval and Renaissance music. Contemporary terminology regarding the modes, however, has relatively little historical basis. We shall focus now solely upon the twentieth-century idea of the church modes.

The most common names currently in use to designate the seven church modes are Dorian, Phrygian, Lydian, Mixolydian, Aeolian, Locrian, and Ionian. Each refers to a scale duplicating the order of half and whole steps occurring without accidentals above the tonics D, E, F, G, A, B, and C, respectively (Example 3-13).

These modes are encountered in the work of composers such as Béla Bartók, Claude Debussy, Ralph Vaughan Williams, Jean Sibelius, and Carl Nielsen, all of whom sought to imitate early music or folk song. In their works modality is primarily a melodic phenomenon. The finale of Vaughan Williams's *Pastoral* Symphony, for example, con-

Example 3-12.   The pentatonic mode of old Hungarian peasant music.

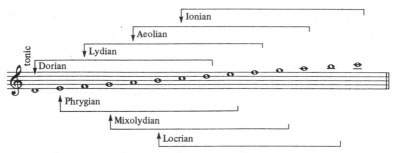

Example 3-13.   The seven diatonic modes.

tains a principal theme in the Dorian mode on D (Example 3-14). Despite the chromatic inflection of the note B♭ near the end of the melody, its pitch content generally duplicates that of the natural diatonic set. The note D is heard as a tonic because of its frequency of recurrence, its use as the last note, and its metric emphasis in several measures; D is also reinforced by the prominence of its dominant note A toward the beginning.

Modality in twentieth-century music normally exerts less influence on the harmonic than on the melodic dimension. Modal melodies are sometimes harmonized by triads within the mode, which may be strung together in root position. The opening of Bartók's *Bagatelle*, op. 6, no. 4 (Example 3-15), is of this type. Its theme is a folk song in the Aeolian mode on D, which is harmonized in the first two measures by a succession of root position triads. These chords express the centricity of D much more dimly than does the melody, since the mode lacks a dominant chord with leading tone which could strongly direct the harmonic motion toward a cadential tonic. The next phrase (measures 3-4) uses the same outer voices for the first two measures, only enriching the sound of the triads by the addition of sevenths and ninths.

Example 3-14.   Vaughan Williams, *Pastoral* Symphony, fourth movement, finale, measures 21–28. Copyright 1924 by J. Curwen & Sons Ltd. U.S. copyright renewed 1952. Used by arrangement with G. Schirmer, Inc., U.S. agent for J. Curwen & Sons Ltd., London.

Example 3-15.   Bartók, *Bagatelle,* op. 6, no. 4, measures 1–4.

Other harmonizations of modal themes by twentieth-century composers make few references to the structure of the melody. They are instead entirely atonal. In Bartók's *Improvisation*, op. 20, no. 7 (Example 9-1), a Hungarian peasant melody in the Phrygian mode on C is elaborated by a harmonic setting that does not refer to the modality of the theme. The accompanimental chords draw freely upon all chromatic pitches, and the note C does not receive special emphasis. The principal chords, furthermore, are not subsets of the diatonic collection.

A phenomenon related to modality is the use of a diatonic set—normally the notes of a C-major scale—without the assertion of a clear and stable tonic which would posit a mode. The term *pandiatonicism* was coined by Nicolas Slonimsky to identify this technique, which was prefigured in works by Debussy and Satie and used extensively in

Example 3-16.   Debussy, "La cathédrale engloutie" ("The Sunken Cathedral") from *Préludes*, book 1, measures 1–6.

music of Stravinsky and other neoclassicists in the 1920s and 1930s.

The opening of Debussy's piano prelude "La cathédrale engloutie" ("The Sunken Cathedral") uses all notes of the C-major scale, but projects no tonic note by which a key or mode could be inferred (Example 3-16). As in much of Debussy's diatonic music, pentatonic subsets are emphasized (for example, the quarter notes of the first measure constitute one of the three pentatonic sets—D E G A B—contained in a C-major scale). These pitches are arranged into chords in open fourths and fifths, which help to create the effect of a "gently sonorous mist" mentioned at the beginning of the score. The pandiatonic collection of pitches is not at all static. Harmonic motion is strongly directed by the bass line, which moves inexorably downward by step from the initial bass note G to B at the beginning of the middle section (measure 16).

Tonality and Atonality

There is no term in twentieth-century musical theory that has received more varied interpretations than *tonality*. The word is most commonly used in two ways, one specific, the other general. In the former sense it refers to the expression of key by methods that were common among composers of the eighteenth and nineteenth centuries. Some of these techniques were outlined in Chapter 1. In the latter and more general sense, it refers to the power of one or a few pitches to be heard through some span of a piece as central to its organization.

Common-practice tonality has continued to exist in this century, although as a relatively minor phenomenon. Many composers who were trained in the nineteenth century, such as Richard Strauss, chose to continue their earlier approach to key rather than to follow the more general trend away from traditional tonality. Certain works by European and American neoclassicists of the years between the world wars are also of this type, and in the 1970s and 1980s composers such as David Del Tredici and George Rochberg have written tonal music.

Music that does not express a key by these compositional principles is *atonal*. This term was first used in German musical criticism shortly before 1920 to refer pejoratively to a variety of modern works. The definition given shortly thereafter by the Viennese composer and theorist Josef Matthias Hauer in his *Lehrbuch der atonalen Musik* (1923) is still usable: "In atonal music there is no longer tonic, dominant, subdominant, scale step, resolution, consonance, or dissonance: instead, only the twelve intervals of equal temperament. Its 'scale' consists of twelve tempered semitones."

Although Hauer readily accepted the term atonal to describe his music, it was rejected by Schoenberg and his circle because of its negative connotation. In a radio lecture titled "What is Atonality?" (1930), Alban Berg deemed the term "diabolical" since it falsely implied a rejection of all older musical values and structural principles. Berg concluded that much atonal music was unpopular not because of its lack of key, but because of the absence of triadic consonances. Atonality is nevertheless a useful term, and it has long shed whatever pejorative connotations it possessed earlier. It will be used in this book to designate twentieth-century music that is nontonal and nonserialized.

In a more general sense, tonality refers to the centricity of one or a few pitches in parts of a musical work. Under this definition, virtually all music in Western history is to some degree tonal. The most common way such tonality is expressed in the twentieth century is by *assertion*, that is, by repeating a central pitch or otherwise emphasizing it by means of instrumentation, register, rhythmic elongation, or metric accent. Tonality by assertion is normally heard in the thematic or linear dimension of an otherwise "atonal" work. The third movement of Bartók's Piano Suite, op. 14 (opening measures in Example 2-17), strongly asserts the note D as its tonic by frequent recurrences, metric emphasis, placement in the lowest register of the piano, and by priority of place as the first and last note of themes and accompanimental lines.

Other twentieth-century works express a "key" by maintaining vestiges of common-practice tonality, for example, beginning and ending on the same triad, references to dominant or tonic pedal points, or contrapuntal motion within or around some central chord (often a triad). Such references are usually insufficient to establish a key in the traditional manner, and the musician must rely upon careful listening to judge whether the work is tonal or atonal. No single approach to tonality by assertion has become widespread in this century.

Key signatures may be found in twentieth-century music that is either tonal or atonal. A key signature does not create a key. It only simplifies notation, reducing the need for accidentals. Signatures imply that a diatonic collection of seven pitch classes has greater frequency or priority over the remaining five pitch classes. In atonal music that avails itself freely of all twelve pitch classes—as in the post-tonal works of Schoenberg—key signatures are not found. But other works that emphasize a single diatonic set or subset may use a signature to simplify notation despite little or no reference to a key. The "Augurs of Spring" from Stravinsky's ballet *Rite of Spring,* for example, uses a signature of three flats, despite its lack of significant references to a key. The bass line at rehearsal 16 and 28 dwells on the notes B♭ and E♭, but this suggestion of an E♭ triad is temporary and confined entirely to this one voice.

Other occurrences of key signatures in the atonal literature are intentionally enigmatic. The first three of Alban Berg's Four Songs, op. 2, use signatures despite Berg's application of an accidental to every note. His purpose for this apparent superfluity may have been programmatic rather than purely musical—in this case, a secretive homage to his teacher Arnold Schoenberg which is explained in Chapter 7.

Bitonality refers to the superposition of two different diatonic collections in different strata of a piece, each of which makes an allusion to a different key. This device was fashionable among composers living in France early in the century, especially Charles Koechlin (1867–1950), Igor Stravinsky, and Darius Milhaud. In his article "Polytonalité et atonalité" (1923), Milhaud traces this tonal device back to the canons of Bach, in which a consequent voice at the interval of a fifth is superimposed over a leading voice. Milhaud's dance for piano "Botafogo" from *Saudades do Brazil* (Anthology no. 5) begins with an F-minor collection in the left hand, which accompanies a melody in the right hand in F♯ minor. These two strata maintain distinct harmonic relations: the left hand reiterates a tonic–dominant–tonic motion in its key, and the melody in the right hand emphasizes scale degrees one and five, reinforcing its key of F♯ minor. The chords formed by vertical conjunction of these strata do not create structurally significant sets.

Bibliography

An important early study of the relationship between tonal and atonal music in the twentieth century is Rudolph Reti's *Tonality, Atonality, Pantonality: A Study of Some Trends in Twentieth-Century Music* (New York and London, 1958). Reti's view of atonality is somewhat more narrow than the one advanced in this book, and he supplements it with the notion of "pantonality"—brought to twentieth-century music by Debussy—in which a purely melodic type of tonality is made pervasive. Early theoretical writings on atonality are generally unavailable in English; important among them are Josef Matthias Hauer's *Vom Wesen des Musikalischen: Ein Lehrbuch der atonalen Musik* (Leipzig, 1920; rev. Berlin, 1923), Herbert Eimert's *Atonale Musiklehre* (Leipzig, 1924), and Edwin von der Nüll's *Moderne Harmonik* (Leipzig, 1932).

Discussions of polytonality by two composers who used this technique are Darius Milhaud's "Polytonalité et atonalité," *Revue musicale*, 4 (1923) and Charles Koechlin's "Évolution de l'harmonie: période contemporaine," in the *Encyclopédie de la musique et dictionnaire du conservatoire*, ed. Albert Lavignac and Lionel de La Laurencie (Paris, 1923). Koechlin's lengthy study also emphasizes the application of modes to late-nineteenth- and early-twentieth-century French music.

Differing views on how triadic harmony can relate to twentieth-century practices are put forth by Paul Hindemith in his *Craft of Musical Composition*, vol. 1, trans. Arthur Mendel (New York, 1942) and by Felix Salzer in *Structural Hearing: Tonal Coherence in Music*, 2 vols. (New York, 1952). Arnold Whittall's *Music Since the First World War* (London, 1977) emphasizes the ways in which triadic harmonies can create tonality in modern music. John Clough's articles "Aspects of Diatonic Sets," *Journal of Music Theory*, 23 (1979), and "Diatonic Interval Sets and Transformational Structures," *Perspectives of New Music*, 18 (1980), present technical discussions of diatonic sets.

Nicolas Slonimsky's discussion of pandiatonicism is located in his *Music Since 1900* (New York, 1971).

◆ 4 ◆

SERIALISM

Serialism is a method of composition by which the order of occurrence of one or more musical elements is determined by a preexistent arrangement. The musical elements that can be disposed serially include pitch, duration, attack, instrumentation and timbre, and overall form. Serialism was applied to music of the twentieth century at first to compensate for the absence of common-practice tonality. Like tonality, it produced unity of design and offered the composer a practical guide to musical expansion. After the Second World War, it was applied in a broader way to the compositional process. Serialism is thus a structural element and compositional method that does not produce any single musical style.

Antecedents of serialism exist in common-practice music. For example, the background harmonic progression *tonic–dominant–tonic* is a preexistent series used time and again by composers of the eighteenth and nineteenth centuries to guide them in organizing large spans of musical space. When composers of the twentieth century ceased to apply this tonal series, many felt the need for analogous (though less widely stereotyped) sequences that would direct them in the creation of syntactically comprehensible works.

We shall begin our discussion of serialism by an investigation of the twelve-tone method: a way of serializing pitch introduced by Arnold Schoenberg and freely adapted by other composers. Subsequently, we shall turn to non-twelve-tone serialization of pitch, a technique that was used in music both before and after the development of the twelve-tone method, and, finally, to "integral serialism," in which musical elements other than pitch are predetermined in their order of appearance.

The Twelve-Tone Method

In a lecture on "Composition with Twelve Tones" (1941), Schoenberg stated:

> After many unsuccessful attempts during a period of approximately twelve years, I laid the foundations for a new procedure in musical construction which seemed fitted to replace those structural differentiations provided formerly by tonal harmonies. I called this procedure *Method of Composition with Twelve Tones which are Related Only with One Another.* This method consists primarily of the constant and exclusive use of a set of twelve different tones.

According to Schoenberg's method, most or all pitches of a composition occur in an order derived from forms of a *row* (or *series* or *set*). This "basic set," as it was called by Schoenberg, is a predetermined ordering of the twelve pitch classes, each occurring once. The term *dodecaphonic* also designates music composed according to this method. In the following discussion, the terms row and series will be used synonymously, but we shall avoid the term "set," since it has been used earlier to refer to an unordered harmonic unit.

Schoenberg's method was applied tentatively in movements of his Suite for piano, op. 25, in 1921, and it was more fully developed by 1923. Most (but not all) of his compositions after that time use the method, although his interpretation of it later changed in several fundamental ways. In his 1941 lecture, Schoenberg stated that his first thought or inspiration for a piece of this type was motivic in nature, from which the basic row could then be extracted. "The basic set functions in the manner of a motive," he said. "This explains why such a basic set has to be invented anew for every piece. It [the motive] has to be the first creative thought."

The basic series is abstracted from its motivic origins and then generates as many as forty-eight related *row forms*. These are derived, first, by performing three operations upon the basic series: retrograde arrangement, (symmetric) inversion, and retrograde arrangement of the inversion. Let us illustrate these operations by considering the basic series of Schoenberg's Fourth String Quartet, op. 37 (first movement, Anthology no. 25). The motivic shape in which the row was conceived is heard in the first violin in measures 1–5. From this line we can readily extract the order of twelve pitch classes that constitutes the basic series. We shall call this basic series the *prime* form of the row, abbreviated P. (These abbreviations, by the way, are not widely standardized.)

Prime form row)

P: D C♯ A B♭ F E♭ E C A♭ G F♯ B

The *retrograde* of P (abbreviated RP) may be obtained by reading the series from right to left:

RP: B F♯ G A♭ C E E♭ F B♭ A C♯ D.

The *inversion* of the prime form (abbreviated I) may be obtained by intervallic rotation about some fixed pitch class within P. We shall allow the first pitch class D to remain fixed as the first pitch class within I. The second pitch class of P is one semitone *below* D, so the second pitch class of I will be one semitone *above* D, that is, E♭. The third pitch class is a fifth above D, so the third pitch class in I will be G, a fifth below D—and so forth through all pitch classes of the prime form:

I: D E♭ G F♯ B C♯ C E A♭ A B♭ F.

The *retrograde inversion* (abbreviated RI) may be obtained by reading the inversion from right to left:

RI: F B♭ A A♭ E C C♯ B F♯ G E♭ D.

The four basic forms of the row—P, RP, I, and RI—can then spawn a total of forty-eight forms by transposition of each to all of the twelve available levels of pitch. The prime form of the row from the Fourth String Quartet, for example, can be transposed up three semitones to render a new row form. We shall use the abbreviation P_3 to identify this transposition and refer to the basic (untransposed) form as P_0:

P_0: D C♯ A B♭ F E♭ E C A♭ G F♯ B
P_3: F E C C♯ G♯ F♯ G E♭ B B♭ A D.

These forty-eight forms of the basic series are equally available to the composer for the purpose of establishing the order in which pitches will occur in a twelve-tone piece. The forms are closely related. The intervals between pitch classes in the prime form recur in all of the other forms, although they may be reversed in order. Thus a work based on the twelve-tone method will have a powerful intervallic unity.

Before continuing with a survey of Schoenberg's applications of the row, we shall briefly examine the circumstances that led him to his method. It will be especially instructive to compare the premises of twelve-tone composition with Schoenberg's compositional procedures in his "atonal" period, the latter extending from about 1908 to 1921. Many of the same techniques and assumptions underlie both types of composition. In both, dissonance is emancipated and suggestions of a keynote are usually suppressed. In both, transpositions and inversions of sets of pitches contribute to diversity and unity among lines and chords. In most respects, the twelve-tone method only provides more "conscious control" (to use Schoenberg's terms) over the materials of composition than was the case in his largely intuitive atonal language.

The twelve-tone method differs from atonal composition primarily in two ways: it guarantees a more complete recirculation of all twelve pitch classes, and it applies a rigorous criterion of order to pitches as they unfold in the music from the background chromatic set. The first of these phenomena continues a pronounced historical trend toward chromaticism, especially among German and Austrian composers of the generation after Wagner. Numerous works of the late nineteenth and early twentieth centuries contain themes that touch upon every note of the chromatic scale. The beginning of Liszt's *Faust* Symphony (1854), the fugal subject "On Science" from Strauss's *Also sprach Zarathustra* (1895), and the passacaglia theme from Act 1 of Berg's *Wozzeck* (1917–22) are important examples.

In the early decades of the twentieth century, this trend toward chromaticism led to systems that were intended to insure total chromatic saturation of themes. While these techniques are related to Schoenberg's twelve-tone method only in the most superficial way, they are evidence of a broad concern for total chromaticism. The Viennese composer Josef Matthias Hauer (1883–1959), for example, devised a "law" governing atonal melody: "Within a given [melodic] succession of pitches," he stated in his *Vom Wesen des Musikalischen* (1923), "no pitch may be repeated and none may be omitted. . . . Over and over again, all twelve pitches of the tempered scale must be heard." By 1924 Hauer had further refined his method for insuring complete chromatic recirculation by basing his works upon one or more "tropes." These were divisions of the chromatic set into forty-four different pairs of complementary, unordered hexachords. Hauer's tropes contain no system of order within the twelve-tone set, and his music is more closely related to Schoenberg's atonal idiom than to his twelve-tone works.

The twelve-tone method differs most strikingly from atonal composition by its principle of order. The row establishes an unvarying succession of intervals, which is repeatedly presented, either directly, in inversion, or in retrograde. Such intervallic order also has historical precedents, for example, in the strict canonic writing of the Renaissance or in certain motivic practices of eighteenth- and nineteenth-century composers. In his lecture of 1941, Schoenberg cited the primary motive from the finale of Beethoven's String Quartet in F major, op. 135, which is deployed in an inversion and in a varied retrograde. But order in the twelve-tone method did not arise primarily through historical considerations. It was instead the result of Schoenberg's decision to make the basic sets in his music encompass the entire chromatic as opposed to his earlier practice of utilizing primarily four-, five-, and six-note collections. An unordered twelve-note set is, in fact, very limiting. It has no inversion, no transpositions, no complement, and it possesses an undistinctive intervallic content. To use it as Hauer did—as an ever-present unordered set—might have led to music that was monotonous and unstructured. So Schoenberg added to it a principle of order, thus creating a new dimension of variety and differentiation.

Schoenberg's method was later adopted by many composers, including Alban Berg, Anton Webern, Ernst Křenek, Luigi Dallapiccola, and a large group of avant-garde musicians in Europe and America after the Second World War. Among them the method has proved enormously flexible. Other than the necessity of deriving the order of most pitches from preconceived arrangements of the total chromatic set, there are few if any firmly established principles that have been widely and consistently observed. The method has instead become a general approach to order and chromatic pitch content. It will be useful, nevertheless, to survey various interpretations of the method in works of major composers, focusing primarily upon the twelve-tone compositions of Schoenberg.

Construction of the Row

The row of Schoenberg's Fourth String Quartet—D C♯ A B♭ F E♭ E C A♭ G F♯ B—is typical of his series in its succession of intervals. There is diversity of intervallic content and avoidance of triadic or diatonic segments.

Some interval classes, here the semitone and major third, are emphasized. Schoenberg's construction of rows after about 1925 was guided by the principle of combinatoriality, which will be discussed shortly.

Other composers deliberately incorporated diatonic shapes into their rows, giving their music more familiar sonorities. The series of Berg's Violin Concerto consists of interlocking major and minor triads concluded by three whole tones: G B♭ D F♯ A C E G♯ B C♯ D♯ F. One of the rows from his opera *Lulu* begins with the first six notes of an F-minor scale: F G A♭ B♭ C D (F♯ D♯ E A B C♯).

The rows employed by Webern are often made from segments with the same succession of intervals. An example is the row of his String Quartet, op. 28: B♭ A C B D♯ E C♯ D G♭ F A♭ G. Its first four notes (spelling BACH in German) are identical at I_5 to the second four notes and, if transposed up eight semitones, to the final four notes. A row of this type, which can be generated by operations on an initial segment, is said to be *derived*: its symmetry reduces its number of different intervals—this series contains only minor seconds, minor thirds, major thirds, and their inversions. Derived series present the composer with many possibilities for motivic relationships within different segments of different row forms.

An opposite tendency from Webern's reduction of intervallic variety is found in rows that state every interval. The row from the first movement of Berg's *Lyric* Suite is such an *all-interval series*: F E C A G D A♭ D♭ E♭ G♭ B♭ B. If we count the number of semitones from each pitch class upward to the next pitch class, we obtain the intervals 11 8 9 10 7 6 5 2 3 4 1, which shows that each interval within the octave occurs once. Several composers after World War II favored all-interval rows of symmetrical construction. The row of Luigi Nono's *Il canto sospeso* (1956) expands chromatically in both directions to form an all-interval series. Its shape can be observed in the staff notation in Example 4-1.

Example 4-1.   Basic series of Luigi Nono's *Il canto sospeso.*

Supplementary Row Forms

Composers of twelve-tone music have felt the need in some works to expand the number of forms of a row beyond the forty-eight variations upon a single basic series posited by Schoenberg. A simple way to accomplish this expansion is to use more than one basic series in a composition. Schoenberg—who generally opposed the use of more than one basic row in a work—resorted to several interrelated basic series in his Third String Quartet, op. 30, and String Trio, op. 45. Berg used several rows in his *Lyric* Suite and opera *Lulu*. The rows of *Lulu* are each associated with a character in the drama. In a letter to Schoenberg of 1928, Berg stated that these rows were derivable from one central series by a variety of imaginative procedures. The row associated with the character Alwa, for example, is constructed from every seventh note of the basic series, the latter identified with Lulu. But, regardless of their method of derivation, these rows function as mutually independent elements.

Another way to expand the number of row forms is to devise operations on a basic series that supplement inversion and retrograde arrangement. The most common and widespread of these additional operations has been *cyclical rotation* (sometimes called *cyclical permutation*). A row form is cyclically rotated when one or more consecutive pitch classes at the beginning are made to go, as it were, to the end of the line. Consider as an example the following row form from Berg's "Lied der Lulu" (Anthology no. 20), which is I_{10} of the basic series of the work:

I_{10}: B♭ G♭ F A♭ D♯ C♯ E D B C G A.

There can be as many as eleven additional cyclical rotations of this row, beginning with G♭, F, A♭, and so forth, rotating preceding pitch classes in order to the end. We shall designate these rotations by two numbers in parenthesis, the first showing which pitch class begins the rotation, the second designating which pitch class ends the

Example 4-2.   Berg, *Lulu*, Act 2. Copyright 1936 by Universal Edition, © renewed 1964 by Universal Edition, all rights reserved. Used by permission of European American Music Distributors Corp., sole U.S. agent for Universal Edition.

new row form. Thus, I_{10} (5-4) refers to the rotation which begins with the fifth note of I_{10} (D♯) and ends with the fourth (A♭):

I_{10} (5-4): D♯ C♯ E D B C G A B♭ G♭ F A♭.

Berg uses cyclic rotations of basic series in his opera *Lulu* in addition to the normal forty-eight forms. The first vocal phrase of the "Lied der Lulu" begins with a statement of the central series at P_0, which is then followed by the rotation of I_{10} shown above. A subsidiary line in the celli and bass clarinet uses I_7 (Example 4-2). This passage is typical of music from *Lulu* and of Berg's twelve-tone music in general in that subsidiary inner parts (and some important lines) may be atonal rather than dodecaphonic. Most of the chords of measures 492–97 are whole-tone subsets, which are not segments of any tone rows in this work. In measures 495–96 the basses and piano repeat the notes D G A♭ D♭, which is a primary set in the opera representing Lulu's seductivity. It is not part of a tone row. A further discussion of this aria will be found in Chapter 7.

A special way of using cyclic rotations was devised by Ernst Křenek in his *Lamentatio Jeremiae* (1941) and used later by Igor Stravinsky beginning with his *Movements* (1959). According to this procedure, the composer supplements the forty-eight basic row forms and their cyclic rotations by four matrices, each consisting of six hexachords. The hexachords within each matrix are transposed rotations of the first and last hexachords of the basic series and its inversion.

Let us illustrate with the basic series of Stravinsky's Variations for Orchestra by constructing a matrix from its first hexachord:

P_0: *D C A B E A♯* (*G♯ C♯ D♯ G F♯ F*)

This hexachord is first rotated its maximum of five times:

D	C	A	B	E	A♯
C	A	B	E	A♯	D
A	B	E	A♯	D	C
B	E	A♯	D	C	A
E	A♯	D	C	A	B
A♯	D	C	A	B	E

The rotations are then transposed so that they will all begin with the first pitch class of the source hexachord (in this case D):

D	C	A	B	E	A♯
D	B	C♯	F♯	C	E
D	E	A	D♯	G	F
D	G	C♯	F	D♯	C
D	G♯	C	A♯	G	A
D	F♯	E	C♯	D♯	G♯

The matrix is used by Stravinsky in various ways in his Variations, especially to guide him in constructing chords by duplicating the content of pitches found in vertical columns of the matrix. These verticalities greatly expand the harmonic vocabulary derivable from the row. The third and fifth columns of the matrix, for example, form major/minor tetrachords—a set that had long been favored by Stravinsky and that was thus brought into the twelve-tone idiom of his Variations despite its absence as a segment of any row form.

Combinatoriality and Invariance

The terms combinatoriality and invariance, both brought into the study of music by Milton Babbitt, refer to properties of twelve-tone rows and relationships among row forms that have proved to be of great consequence to many twelve-tone composers. *Combinatoriality* is the capacity of a segment of a series to form a collection of all twelve pitch classes when it is combined with the corresponding segment of one or more of its row forms. The basic series of Schoenberg's Fourth String Quartet is thus combinatorial, since its first hexachord combines with the first hexachord of I_5 to form the chromatic set (which Babbitt has dubbed the *aggregate*):

	first hexachord:	second hexachord:
P_0:	D C♯ A B♭ F E♭	(E C A♭ G F♯ B)
I_5:	G G♯ C B E F♯	(F A C♯ D D♯ B♭)
	aggregate	aggregate

It will be obvious from this example that the second hexachord must also be combinatorial with the second hexachord of the related row form (I_5). Furthermore, any transposition of P will be combinatorial with the same transposition of I plus five semitones. P_3, for example, will be combinatorial at I_8. And, finally, it can be observed that combinatoriality does not depend upon the order of pitch classes within the hexachord—only upon its total content of pitches. In other words, any reordering of the notes D C♯ A B♭ F E♭ will also form an aggregate when combined with its transformation at I_5.

Combinatoriality has been extensively exploited in the music of Schoenberg, Babbitt, and other contemporary Americans. Schoenberg focused solely upon inversional, hexachordal combinatoriality as illustrated above. Combinatorial relations have been applied much more broadly in Babbitt's music, where they are central to its construction and meaning. Combinatoriality had a decisive influence on Schoenberg's construction of rows beginning with his Suite, op. 29 (1924–26). A few years thereafter his selection of basic series became even more restrictive as he only used rows whose hexachords were combinatorial at I_5.

Schoenberg stated in his 1941 lecture that his purpose in using combinatorial row forms was to insure that no pitch class would inadvertently be doubled if, for example, a hexachord from one form were accompanied by the corresponding hexachord from the related row form. His use of combinatorial series, however, is more extensive

than this fundamental circumstance. Combinatoriality became Schoenberg's primary criterion for *association* of row
forms, that is, which of the forty-eight forms should be used
in the same region of a composition or used at the same
time. In the Fourth String Quartet we see a P form
consistently paired with its combinatorial I form, the two
heard either simultaneously or in succession.

Schoenberg's later twelve-tone music reveals a fascination with the creation of aggregates by combinatorial
conjunction of hexachords such that the principle of order
in a twelve-tone series plays a decidedly secondary role. In
works such as the String Trio, op. 45, and Violin Fantasy,
op. 47, the unordered hexachord becomes the primary
structural unit.

Invariance refers in general to the existence of elements of a series that remain unchanged subsequent to the
operations of inversion, transposition, or retrograde arrangement. An example of this phenomenon is the preservation
of certain pitch classes at the same position in the row
after it is inverted. Any row will maintain two pitch classes
in the same position if it is inverted and transposed to an
even number of semitones (I_0, I_2, I_4, and so forth). These
invariant pitch classes will always be a tritone apart:

P_0:   D   C♯ | A   B♭   F | E♭ | E   C   A♭   G   F♯   B
I_2:   E   F | A   G♯   C♯ | E♭ | D   F♯   B♭   B   C   G

tritone

This type of invariance has compositional significance in
the Musette from Schoenberg's Piano Suite, op. 25, in which
a P form is associated with an I form at an even-numbered
transposition level. The two invariant pitch classes are
reiterated in a very prominent manner.

More important for the later twelve-tone music of
Schoenberg and for the works of Berg and Webern is
segmental invariance. This type of invariance obtains when
a continuous segment of two or more notes reappears as a
segment in another row form. Any of the prime forms of
the row of Schoenberg's Fourth String Quartet contains two
trichordal invariants in comparison with the corresponding

RI form five semitones higher. Let us illustrate by comparing P_1 to RI_6:

P_1: | E♭ D A♯ | B F♯ E F | C♯ A G♯ | G C

RI_6: B E | E♭ D A♯ | F♯ G F C | C♯ A G♯ |

These invariant segments are used to construct principal lines and to bring about motivic continuity despite changes in row forms. In measures 153–54 of the first movement of the Fourth String Quartet, the principal line in the viola consists of these two disjunct trichords in P_1, while the other parts fill in the remaining pitch classes of this row form. The next two measures unfold RP_6, and the same line is heard an octave higher in the first violin. This recurrence is possible since the two trichords that underlie this line are still available in that row form.

Application of the Row to Lines and Chords and Choice of Row Forms

The twelve-tone method is most applicable to the melodic lines of a composition. Schoenberg usually begins his twelve-tone works with a principal melody which unambiguously states the basic series while the subsidiary parts unfold the same or another row form. Immediate repetitions of notes or groups of notes are common, since these are motivic details that cause no fundamental distortion in the order in which a row form is presented. The opening of Schoenberg's Fourth String Quartet unfolds the basic series in the principal line (first violin) while segments of the same row form are heard simultaneously in the accompanimental chords. The composer also initiates in these first measures a characteristic division of the row—four segments of three notes each—which will be continued throughout the entire movement. In the diagram that follows, it will be seen that these trichords (labelled *a*, *b*, *c*, and *d*) subdivide both vertical and horizontal dimensions:

	a			b			c			d		
P₀:	D	C♯	A	B♭	F	E♭	E	C	A♭	G	F♯	B

measure:	1	2	3	4–6
principal line:	a———	b———	c———	d———
accompanimental chords:	b c d	c d a	d a b	a b c

In measure 6 the principal line passes to the second violin, which then unfolds I₅. Schoenberg's decision to follow P₀ with I₅ is no doubt based on the fact that these two row forms are combinatorial. His selection of forms later in the work is also influenced by motivic considerations. The basic shape of the Fourth String Quartet strongly emphasizes the descending semitone, two occurrences of which are marked by rhythmic elongations (Example 4-3). When this theme makes its first important return at measure 165, Schoenberg chooses to state it at P₆ so that the figure A♭–G will then be thrust into the leading position.

Other composers such as Berg and Webern often choose row forms that elide with one just heard. In other words, they select a form whose first pitch class is the same as the last pitch class of the row just concluded. In the sixth movement of Webern's Second Cantata, op. 31, for example, the soprano line begins with a prime form which is followed by the prime form six semitones distant. The composer has P₆ follow P₀ since in that succession they share the note C:

P₀

F♯ A F E G♯ D♯ G B B♭ D C♯ | C | E♭ B B♭ D A C♯ F E G♯ G F♯

P₆

Another consideration guiding composers in their choice of row forms is their desire to create certain harmonic sonorities. At the beginning of the fifth movement of Webern's Second Cantata (Anthology no. 22) the four choral parts simultaneously state P₀, P₂, P₅, and P₆

Example 4-3.   Schoenberg, Fourth String Quartet, op. 37, first movement. Copyright 1939, by G. Schirmer, Inc. International copyright secured. Reprinted by permission.

(Example 4-4). Webern probably chose these transpositions because they create a succession of all-interval tetrachords of type A, which we hear as the six verticalities of this opening passage. The all-interval tetrachord, which was prominent in Webern's vocabulary of atonal harmonies, does not occur as a segment of the row used by the composer in this piece, but it is brought nonetheless into the music as a prominent sonority by the choice of row forms.

The derivation of chords from row forms is often less systematic than the construction of melodies. Schoenberg usually creates chords from segments of a row, that is, from two or more consecutive pitch classes. But their vertical order does not consistently reflect the intervallic order of the series. In music by Milton Babbitt, on the other hand, the vertical arrangement of chordal pitches is strictly determined by serial order. In many cases, chords will be made from invariant segments of two row forms that are operative in the same area of a work, or, as we have seen in the whole-tone harmonies in Berg's "Lied der Lulu," they may be independent of the row.

Example 4-4.   Webern, Second Cantata, op. 31, fifth movement, measures 1-3, rhythm omitted. Copyright 1951 by Universal Edition, Wien. Copyright renewed. All rights reserved. Used by permission of European-American Music Distributors Corp., sole U.S. agent for Universal Edition.

Non-Twelve-Tone Serialism

Series of greater or fewer than twelve pitch classes were important elements in the organization of music by Schoenberg and Stravinsky prior to their adoption of the twelve-tone method. Nondodecaphonic serialism also plays a role in music by the American composer Carl Ruggles (see Chapter 11). Schoenberg began to apply series of this type in several incomplete works around 1915 and later in his Piano Pieces, op. 23 (1920–23), and Serenade, op. 24 (1920–23). Stravinsky's music from the Cantata (1952) to his first twelve-tone composition, *Threni* (1958), mixes atonal and nondodecaphonic serial procedures.

Schoenberg's Serenade for seven instruments and bass voice is in seven movements grouped symmetrically about a vocal setting of a Petrarchan sonnet. Two experimental approaches to serial composition are encountered in this work: one in the sonnet, where the vocal part reiterates an untransformed twelve-note row, and the other in the third movement, Variations, which is based upon a fourteen-note series. The theme of the Variations (Example 4-5) consists of this row joined to its retrograde, in imitation of the antecedent and consequent phrases of a classical period. Compared to Schoenberg's later twelve-tone procedures, application of the row in the five variations and coda that follow is decidedly primitive. Only the untransposed prime form, untransposed inversion, and their retrogrades are used, and, toward the middle of the movement, these row forms are scattered in free order among several contrapuntal lines.

Example 4-5.   Schoenberg, *Serenade*, op. 24, third movement, measures 1–11. Copyright 1924 by Wilhelm Hansen, Copenhagen. Reprinted by permission.

Example 4-6.   Stravinsky, *In Memoriam Dylan Thomas*, second
movement (song, "Do not go gentle," poem by Dylan
Thomas) © Copyright 1954 by Boosey & Hawkes, Inc.;
renewed 1982. Reprinted by permission. From *Collected
Poems of Dylan Thomas*, by permission of J.M. Dent and
Sons.

Igor Stravinsky's *In Memoriam Dylan Thomas* (1954) is
a work in three movements which uses a five-note set: E Eb
C C♯ D. The outer movements, "Dirge-Canons," imitate
instrumental *equali* of the eighteenth century, of which
Beethoven's *Three Equali for Four Trombones* are the best
known examples. The middle movement is a setting for
tenor and string quartet of Thomas's "Do not go gentle into
that good night."

Several transpositions of all four basic transformations
of the row are strictly applied to the polyphonic lines.
Stravinsky's elisions of row forms reflect the row technique
of Webern; as in the music of Webern, these elisions often
encompass larger segments. The first vocal phrase of the
second movement (Example 4-6) is an illustration. Despite
the chromatic content of the row, the composer's choice of
row forms insures that diatonic subsets will be evident,
especially as harmonies at major cadences. The brass
cadences in the first movement and string cadences in the
finale are mainly on triads. Other passages come to a rest
on diatonic segments such as C–D–E or (in the song)
B–D–E.

Integral Serialism

Shortly after the conclusion of World War II, the
revival of a musical avant-garde stimulated renewed interest in serial composition. In Europe the long suppressed
twelve-tone works of Schoenberg, Webern, and Berg were
performed and studied, and the method underlying their

composition was spread by former students of Schoenberg including René Leibowitz and Josef Rufer. In America a younger generation of composers including Milton Babbitt and Gunther Schuller had become devoted and resourceful serialists.

There arose among musicians on both sides of the Atlantic similar though independent movements to extend the serial principle to embrace multiple elements of a composition, such as duration, placement of attacks, dynamics, tempo, and timbre. This application of serialism to several dimensions of a work will be called *total* or *integral serialism.*

Postwar integral serialism was prefigured by the twelve-tone works of Schoenberg, Berg, and Webern. The row in Schoenberg's music strongly (although unsystematically) influences melodic phrasing, rhythm, meter, attack, register, timbre, and form. The influence of the row on these elements is more systematically explored in works of Webern, whose desire to achieve the greatest possible conciseness of materials led in some pieces to a consistent interrelation of intervallic structures with other musical elements. His sparse and disconnected textures were also very appealing to the postwar European avant-garde.

Music by Olivier Messiaen of the late 1940s was also influential upon the emerging movement of European serialism. In his piano prelude "Mode de valeurs et d'intensités" (1949), Messiaen devised a way to integrate the different elements of a work, although these were not disposed serially. In this piece an unchanging dynamic level, duration, type of attack, and register are assigned to each pitch class in each of three strata. These pitch classes are not deployed in a serial order, but their prearranged integration with other variables of composition was an idea that Messiaen's students (including Pierre Boulez and Karlheinz Stockhausen) soon allied to serial methods.

Systems of integral serialism did not attain widespread standardization. We shall thus focus on two representative approaches: those of Milton Babbitt and Pierre Boulez. By the late 1940s, Babbitt had devised a mathematical model that concisely represents the manipulations of pitch in a twelve-tone piece. He used these same numerical operations to generate rhythm and dynamics in his Three

Compositions for Piano (1947), which produced a highly integrated structure. His goal in this and later compositions, as he wrote in the article "Some Aspects of Twelve-Tone Composition" (1955), is "a completely autonomous conception of the twelve-tone system, and . . . works in which all components, in all dimensions, would be determined by the relations and operations of the system."

Babbitt begins by constructing a basic series that is rich in structural relationships. Some series, as in the first of his Three Compositions for Piano, are all-interval rows. Most of Babbitt's basic series are what he calls *all-combinatorial*: their hexachords can create aggregates when combined with at least one transposition each of P, RP, I, and RI.

Babbitt then extends the structural features of the row to other aspects of composition by interpreting pitches and their relationships in terms of modular arithmetic and mathematical group theory. The pitch classes of a tone row are represented by integers from 0 to 11, each corresponding to the number of semitones of a pitch class above the initial one in the basic series, which is postulated as 0. Row forms can then be derived by simple arithmetic functions. The inversion of the row can be obtained by subtracting each number from 12 (the first element remains 0). Transpositions are figured by adding the number of semitones by which the row is to be transposed to each integer, reverting to 0 when 12 is reached. The basic series of Schoenberg's Fourth String Quartet, its inversion, and the inversion transposed up five semitones, for example, would be represented:

$(P_0:$	D	C♯	A	B♭	F	E♭	E	C	A♭	G	F♯	B)
$P_0:$	0	11	7	8	3	1	2	10	6	5	4	9
$I_0:$	0	1	5	4	9	11	10	2	6	7	8	3
$I_5:$	5	6	10	9	2	4	3	7	11	0	1	8

These arithmetic procedures simultaneously underlie the construction and application of rhythms, successions of dynamics, and overall form. We shall return to Babbitt's serialized music in Chapter 5 to explain how rhythms are derived from his mathematical model.

Pierre Boulez's involvement with integral serialism was more short-lived than Babbitt's. Boulez's *Structures Ia* for two pianos (1952) was his most detailed essay in this method of composition, and it will show both the similarities and differences of European postwar serialism with its American counterpart.

Boulez's basic series in *Structures Ia* is borrowed from one of the "modes" or sets used by Messiaen in his "Mode de valeurs et d'intensités." Boulez, like Babbitt, uses the series in the forty-eight classical transformations, and, also like Babbitt, he relates these rows to the serialization of other elements of the work by mathematical means. Boulez's system, however, is entirely different from Babbitt's. Boulez assigns the numbers 1 to 12 to each pitch class in the basic series in the *order* of their occurrence:

P_0:	E♭	D	A	A♭	G	F♯	E	C♯	C	B♭	F	B
	1	2	3	4	5	6	7	8	9	10	11	12

He then constructs two twelve-by-twelve matrices of numbers, each of whose rows represents a transposition of either the P or I forms of the basic series. In the P matrix, for example, a transposition of P_0 up one semitone results in a number series representing how this transposition changes the *order* of elements in P_0:

P_0:	1	2	3	4	5	6	7	8	9	10	11	12
P_1:	7	1	10	3	4	5	11	2	8	12	6	9
	(E	D♯	A♯	A	G♯	G	F	D	C♯	B	F♯	C)

The first integer of P_1 is 7 because its first pitch class E is numbered 7 in P_0. The matrices are then completed in this way:

P Matrix

[P₀]											
1	2	3	4	5	6	7	8	9	10	11	12
2	8	4	5	6	11	1	9	12	3	7	10
3	4	1	2	8	9	10	5	6	7	12	11
4	5	2	8	9	12	3	6	11	1	10	7
5	6	8	9	12	10	4	11	7	2	3	1
6	11	9	12	10	3	5	7	1	8	4	2
7	1	10	3	4	5	11	2	8	12	6	9
8	9	5	6	11	7	2	12	10	4	1	3
9	12	6	11	7	1	8	10	3	5	2	4
10	3	7	1	2	8	12	4	5	11	9	6
11	7	12	10	3	4	6	1	2	9	5	8
12	10	11	7	1	2	9	3	4	6	8	5

[P₀]
[P₁₁]
[P₆]
[etc.]

I Matrix

1	7	3	10	12	9	2	11	6	4	8	5
7	11	10	12	9	8	1	6	5	3	2	4
3	10	1	7	11	6	4	12	9	2	5	8
10	12	7	11	6	5	3	9	8	1	4	2
12	9	11	6	5	4	10	8	2	7	3	1
9	8	6	5	4	3	12	2	1	11	10	7
2	1	4	3	10	12	8	7	11	5	9	6
11	6	12	9	8	2	7	5	4	10	1	3
6	5	9	8	2	1	11	4	3	12	7	10
4	3	2	1	7	11	5	10	12	8	6	9
8	2	5	4	3	10	9	1	7	6	12	11
5	4	8	2	1	7	6	3	10	9	11	12

[I₀]
[I₁]
[I₆]
[etc.]

By certain precompositional decisions based on these matrices, the order of occurrence of durational values, dynamics, types of attacks, and row forms is established. Other precompositional decisions dictate the order of tempi, texture, and overall form. Some elements of the piece—such as the succession of meters—are freely or intuitively chosen. In his application of structures of pitch to the other variables of composition, Boulez's method differs strikingly from Babbitt's. Boulez makes no attempt to establish a logical connection between these components: they are all interrelated, but in an essentially arbitrary way. We shall illustrate this point in Chapter 5, where we shall see how the matrices of *Structures Ia* dictate its rhythmic structure.

Bibliography

An authoritative introduction to serialism is provided by Ernst Křenek in his article on this subject in the *Dictionary of Contemporary Music*, ed. John Vinton (New York, 1974). Josef Rufer's *Composition with Twelve Notes*, trans. Humphrey Searle (London, 1954) focuses on the music of Schoenberg, and it also contains a detailed analysis (emphasizing motivic and formal matters) of Schoenberg's Fourth String Quartet (pp. 140–54). Also see George Perle, *Serial Composition and Atonality*, 4th ed. (Berkeley and Los Angeles, 1977) and Reginald Smith Brindle, *Serial Composition* (London, 1966).

The article by Brian Fennelly on "Twelve-Tone Techniques" in the *Dictionary of Contemporary Music* is a concise and lucid explanation of concepts put forth by Milton Babbitt. Babbitt's ideas also underlie Charles Wuorinen's *Simple Composition* (New York and London, 1979).

Among composers' descriptions of twelve-tone techniques, see Arnold Schoenberg, "Composition with Twelve Tones," in *Style and Idea*, ed. Leonard Stein (London, 1975), Ernst Křenek, "Extents and Limits of Serial Techniques," in *Problems of Modern Music*, ed. Paul Henry Lang (New York, 1960), and Pierre Boulez, "Eventually . . ." (1952), in *Notes of an Apprenticeship*, trans. Herbert Weinstock (New York, 1968). Most of Milton Babbitt's writings deal with compositional resources of the twelve-tone system, but they also have extensive analytic applications. He discusses the phenomenon of invariance in "Twelve-Tone Invariants as Compositional Determinants," in *Problems of Modern Music* and combinatoriality in "Set Structure as a Compositional Determinant," in *Perspectives on Contemporary Music Theory*, ed. Benjamin Boretz and Edward T. Cone (New York, 1972). A concise overview of his goals in twelve-tone music is found in "Some Aspects of Twelve-Tone Composition," *Score*, 12 (1955).

A detailed analysis of compositional method in Boulez's *Structures Ia* has been made by György Ligeti in *Die Reihe*, 4 (1958; English trans., 1960).

◆ 5 ◆

RHYTHM AND METER

The revolution in musical style of the early years of the twentieth century had no less effect upon rhythm and meter than it did upon harmony and tonality. The emancipation of dissonance that we have observed in music of the late nineteenth and early twentieth centuries was accompanied by a freeing of regular beat and an unsettling of stable metric organization in music of the same period. In this chapter we shall sketch some features of this disruption of earlier conventions of rhythm and survey some notable constructive systems devised by major twentieth-century composers to reorganize the dimension of time in their music.

The Emancipation of Rhythm

In music of the common-practice period, rhythm is organized essentially in three interconnected levels. The central level is a regularly recurring beat or pulse. Beat is expressed in music primarily by a regular onset (or "attack") of notes; the beat may also be clarified by frequent occurrence of note values that extend without interruption from one beat to the next.

rhythm: ♩ ♫♩ ♫ ♫.♫ ♪ ♪♫♫ ♩ ♫♪♩ ♪ ♪

beat: ∧ ∧ ∧ ∧ ∧ ∧ ∧ ∧ ∧ ∧ ∧ ∧ ∧ ∧

Example 5-1.   Rhythm and beat in Schubert's "Kennst du das Land."

Let us see how a pulse is expressed musically by observing the rhythm of the main theme of Schubert's song "Kennst du das Land" (Example 5-1). The score of the first two stanzas of this song is found in Example 1-1. If this rhythm is performed at a moderate tempo, the listener will hear the recurrence of a beat as shown in the lower line of Example 5-1. The beat is expressed by the regular pattern of recurrent attacks and by the prominence of the quarter-note value—a duration, that is, which spans without interruption the distance from one beat to the next. Frequency of beat also depends upon tempo. If the speed of this passage were very slow, for example, beats would be heard twice as often as would occur if the tempo were fast.

A lower level of rhythmic organization in music is created by a characteristic *division* of the beat into groups of either two or three values or their multiples. A beat in the rhythm shown in Example 5-1 has a characteristic *duple* division on account of the many eighth and sixteenth notes—in other words, values that divide the beat into subgroups of twos and fours.

A third and higher level of temporal organization is a recurrent *grouping* of beats into larger units of the same size. This characteristic grouping and its expression in music is called *meter.* The first four measures of "Kennst du das Land" reveal that the recurrent metric group consists of two beats (Example 5-2). This grouping is expressed musically by several factors. At the beginning, a recurrent pattern is established which consists of a quarter note followed by two eighths. This pattern spans two beats, which tells us that the metric unit will probably be of this duration. Another factor that articulates meter is an emphasis on the first note of the metric group. In Schubert's song the emphasis is created by elongation of the initial note of

metric
group: ⌐‾‾‾¬ ⌐‾‾‾¬ ⌐‾‾‾¬ ⌐‾‾‾¬

rhythm: ♩ ♫♩ ♫ ♫.♫.♫♫ ♪

beat: ∧ ∧ ∧ ∧ ∧ ∧ ∧ ∧

Example 5-2.   Metric grouping in Schubert's "Kennst du das Land."

the metric pattern, as we see in the opening figure quarter-eighth-eighth.

In order to clarify the rhythmic-metric structure of a piece, performers often make the beginning of a metric group even more emphatic by adding to it a slightly percussive accent. This practice coincides with a widespread belief among musicians that the very beginning of a metric group is "stronger" than the remaining beats in the group.

Time signatures are chosen to conform to this three-level rhythmic structure: the time signature of $\frac{2}{4}$ in "Kennst du das Land" acknowledges that the metric group consists of two beats and that the characteristic division of the beat is duple. Music in which the metric group consists of two beats and that has a triple division of the beat is normally given a $\frac{6}{8}$ signature; metric groups of three beats having a duple division of the beat normally call for a $\frac{3}{4}$ signature; and so forth.

A time signature is a practical notational device assisting the performer to read note lengths and to visualize (by virtue of bar lines) the metric group. It is analogous to key signature. Both reflect structures of pitch or time that predominate in the music, but neither type of signature creates these structures nor does it rule out temporary deviations from them.

Just as music in a key normally passes through other temporary tonics, music with a prevailing rhythmic-metric organization frequently undergoes temporary or superficial metric changes. In the common-practice period, these deviations include flexible or rubato tempo, syncopation, and hemiola. An example of the last of these—a simultaneous duple and triple division of the beat—occurs in "Kennst du das Land" at measure 8 and following. In these measures the voice and left hand of the piano express primarily a duple division of the beat; the right hand of the piano, primarily a triple division. The fluttering motion that results graphically captures the meaning of the words of measures 8–11 of the first stanza: "a gentle breeze wafts from the blue heavens." It is also entirely typical of tonal music that this change of rhythmic design coincides with and underscores an important harmonic and structural juncture—the end of the expository thematic period and the beginning of a passage where a dominant preparation is in effect.

In late-nineteenth- and early-twentieth-century music, conventions of rhythmic organization were increasingly disregarded. Perhaps the most radical innovation in rhythm of this time was the suspension or outright avoidance of a clear beat, without which meter cannot exist. The opening of Ravel's ballet *Daphnis et Chloé* (1909–12, Example 5-3) depicts a fanciful scene from Greek mythology. To capture its supernatural aura, Ravel avoids a clear beat by entrances of parts at irregular intervals of time and by

Aristide Maillol, *Daphnis Plays to his Goats.* (Courtesy of the Print Collection, The New York Public Library, Astor, Lenox and Tilden Foundations.)

Example 5–3.   Ravel, *Daphnis et Chloé*, measures 1–11. © 1910 Durand
S.A. Editions Musicales, Editions Arima and Durand S.A.
Editions Musicales. Joint Publication. Used by Permission of the Publisher. Theodore Presser Company, Sole
Representative U.S.A. and Canada.

syncopated or irregularly divided note values. The chimeri-
cal quality of the scene is further enhanced by its lack of
triadic harmonies and the use instead of chords in superimposed fourths and fifths.

Music by German and Austrian composers such as
Reger, Schoenberg, and Zemlinsky at the turn of the
century often had a dense and hyperactive texture that
obscured the beat. In his essay "Brahms the Progressive,"
Schoenberg referred to works of this type as "musical
prose," since they are dense in texture and asymmetrical
in phrasing. Schoenberg's atonal music continued to incorporate prose-like textures. The perception of a beat in
his Piano Piece, op. 23, no. 4 (Anthology no. 6), for example,
is made dim by a busy texture in which different divisions of
the beat often conflict, by the large number of changes of
tempo, and by frequent placement of rests on downbeats.

The atonal and twelve-tone music of Webern is even
more radical in its elimination of beat through its sparse
texture and profusion of rests. The rhythm of the opening
measures of the fifth movement of his Second Cantata
(Anthology no. 22) is shown in Example 5-4; regular pulse
plays only a minor role in these figures due to the use of
rests on downbeats, syncopation, and irregular accents.

Avant-garde composers after the Second World War
intensified Webern's disruption of pulse as a perceptible
means of rhythmic measurement. In the "pointillist" style
of Stockhausen, Boulez, Messiaen, and other European
serialists (see Chapters 6 and 12), regular beat is completely
absent. The music of Elliott Carter intensifies the turgid
polyphony of Schoenberg's musical prose. Other experimental trends in composition after the war—including the
textural compositions of Krzysztof Penderecki and György
Ligeti, the studies in sound of Morton Feldman, and the
rhythmically indeterminate works of Earle Brown and John
Cage—are also generally devoid of conventional pulse.

Example 5-4.   Rhythmic elements in Webern's Second Cantata, fifth
movement, measures 1-6.

But a majority of twentieth-century composers have maintained beat and metric organization in their music, albeit in a freer way than their forebears. Music in which a beat is strongly evident may still bypass the conventions of common-practice music by employing rapidly changing meters, irregular placement of the beat, or both simultaneously. Changing meters were prefigured in the nineteenth century by the appearance of themes having five or seven beats per metric unit. Composers who quoted folk songs or who were influenced by folk music—including Brahms, Tchaikovsky, and Musorgski—often used such meters. The Hungarian theme quoted by Brahms in his Variations for piano, op. 21, no. 2, consists of a metric group of seven beats, which Brahms notates by alternating measures of $\frac{3}{4}$ and $\frac{4}{4}$. The Scherzo of Tchaikovsky's Sixth Symphony uses a meter with five beats, which reflects the profile of certain Russian folk songs.

The "Sacrificial Dance" from Stravinsky's *Rite of Spring* is a monumental and widely imitated example of irregular beat and changing meter in twentieth-century music. Example 5-5 shows a composite of the rhythm of the opening twenty measures, using Stravinsky's time signatures and note values from the original score of 1921. An interpretation of the location of beats and metric groups is placed below and above this rhythm. The unit of measurement is not the beat, but instead the sub-beat value of the sixteenth note; these particles are joined in various quantities to

Example 5-5.   Rhythm and meter in Stravinsky's *Rite of Spring*, "Sacrificial Dance."

Example 5-6. Berlioz, *Symphonie fantastique*, fifth movement, measures 399–403.

make up beats, whose occurrence is made more asymmetrical by the placement of rests. The beats are gathered into metric segments in a highly irregular manner that is open to various interpretations. The analysis of meter found in Example 5-5 is based upon the opening idea in measures 2–5, which is repeated almost exactly in measures 6–9. The figure that terminates this group (measures 4–5) is interpreted as the closing of metric groups for the remainder of the passage. Stravinsky's choice of time signatures and placement of bar lines in this dance does not directly correspond to the perception of pulse or meter; the arbitrariness of notation is confirmed by his revision of the score for publication in 1943, in which the music remains the same but the barring and time signatures are revised.

An innovation often seen in music by Stravinsky, Ives, Carter, and Copland is *polyrhythm*, or the simultaneous use of two or more distinct modes of rhythmic-metric organization. Polyrhythms are encountered occasionally in music of the nineteenth century. In the finale of Berlioz's *Symphonie fantastique*, for example, the orchestra is divided at measure 399 into two groups, which express conflicting locations of the beat (Example 5-6). Passages with more than two simultaneous meters are common in Stravinsky's *L'histoire du soldat* (1918). At rehearsal 10 in the first Soldier's March, for example, four simultaneous lines incorporate either different meters or different placements of the pulse. The score to this passage is shown in Example 5-7, below which is an interpretation of the different meters in its four strata.

The diversity of approaches to rhythm among composers early in the twentieth century has not led to a reconsolidation into a common rhythmic practice. Several major composers of the century have nevertheless pursued their own systems of rhythmic and metric construction. We shall now survey three of the most important of these new avenues of temporal organization.

Example 5-7. Stravinsky, *L'histoire du soldat.* Reprinted by kind permission of the copyright owner J & W Chester/Edition Wilhelm Hansen London Ltd.

Systematic Changes of Tempo and Meter: Berg, Ives, and Carter

Twentieth-century composers have generally been more specific in their indications of tempo than have earlier musicians. Rather than allowing the performer the traditional selection of tempo within general guidelines, composers of this century have been inclined to dictate precise metronomic speeds. These speeds are sometimes linked to a large-scale plan according to which every tempo has a simple numerical relationship to its neighboring tempos.

Alban Berg was a pioneer in such proportional systems of tempo. The changes of speed in his opera *Wozzeck* are normally linked by ratios that facilitate smooth transitions. A change of tempo in the tavern scene of Act 2, scene 4, between a *Ländler* rhythm and a passage of drunken philosophizing among apprentices, is accomplished in several stages. An irregular division of the beat (eighth-note triplets) is first established (measures 447–55), through which a ritardando slows the tempo by measure 455 to a metronomic marking of 54. The irregular division of the beat—an eighth note within a triplet—then becomes at the same speed a regular division of the beat in a new meter and rhythmic design. These relationships are shown schematically in Example 5-8; they directly prefigure the

Example 5-8.   Systematic change of tempo in Berg's *Wozzeck*, Act 2.

method of changing tempo used later by Elliott Carter, which will be described shortly.

A passage in Act 1, scene 2 of Berg's opera *Lulu* (measures 669–956), in which the Painter commits suicide, is labeled by Berg a "Monoritmica." This term refers to the use of a single rhythmic motive, which recurs in various guises throughout the passage. This figure—symbolic of fate and violent death—is shown in Example 5-9. Berg organizes tempos in the Monoritmica in a symmetrical manner reminiscent of the symmetrical shapes that are pervasive elsewhere in this work. The first half of the Monoritmica (measures 666–842, including its three-measure introduction) consists of eighteen sections, which increase in tempo from an eighth note at the metronomic rate of 76 to a half note at 132. The second half (measures 843–956) reverses the eighteen tempos, but links them by a gradual ritardando rather than by stepwise changes.

Berg's sketch for the metronomic speeds of this passage (Vienna, Austrian National Library) shows that he was guided in constructing the tempos by a numerical sequence in which the difference between any two adjacent terms is one greater than the preceding difference. His sequence begins with the number forty—usually the slowest tempo available on a common metronome. He then derives tempos by approximating the terms of the sequence by even numbers with which metronomes are calibrated:

original numerical sequence:
40 42 45 49 54 60 67 75 84 94 105 117 130 144 159 175 192 210
metronomic approximation ($\quad$ =):
38 42 46 50 54 60 66 76 86 96 106 118 132 152 172 192 224 264.

♩. ♩. ♫

Example 5-9.   Motive of fate and violent death in Berg's *Lulu*.

He begins the Monoritmica with the eighth note as the temporal unit and changes to quarter and half notes as the speeds increase.

Independently of the Europeans, Charles Ives devised related methods for linking changes of tempo in his music composed before the First World War. His *Robert Browning Overture* (1911) contains a change of speed akin to the one we observed in Berg's *Wozzeck*. At measure 55 (Example 5-10) the tempo slows by allowing the quarter-note beat in the old tempo to remain at the same duration and as the same value in a quarter-note triplet in the new tempo. The new tempo is thus one-third slower than the old tempo.

This change of tempo ushers in a polyrhythmic passage of two distinct speeds. Example 5-11 shows the location of the beat and metric groupings of the two strata, which begin in measure 55. The upper line represents the principal beat and meter, which proceeds at the slower rate of 66. At the same time other instruments play, in Ives's words, "a kind of fast march" in a different meter and at a quicker speed. The march is represented by the lower line in Example 5-11.

Ives's use of polyrhythms linked by fractional changes of tempo was developed and refined in the music of Elliott Carter beginning in the late 1940s. Carter's Cello Sonata (1948) was his first major work to apply the device that he termed *metric modulation* (which Carter now calls "tempo modulation"). A metric modulation is a change of tempo (often accompanied by a change of meter) in which an irregular division of the beat in the previous tempo becomes a regular division and remains at the same durational length in the new tempo. Metric modulations consist of three stages, which are illustrated by the paradigm in Example 5-12. The first stage is characterized by a regularly divided beat; the second stage, which we shall call the "transition," establishes an irregular division of the beat. The final stage completes the modulation, as a note value within the irregular division of the beat becomes part of a regular division of a new beat and maintains its earlier duration, thus bringing about a new tempo.

Example 5-10. Ives, *Robert Browning* Overture. Copyright © 1959 by Peer International Corp. International copyright secured. Reprinted by permission.

Example 5-11.   Change of tempo in Ives's *Robert Browning* Overture.

In his lecture "The Time Dimension in Music" (1965), Carter remarked that metric modulations were analogous to modulations in key in earlier music. He pursues this analogy in his First String Quartet, for example, by returning near the end to the tempo of the beginning, just as a tonal work returns to the tonic at its conclusion. In his interview *Flawed Words and Stubborn Sounds*, Carter elaborates on his purposes behind the use of metric modulations:

> I tried to think in larger-scale time-continuities of a kind that would be still convincing and yet at the same time new in a way commensurate with, and appropriate to, the richness of the modern musical vocabulary. This aim led me to question all the familiar methods of musical presentation and continuation—the whole so-called musical logic based on the statement of themes and their development. In considering constant change-process-evolution as music's prime factor, I found myself in direct opposition to the static repetitiveness of much early twentieth-century music, the squared-off articulation of the neoclassics, and indeed much of what is written today in which "first you do this for a while, then you do that." I wanted to mix up the "this" and the "that" and make them interact in other ways than by linear succession.

Example 5-12.   Metric modulation.

Example 5-13.   Carter, First String Quartet. Copyright 1955, 1956 by Associated Music Publishers, Inc. All rights reserved. Reprinted by permission.

Carter's First String Quartet is one of his earliest essays in these "larger-scale time-continuities." In this work two independent temporal devices are explored: polyrhythm and metric modulation. Each of the four instruments follows its own tempo, meter, and rhythm, only occasionally merging into unified structures. The polyrhythmic aspects of this quartet are discussed further in Chapter 12.

Let us focus upon the initial metric modulation, which occurs in the cello part in measure 17. Carter's notation of this part in measures 13–22 is shown in Example 5-13, below which a revision of the time signatures and bar lines is added in order to clarify its rhythmic structure. The first thirteen measures establish a regular quarter-note beat at the metronomic rate of 72. Measures 14–16 constitute the transition, during which the beat is divided into groups of five equal values. Modulation to the new tempo is completed at measure 17 as the sixteenth note within the quintuplet becomes the eighth note in a $\frac{6}{8}$ meter, thus producing a tempo of 120. A change from $\frac{6}{8}$ to $\frac{4}{4}$ in the next few measures adds a complication to the third stage in this passage, but it does not involve a change of tempo, which remains at 120.

The Rhythmic Language of Messiaen

The music of Olivier Messiaen contains many works without a perceptible pulse or regular meter. In order to avoid these conventional modes of temporal organization, he uses rhythms that are sometimes borrowed from pre-existent sources (such as Indian talas), rhythms constructed from series of numbers, or those freely devised according to self-imposed guidelines. These principles of rhythmic construction—upon which we shall focus in this section—have been imitated by several of his students, including Pierre Boulez. They are outlined in Messiaen's *Technique of My Musical Language* (ca. 1942), upon which this survey is based.

Messiaen's rhythmic style is aimed at dispelling regular pulse and its conventional division into smaller values. "We shall replace the notions of 'measure' and 'beat,'" he writes, "by the feeling of a short value (the sixteenth note, for example) and its free multiplication, which will lead us toward a music more or less 'ametrical.'" Messiaen found a model for this freely multiplicative rhythm in Stravinsky's *Rite of Spring,* a work whose analysis has been a fundamental part of his teaching.

Messiaen's music consists of short rhythmic figures that are superimposed or pieced together. These figures are often built from a prime number (five, seven, and so forth) of small values. The basic figures are then varied or reshaped by a combination of four processes: retrograde arrangement, added values, augmentation, and diminution. An *added value* is produced by interpolating a brief rest, a dot of augmentation, or an additional small note value into the basic figure. Illustrations of added values are seen in Example 5-14. Augmentation (or diminution) can be either exact, in which all note values of the basic figure are increased or decreased by the same multiple, or inexact, in which the values are increased or decreased by differing multiples (Example 5-15).

basic figure: [musical notation]   added values: [musical notation]

[musical notation]

[musical notation]

Example 5-14. Added rhythmic values.

Although Messiaen uses retrograde arrangement as a means of varying rhythmic figures, he also favors rhythms that are palindromic, that is, those whose retrogrades are identical to their original shapes. He calls such figures "nonretrogradable rhythms" and describes the limitations that constrain their variation as having the "charm of impossibilities." They are rhythmic equivalents to his "modes of limited transposition" (see Chapter 15), which similarly contain restrictions upon the ways in which they can be varied.

Serialized Rhythm

Music in Europe and America following World War II emphasized experimental styles that were often organized by serial procedures. The twelve-tone method at this time became a widespread compositional technique, and the serial idea upon which it is based was often applied systematically to patterns of attack, durational successions, and metrical groups.

In Chapter 4 we sketched two approaches to "integral" serialism: Pierre Boulez's highly automated technique of composition of his *Structures Ia* and the mathematical model of Milton Babbitt. Let us now continue that discussion to explore ways in which Boulez and Babbitt use a series of pitches to influence the creation of rhythmic ideas. The methods of Boulez and Babbitt are representative of techniques of serialization among their fellow composers in

basic figure: [musical notation]   exact augmentation: [musical notation]

inexact augmentation: [musical notation]

Example 5-15. Rhythmic augmentations.

Europe and America, respectively; their rhythmic styles are similarly representative. Boulez—like many European composers after the war—uses serial procedures to obliterate pulse and meter. Babbitt—like many of his American colleagues—uses serialism to produce rhythms in which traditional means of organization are still much in evidence.

In Chapter 4 we saw that the basic series of Boulez's *Structures Ia* is used to construct two twelve-by-twelve matrices of numbers. Each row of numbers in these arrays may be used to create a rhythmic pattern. A number in a row represents a multiple of a thirty-second-note value. The number one, for example, signifies a thirty-second note; the number two, a sixteenth note; and so forth. The rhythmic figure corresponding to the first row in the I matrix, for example, is shown in Example 5-16. The rhythms that result from this method are plainly devoid of regular beat or meter, thus accomplishing by an arithmetic method what Messiaen accomplished in his music of the 1930s and early 1940s by intuitive processes.

The order in which these rhythmic series occur is determined in advance by an arbitrary plan. In piano I, for example, the durational rows are used at first in the order in which they appear in the I matrix, moving from bottom to top and read in retrograde from right to left. The rhythm in the first piano part in the opening section (Example 5-17) can be seen to derive from the numbers 12 11 9 10 3 6 7 1 2 8 4 5, which is the retrograde of the bottom row in the I matrix. A similar plan governs the order of durational row forms of piano II.

Milton Babbitt's system differs from Boulez's primarily in Babbitt's attempt to establish a more logical connection between transformations of rows of pitches and those of rhythms. He was critical of the procedures of European serialists, who, like Boulez, manipulated rhythms by what seemed to Babbitt to be arbitrary decisions. Babbitt's Three Compositions for Piano (1947) are early examples of his closed system. In the first piece in this set, Babbitt derives

Example 5-16. Rhythmic construction in Boulez's *Structures Ia*.

Example 5-17.   Boulez, *Structures Ia,* measures 1–7. Copyright 1955 by
Universal Edition (London) Ltd., London. Copyright
renewed. Used by permission of European American
Music Distributors Corp., sole U.S. agent for Universal
Edition.

rhythms from the numerical row 5 1 4 2. Each number is
interpreted as a group of that number of sixteenth notes or
its equivalent; the group is terminated by a rest, a longer
value, a new phrase mark, an accent, or by some other
means of articulation. The rhythmic row is "inverted" by
subtracting each number from the value 6, just as a row of
pitches in Babbitt's system is inverted by subtracting the
integer by which a pitch class is represented from 12. Retrogrades of these P and I forms and cyclic rotations of all
forms are also available.

   While this method of serializing rhythm has analogies
to operations of the twelve-tone system, it did not com-

pletely satisfy "the necessity of temporal interpretation translating completely the attributes of the pitch system into temporal terms," upon which Babbitt insisted in his article "Twelve-Tone Rhythmic Structure and the Electronic Medium" (1962). Therefore, in certain instrumental and electronic compositions of the 1950s and 1960s, he used what he called the *time-point* system of serializing attacks. A time-point row consists of twelve integers, each of which governs the place in a measure where an attack may occur. The basic time-point row is identical to a row of numbers expressing the intervals between pitch classes of the basic (pitch) series. The first element of this intervallic or time-point row is postulated to be 0, and each number that follows is the number of semitones from a pitch class upward to the next pitch class. If the basic series is an all-interval row, the intervallic series will contain all of the integers from 0 to 11. Let us illustrate with the basic series of Babbitt's Three Compositions for Piano, no. 1:

P_0: B♭ E♭ F D C D♭ G B F♯ A G♯ E

    0   5   2   9 10   1   6   4   7   3 11   8

The composer then picks a basic note value (such as the sixteenth note) and a measure length (such as $\frac{3}{4}$) which will contain twelve basic values. Let us use the assumption of a basic value of the sixteenth note to illustrate how the intervallic or time-point row determines where in a measure a note can begin. Example 5-18 shows how the integers from 0 to 11 correspond to a point in a $\frac{3}{4}$ measure. Since the first element of the time-point row is 0, the first note will begin on the downbeat of the first measure; the next integer of the row (5) commands that the next attack be on the fifth sixteenth of the measure; the next element (2) requires the next attack on the second sixteenth of a fol-

0 1 2 3 4 5 6 7 8 9 10 11 0 1 2 3 4 5 6 7 8 9 10 11 0 1 2

Example 5–18. Rhythmic "time points."

Example 5-19.   Rhythm derived from a numerical series.

lowing measure. One rhythmic interpretation of the intervallic row is shown in Example 5-19.

The time-point series does not literally control durations, only points of attack within the measure. The space between attacks can be filled freely by a sustained tone or by a shorter value followed by a rest. Furthermore, attacks do not have to occur in each measure; for example, the second element of the time-point row (5) can be realized by an attack in the second measure, thus allowing for a more sparse texture. The time-point series can be transformed by "transposition," "inversion," or "retrograde" arrangement through arithmetic functions analogous to those used on numerical representations of pitch series. An inversion is obtained by subtracting each of the integers of the time-point row from twelve, and "transposition" delays the onset of the first attack point by some number of basic values. Babbitt's system, unlike Boulez's, produces music with a definite pulse and the potential for conventional metric organization.

Bibliography

Howard E. Smither's article on "Rhythm" in the *Dictionary of Contemporary Music,* ed. John Vinton (New York, 1974) is a concise introduction to rhythmic innovations in the twentieth century. It distills ideas more fully presented in his "Rhythmic Analysis of 20th-Century Music," *Journal of Music Theory,* 8 (1964), which is drawn from his dissertation entitled "Theories of Rhythm in the Nineteenth and Twentieth Centuries" (Cornell University, 1960). Also see Arnold Elston, "Some Rhythmic Practices in Contemporary Music," *Musical Quarterly,* 42 (1956). General theories of rhythm are contained in books on this subject by Paul Creston (New York, 1964) and Grosvenor Cooper and Leonard Meyer (Chicago, 1960).

Regarding rhythmic procedures in Berg's *Lulu*, see Douglas Jarman, "Some Observations on Rhythm, Metre and Tempo in *Lulu*," in *Alban Berg Studien*, vol. 2, ed. Franz Grasberger and Rudolf Stephan (Vienna, 1981). Carter's innovations are discussed by David Schiff in his book *The Music of Elliott Carter* (London, 1983) and in Richard Franko Goldman's contribution to the Current Chronicle (regarding Carter's Cello Sonata) in *Musical Quarterly*, 37 (1951). Also see Carter's lecture "The Time Dimension in Music" (1965), in *The Writings of Elliott Carter*, ed. Else and Kurt Stone (Bloomington and London, 1977) and his article "The Rhythmic Basis of American Music," *Score*, 12 (1955). The latter article discusses innovations in rhythm in music by Ives, but it does not mention Ives's experiments with metric modulation.

The concept of a musical prose has long been used by German writers on musical form. It is discussed by Carl Dahlhaus in his article "Musikalische Prosa," *Neue Zeitschrift für Musik*, 125 (1964). Messiaen's doctrine of rhythm in his music of the 1930s and early 1940s is given out in Chapters 2–7 of his *Technique of My Musical Language*, 2 vols., trans. John Satterfield (Paris, ca. 1956).

Babbitt's proposal for his time-point system of rhythmic serialization is contained in his article "Twelve-Tone Rhythmic Structure and the Electronic Medium" (1962), in *Perspectives on Contemporary Music Theory*, ed. Benjamin Boretz and Edward T. Cone (New York, 1972). It is more clearly stated by Charles Wuorinen in *Simple Composition* (New York and London, 1979). The rhythmic construction of Boulez's *Structures Ia* is analyzed by György Ligeti in *Die Reihe*, 4 (1958; English trans., 1960).

◆ 6 ◆

ORCHESTRATION, TONE COLOR, AND TEXTURE

We turn in this chapter to a primary element in twentieth-century composition: sound. Modern composers are unrivaled in their efforts to refine and diversify the audible fabric of music. Increasingly throughout the century, distinctive qualities of sound have become basic compositional materials and structural components, at times outweighing in importance the more traditional elements of pitch, interval, line, and chord.

The primacy of this "sonorous image" in modern music is underlined by Aaron Copland in his book *Music and Imagination:*

> The sonorous image is a preoccupying concern of all musicians. In that phrase we include beauty and roundness of tone; its warmth, its depth, its "edge," its balanced mixture with other tones, and its acoustical properties in any given environment. . . . A deliberately chosen sound image that pervades an entire piece becomes an integral part of the expressive meaning of that piece.

To Copland's list of constituents of the sonorous image, we may add the broad and interrelated areas of orchestration, tone color, and texture. *Orchestration* is the art of realizing a musical idea for a specific group of instruments. *Tone color* or *timbre* is the distinctive quality of a musical sound, and *texture* refers to the sonorous aggregate of lines, chords, or other audible events as they interact with one another.

Orchestration

The orchestra of the later nineteenth century underwent an expansion in size that gave it greater force and diversity and enabled its basic subdivisions—choirs of brass, woodwinds, and strings—to be deployed independently. But, more often than not, this enlarged and diversified medium was used to create a relatively limited range of homogenized sounds. Like the painter who mixes his primary colors prior to putting them on the canvas, the nineteenth-century orchestrator was inclined to blend the pure colors of his instruments into a much smaller number of composite hues.

Multiple doublings of essential parts, especially in passages where the full orchestra plays, create a uniformity of timbre in the nineteenth-century symphony. Among German composers such as Richard Wagner, a line or chord is often taken simultaneously by instruments from two or even three of the principal choirs. French and Russian symphonists, on the other hand, typically doubled parts among instruments of the same family or choir. We see the Germanic style of orchestration at the beginning of Anton Dvořák's Symphony in G major, op. 88 (1889), shown in Example 6-1. The melody is played in unison by selected woodwinds, brass, and strings (clarinets, bassoon, horns, and cellos); no one instrument stands out as a distinctive color, and the line is heard instead as a blended composite. The underlying harmonies are realized similarly by other members of all three choirs.

Nineteenth-century standards of orchestration endured well into the twentieth century in symphonic works by

Example 6-1. Dvořák, Symphony in G major, op. 88, first movement, measures 1–15.

Shostakovich, Prokofiev, Bartók, Hindemith, Sibelius, and Vaughan Williams. But a new handling of the orchestra, which would be immensely influential upon early twentieth-century composers, was initiated at the end of the romantic period by Claude Debussy and Gustav Mahler. Debussy wrote for an orchestra of moderate size, often omitting instruments that did not contribute to the image which his music was to evoke. In *Nocturnes* (1893–99), for example, the gray sameness of "Nuages" is suggested by its ensemble of woodwinds, horns, and strings; the brilliant revelry of "Fêtes" by the addition of a band of trumpets, trombones, tuba, and percussion; and the mysterious seascapes of "Sirènes" by the unexpected appearance of a female chorus.

The full orchestra in Debussy's scores rarely plays loudly for long stretches, seeking instead a refined understatement which is characteristic of all of his music. Debussy lavishes great attention upon the woodwinds, which often replace the strings as primary bearers of melodic material. In soft or thinly scored passages, Debussy usually avoids doubling melodic lines, preferring the pure colors of solo instruments. Only in passages where the full orchestra plays are doublings common, as at the beginning of the middle section (measure 55) of the Prelude to *The Afternoon of a Faun.*

Among German and Austrian composers of the later nineteenth century, Mahler was unrivaled as an innovator in orchestration. Each of his symphonic works uses orchestral devices uniquely geared to express the idea of that piece. The triumph of human spirit depicted by the end of the Eighth Symphony is expressed by the force of its gigantic orchestra and chorus. And how poignantly do the cowbells in the Sixth Symphony express the isolation of the artist, which prefigures his destruction—symbolized by blows of a hammer—in the finale of that work. The audience of the Second Symphony is itself brought into the grim procession of mankind toward its final judgment by Mahler's diverse placement of brass instruments offstage.

Mahler's manipulation of spatial effects and his use of unorthodox instruments anticipated developments in orchestration after the Second World War. Of greater importance to the direction of orchestration in the early twentieth century, however, was his tendency to use small, heterogeneous subdivisions of the orchestra independently and to clarify the contrapuntal content of his scores by fewer doublings and more clearly etched soloistic timbres. These practices are seen in the opening of his Ninth Symphony (1908–10), illustrated in Example 6-2. This passage, which introduces motives upon which the first movement is based, contains no doublings. It consists of a disjunct and fragmentary play of rhythms, colors, and intervals, in a manner that is remarkably akin to the "pointillistic" textures later developed by Anton Webern.

The relatively small number of instruments that Mahler usually calls into play at any one time—as at the beginning of the Ninth Symphony—marks a transition between the large orchestra of the nineteenth century and a widespread preference for the *chamber ensemble* among composers of the first quarter of the twentieth century. European composers of the modern period turned to small ensembles for many reasons: rebellion against romantic overstatement and giganticism, economic deprivation which descended upon Europe after the First World War,

Example 6-2. Mahler, Symphony IX, first movement. Copyright 1912 by Universal Edition A.G. Wien. Copyright renewed 1940, assigned 1952 to Universal Edition (London) Ltd., London. This edition revised by the Internationale Gustav Mahler-Gesellschaft, Copyright 1969 by Universal Edition A. G. Wien, and Universal Edition (London) Ltd., London. All rights reserved. Used by permission of European American Music Distributors Corporation, sole U.S. agents for Universal Edition.

the tastes and requirements of several influential patrons, interest in popular music, a revival of the sonority of music of the baroque and early classical periods, and the need for a medium that could best convey clear and concise polyphonic fabrics or lightness of spirit.

After *The Rite of Spring* (1911–13), Stravinsky made a

clean break with the large orchestra, to which he did not return until the late 1920s. Between 1913 and 1917 he composed a series of songs on Russian words—*Three Japanese Lyrics, Pribaoutki,* and *Cat's Cradle Songs*—each accompanied by diverse chamber groups. The orchestration of the first of these, which is for voice, piano, woodwinds, and strings, may have been influenced by Schoenberg's *Pierrot lunaire,* which Stravinsky had heard in 1912 in Berlin and later deemed a "brilliant instrumental masterpiece." Stravinsky's ensemble songs were much admired by the Viennese atonalists, who heard them between 1919 and 1921 in Schoenberg's Society for Private Musical Performances (a Viennese concert organization dedicated to performances of modern music). In a letter to Berg dated June 9, 1919, Webern describes a performance by the Society:

> Stravinsky was magnificent. These songs are wonderful. This music moves me completely beyond belief. I love it especially. The cradle songs are something so indescribably touching. How those three clarinets sound! And "Pribaoutki." Ah, my dear friend, it is something really glorious. [From Hans Moldenhauer, *Anton Webern* (New York: Alfred A. Knopf, 1979), p. 229.]

It is likely that Webern's predilection for the song with accompaniment by chamber ensemble (used in his opp. 8, 13, 14, 15, 16, 17, and 18) stems from his enthusiasm for these works by Stravinsky.

Toward the end of the First World War, Stravinsky also composed several dramatic works for small ensemble. The first of these was *Reynard* (1915–16) for fifteen instrumentalists, singers, and actors, followed by *Les noces* and *L'histoire du soldat. Reynard* owes its medium in part to the wishes of the French-American patron Princess Edmond de Polignac, who commissioned the work. She writes in her *Memoirs:*

> My intention at that time was to ask different composers to write short works for me for a small orchestra of about twenty performers. I had the impression that, after Richard Wagner and Richard

Strauss, the days of big orchestras were over and that it would be delightful to return to a small orchestra of well chosen players and instruments. [*Horizon: A Review of Literature and Art,* 12 (1945).]

The Princess de Polignac—who, ironically, was one of the leading enthusiasts in France in the 1880s and 1890s for the music of Wagner—catalyzed the French change of taste after the First World War in favor of small orchestral ensembles. In addition to Stravinsky's *Reynard,* she commissioned Satie's *Socrate* (1918), Falla's puppet show *El retablo de Maese Pedro* (1919-22), and Milhaud's chamber opera *Les malheurs d'Orphée* (1924).

No two of Stravinsky's works involving small orchestras in the decade following the war use the very same instrumentation. During these years he explored a series of novel orchestral combinations, which have in common the clear outlines and rhythmic drive created by his emphasis upon woodwinds, brass, and percussion. His style of orchestration was influential upon native French composers of the 1920s and 1930s, who found in it a model for the clarity, lightness, and unemotional objectivity that they sought in their own works. In an article on Stravinsky written in 1922, Erik Satie praises the "extraordinary cleanness" of Stravinsky's orchestrations. Satie continues:

> One of the characteristics of the music of Stravinsky is its sonorous transparency. This quality is always found among pure masters, who never allow residue in their sonorities—residue which you will always find in the musical substance of impressionist composers and even in that of certain romantic musicians. [Erik Satie, *Ecrits,* ed. Ornella Volta, rev. ed., Paris, 1981.]

Stravinsky's emphasis upon percussion and his other innovations in orchestration found a fertile ground in the music of Darius Milhaud at about the time of the First World War. Milhaud was the earliest major composer to use the percussion as an independent choir within the orchestra. In sections of his music (1913-22) to Paul Claudel's translation of the *Oresteia* by Aeschylus, striking dramatic effects are produced by narration joined to music solely for percussion ensemble. Edgard Varèse's emphasis upon percussion—most notably in his *Ionisation* (1931)—reflects Milhaud's innovations. Music for percussion ensembles was also written by American composers on the West Coast such as John Cage and Lou Harrison in the 1930s and 1940s. These works are informed by a resourceful interest in new sounds and formal experimentation as well as by oriental music, in which percussion plays a large role.

Arnold Schoenberg was especially devoted to the chamber orchestra, for which he composed two Chamber Symphonies, a Serenade, Suite, and numerous works using voices. In these pieces Schoenberg's mature style of orchestration is most evident: there is little octave doubling of parts, a rapid change of colors, and, in general, an attempt to clarify and differentiate contrapuntal or motivic elements. Schoenberg writes in his *Interview mit mir selbst*:

> My goal has for some time been to find for my orchestral structures a form such that the fullness and saturation of sound shall be obtained only through the use of relatively few voices. . . . Coloristic changes serve, while animating the expression, to clarify the musical idea. That is their principal function.

In music by American composers such as Charles Ives, Henry Cowell, Edgard Varèse, Harry Partch, and John Cage, the chamber orchestra became a medium of experimentation with new sounds, textures, and structural principles. Ives composed over twenty-five works for small ensembles between 1900 and 1917. In his *Memos* he refers to them as "sound-pictures": "Some of these . . . chamber music pieces were in part made to strengthen the ear muscles, the mind muscles, and perhaps the Soul muscles too. . . . [They] gave the ears plenty of new sound experiences."

A major development in orchestration after the Second World War was the exploitation of *spatial effects:* dividing the orchestra into several groups which play from different parts of the stage or auditorium. The use of multiple sources of sound in music has a history dating from the

Renaissance. In nineteenth-century music, offstage instruments were frequently used to create realistic effects. The offstage trumpet in Beethoven's *Fidelio* and offstage brass in requiems by Berlioz and Verdi are stirring examples of the nineteenth-century composer's use of multidimensional space.

Charles Ives applied these dramatic spatial devices in his *Unanswered Question* (ca. 1906). In the Foreword to the score, the composer states that the strings are to be offstage and separated physically from the other instruments, which consist of a solo trumpet and a choir of flutes. The music played by these three orchestral groups is also made independent in character and relatively uncoordinated in time. Each of the three strata represents an actor in a metaphysical drama in which mankind (flutes) is confronted by recurrent existential doubt (the "question" stated by the trumpet) within the continuum of space and time represented by the offstage strings.

In his *Music for Strings, Percussion, and Celesta* (1936) Béla Bartók indicates a detailed seating plan in which two small string ensembles flank the percussion and keyboard instruments. These resources are then treated with great attention to the opposition, alternation, and union of bodies of sound. Unlike Ives's *Unanswered Question*, however, the spatial element in Bartók's work has no overt programmatic meaning.

Following the Second World War these initiatives in spatial arrangement were developed in many experimental directions both by European and American composers. Boulez manipulates divided orchestral groups in his *Doubles* (1958), *Domaines* (1968–69), and *Rituel* (1974), in which ensembles of various sizes engage in antiphonal repartee. Stockhausen's use of divided orchestras in *Gruppen* and *Carré* was anticipated by the spatial effects in his electronic work *Gesang der Jünglinge*, whose original version called for five distinct channels of sound to surround the audience. Stockhausen makes a grandiose extension of spatial effects in his *Sternklang* (1971), in which five ensembles perform in distant locales of an outdoor park.

A series of orchestral works by Iannis Xenakis beginning with *Terretektorh* (1966) calls for the instrumentalists to be scattered throughout the audience. These pieces extend the spatial effects used by this composer in his earlier *Duel* (1959) and *Stratégie* (1962), in which two orchestras engage in a game-like competition.

Spatiality has been a major concern of the Canadian-American composer Henry Brant (1913–   ). Virtually all of his orchestral music since the early 1950s uses multiple ensembles situated in different areas of an auditorium, in which each ensemble carries on its own distinct musical discourse. In his article "Space as an Essential Aspect of Musical Composition" (1967), Brant investigates the ways in which unorthodox placement of performers can create novel acoustic effects. Unlike Ives's *Unanswered Question* (which Brant cites as his model), Brant's orchestrational medium does not suggest dramatic or theatric ideas. Placement of the instrumentalists is intended instead to enhance the acoustic experience of the listener. He writes:

> The spatial elements in concert music, if exploited fully and expressively, could make their points much more strongly if the sounds could be heard in complete darkness, without the disturbing and confusing intervention of merely functional visual impressions . . . that are irrelevant to the actual communication of the music in terms of its sound.

Tone Color

At the conclusion of his *Theory of Harmony* (1911), Arnold Schoenberg enters into a speculative discussion on the role of tone color in music of the future. He states:

> It must also be possible to make [melodic] progressions out of tone colors . . . , progressions whose relations with one another work with a kind of logic entirely equivalent to that logic which satisfies us in the melody of pitches. That has the appearance of a futuristic fantasy and is probably just that. But it is one which, I firmly believe, will be realized. I firmly believe it is capable of heightening in an unprecedented manner the sensory, intellectual, and spiritual pleasures offered by art. . . . Tone-color melodies [*Klangfarbenmelodien*]! How acute the

senses that would be able to perceive them! How high the development of spirit that could find pleasure in such subtle things!

As Schoenberg predicted, the importance of tone color rose to unprecedented heights later in the twentieth century. In addition to the creation of tone-color melodies which Schoenberg advised, composers have increasingly called upon the voice and traditional instruments to produce unorthodox sounds, to play in registral extremes, and to master high levels of technical complication. The twentieth century has also witnessed a revolution in musical instruments in which electronic devices for the production of sound have rivaled conventional instruments. The percussion has undergone a dramatic increase in its variety and independent use, and other sources of noise or sounds of unfixed pitch have lent their timbres to the modern composer. In experimental compositions by European and American composers before and after the Second World War, timbre has sometimes become the sole compositional material.

Klangfarbenmelodie ("tone-color melody") is a term coined by Schoenberg, who suggests by it (see the preceding quotation) that melodic elements can be created by a succession of different colors as well as by different pitches. The third of Schoenberg's Five Pieces for Orchestra, op. 16 (1909)—which he alternately titled "Chord Colors," "Colors," "Summer Morning by a Lake," and "The Changing Chord"— is Schoenberg's primary example of this concept. The movement is in a ternary form in which the outer sections (beginning at measures 1 and 32) contain relatively long-held notes which dovetail into a kaleidoscope of changing colors and chords. The middle section (measures 12–31) is animated by a filigree of short figures in a more pointillistic texture. Although the mottled play of colors of this orchestral panorama first captures our attention, the work is structured by recurrent harmonies and brief motives. The principal chord is the initial pentad G♯ A B C E, which returns transposed at the end of the first section and in the reprise; the primary motive is the figure A B♭ A♭, heard in long values and in different transpositions in all parts in the A section and in fleeting diminutions in the middle part. This movement, accordingly, is not a pure exercise in

Example 6–3.   Bach, *Fuga (Ricercata) no. 2 aus dem "Musikalischen Opfer" von Joh. Seb. Bach.* Transcribed for orchestra by Anton Webern. Copyright 1935 by Universal Edition. Copyright renewed 1963. All rights reserved. Used by permission of European American Music Distributors Corporation, sole U.S. agents for Universal Edition.

timbral composition, but it is indeed unique in Schoenberg's music in the degree to which normal motivic exposition and development are hidden by rhythmic and coloristic devices.

The music of Anton Webern contains a different type of tone-color melody. Webern's lines are often constructed of small segments which are passed among several instruments, with further variety added by a large number of rests and disjunctions in register.

Webern's orchestration of the subject of the six-voice ricercar from Bach's *Musical Offering* (Example 6-3) illustrates his use of changing colors within a single theme. The line is passed back and forth among three muted brass instruments and punctuated by the harp harmonic in measure 5 before it is turned over to the contrasting colors of flute and violin in measure 9. In a letter to Hermann Scherchen dated January 1, 1938, Webern states that in his Bach arrangement the "instrumentation attempts to reveal motivic coherence." Webern asserts, in other words, that color serves to clarify structures of pitch; it is not an independent element.

Each change of color occurs at a point at which Webern perceived a juncture in the motivic structure of the theme. In his letter to Scherchen, Webern explains that he considered the opening of the theme to consist of three groups of five notes each: C E♭ G A♭ D / G F♯ F E E♭ / (E♭) D D♭ C B. The first group—terminated by a rest—is given to a single instrument. Each of the pairs of descending semitones of the second group is emphasized by alternative statements in the horn and trumpet. This second group overlaps with the third segment on the note E♭, a juncture that Webern underscores by doubling the note with a harp harmonic. The beginning of the next structural unit of the fugue—the answer and countersubject in measure 9—is signaled by contrasting string and woodwind sonorities.

Experiments and innovations in musical sound were in abundance in Europe in the early years of the twentieth century. The Italian Futurist artist and composer Luigi Russolo (1885–1947) used noise to create musical works that celebrate the machine and life in an industrial society. Bartók, Schoenberg, Berg, and Stravinsky devised new playing techniques on traditional instruments, which provided these composers with a more diverse palette of colors. But it was among experimental composers in America that sound was used in the most original way. In works by Edgard Varèse, Henry Cowell, John Cage, Morton Feldman, George Crumb, and others, a movement was established in which tone colors were freed from their traditional role of clarifying structures of pitch and rhythm and became instead independent structural elements. George Rochberg alludes to this development in his article "The New Image of Music" (1963): "Today, the sound material of music enjoys an autonomy never before accorded it. . . . This liberation permits sounds to create their own context, a reversal of the traditional procedure in which the train of thought largely determined the individual sounds and their succession."

Edgard Varèse was a pioneer of this movement, who crusaded for "the liberation of sound and for my right to make music with any sound and all sounds." Prior to his late pieces in electronic media, Varèse felt constrained by the unavailability of musical instruments that could produce sufficiently varied sounds. When such instruments were perfected, he predicted, musical forms would be shaped solely from the manipulation of masses of sound. In a lecture at Santa Fe in 1936, he said: "The role of color or timbre [will] be completely changed from being incidental, anecdotal, sensual or picturesque; it [will] become an agent of delineation like the different colors on a map separating different areas, and an integral part of form."

Varèse's ensemble music of the 1920s and 1930s contains vivid timbral elements, such as the appearance of sirens in his *Ionisation* and the dramatic climaxes for *ondes Martenot* in *Ecuatorial*. But Varèse's theories regarding the liberation of sound were realized only at the end of his career in his electronic works, of which *Poème électronique* (1958) is the masterpiece.

A series of experimental works by Henry Cowell written for the strings of a piano prefigure the liberation of sound of electronic music. Cowell's *Banshee* (1925, Anthology no. 7) is typical of these studies. Noise from the piano strings creates an eerie effect, which forms a backdrop to short melodic motives made by plucking the strings.

Among American composers after World War II, Morton Feldman (1926–   ) typifies the fascination with sound that had long characterized his American forebears. His music consists primarily of studies in contrasting timbres, normally in hushed dynamics and devoid of motivic development, regular pulse, or dramatic climaxes. Feldman's devotion to sound has led him to bypass systematic constructive methods of composition and, in their place, to embrace indeterminate procedures. "An indeterminate music can lead only to catastrophe," he writes in the article "Pre-Determinate/Indeterminate" (1966). "This catastrophe we allowed to take place. Behind it was sound—which unified everything. Only by 'unfixing' the elements traditionally used to construct a piece of music could the sounds exist in themselves—not as symbols, or memories which were memories of other music to begin with."

Certainly, the most important outcome of the liberation of sound in the twentieth century is the medium of electronic music—a development beginning about 1950 which is surveyed in Chapter 14. The electronic experience influenced the works in nontaped media by American composers, who continued to seek new vistas in the art of sound. The music of George Crumb, for example, combines a panoply of conventional and unorthodox instruments and innovative vocal techniques to create his vivid and dramatic soundscapes.

Yet other composers in America have remained aloof from the revolution in new timbres. Schoenberg—who, ironically, had eagerly foretold the liberation of sound in his *Theory of Harmony*—later recanted and proclaimed that color was not basic to the vocabulary of musical thought. In his essay "Composition with Twelve Tones" he writes: "More mature minds resist the temptation to become intoxicated by colors and prefer to be coldly convinced by the transparency of clear-cut ideas." Similarly, Elliott Carter has stated in the interview *Flawed Words and Stubborn Sounds:* "As far as color goes, I still believe that the real interest of music lies in its organization. . . . I don't believe in novelty of sound for its own sake; that is always the easiest thing to bring off and loses its interest very quickly."

Texture

Western music prior to the twentieth century utilized three primary textures: *monophony,* which consists of a single melodic line; *homophony,* in which one predominant line stands forth from a backdrop of chords or other accompanimental strata; and *polyphony* or *counterpoint,* in which two or more distinct lines are heard simultaneously. Throughout the classic and romantic periods, homophonic textures were most common. These endured in the twentieth century, especially in the hands of composers for whom clarity and lightness of spirit were paramount.

In the late nineteenth and early twentieth centuries, there began a revival of polyphonic writing among composers in several different styles. In works by neoclassicists such as Hindemith and Stravinsky, counterpoint often evoked baroque music. Paul Hindemith took the orchestral music of Bach as a point of departure for his busy, linear *Kammermusik* series (1924-27)—a cycle of concertos for different instruments and chamber orchestra. Counterpoint in Stravinsky's neoclassic works served to dispel pictorial connotations within the music and to create the unemotional and objective tone that he intended his music to convey. In an article entitled "Some Ideas about my Octuor [Octet]" (1924), Stravinsky writes: "Form in my music derives from counterpoint. I consider counterpoint as the only means through which the attention of the composer is concentrated on purely musical questions. Its elements also lend themselves perfectly to an architectural construction" (from Eric Walter White, *Stravinsky* [Berkeley and Los Angeles, 1969], p. 530).

German and Austrian modernists beginning with Gustav Mahler and Richard Strauss adopted the dense part writing of Brahms and contrapuntal passages from Wagner's works such as *Die Meistersinger* and *Siegfried Idyll* as models for further development. The texture of Mahler's later symphonies is dominated by a free and dense polyphony. Principal melodic lines are commonly accompanied by one or more subsidiary lines, all of which share common motivic elements. This style of polyphony was developed by Schoenberg and his school. "It is apparent and will probably become increasingly clear," Schoenberg writes in his *Theory of Harmony*, "that we are turning to a new epoch of polyphonic style, and as in the earlier epochs, harmonies will be a product of voice leading." Schoenberg's polyphony may be studied in his First String Quartet, of which the opening ten measures are shown in Example 6-4. The principal line is contained in the first violin, with important subsidiary lines presented in the viola and cello. Later in this work, motives and shapes from all three lines recur in new forms within densely polyphonic textures. In most such passages one line is still predominant. Schoenberg and his student Alban Berg later used the notation H⁻ (for *Hauptstimme* or "principal voice") and N⁻ (*Nebenstimme,* "subsidiary voice") to clarify the relative importance of the lines within their complicated polyphony.

The strict imitative forms of canon and fugue have been maintained or reinterpreted by twentieth-century composers. Canon has proved to be a basic means for contrapuntal elaboration in modern music, especially in works that use the twelve-tone method. The sixth movement of Webern's Second Cantata, op. 31, for example, is a four-voice canon in which the lines are interrelated by inversion and retrograde. Schoenberg's "Mondfleck" from *Pierrot lunaire*—an atonal, pre-twelve-tone composition—combines canonic lines in the strings and woodwinds with a fugue in the piano.

Fugue—more than canon or free polyphonic writing—

Example 6-4. Schoenberg, First String Quartet, measures 1–10.

is intimately related to traditional tonality. All the same, modern musicians have mingled traditional elements of fugue—subject and answer separated by the interval of a fifth, alternating statements of subjects and episodes, and stretti, to name a few—with a liberated harmonic and tonal idiom. Stravinsky, for example, writes fugues and fugatos in his Octet, *Symphony of Psalms*, *Dumbarton Oaks* Concerto, and *Orpheus*. Hindemith's *Ludus tonalis* for piano (1942) contains a cycle of twelve three-part fugues which integrate traditional and nontraditional features. The first movement of Bartók's *Music for Strings, Percussion, and Celesta* (1936) is an especially ingenious adaptation of fugal principles to liberated tonality and symmetrical form. The subject—a chromatic figure beginning on the note A—is answered first on E, then on D, and continues through a cycle of fifths both above and below the starting point. The second half of the movement introduces freely inverted forms of the subject, which return through a cycle of fifths to the central "tonic" A.

A momentous change in twentieth-century musical style occurred when composers began to dispense with the traditional textures of homophony and polyphony and to experiment with various alternatives. Americans such as Varèse and Cowell were pioneers in this stylistic revolution as they delved into textures made from masses of sound rather than from intervals, lines, and chords. In Europe, Anton Webern was pivotal in the "liberation of texture" which characterized postwar European developments.

Webern's instrumental music disguises polyphonic textures beyond recognition. The beginning of his Symphony, op. 21 (Example 6-5), illustrates this phenomenon. The texture consists of several lines, each of which is made discon-

*) Sounds as written

Example 6-5.   Webern, Symphony, op. 21, first movement. Copyright 1929 by Universal Edition. Copyright renewed 1956. All rights reserved. Used by permission of European American Music Distributors Corporation, sole U.S. agents for Universal Edition.

Pointillism in nineteenth century French painting: Georges Seurat, *Bridge and Quays at Port-en-Bessin.* (Courtesy of The Minneapolis Institute of Arts.)

tinuous by the placement of rests, large leaps, disjunctions in register, and rapid changes of color. It is, in fact, difficult to perceive any lines in the traditional sense, and the listener's attention is at first drawn to a mottled array of individual sounds or intervals. Webern's textures of this kind may be described as *pointillistic.* This term comes from art criticism, where it refers to a technique of painting used by Georges Seurat (1859–91) and Paul Signac (1863–1935), in which subjects are represented by a multitude of dots of pure color. The mosaic of dots appears at a distance to merge into recognizable forms.

Although it is unlikely that Webern intended works such as the Symphony to obliterate conventional textures, these pieces guided European composers after the Second World War in their elimination of traditional musical argument based on thematic statement and elaboration.

György Ligeti writes in his article "Weberns Melodik" (1966) that Webern's fragmentation of line created a new "global" texture in which the mosaic of independent colors and intervals is amalgamated into a large static mass. "Global form has no characteristics of traditional musical form because of the relative autonomy of its constituent parts. In it there is no longer a flow of music through time. It has no real termination; rather, it is summation and structure made from individual moments. The music appears to stand still, to effect a stoppage in the stream of time."

Ligeti, Stockhausen, Boulez, and many of their European contemporaries eagerly adopted into their own music the global texture made from autonomous moments of sound which they found in Webern. Stockhausen's *Kreuzspiel* (1951, excerpt in Anthology no. 26) is an example of postwar pointillism. In this music there is no line, accompaniment, counterpoint, or motivic development in the traditional sense (although the part for tumbas at the beginning provides a linear measurement of durational values). The texture instead projects a maximal differentiation of pitches, durations, registers, colors, and other musical elements, which focuses our attention upon isolated moments rather than upon linear continuities.

By the later 1950s many among the European avantgarde had become concerned that their pointillistic textures were too uniform. Composers such as Ligeti recognized that the maximum differentiation and variety that they sought had ironically produced a deadening sameness. While figures such as Stockhausen and Boulez were bringing indeterminacy to their music for the sake of variety, others such as Ligeti and Krzysztof Penderecki developed new ways to govern masses and textures of sound. Their experiments in *textural composition* were widely imitated in both Europe and America, and they represent the outcome of an evolution of texture begun by Webern.

Ligeti's music beginning with his orchestral studies *Apparitions* (1958–59) and *Atmosphères* (1961) is concerned primarily with textures. The specific intervals, lines, and colors from which they are made are subsumed into a totality of sound which becomes the elemental compositional material. The textures are created mainly by sustained chromatic clusters or by busy chromatic figures distributed over fifty or more orchestral voices, and these masses then interact by collision, penetration, dissipation, merging, or other vividly dramatic gestures.

In his article "Zustände, Ereignisse, Wandlungen" (1967), Ligeti writes: "The transformation of optical and tactile sensations into acoustic phenomena often occurs to me involuntarily. I almost always associate sounds with color, form, and consistency, and, conversely, every acoustic sensation has form, color, and material qualities."

His *Apparitions* is a musical interpretation of the texture of a vast web of filaments, which is transformed into new shapes by a series of sonic jolts. *Volumina* for organ (1961–62) uses graphic notation (see Chapter 13) to represent its textures and their transformation. In later works such as the wordless dramas of *Aventures* (1962) and *Nouvelles aventures* (1962–65), Ligeti returns to textures of a more pointillistic type.

Bibliography

General historical surveys of orchestration are found in Gardner Read's *Style and Orchestration* (New York, 1979); the book-length article "Histoire de l'orchestration" by Gabriel Pierné and Henry Woollett in the *Encyclopédie de la musique et dictionnaire du conservatoire*, ed. Albert Lavignac and Lionel de La Laurencie, part 2, vol. 4, 2215–2286 and 2445–2818 (Paris, 1929); and Egon Wellesz's *Die neue Instrumentation*, second ed. (Berlin, 1928). Aaron Copland's discussion of the sonorous image of modern music is found in *Music and Imagination* (Cambridge, Mass., 1952).

The autobiographical "Memoirs of the Late Princesse Edmond de Polignac" are found in *Horizon: A Review of Literature and Art*, 12 (1945). Charles Ives's *Memos* (ed. John Kirkpatrick, New York, 1972) were written in 1931 and 1932 as a private rejoinder to journalistic critiques of his music. A list of published music for chamber orchestra is given by Cecilia and Henry Saltonstall in their *New Catalog of Music for Small Orchestra* (Clifton, N.J., 1978).

Henry Brant's "Space as an Essential Aspect of Musical Composition" is in the collection *Contemporary Composers* on *Contemporary Music,* ed. Elliott Schwartz and Barney Childs (New York, 1967). The untitled article by Satie on Stravinsky is published in French in Satie's *Ecrits,* ed. Ornella Volta, rev. ed. (Paris, 1981). Varèse's lecture in Santa Fe in 1936 is excerpted in "The Liberation of Sound," *Perspectives of New Music,* 5 (1966). Schoenberg's "Interview mit mir selbst" is in the Schoenberg *Gesammelte Schriften,* ed. Ivan Vojtech, vol. 1 (n.p., Fischer, 1976).

Ligeti's article "Weberns Melodik" is in *Melos,* 33 (1966), and "Zustände, Ereignisse, Wandlungen" by the same author is in *Melos,* 34 (1967). Morton Feldman's remarks on the purity of musical sound are found in "Pre-Determinate/Indeterminate," *Composer,* 19 (1966). In Allen Edwards's *Flawed Words and Stubborn Sounds: A Conversation with Elliott Carter* (New York, 1971), Carter speaks slightingly about timbral composition. George Rochberg's article on the liberation of sound and the "spatialization" of new music, entitled "The New Image of Music," is in *Perspectives of New Music,* 2 (1963).

P · A · R · T
T · W · O

♦

Music from 1900 to 1945

♦

◆ 7 ◆

AVANT-GARDE COMPOSITION IN GERMANY AND AUSTRIA

At the turn of the twentieth century, German musical culture was preeminent in the Western world. German music was widely admired and imitated by composers of virtually every Western nationality. The works of Richard Wagner had become a beacon of modernism, an inspiration for a generation of young writers and artists as well as musicians. The music of Brahms honored a distinguished past by preserving traditional forms and genres, but transformed them in such a way as to defy distinctions between old and new. As the twentieth century began, there was great confidence that Germany would continue to be the source of new musical ideas.

Modern music, like modern developments in the other arts, was centered mainly in the large cities of the German-speaking world, especially Vienna and Berlin. Vienna, or the "Music City," as it was known, was by longstanding reputation conservative in its tastes, and here modernism had the tinge of a youthful rebellion against values of the older generation. Stefan Zweig writes in his memoirs *The World of Yesterday:*

Suddenly the old, comfortable order was disturbed, its former and infallible norms of the "aesthetically beautiful" (Hanslick) were questioned, and while the official critics of our correct bourgeois newspapers were dismayed by the often daring experiments and sought to dam the irresistible stream with such epithets as "decadent" and "anarchistic," we young ones threw ourselves enthusiastically into the surf where it foamed at its wildest. We had the feeling that a time had set in for us, our time, in which youth had finally achieved its rights.

In Berlin, on the other hand, experiment was tolerated, so that many of Vienna's younger musicians looked enviously across the border at a more sympathetic atmosphere for their endeavors. In 1904 a number of young Austrian musicians—among them Arnold Schoenberg and Alexander von Zemlinsky—set about to create a society for the advancement of modern music. The organizers presented their case to the conservative Viennese theorist Heinrich Schenker:

Whoever compares the musical situation in Vienna with that in even the smaller cities of Germany will recognize that the "Musikstadt" has for a long time lagged behind. It has lacked that minimal progress which one demands of all cultural centers, even those that rest on their laurels of yesteryear. Those who suffer most for this are the young creative artists, the rising generation of composers, not only of Vienna but of the Empire. In Germany the public and the press regard serious modern artists not simply with snobbish condescension, but show their favor with warmth and high regard. Here their efforts are greeted at all times with silence. [Oswald Jonas Memorial Collection, University of California, Riverside.]

Developments in modern music in Germany and Austria were closely allied to modernism in the other arts, an affinity that was stimulated by the unusually close personal contact among younger musicians, architects, writers, and painters. The architectural style of Adolf Loos

(1870–1933), for example, with its austere geometrical shapes and rejection of ornament, has much in common with the musical idiom of his close friend Arnold Schoenberg, who similarly eliminated all but the essentials of musical expression. The operas of Alban Berg deal with themes of social criticism, sexuality, and the degradation of the individual, which were matters addressed by contemporary Expressionist playwrights. Schoenberg's aesthetics of intuitive subjective expression are remarkably akin to those of Expressionist painters such as his friend Vasili Kandinski (1866–1944).

This chapter will follow the musical accomplishments of a group of German and Austrian composers who placed great value on the progress of style. They formed an avant-garde in that they consciously sought to expand and reinvigorate their inherited musical language. Yet none of them was an experimentalist: their innovations and artistic outlook were grounded instead in their musical past.

Their movement may be divided into three chronological and stylistic phases. The first is an extension of progressive tendencies among German composers of the late nineteenth century; the second, atonality and its associated styles; and, third, a postwar stylistic consolidation which coincided with the early years of twelve-tone composition. The avant-garde movement in Germany and Austria was brought to a decisive halt in the 1930s by the Nazis. From then until the end of the Second World War, only the most traditional composers were tolerated.

The Progressive Romantics

The music of Wagner and Brahms proved to be a compelling model for progressive German and Austrian composers born in the second half of the nineteenth century. The older figures in this group, such as Gustav Mahler (1860–1911), Hugo Wolf (1860–1903), and Richard Strauss (1864–1949), typically singled out Wagner as the spiritual leader of modernism and rejected—often vehemently—what they saw as the conservative direction of Brahms. But the younger composers—Alexander von Zemlinsky (1871–

1942), Max Reger (1873–1916), Arnold Schoenberg (1874–1951), and Franz Schreker (1878–1934)—were inclined to see both Brahms and Wagner as models for future developments in music.

From Brahms they inherited a renewed confidence in the power of absolute instrumental music. Also from Brahms came a revival of interest in the string quartet and other chamber genres, notably among the works of Reger, Zemlinsky, and Schoenberg. From Wagner they took their harmonic idiom and attenuated tonality, the leitmotif technique, massive lengths and media, and mythic subjects. Most of their works shared Wagner's affirmation of the power of the individual artist to control his world and destiny. They were progressives in their determination to preserve and advance those ideals of composition which were so strikingly innovative in the music of their models.

The musical idiom of these "progressive romantics" was not limited to the years at the turn of the century. Indeed, in works by Richard Strauss it continued into the 1940s. Thus it existed side-by-side with other styles: atonality, on one hand, and the traditionalism of composers such as Hans Pfitzner (1869–1949) and the German neo-classicists of the 1920s and 1930s on the other. Their idiom has itself been revived in the 1970s by American composers such as Thomas Pasatieri, David Del Tredici, and George Rochberg.

Gustav Mahler's ten symphonies mark the end of a symphonic tradition among Viennese composers which included masterworks by Haydn, Mozart, Beethoven, Brahms, and Bruckner. Although Mahler was an ardent supporter of Wagner and a great conductor of his music, Beethoven was his model for symphonic composition, a model that he enriched by the addition of elements from the music of Bruckner, Wagner, Tchaikovsky, Liszt, popular Austrian music, and Jewish ghetto music.

Mahler's symphonic genres—the absolute symphony, programmatic symphony, and symphony with voices—all have precedents in the works of Beethoven. The expansive slow movements of the Third, Fourth, and Ninth Symphonies take their departure from the Adagio of Beethoven's Ninth Symphony, and the scherzo with multiple trios, used by Mahler in most of his works, is suggested by the

GUSTAV MAHLER
(Kalište, 1860—Vienna, 1911)

Mahler was born to the family of a merchant and innkeeper and lived as a child in Bohemia and Moravia, north of Vienna. He exhibited a prodigious talent on piano, which he continued to study at the Conservatory of the Gesellschaft der Musikfreunde in Vienna from 1875 to 1878. He also attended lectures at the University of Vienna, where he became acquainted with Anton Bruckner. After his days as a student, Mahler put aside his plans to be a concert pianist and concentrated instead upon conducting and composition. He served as a conductor in Kassel, Prague, Leipzig, Budapest, and Hamburg before his appointment in 1897 as director of the Vienna State Opera. From 1907 until 1911 he conducted at the Metropolitan Opera in New York and served briefly as conductor of the New York Philharmonic.

Selected Works

Symphonies. Ten symphonies (1888–1910); *Das Lied von der Erde* ("a symphony for tenor, contralto and orchestra," 1908).

Songs. Cycles: *Lieder eines fahrenden Gesellen* (texts by the composer, 1884) and *Kindertotenlieder* (Rückert, 1904). Other songs on texts from *Des Knaben Wunderhorn* and on poetry by Mahler, Leander, Tirso de Molina, and Rückert. The early songs are for the medium of voice and piano, the later songs for voice and piano or orchestra.

scherzi of Beethoven's Fourth and Seventh Symphonies. Mahler's characteristic juxtaposition of the ecstatic and the mundane is prefigured by passages such as the Turkish march in the finale of Beethoven's Ninth Symphony, and his technique of recapitulating themes from first movements in finales (as in his First, Second, Fifth, Seventh, and Eighth Symphonies) is also seen in Beethoven's Ninth.

Mahler's attitude toward programmatic music was ambivalent. His early symphonies are intensely programmatic, and he remarked in a letter of 1897 to Arthur Seidl that he needed a verbal idea to guide and motivate his work. Nevertheless, he meticulously eliminated programmatic details from the published scores of all of his music, bringing it still closer to the tradition of Beethoven and the Viennese symphony. By doing so, he hoped to bypass the inclination of audiences of his day to invent elaborate verbal explanations of instrumental music. Mahler summarized his views on programmatic music in a letter to Max Marschalk of 1896:

> I know that, so far as I myself am concerned, as long as I can express an experience in words, I should never try to put it into music. The need to express myself musically—in symphonic terms—begins only on the plane of obscure feelings, at the gate that opens into the "other world," the world in which things no longer fall apart in time and space. Just as I find it banal to compose programme music, I regard it as unsatisfactory and unfruitful to try to make programme notes for a piece of music. This remains so despite the fact that the reason why a composition comes into existence at all is bound to be something the composer has experienced, something real, which might after all be considered sufficiently concrete to be expressed in words.

In his Eighth Symphony (1906–1907), dubbed the *Symphony of a Thousand* on account of its immense instrumental and vocal requirements, Mahler returns to a metaphysical theme—the nature of divine spirit—comparable with those that he addressed in his earlier works. This symphony is his swan song to Wagnerian romanticism in its grandiloquence and larger-than-life affirmation. It is a style to which Mahler did not return: the summer after completing this magnificent statement of faith, he learned that he had an incurable heart ailment that would soon bring about his own death. His works after this time—*Das Lied von der Erde,* Symphony no. 9, and the incomplete Symphony no. 10—reflect the personal anxiety and skepticism that would impel him in new stylistic directions.

The Tenth Symphony was left in a fragmentary state after Mahler's work on it during the summer of 1910. The manuscripts suggest a five-movement piece in F♯ major, of which the first movement (Adagio) was the most completely scored. This movement is often performed alone, although a version of the entire symphony has been successfully reconstructed by Deryck Cooke from the drafts and sketches.

The Adagio from the Tenth Symphony deviates strikingly from the idiom of Mahler's earlier works. Its form is unlike any of his other first movements. Here an introductory viola theme (A) returns in cyclic fashion, alternating with two other principal themes B and C. These themes are shown in Example 7-1. Elements of sonata form are present

Example 7-1. Mahler, Symphony no. 10, Adagio. Copyright 1951 by Associated Music Publishers, Inc. Reprinted by permission.

in the development of themes in measures 112–40 and in the reprise of themes B and C beginning at measure 141.

The modern spirit of the work resides in its abstract mood, wide and angular leaps in the principal themes, intensely polyphonic texture, and chromatic content of both lines and chords. The relationship of lines to underlying harmonies is sometimes remote, as a result of Mahler's typically free handling of embellishing tones (see Chapter 1).

Principal melodic ideas of this Adagio are motivically interrelated, which was a feature of much German music of the nineteenth century that would be of immense importance for early atonal composition. All of the themes of the movement grow out of motives of the viola's introduction. With respect to contour and rhythm, theme C begins almost identically to A. The head motive of theme B is constructed out of the emphasized notes of A as shown by the bracket in Example 7-1. Themes B and C then become the basis for new variants, some of which for theme B are illustrated in Example 7-2. The head motive of theme B is inverted at measure 20, for example, and its second measure is spun into a diminution at measure 28.

The Adagio of the Tenth Symphony illustrates clearly how Mahler replaces the distinct thematic areas of the classical symphony with a web of themes that derive by

Theme B

Inversion (m. 20)

Diminution (m. 28)

Example 7–2.   Mahler, Symphony no. 10, Adagio. Copyright 1951 by Associated Music Publishers, Inc. Reprinted by permission.

motivic variation from a common source. It was precisely this formal procedure that Schoenberg dubbed "developing variations" and that he would apply in all of his own works, whether tonal or atonal.

If Mahler's model as a composer was Beethoven, then Richard Strauss's model was Mozart, with whom he shared an effortless lyricism and great technical virtuosity. Strauss began his career as a composer of tone poems, brilliantly reviving the genre established by Liszt, and lieder, where he was a worthy successor to Schubert and Schumann. After two early operas in the Wagnerian vein, *Guntram* (1893) and *Feuersnot* (1901), he turned his attention almost exclusively to the stage. His next two operas, *Salome* and *Elektra*, continue to use the Wagnerian technique of the leitmotif, but they are strikingly original in their subject matter, free use of dissonance, and extended tonality.

Strauss then returned to the model of Mozart's Italian operas and *Singspiele* in a collaboration with the Viennese poet and playwright Hugo von Hofmannsthal (1874–1929), first with the immensely popular *Der Rosenkavalier* (1910), which was then followed by five other works. In these and in his later operas, Strauss adopts a tuneful, predominantly consonant, and tonal idiom, with few references to the experimental style of *Salome* or *Elektra*. Later in this chapter we shall return to the opera *Salome* as a forerunner of Expressionist musical theater.

Max Reger's short but prolific career is marked by a multiplicity of stylistic directions. At various times he was an outspoken advocate of conservative trends in late nineteenth-century music and also of the more progressive tendencies associated with Wagner and the "New German School." But Reger was primarily a follower of Brahms, who had once praised his youthful compositions. He returned time and again to genres and media of the classical era— chamber music, the sonata, and variations forms—and his admiration for the music of Bach and earlier contrapuntal masters is shown by his many fugal works. His music, nevertheless, is marked by asymmetric phrasing, irregular rhythm and meter, organically unified motivic work, and, above all, a harmonic idiom that achieves remarkable freedom from diatonic progressions. In this last area he goes

MAX REGER

(Brand, 1873—Leipzig, 1916)

Reger's early years were spent in the Bavarian town of Weiden; his father was a schoolmaster and musical amateur, and Reger received keyboard lessons from a local organist Adalbert Lindner. In 1890 he moved to Sondershausen to study with the renowned scholar and composer Hugo Riemann, and he followed Riemann shortly thereafter to Wiesbaden. From 1901 to 1907 he lived in Munich, attempting to make his way as a composer and pianist. He subsequently was appointed Professor of Composition and Director of Music at the University of Leipzig and, in 1911, conductor of the orchestra in Meiningen. In 1915 he moved to Jena, but retained teaching duties in Leipzig.

Selected Works

Orchestral Music. Concertos (violin and piano), overtures, variations, tone poems.

Choral Music. Part songs, cantatas, miscellaneous music for the Latin liturgy.

Chamber Music. Five string quartets (1900–11); sonatas for violin alone, violin and piano, cello and piano, clarinet and piano; Clarinet Quintet (1915).

Songs. Over 250 songs, including the *Schlichte Weisen*, op. 76. Some are orchestrated.

Music for Piano Solo. Variations and fugues on themes by Telemann, Mozart, Beethoven, and Bach; dances; character pieces, études.

Music for Organ. Two sonatas (1899, 1901); chorale fantasies; fugues.

considerably beyond Brahms and establishes a style where triads within a prevailing key are infrequently heard and serve as points of orientation amid long stretches of dissonant, chromatic part writing.

These features are seen in Reger's five string quartets, which span his career as a composer. The genre of string quartet did not enjoy great popularity among progressive composers of the nineteenth century, but at the hands of the post-Brahmsian romantics such as Reger, Schoenberg, and Zemlinsky, it regained a central importance. The String Quartet no. 5 in F♯ minor, op. 121 (1911), is a four-movement work of which the first movement is a sonata form with a conventional large-scale tonal plan. The exposition moves from an initial statement of the tonic F♯ to the relative major A (subsidiary theme, measure 76), in which key the exposition ends. The development section (measures 128–240) leads to a return of the tonic at the beginning of the reprise (measure 241) and coda (measure 342). But between these principal tonal guideposts, the sense of a controlling key is not at all strong.

Reger links together a large number of loosely related themes, which project rapidly differing moods ranging from the brief whole tone idea at measures 10–12 to the *Ländler* at measure 76. The themes are constructed in the manner of a "musical prose"—a characteristic of Reger—in their asymmetrical and nonperiodic phrasing and irregularity of rhythm and meter.

Reger's music often has a singsong quality created by the effusion of themes and sudden changes of mood, sections of turgid counterpoint, and the lack of strongly directed harmonic motion. His music was nevertheless influential upon later German composers such as Schoenberg and Paul Hindemith, who saw in it a logical development for musical style between the age of Brahms and Wagner and the twentieth century.

Arnold Schoenberg is the greatest of the late romantic German composers born into the generation after Strauss and Mahler. Schoenberg's early music draws upon the styles of both Wagner and Brahms, but, unlike his contemporaries Zemlinsky, Reger, and Schreker, he eventually went beyond this hybrid language and transformed it in an entirely new way. We will thus have occasion to return to

ARNOLD SCHOENBERG
(Vienna, 1874—Los Angeles, 1951)

Schoenberg was largely self-taught as a musician. He received a few lessons from his future brother-in-law Alexander von Zemlinsky, but otherwise developed his musical skills by an intense and independent study of the works of the masters. Until he was forced to flee Europe for America in 1933, he lived alternately in Berlin and Vienna. His last residence in Berlin was from 1926 to 1933, when he was Professor of Composition at the Academy of Arts. Schoenberg continued his teaching in America, primarily at the University of California, Los Angeles.

Selected Works

Operas. *Erwartung* (1909), *Die glückliche Hand* (1910–13), *Von Heute auf Morgen* (1929), *Moses und Aron* (1932, incomplete).

Orchestral Music. *Pelleas und Melisande* (1903); Five Pieces, op. 16 (1909); Variations, op. 31 (1928); Concertos for violin (1936) and piano (1942).

Chamber Music. Five string quartets (1897–1936; the earliest has no opus number), sextet *Verklärte Nacht* (1899), two chamber symphonies, Serenade (1923), woodwind quintet (1924), Suite (1926), String Trio (1946).

Piano and Organ Music. Five collections for piano solo (opp. 11, 19, 23, 25, 33 [two versions]), Variations on a Recitative (organ, 1941).

Songs. Eight collections of lieder for voice and piano (opp. 1–3, 6, 12, 14, 15, 48), orchestral songs (opp. 8, 22), *Herzgewächse* (1911).

Choral Music. *Gurrelieder* (1900–1911), *Friede auf Erden* (1907), six miscellaneous collections.

Works for Speaker and Instruments. *Pierrot lunaire* (1912), *Survivor from Warsaw* (1947), *Ode to Napoleon* (1942), *Kol Nidre* (1938), *Modern Psalm* (1950).

Schoenberg's music under several different headings in this chapter.

Schoenberg remarked that his works fell into three stylistic periods: extended tonality until about 1908, atonality from 1908 until about 1921, and twelve-tone composition after 1921. We focus now upon the first of these three. Schoenberg's period of tonal composition produced seven published collections of lieder, two programmatic works (the string sextet *Verklärte Nacht* and symphonic poem *Pelleas und Melisande*), chamber music (two string quartets and a chamber symphony), the chorus *Friede auf Erden*, and the massive cantata *Gurrelieder*. By Schoenberg's admission his models were Brahms and Wagner and, later, Strauss and Mahler. It is unclear whether he knew much of Reger's music early in his career, but he later expressed great admiration for it.

His early style is exemplified by the String Quartet no. 1 in D minor, op. 7 (1905). The key of D had a special importance for Schoenberg at this time. It is also the key of an earlier string quartet (1897), the sextet *Verklärte Nacht*, and the symphonic poem *Pelleas und Melisande*. Later it would be used by him and his students to refer in a general way to his accomplishments of this period.

Even in the first measures of this quartet, Schoenberg's superior command of the late romantic idiom is plain. The impetuous first theme is the start of a breathless inspiration which continues unabated to the end. The work is in one movement, whose sections combine features of both the sonata-allegro form and the movement types of a traditional four-movement quartet or symphony. This formal amalgam is found in the nineteenth century, for example, in Liszt's Piano Sonata in B minor, and it was used on sev-

eral other occasions by Schoenberg and his contemporaries.
The music to rehearsal E corresponds to the first movement of a traditional quartet and at the same time to the
exposition of a sonata form; the music from E to K is both
developmental and in the manner of a scherzo; from K to M
is the slow "movement" and continued development, and
the passage from M to O is a rondo finale. A coda begins at
letter O.

Rhythm, meter, and phrase structure in this quartet
create examples of "musical prose" also observed in Reger's
Fifth String Quartet. The themes are nonperiodic and
asymmetrical, rhythm and meter are fluid, and the polyphony restless and turbulent. Periodic themes, which consist of symmetrical antecedent and consequent phrases, are
replaced here by freely developmental forms, some of
which are examples of what Schoenberg called "sentences"
(see his *Fundamentals of Musical Composition*, Chapters 5
and 8). A sentence consists of three parts: an initial phrase
containing the basic motive(s) and expressing the tonality,
tempo, and meter; a simple or varied repetition of the first
phrase; and a continuation which develops the basic
motives into more varied shapes and leads to a cadence.
The principal theme in the first violin in measures 1–10
(Example 7-3) is such a sentence.

As in Reger's Quartet in F♯ minor, diatonic harmonies
support the dissonant voice leading. But basic triads themselves rarely come to the surface of the music, being sub-
merged instead beneath the chromatic counterpoint. In his

Example 7-3.   Schoenberg, First String Quartet, measures 1–10 (violin 1).

Example 7-4. Schoenberg, First String Quartet, harmonic reduction of measures 1–3.

analysis "Why is Schoenberg's Music So Difficult to Understand?" written for the Festschrift honoring the composer's fiftieth birthday, Alban Berg produced a reduction of the chords of the first ten measures of this quartet, intending to show that frenetic rhythmic activity and diminutions of part writing conceal a normal harmonic progression in D minor. The beginning of Berg's analysis (covering measures 1–3 of the quartet) is shown in Example 7-4, which illustrates the harmonic motion from I to V of the first phrase of the sentence.

Harmonic complexities are nevertheless in abundance in the continuation of the sentence. Its cadence in measure 10 occurs upon a whole-tone harmony F♯ D B♭ G♯. This chord may be understood to represent the tonic D-major triad in first inversion. It is typical of Schoenberg's harmonic practice that a literal statement of the triad does not occur. It is instead suggested by an ellipsis—the ear must complete the voice leading hypothetically by imagining the B♭ and G♯ moving to octave A's in order to interpret the diatonic role of the chord.

Perhaps the most remarkable feature of this quartet is the extent to which themes and contrapuntal part writing grow out of motives stated in the principal subject of the first ten measures. Schoenberg's degree of motivic integration goes far beyond Reger and relates more to the music of Brahms, Mahler, and, ultimately, Beethoven. In program notes to his quartets, Schoenberg wrote that he was guided in this work by the "spiritual essence" of the first movement of Beethoven's *Eroica* Symphony. "The *Eroica* was the solution to my problems: how one produces diversity out of unity, how one creates new forms from basic material, and how much can be made from often insignificantly small shapes by small modifications, if not by outright developing variations."

Example 7–5.   Schoenberg, First String Quartet, motivic development.

Some of the themes produced by developing variations are illustrated in Example 7-5. Three important motives in the main theme are bracketed and labeled *a, b,* and *c.* In a transformation of the theme in measure 85 (part of a passage that Schoenberg would have called a "liquidation" because of its progressive elimination of distinctive features of the main theme), the head motive *a* is followed immediately by motive *b*, characterized by the descending tritone. The passage at rehearsal A is a transition in the manner of a fugato on two themes—the first is derived from motive *b* and the second from motive *c*—followed by a new motive *d*. The first subsidiary theme (m. 153) picks up motive *d* from the transition and ends with a new motive *e*, which is the basis for the second subsidiary theme (m. 167). Such intense motivic unity was a guiding formal principle in all three of Schoenberg's periods of style, and it was of great importance in leading him finally to his twelve-tone method of composition.

Another way in which Schoenberg attained "diversity out of unity" is his use of varied rather than literal repetitions. All of the recapitulations or restatements of themes in the D-minor quartet are varied by seemingly endless invention. Schoenberg considered repetition to be the basis of all musical form; however, it was his belief that the literal repetitions used by earlier composers were no longer valid means of musical expansion and that they must be replaced by varied repetitions.

Schoenberg may well have been indebted to Mahler for these principles of musical form. Anton Webern noted in his diary in 1905 a discussion between Mahler and Schoenberg:

> The conversation turned to counterpoint, as Schoenberg said only the Germans could write counterpoint. Mahler refers to the old French composers (Rameau, etc.) and will accept only Bach, Brahms, and Wagner as great contrapuntalists among the Germans. "Our model in this matter is nature. Just as the whole universe has developed from the original cell—through plants, animals, men, to God, the highest being—in music too a whole piece should be developed from a single motif, a single theme, which contains the germ of all that is to follow. . . ." Variation is the most important element of musical work, he said. A theme has to be quite exceptionally beautiful—a few by Schubert, for example—to make a repeat of it without alteration successful. [From Kurt Blaukopf, *Mahler: A Documentary Study*, New York and Toronto, 1976, p. 240.]

Alexander von Zemlinsky divided his career between conducting opera, composing, and teaching. In this last capacity he is best known as the teacher of Alma Mahler and Arnold Schoenberg. His compositions—primarily operas, songs, and chamber music—are in the late romantic idiom. The Six Songs, op. 13, on texts by Maurice Maeterlinck; Second String Quartet, op. 15; and *Lyric* Symphony, op. 18, are among his most advanced works. The Second String Quartet was dedicated to Schoenberg, and it utilizes the same one-movement form as Schoenberg's D-minor quartet, to which it is also related in style. The *Lyric* Symphony is a work in the vein of Mahler's *Das Lied von der Erde*, using large orchestra and solo voices on texts by Rabindranath Tagore. Zemlinsky immigrated to America in 1938, where he lived until his death in 1942.

Franz Schreker, like Zemlinsky, was a conductor, teacher, and composer. He was educated at the Conservatory in Vienna, where he lived until his appointment as director of the Hochschule für Musik in Berlin in 1920. His early compositions were mainly songs in the manner of Richard Strauss. Later he turned to operatic composition, a genre in which he completed nine works between 1900 and 1932. The best known is *Der ferne Klang,* whose libretto (written by Schreker) and leitmotif technique are indebted to Wagner, but whose musical style otherwise reflects Schreker's interest in French Impressionism.

Atonality

Works of late romantic composers at the turn of the century show that tonality was waning in importance. The tonic–dominant axis (see Chapter 1), which had earlier organized harmonic motion throughout entire pieces or movements, was increasingly disrupted. Dissonant chords were exchanging roles with consonances as central elements in the harmonic vocabulary, and these were often unfamiliar combinations composed of five or more notes. Even in those areas where a diatonic triad was perceptible, its significance tended to be local rather than a guide to the organization of an entire movement. Indeed, it was a relatively short step toward the complete elimination of key. This final step was taken by Arnold Schoenberg approximately in 1907 or 1908, at about the same time as composers elsewhere in the world including Scriabin, Ives, and Bartók had similarly disposed of key. Schoenberg's innovations were quickly adopted by his students Alban Berg and Anton Webern and, at least briefly, by others such as Ferruccio Busoni.

Schoenberg considered atonality a historical necessity— a product of the "evolution" toward dissonant harmony. He wrote in "My Evolution":

> The overwhelming multitude of dissonances [in music at the turn of the century] cannot be counterbalanced any longer by occasional returns to such tonal triads as represent a key. It seemed inadequate to force a movement into the Procrustean bed of a tonality without supporting it by harmonic progressions that pertain to it. This dilemma was my concern, and it should have occupied the minds of all my contemporaries also. That I was the first to venture the decisive step will not be considered universally a merit—a fact I regret but have to ignore.
>
> This first step occurred in the Two Songs, op. 14, and thereafter in the *Fifteen Songs of the Hanging Gardens* and in the Three Piano Pieces, op. 11. Most critics of this new style failed to investigate how far the ancient 'eternal laws' of musical esthetics were observed, spurned, or merely adjusted to changed circumstances. Such superficiality brought about accusations of anarchy and revolution, whereas, on the contrary, this music was distinctly a product of evolution, and no more revolutionary than any other development in the history of music.

A comparison of Schoenberg's music from before and after his decision to forgo the use of key supports his assertion that atonality was not a revolutionary stylistic change. Many features of his music remained unchanged: the contrapuntal textures, motivic unity, avoidance of literal repetitions, and "prose"-like rhythm and meter. But after 1907 he rarely made any further use of triads or other familiar chords, preferring instead to treat dissonances as stable or referential sonorities. He began immediately to settle upon a repertory of favored dissonances that would characterize his style, and he intuitively developed ways of interrelating these dissonant chords so that the unity he had attained in the thematic dimension would also be preserved harmonically. A further examination of his "emancipated" use of dissonance and of techniques of harmonic relation is found in Chapter 2.

Schoenberg's transition to atonality was provoked not only by his view of its historical inevitability, but also by a great personal crisis. In the summer of 1908, his wife Mathilde left him for the painter Richard Gerstl; she subsequently returned, whereupon Gerstl committed suicide. Schoenberg worked out his feelings of betrayal not only by breaking with the idiom of the late romantic period, but also by setting to music several texts that referred to his dilemma, thus undertaking the sort of public self-examination common to Expressionist painters and writers at this time. The most notable of these are his two operas *Erwartung* (1909) and *Die glückliche Hand* (1910–13). Symbolic references to his plight are also found in his choice of song texts, as in the cycle of *Fifteen Poems from The Book of the Hanging Gardens*, op. 15 (1908–1909). These songs, on poetry by Stefan George (1868–1933), were begun at the height of Schoenberg's crisis. The first poem that he set to music, "Du lehnest wider eine Silberweide," speaks of the separation of lovers, and the cycle ends with a piano postlude in a tone of bitter resignation to a fate that had destroyed love.

Schoenberg and others in his circle of composers were strongly attracted to the poetry of George, with its mysterious symbolism, elegant perfection of language, and inherent musicality. George's *Book of the Hanging Gardens* is a cycle of thirty-one poems telling of initiation to love, its consummation, and ultimate destruction. In the eighth poem of Schoenberg's cycle, the initiate has entered the garden sanctuary of love and tells of his tortured anxiety for fulfillment. George's free verse is accentuated by frantic rhythms and dynamic outbursts. The music is through composed, but with a hint of ternary form. Typically, it contains subtle word paintings in the piano part, such as the alternation of B and F on the word *wankend* ("wavering") in measure 19. The harmonics make free use of the whole-tone idea of the opening motive.

The tenth poem ("Das schöne Beet") is the climax of the cycle: here the lovers consummate their passion, which is expressed poetically by erotic references to flowers of the garden. Schoenberg's musical treatment makes a startling return to the idiom of late romanticism. The song expresses the key of D major/minor—Schoenberg's motto key—thus reinforcing his kinship with the persona of the poem.

Among vocal works of Schoenberg's atonal period, *Pierrot lunaire* (1912) treats the voice in the most original manner. This is a setting of twenty-one Expressionistic poems by Albert Giraud for speaker and mixed instruments. The work captures the atmosphere of the German artistic cabaret as the speaker evocatively couples the tragic with the clown-like. The actor is called upon to use a form of recitation called *Sprechstimme* ("speaking voice"), in which rhythmic values are to be strictly observed and pitches approximated.

Of Schoenberg's nine completed works that are entirely atonal (opp. 11 and 15 through 22), only three are instrumental: two collections of piano music, opp. 11 and 19, and Five Orchestral Pieces, op. 16. The composer remarked in his lecture "Composition with Twelve Tones" (1941) that he needed a text to guide him in constructing larger forms, since he was using his musical materials intuitively rather than systematically. Schoenberg calls each of the instrumental collections "pieces": the most neutral and abstract of titles. Thus he rejects the programmatic implications with which he imbued much of his own earlier instrumental music, and he suggests that these works will be solely "about" their own compositional content. He was later asked by his publisher Peters to supply titles to the orchestral pieces of opus 16. He did so, although he was "on the whole unsympathetic to the idea. . . . Whatever was to be said has been said by the music."

Unlike Schoenberg, Alban Berg had only a brief period of tonal composition behind him when he turned to atonality. His early works consist of songs reminiscent of the style of Hugo Wolf. In 1904 he began to study with Schoenberg, marking the beginning of his career as a

ALBAN BERG
(Vienna, 1885—Vienna, 1935)

Berg's early years in Vienna were largely devoted to his passionate love of literature and music, at which he was self-taught before becoming a private student of Schoenberg in 1904. Prior to the great success of his opera *Wozzeck* in 1925, Berg was virtually unknown as a composer, working instead as a teacher of music, journalist, and consultant for the publisher Universal Edition. Berg was one of the leaders of Schoenberg's Society for Private Musical Performances from its founding in 1918. His final years were devoted to the opera *Lulu*, which was left unfinished, and to his Violin Concerto, which was dedicated to the memory of the daughter of Alma Mahler and Walter Gropius. Much has been written in recent years about Berg's relationship with Hanna Fuchs-Robettin, to which he refers in all of his late works in the manner of secretive programs.

Selected Works

Operas. *Wozzeck* (1917–22), *Lulu* (incomplete, 1928–1935).

Concertos. Chamber Concerto for piano, violin, and thirteen wind instruments (1925), Violin Concerto (1935).

String Quartets. String Quartet op. 3 (1910); *Lyric* Suite (1926).

Songs. Seven Early Songs (1905–1908); "An Leukon" (1907); "Schliesse mir die Augen beide" (two versions, 1907, 1925); Four Songs, op. 2 (ca. 1908–10), Five Orchestral Songs, op. 4 (1912); *Der Wein* (concert aria, 1929).

Miscellaneous. Piano Sonata, op. 1 (1908); Four Pieces for Clarinet and Piano, op. 5 (1913); Three Pieces for Large Orchestra, op. 6 (1915); numerous piano-vocal scores prepared for Universal Edition and other arrangements.

Writings. Thematic analyses of Schoenberg's *Pelleas und Melisande*, First Chamber Symphony, and *Gurrelieder*; miscellaneous lectures and essays.

---

serious composer, and about 1909 he followed his teacher on the path to atonality. Berg's studies with Schoenberg were exceptionally thorough: they began with exercises in harmony and later emphasized tonal counterpoint, at which Berg was especially gifted. He was a slow worker who produced a relatively small number of compositions, but each of great depth and artistry. In the atonal style, which he pursued between 1909 and about 1925, he completed only seven works: chamber music, songs, orchestra pieces, and the opera *Wozzeck*. This masterpiece and its companion *Lulu* will be discussed in the section on Expressionist opera later in this chapter.

Berg's Four Songs, op. 2, were written about 1908–10, toward the end of his period of study, and they exemplify his transition from tonality to atonality. The poetry by Friedrich Hebbel (1813–63) and Alfred Mombert (1872–1942) is unified by images of sleep which increasingly become Expressionistic nightmares. The final poem—Mombert's "Warm die Lüfte" (Anthology no. 11)—also has a general similarity to the text of Schoenberg's opera *Erwartung*, a work that was composed at about the same time as these songs. Both deal with themes of a lover's betrayal, isolation, and death.

Berg's music is also unified as a cycle by the recurrence in the final song of harmonic materials used earlier in the cycle. The first song of opus 2 begins and ends with D-minor triads, which establish a tonal framework. No other references to the key of D minor are made, however, as the interior regions of the song emphasize all-interval tetrachords (measures 5–10), whole-tone sets linked by a bass in ascending fourths (measures 11–14), and fourth chords (measures 18–19). The second song dwells upon the whole-tone harmonies introduced in the first piece: almost every chord in the accompaniment is a subset of a whole-tone scale. The third song emphasizes the triad: it begins by outlining an A♭-minor chord, passes in measures 4 to 8 through a cadential progression whose goal is D minor, and then moves to an E♭-major triad at the end.

The final song makes no reference to any key or triad, nor does it contain the varied reprise found in each of the earlier songs. The climactic passage from measure 17 to the end recapitulates several of the pitch structures of the first two songs: whole-tone segments (measures 17–19), all-interval tetrachords (20–22), and a bass line ascending in fourths (20–22). The work concludes with the same five-note chord heard in the first song at measure 5, transposed down a minor third.

The songs of Berg's opus 2 also contain a hidden tribute to his teacher Arnold Schoenberg. The first song is in an extended D minor, the favored key of Schoenberg's earliest works; the last song is entirely atonal, as are Schoenberg's later compositions. The second song uses a key signature suggesting E♭ minor, despite the presence of an accidental on every note and the lack of any reference to a key other than the bass note E♭ of the final whole-tone chord. The note E♭ (*Es* in German) may be understood symbolically to refer to the first letter of the name Schoenberg. This symbolism is carried into the third song as well, which progresses from a statement of an A♭ triad (*As* in German: *A*rnold *S*choenberg)—reinforced by an otherwise superfluous key signature—through a progression in D minor, to an E♭ triad at the end, thus thrice referring to Berg's mentor.

The atonal compositions of Schoenberg and his students were utterly baffling to most audiences and alienated them even from musicians who had sympathetically followed their achievements up to 1907. Bruno Walter wrote in his memoirs:

> Much as I admired Schoenberg's courage and unwavering attitude, profoundly though I was impressed by his exquisite musicianship, and attracted though I was by much of his later chamber music and vocal compositions, I felt increasingly unable to follow him on his way because I considered it a devious way. . . . I am quite serious when I say that I should be happy if in a future existence, in which I

might have the benefit of superior organs of musical perception, I were to be able to ask his forgiveness for my primitive mundane lack of understanding.

Nevertheless, the strikingly original language of atonality was influential upon certain composers outside of Schoenberg's circle. Alois Hába (1893–1972) became familiar with Schoenberg's music during his period of study with Franz Schreker, and he utilized aspects of the atonal style in his own works prior to his experiments with quartertone music. Paul Hindemith took a brief excursion through Expressionism and atonality in the years immediately after World War I in several one-act operas and in his Second String Quartet (1921). This style and its attendant aesthetic were never congenial to his artistic temperament, and he shortly became the leading German neoclassicist. Ernst Křenek (1900–), like Hába a student of Schreker, wrote atonal symphonies and quartets before turning to neoclassicism and, later, to serialism.

Composers of an older generation were also attracted to Schoenberg's innovations. Giacomo Puccini (1858–1924) was especially supportive and cordial after hearing *Pierrot lunaire* in Florence in 1924. Ferruccio Busoni (1866–1924) also expressed admiration for Schoenberg's atonal works. Busoni was a piano virtuoso in the mold of Franz Liszt, whose accomplishments also included composition, teaching, arranging, and writing on music. His attitude toward modernism was ambivalent. While he supported younger composers with exceptional generosity and conducted new music with the Berlin Philharmonic Orchestra, his own compositions were generally conservative, and he resolutely avoided twentieth-century works in his own piano repertory. Schoenberg's atonal style exerted considerable fascination on him. In 1910 he prepared an arrangement or "Concert Interpretation" of Schoenberg's Piano Piece, op. 11/2, intending to make the original more idiomatic for the instrument.

Busoni's awareness of new stylistic directions is also apparent in his *Sonatina secunda* of 1912. This powerful and entirely eclectic work for piano shows aspects of the recent music not only of Schoenberg, but also of Alexander Scriabin and Béla Bartók. From Bartók and Scriabin comes

FERRUCCIO BUSONI
(Empoli, 1866—Berlin, 1924)

Busoni was born in the Tuscan region of northern Italy to a family of professional musicians, and for his entire life he attempted to balance his German and Latin proclivities. After establishing his reputation as a child prodigy on piano, he took a variety of teaching positions in both Europe and America, settling permanently in Berlin in 1894. From 1919 until his death in 1924 he held the position of Professor of Composition at the Academy of Arts. His repertory as a pianist was based upon works by Bach and Liszt: in his words, the "alpha and omega" of music for that instrument. Although he did not perform piano music by the twentieth-century avant-garde, he greatly encouraged younger composers in all styles, and he conducted a notable series of orchestral concerts featuring modern compositions with the Berlin Philharmonic Orchestra from 1902 until 1909. His essay *Sketch of a New Esthetic of Music* (1907) proclaimed absolute freedom for the composer in materials and approaches—a position that he recanted in later writings. His music is generally tonal, although certain works mirror more experimental directions.

Selected Works

Operas. *Die Brautwahl* (1910), *Turandot* (1917), *Arlecchino* (1917), *Dr Faust* (incomplete, 1916–).

Orchestral Music. *Nocturne symphonique* (1912), Suites, *Berceuse élégiaque* (1909).

Concertos. Violin Concerto in D (1897), Concerto for Piano and Male Choir, miscellaneous concerted works for piano.

Chamber Music. String quartets (2), sonatas for violin and piano (2).

Piano Music. Sonatinas (6, 1910–20), Toccata in A minor (1921), Exercises, Elegies, *Fantasia contrappuntistica* (1910, later revised), artistic arrangements.

Writings. *Sketch of a New Esthetic of Music* (1907); *Futurism in Music* (1911); miscellaneous essays, reviews, and polemics.

---

the prominent use of the octatonic scale (see Chapter 2), which is laid out in the opening motive. The piece has the flexible, improvisatory élan of the piano music of Scriabin, using the sort of suggestive instructions ("triste," "lamentoso," "pallido") of which Scriabin was fond. The work consists of two large parts, each of several sections; certain themes recur in new guises in the Lisztian manner of thematic transformation. The *Sonatina* is atonal, with the interval of the major seventh the primary integrative detail. The inversion of this interval forms the boundary points (B to C) of the opening theme as well as the final gesture, and the interval is spelled out in various shapes in every section. The octatonic passages alternate with whole-tone motives, chromatic clusters, and, in the Lento occulto, with triads.

Consolidation: The Twelve-Tone Method

The First World War led to years of unprecedented social and economic turmoil in Germany and Austria. Not only was famine widespread, but a period of uncontrolled inflation caused wild inversions in the social order. Stefan Zweig describes the chaos:

> Every descent into the town [Salzburg] at that period was a moving experience; it was my first sight of the yellow and dangerous eyes of famine. The bread crumbled into black particles and tasted like pitch and glue, coffee was a brew of roasted barley, beer

like yellow water, chocolate like colored sand and the potatoes were frozen. . . .

The first sign of distrust [in the value of currency] was the disappearance of hard money, for people tended to value a bit of copper or nickel more highly than mere printed paper. . . . In consequence of this mad disorder the situation became more paradoxical and unmoral from week to week. A man who had been saving for forty years and who, furthermore, had patriotically invested his all in war bonds, became a beggar. A man who had debts became free of them. A man who respected the food rationing system starved; only one who disregarded it brazenly could eat his fill. [*The World of Yesterday.*]

These disastrous consequences of the war spelled the end of musical progressivism—that tradition of modernism which had reigned supreme in German music from the age of Liszt and Wagner through the time of Mahler and Strauss and which was then carried relentlessly into the realm of atonality by Arnold Schoenberg. After the war this tradition split in two opposing directions: an experimentalism that disdained the moderate values of the earlier progressives and a contrary movement toward retrenchment or consolidation of the stylistic advances of the preceding decades.

Experimentation in Europe in the postwar period did not produce music of lasting value, although the activities of Dadaists, Italian Futurists, and Russian Constructivists of these years prefigured developments among the avant-garde following the Second World War. In fact, artists and musicians in Germany and Austria cast an increasingly suspicious eye at uninhibited experiment and progress. Busoni totally retracted the declaration of artistic freedom that he had made in his pre-war *Sketch of a New Esthetic of Music*, and Hindemith excoriated music that appeared elitist and excessively abstract. This postwar conservativism will be traced more fully in Chapter 10.

Even the music of Schoenberg—the most steadfast of modernists—entered a phase of consolidation and systematization of his earlier advances. This new period in Schoenberg's work coincides with his adoption of the twelve-tone method of composition, whose technical features are surveyed in Chapter 4. Beginning in the early 1920s, Schoenberg returned predominantly to instrumental composition, and he no longer distilled his music into aphoristic fragments. These new, full-blown instrumental pieces return, furthermore, to the traditional instrumental genres that he had earlier bypassed. No longer were his works called simply "pieces"; instead, he wrote quartets, suites, variations, and concertos. In vocal media he composed operas, choruses, and works for speaker; with only one exception (op. 48) he avoided lieder, which earlier had been his favored vocal genre. He also renewed his interest in traditional forms, such as the sonata-allegro. In some works such as the Piano Suite, op. 25, he even uses exact sectional repetitions, a formal device that he had absolutely ruled out earlier.

The first movement of the Fourth String Quartet, op. 37 (1936, Anthology no. 25), exemplifies this stylistic retrenchment of the twelve-tone period. Like his Third Quartet, this work was commissioned by Elizabeth Sprague Coolidge (1864–1953), America's greatest patron of modern chamber music. The quartet is in four movements in the classical sequence of sonata form/scherzo/adagio/rondo-finale, and it is entirely based on a single tone row.

The main theme, heard at the outset in the first violin, has a regularity of rhythm and meter that contrasts plainly with Schoenberg's earlier "musical prose." Its structure is virtually periodic: it is sixteen measures in length and is divided into three phrases (at measures 6 and 10) which create an A B A' shape. The substance not only of this theme but the entire movement is contained in its first five measures, which the composer would have called the "basic shape" of the composition. From it can be abstracted the tone row, basic rhythms, and fundamental motivic elements.

The rhythm and meter of the main line in these five measures recur first to round off the theme itself (measures 10–14, violin 1) and later to identify reappearances of the theme at major structural junctures (measures 95, 165, 239). The basic shape is made up of several smaller rhythmic motives that are subsequently developed independently. Primary among them is the group of three eighth notes on the note A in measure 2. This rhythmic motive also underlies the rhythm of the accompaniment at the beginning, the triplets in the transitional passage at measure 21, and numerous other developmental areas.

The principal line in measures 1 to 5 also contains two intervallic motives which will become the crux of the musical argument that follows. These frame the line: first, the descending semitone in measure 1 and, second, the ascending fourth (F♯–B) in measure 4. These two intervals are the first and last intervals of the row. But they do not derive their importance from serial considerations, rather, from a more basic conception. These intervals guide, for example, the bass line in each of the first two measures; later, the choice of forms of the row and much of the development of rhythm and meter will be made to assert them and their derivative shapes.

Schoenberg uses a very free adaptation of sonata-allegro form in this movement. The lyrical second theme begins at measure 66, an episode begins at 116, and there are two recapitulations at measures 165 and 239. The composer was faced with a major difficulty in adapting sonata form to the nontonal idiom, since this structure earlier had been delineated more by tonal plan than by theme. As a solution, he uses transposition levels of row forms analogously to relations among keys. The second theme, for example, states the row a fifth "higher" than the main theme, just as the second theme of the classical sonata form is normatively in the dominant. Comparable to the return of the tonic, the untransposed prime form of the row is brought back at the principal reprise in measure 239.

Schoenberg was chary about the importance of row techniques to an understanding of his dodecaphonic music. To Rudolf Kolisch he wrote, "I can't utter too many warnings against overrating these analyses [of row technique], since after all they only lead to what I have always been dead against: seeing how it is *done,* whereas I have always helped people to see what it *is!*" Although Schoenberg may have overstated this point, not wishing the twelve-tone method to be perceived as a preprogrammed way of writing music, he raises an important point: the method does not in itself dictate a style, but is susceptible to widely varying modes of application, which produce music of many different types.

The twelve-tone method was immediately adopted by

[handwritten marginalia: 12 tone adopted quickly]

Schoenberg's leading students, among them Berg and Webern and, prior to the Second World War, by a few other European composers such as Ernst Křenek. In the later music of Berg—*Lyric* Suite, the aria *Der Wein*, Violin Concerto, and the opera *Lulu*—the method was joined to a renewed emphasis upon tertian harmonies and lyricism of the age of Mahler. Berg's application of the method was relatively free. For example, he made the method accommodate his favored chordal sonorities such as whole-tone harmonies and triadic tetrachords, and he frequently quoted preexistent tonal melodies. His dodecaphonic opera *Lulu* will be discussed in more detail later in this chapter.

The twelve-tone technique found its most devoted follower in Anton Webern. Like Berg, Webern did little serious composition before becoming a private student of Schoenberg in 1904, and both he and Berg turned to atonality in 1909. His music from this time until his definitive adoption of the twelve-tone method in 1924 is about equally divided between songs and instrumental works. The latter are among the most original creations in the entire history of music: their length dwindles often to a few measures, and the customary notions of musical line, pacing, and form are called into question. The composition of brief or "aphoristic" pieces was virtually a compulsion for Webern. Beneath their fleeting surface lie a profound network of structural relations and whirlpools of personal sentiment. Their melodic content is no less original. Melodic ideas are often passed from instrument to instrument and thus completed in a disjunct manner in which rests and changing colors are of heightened importance.

Webern experimented with the twelve-tone method beginning in 1922, and he adopted it as his sole compositional approach in 1924. His application even exceeds Schoenberg's in its strictness and in the extent to which the structural potential of a tone row is explored. But, as with Schoenberg, his use of the method also brought about more traditional thematic expansion and the application of conventional forms and genres.

These retrospective features are seen in his Second Cantata, op. 31 (1943), a six-movement work for mixed chorus, soprano and bass soloists, and orchestra. It would be his last completed composition before his tragic death in 1945. The composer selected poetry by his confidante Hil-

ANTON WEBERN
(Vienna, 1883—Mittersill, 1945)

As a young man in Vienna, Webern was greatly attracted to the music of Wagner, in whose style he made his earliest essays as a composer. He pursued a Ph.D. degree in musicology at the University of Vienna under the guidance of Guido Adler, which he completed in 1906. During his university studies he became a student of Schoenberg, forming a lifelong friendship.

Webern's career is a study in total dedication to music, despite considerable obstacles posed by the unprecedented originality of his compositions. He lived primarily by teaching, consulting for Universal Edition, and conducting, at which he was especially gifted. Toward the end of the Second World War he left Vienna to live with his daughter in the Tyrolean village of Mittersill. On September 15, 1945, he was accidentally shot to death there by an American occupation soldier.

Selected Works

Orchestral Music. Passacaglia, op. 1 (1908); Symphony, op. 21 (1928); Variations, op. 30 (1940); collections of short pieces (opp. 6, 10).

Chamber Music. String Quartet, op. 28 (1938); other works for string quartet (opp. 5, 9); Concerto for nine instruments, op. 24 (1934); Variations for piano, op. 27 (1936).

Songs. Five collections for voice and piano, seven collections for voice and instruments.

Choral Music. Two cantatas (1939, 1943), *Das Augenlicht* (1935).

Works without Opus Numbers. Webern usually conferred an opus number on a completed work with which he was satisfied. There are thirty-one such pieces or collections, some of which were not published during his lifetime. A larger number of compositions have come to light since his death in 1945, and many of these have now been published.

degard Jone, whose work and thought inspired all of his late vocal music. The verses chosen for this work, like much of Jone's poetry, are mystically religious. The fifth movement, "Freundselig ist das Wort" (Anthology no. 22), is an apostrophe to the Christian Logos or "the Word": mankind seeks the Word searching for love, and, though the Word fell silent on the Cross, it is still the source of life. Webern's setting is ternary, with the middle part an aria-like passage for soprano and instruments and the exterior sections for chorus with soprano and instrumental interpolations.

The outer sections are examples of the severe understatement that characterizes all of Webern's music: here the ephemeral gesture, momentary juxtaposition of colors, the concentrated disjunction of line, and spareness of texture project similar moods in Jone's poetry. In the central "aria" the vocal line is more connected, though filled with expressive leaps and nuances of attack, dynamics, and tempo. It is music of this sort—perhaps more than that of any major composer—which stands or falls on how it is performed. It relies heavily upon the sensitivity with which the performer realizes Webern's intentions, to which the written music is at best an imperfect guide.

The sixth movement, dealing with the Epiphany of Christ, is composed in the manner of a Renaissance motet, a genre with which Webern was intimately familiar through his doctoral thesis on the music of Heinrich Isaac. Webern imitates this archaic style by writing *a cappella;* that is, the instruments only double the four vocal lines. Webern also resorts to Renaissance "white notation," using large note values with the half note or "minim" as the metric unit. The movement, furthermore, is in a simple strophic form. But the most antiquated aspect of this music is its absolute linearity. The four lines are strictly canonic in rhythm and meter, and they each enter at the distance of three minims and at the interval of the major third or minor sixth. The canon creates both an inversion and a retrograde, since the alto and bass invert the subject of the tenor and soprano and the alto-tenor and soprano-bass pairs are exact retrogrades of one another.

The logic of the twelve-tone method seemed inescapable to Schoenberg; in his view, the stylistic evolution of music toward greater chromaticism and reliance on theme as the instrument of unification made the method not just a private compositional principle, rather, a historical necessity which in time would have to be realized and embraced. Thus he confided to his student Josef Rufer in 1921 that his discovery of the method would "insure the supremacy of German music for the next hundred years."

But from the perspective of more than sixty years since Schoenberg's bold assertion, it is now clear that musical style has not unfolded with the predictability that he anticipated. The method unquestionably produced masterpieces by European composers between the world wars, and it was taken up by several Americans before and after World War II. In the decade following the war it inspired a more generalized approach to serialism among most of the leading composers around the world. But the evolution of style has since led composers on new paths, pushing twelve-tone composition, at least for the time, into the background.

The Expressionist Musical Theater

> Man screams from the depths of his soul; the whole era becomes a single, piercing shriek. Art also screams, into the deep darkness, screams for help, screams for the spirit. This is Expressionism.

Thus in 1914 the Austrian critic Hermann Bahr sought to define the most original and influential movement in the arts and letters in Germany in the first quarter of the twentieth century. Bahr's image of the scream is especially apt, since Expressionist art turns on emotional exaggera-

The Expressionist woodcut: Edvard Munch, *The Scream*. (Courtesy of the National Gallery of Art, Washington, D.C., Rosenwald Collection [B-11,106].)

tion and lays bare the secret corners of the human psyche.

Expressionism was a diffuse artistic orientation rather than a coherent movement. The term was first used to describe German painting and graphic art in which the natural appearance of objects was to some extent distorted so as to heighten their emotional significance. In the works of

Nonrepresentational art among Expressionist painters: Vasili Kandinski, *Improvisation 19.* (Courtesy of the Städtische Galerie im Lenbachhaus, Munich. © A.D.A.G.P., Paris/V.A.G.A., New York, 1985.)

painters such as Ernst Ludwig Kirchner (1880–1938) or Erich Heckel (1883–1970), the degree of distortion was relatively small and limited to angular shapes, vivid colors, and bold brush strokes. But in paintings of Vasili Kandinski, abstraction became virtually complete. His works express inner visions, from which they derive their beauty. "The beautiful," wrote Kandinski in *Concerning the Spiritual in Art*, "is that which springs from an inner, emotional necessity. The beautiful is that which is inwardly beautiful."

The new forms and aesthetic of Expressionist painting found a mirror in German literature. Expressionist drama typically dealt with the grotesque, the erotic, the dehumanizing forces of modern society, or the clash of father and son. Such "distortions" of conventional behavior or reality are comparable to the abstractions of Expressionist painting: both allow the artist a more spontaneous statement about the human psyche.

Precursors of the Expressionist theater include Georg Büchner (1813–37), August Strindberg (1849–1912), and Frank Wedekind (1864–1918); later figures include Georg Kaiser (1878–1945), Walter Hasenclever (1890–1940), and Franz Werfel (1890–1945). Characters in their plays often embody principles or generalities, and, for this reason, they often lack names. In Büchner's *Woyzeck* (1837), the basis of Berg's opera *Wozzeck*, we encounter a "Doctor" representing science gone mad, a "Captain" who acts out the hypocrisy of modern society, and a "Drum Major" who symbolizes its brutish elements. Typically, the play is centered on a main character (Woyzeck) who represents all mankind.

In many of these works the theme of sexual perversion was for the first time openly addressed in modern literature. Wedekind's *Earth Spirit* (1895), his *Pandora's Box* (1903), and Oskar Kokoschka's *Mörder, Hoffnung der Frauen* (ca. 1907)—all later used as opera libretti—deal with the clash of male and female life principles. August Stramm's *Sancta Susanna* (1914), later adapted as a libretto by Paul Hindemith, deals with the repressed sexual drives of a nun. Indeed, the emphasis on erotic themes in the Expressionist theater echoes Sigmund Freud's contemporary psychoanalytic theories on the role of sexual repression as a cause of neurotic behavior.

All music of the German avant-garde of this period may appear analogous to Expressionist painting and literature. Its liberation of dissonance, angular melodic lines, vivid orchestration, and bombastic dynamics may well be viewed as distortions of a more natural order in music. But such an interpretation is belied by the high degree of organization that we have observed in this repertory and its continuity in style with the later nineteenth century. These characteristics have little in common with the contrived chaos of nonmusical Expressionism. To be sure, some musicians such as Arnold Schoenberg had close personal contact with the Expressionist movement. Schoenberg was himself a painter and was active in the "Blue Rider" group of Expressionists in Munich around 1912. He wholeheartedly embraced Kandinski's aesthetic of beauty arising from the artist's expression of inner necessity. But, as we have seen, his music maintains a strong bond with his forebears, and it projects a logical order that is essentially non-Expressionist.

The main area of contact between musicians and the Expressionist movement was the genre of opera. Between 1909 and 1935 a number of Expressionist plays were fit to music by Schoenberg, Berg, Hindemith, and Kurt Weill. Libretti that reflected Expressionist themes were also used by composers outside of Germany and Austria, as, for example, in Béla Bartók's *Duke Bluebeard's Castle* (1911) and Dimitri Shostakovich's *Lady Macbeth of the Mtsensk* (1932).

Expressionist plays were attractive to musicians for several reasons. Many had the qualities of good libretti: they were usually brief, they presented striking dramatic situations and clearly drawn characters, and they tended toward mythic universality. They also provided younger composers such as Paul Hindemith and Kurt Weill a convenient way to gain attention by shocking the musical establishment.

The prototype of German Expressionist opera is Richard Strauss's *Salome* (1905). Its libretto is based on Oscar Wilde's play *Salomé* (1891–92), which Strauss had seen performed in Berlin in 1903. Wilde's drama was inspired by the Symbolist plays of Maurice Maeterlinck and by the morbid images of humanity presented by a group of late-nineteenth-century French and English writers known as the "Decadents." In its themes and techniques, this play, which was repeatedly performed in Germany early in the century, formed a link between French Symbolist literature (see Chapter 8) and German Expressionism.

Wilde's story is a grotesque fantasy upon Gospel accounts of the execution of John the Baptist (called by his Hebrew name Jochanaan) at the hands of King Herod, his wife Herodias, and her daughter Salome. In Wilde's play Herod is crazed by superstition, fear, and desire for his stepdaughter, and Salome is swayed by an unquenchable lust for Jochanaan. Herod has promised Salome any wish if she will dance for him. The ensuing "Dance of the Seven Veils," set to music by Strauss in an exotic but arguably facile manner, is frequently performed separately as an orchestral tone poem.

Salome's wish is to have the head of Jochanaan. Among

RICHARD STRAUSS
(Munich, 1864—Garmisch, 1949)

Strauss's career as a musician was shaped by his childhood in Munich, where his father was an internationally renowned French horn virtuoso. Like Mahler he pursued the dual career of conductor and composer, beginning as an assistant to Hans von Bülow in Meiningen and later holding conducting positions in Munich, Weimar, Berlin, and Vienna. With proceeds from his highly successful opera *Salome*, he built a villa in Garmisch, which would be his main refuge for composition after 1908. He acted briefly as an administrator of several governmental organizations during the early years of the Third Reich, but he was dismissed from these positions when he criticized the Nazi's anti-Semitic policies. He resided primarily in Switzerland after the war.

Selected Works

Operas. *Guntram* (1893), *Feuersnot* (1901), *Salome* (1905), *Elektra* (1908), *Der Rosenkavalier* (1910), *Ariadne auf Naxos* (1912, revised 1916), *Die Frau ohne Schatten* (1918), *Intermezzo* (1923), *Die Aegyptische Helena* (1923–27), *Arabella* (1932), *Die schweigsame Frau* (1935), *Friedenstag* (1936), *Daphne* (1937), *Die Liebe der Danae* (1940), *Capriccio* (1941).

Orchestral Music. *Don Juan* (1889), *Tod und Verklärung* (1889), *Till Eulenspiegel* (1895), *Also sprach Zarathustra* (1895), *Don Quixote* (1897), *Ein Heldenleben* (1898), *Sinfonia domestica* (1903), *Alpensinfonie* (1915).

Songs. Approximately 200 songs for voice and piano or orchestra.

Miscellaneous. Concertos for horn (2), oboe, and violin; *Burleske* for piano and orchestra; ballet *Josephs-Legende*; *Metamorphosen* for twenty-three strings.

Expressionist artists and writers, decapitation was understood as a symbol of castration. In the lurid final scene (Anthology no. 18), she sings a rapturous soliloquy to the decapitated head, which she fondles and finally kisses. Herod is at last revulsed and commands that she be killed.

The basic musical idiom that Strauss brings to this disturbing story remains that of Wagner. The work is through composed with a free leitmotif technique dominating the orchestral music. The vocal part leaps over wide, dissonant intervals and demands the power to be heard over a large orchestra. The establishment of keys is still important to the structure of the music, but lines are often highly chromatic and blaring dissonances dominate the harmony.

Strauss goes beyond Wagner, however, by concentrating the action into a relatively brief single act and by intensifying the development of motives into a dense, busy counterpoint. This technique of development may be observed in the handling of Jochanaan's motive (Example 7-6), first heard at the beginning of the third scene when he is fetched out of his prison at Salome's command. The motive then suggests his magisterial self-command and noble purpose. But in the final scene, as Salome gloats over his head, his motive returns (Example 7-7) in a frantic diminution, now contrapuntally subordinated to two of Salome's more expansive motives. Thus, in the orchestral music alone, Jochanaan's grotesque plight and Salome's momentary perverse triumph are made vivid.

The final measures are a famous instance of Strauss's use of harmony and tonality to express Salome's insanity. As the music reaches the central key of C♯ major (rehearsal 359), Salome soars into a triumphant cantilena on the words, "I have now kissed thy mouth Jochanaan." Her music becomes diatonic as she appears victorious over Jochanaan's virtue. But as the orchestra builds to a gigantic cadence, the clash of the nondiatonic chord A C♯ G against

Example 7-6.   Richard Strauss, *Salome*, piano-vocal score. © 1905 by Adolf Fürstner. Renewed 1933. Copyright and renewal assigned to Boosey & Hawkes, Inc. Reprinted by permission.

Example 7-7. Richard Strauss, *Salome,* piano-vocal score. © 1905 by Adolf Fürstner. Renewed 1933. Copyright and renewal assigned to Boosey & Hawkes, Inc. Reprinted by permission.

the diatonic melodic motion in C♯ (Example 7-8) screams out her derangement.

The moon—a recurrent symbol in the play identified with Salome—betrays her by illuminating the ghastly scene. Herod turns and commands that she be killed, and in a tumultuous ten-measure codetta the key shifts without preparation to the distant C minor. With stunning dramatic effect, the older logic of harmonic progression and modulation is cast aside, just as Salome's perversity has shattered the norms of civilized behavior.

Strauss's *Salome* was a milestone in the history of music, for it showed the great dramatic power inherent in a

Example 7-8. Richard Strauss, *Salome,* piano-vocal score. © 1905 by Adolf Fürstner. Renewed 1933. Copyright and renewal assigned to Boosey & Hawkes, Inc. Reprinted by permission.

musical style where dissonance and key were to a large extent liberated. It was an inspiration to composers such as Schoenberg, who studied it intensely. It also pointed the way for other operas of a similar sort, where Expressionist drama found a natural alliance with dissonance and atonality.

Strauss was himself the first to capitalize on the great success of *Salome* with his opera *Elektra* (1908), based upon Hugo von Hofmannsthal's adaptation of the tragedy by Sophocles. In 1909 Schoenberg completed his first of two short Expressionist operas, *Erwartung* (*Expectation*), followed by *Die glückliche Hand* (*The Lucky Hand*). Shortly after the end of the First World War, Paul Hindemith adapted Oskar Kokoschka's *Mörder, Hoffnung der Frauen* and August Stramm's *Sancta Susanna* as one-act operas, and two plays by Georg Kaiser—*Der Protagonist* and *Der Zar lässt sich photographieren* (*The Tsar lets himself be photographed*)—were used as opera libretti by the young Kurt Weill.

The greatest master of Expressionist opera was Alban Berg, whose deep interest in modern theater and genius as a dramatic composer led to the most enduring examples of this genre in his operas *Wozzeck* (1917–22) and *Lulu* (1928–35).

Georg Büchner's play *Woyzeck* is a work of social realism which prefigured the techniques of the Expressionists by almost a century. The main figure Woyzeck (or Wozzeck, as in an edition used by Berg to construct his libretto) is a poor soldier who is assailed by the forces of society and ultimately driven to insanity, murder, and self-destruction. Berg's music is atonal, but it makes passing references to keys and triads and it has a diversity of styles typical of this composer. An elaborate technique of leitmotifs and other musical-dramatic associations helps to give the score its great dramatic power. But Berg dispenses with Wagnerian through composition by using large symmetrical organizations and casting scenes and acts into forms associated with instrumental music.

Many of these techniques recur in the opera *Lulu*, a work of greater abstraction. *Lulu* was left incomplete upon the composer's death in 1935. Only recently has the third act been published (1978) and the complete opera performed (1979), with much of the orchestration of Act 3 realized by Friedrich Cerha.

Berg made up the libretto by joining two related plays of Frank Wedekind, *Earth Spirit* and *Pandora's Box*. The central figure Lulu represents female sexuality in the broadest sense: she enslaves men at will, tyrannically wielding the power of life and death over them. But she is herself ultimately destructible by masculine forces. The three-act libretto is arranged by Berg into a rigidly symmetrical two-part form which emphasizes the alternating dominance of female (part 1) and male (part 2) principles. In the first part Lulu has a succession of three husbands—a Medical Specialist, a Painter, and the editor Dr. Schön. Each is totally in her power, and each is destroyed by jealousy or by a futile attempt to break from her spell.

In the second part of the story, Lulu's fortunes have declined. She is hunted for the murder of Dr. Schön and has fled to Paris and finally to London, where she becomes a prostitute. There she procures three patrons. The last is Jack the Ripper, the notorious murderer of nineteenth-century London, whom Berg identifies by common motives with Dr. Schön. Just as she murdered Schön, symbolically showing the power of her sexuality when it was at its zenith, now he murders her, in an exercise of the brutish power of the male life force.

In this opera as in *Wozzeck*, virtually every detail of musical style and structure is put at the service of the drama. Despite its intense and multifaceted formalism, the listener senses an unbroken continuity through each act. The work is a free application of the twelve-tone method, but with many nondodecaphonic elements.

The "Song of Lulu" from Act 2 (Anthology no. 20) is one of over fifty numbers into which Berg divides this opera. Many of these subdivisions are identified as vocal genres or styles; others suggest specific forms. An aria-like song is appropriate at this point as it is an avowal of Lulu's sensuality. Its musical structure is derived from the poetic form, which is a series of five couplets. Each of the five suggests that Schön and Lulu—representing, as they do, male and female—are opposite sides of the same existential principle. In the first half of each couplet, Lulu sings a theme that is answered in the second half by its inversion, thus an echo of the argumentative parallelisms in the text.

The inversion in the first couplet is illustrated in Example 4-2.

In the first, second, and fourth couplets, the antecedent themes each state a different twelve-tone row, of which the first and third are associated in various thematic guises throughout the opera with Lulu:

Row I (voice, mm. 491–94)   C E F D G A F♯ G♯ B A♯ D♯ C♯

Row II (mm. 498 ff.)   F♯ D C♯ G♯ E C A B♭ C♭ E♭ G F

Row III (mm. 516 ff.)   F E♭ D C B♭ A♭ E G F♯ C♯ B A

Since row I returns in the fifth couplet, the lied is appropriately a ternary or "song" form:

A—	B—	A'—
Couplets 1, 2	Couplets 3, 4	Couplet 5
Mm. 491–507	Mm. 508–21	Mm. 522–38

The third couplet, which begins the middle section, is not twelve-tone. It is instead a succession of octatonic, chromatic, and whole-tone passages which contrasts with the outer sections also by its more florid vocal style.

After Lulu's Song, Dr. Schön demands that she commit suicide. His music states his own tone row, cast into a motive that piles up in a tumultuous stretto. At measure 548 the orchestra welds itself into a unison rhythm (Example 7-9) that is associated throughout with fate and violent death. As he turns his back, Schön is shot to death by Lulu in an expression of her most violent and destructive power.

Expressionist art, literature, and music were totally suppressed by the Nazis in the 1930s, when they were dismissed as degenerate or as examples of "cultural Bolshev-

Example 7-9.   Motive signaling the murder of Dr. Schön in Berg's *Lulu*, Act 2, measures 548–49.

ism." This attitude reflected in part Hitler's own tastes, which in music did not extend beyond the style of Wagner. Among the outstanding living German composers, only Hans Pfitzner and Richard Strauss—who had long turned away from the avant-garde direction of *Salome* and *Elektra*—received official support. The others lived like Webern in total obscurity or like Hindemith and Schoenberg in exile.

A limited revival of opera in the Expressionist vein followed World War II, including Gottfried von Einem's *Dantons Tod* and *Der Prozess*, Hans Werner Henze's *Ein Landarzt*, and Krzysztof Penderecki's *Devils of Loudon*. But by the 1940s the artistic rebellion that had nurtured Expressionism had waned and could not be revived with the shocking audacity of its earlier years.

Bibliography

General studies or reminiscences of the arts in Germany and Austria early in the century may be found in Stefan Zweig's poignant autobiography *The World of Yesterday* (Lincoln, 1964), selected essays by Carl E. Schorske in *Fin-de-siècle Vienna* (New York, 1980), Otto Friedrich's study of Berlin during the Weimar Republic *Before the Deluge* (New York, 1972), and *Wittgenstein's Vienna* by Allan Janik and Stephen Toulmin (New York, 1973). Among the many memoirs of German musicians of these years, Bruno Walter's *Theme and Variations* (London, 1947) is especially recommendable.

The comprehensive writings on Mahler by Henry de La Grange and Donald Mitchell do not yet include his later works, but the *Selected Letters of Gustav Mahler* (New York, 1979) are very informative about his music of this period. Norman Del Mar's *Richard Strauss* (three vols., 1962–72) covers this composer's life and works in detail.

Schoenberg's writings are fundamental to an understanding of his music. His theoretical essays, which deal primarily with tonal music, are surveyed in the Bibliography to Chapter 2. His article "My Evolution" is found in *Musical Quarterly*, 38 (1952); this and other articles and lectures are collected under the title *Style and Idea*, ed.

Leonard Stein (New York, 1975). Also see his *Letters*, ed. Erwin Stein (New York, 1964). H. H. Stuckenschmidt's *Arnold Schoenberg* (New York, 1977) is the most detailed biography, but it contains little technical information about the music. Dika Newlin's *Bruckner, Mahler, Schoenberg* (New York, 1978) is a perceptive study of the works of these three composers by a former student of Schoenberg.

The biography of Alban Berg by his student Willi Reich (New York, 1974) emphasizes Berg's own statements about his works (including his essay "Why is Schoenberg's Music So Difficult to Understand?"), but it does not include sensitive biographical details found in various issues of the Newsletter of the International Alban Berg Society. Douglas Jarman's *Music of Alban Berg* (Berkeley and Los Angeles, 1979) emphasizes the twelve-tone music and develops the analytic approaches of George Perle. Perle is the author of book-length studies of *Wozzeck* (Berkeley and Los Angeles, 1980) and of *Lulu* (Berkeley and Los Angeles, 1985); the former is complemented by the detailed analytic study of *Wozzeck* by Janet Schmalfeldt (New Haven, 1983). Also see Luigi Rognoni, *The Second Vienna School: Expressionism and Dodecaphony*, trans. Robert W. Mann (London, 1977).

Hans Moldenhauer's *Anton von Webern* (New York, 1979) is an admirably thorough study of this composer, containing much information on the music. Among Busoni's voluminous writings on music, see his "Sketch of a New Esthetic of Music" in *Three Classics in the Aesthetic of Music* (New York, 1962) and *The Essence of Music and Other Papers* (London, 1957). Biographies of Busoni include those of his friend Edward Dent (London, 1933) and H. H. Stuckenschmidt (New York, 1970). There are no satisfactory studies of Reger, Zemlinsky, or Schreker in the English language.

John Willett's *Expressionism* (New York, 1970) is a reliable account of this movement, emphasizing developments in painting and drama. Robert Brustein places Expressionist drama in a larger context of modern theater in his *Theatre of Revolt* (Boston, 1964).

◆ 8 ◆

AVANT-GARDE COMPOSITION IN FRANCE AND RUSSIA

France in the nineteenth century was a center of innovation in literature and the visual arts and the guardian of a distinguished musical culture and tradition. In the second half of the century, poets of the Symbolist movement and Impressionist painters created a revolution in their genres that would be felt throughout the world and endure well into the twentieth century. French composers of this time cultivated traditional idioms, invigorating them with imported stylistic ideas and a native gift for color and vividness. By the turn of the century, French musicians looked increasingly toward developments in modern literature and painting as a stimulus for new directions in their work.

[handwritten margin note: looked to lit. & painting]

Symbolism and Impressionism

The Symbolist movement in literature is associated primarily with the poetry of Charles Baudelaire (1821–67),

Stéphane Mallarmé (1842–98), Paul Verlaine (1844–96), Arthur Rimbaud (1854–91), and plays by Maurice Maeterlinck (1862–1949). The works of these writers frequently avoid narration in order to allow sensations or objects to symbolize immaterial states of mind. Meaning is typically blurred by irregular syntax, the unexpected metaphor, and emphasis on the sonority and rhythm of words. Mallarmé's dramatic poem "Afternoon of a Faun" (1876), which inspired Claude Debussy's orchestral Prelude (1894), illustrates the network of sensuous associations that underlies Symbolist poetry. This "eclogue" expresses the fantasies of a mischievous faun who has awakened from a dream of erotic adventure with two nymphs:

> *I would perpetuate these nymphs.*
>
> > *So clear,*
> *Their skin's light bloom, it eddies in the air*
> *Heavy with tufts of sleep.*
>
> > *Did I love a dream!*
> *My doubt, a heap of ancient night, has come*
> *To rest in many a subtle branch, which, still*
> *The very woods, proves me, alas! the fool*
> *Crowning myself with roses, perfect flaw. . . .*

[The remainder may be found in *Mallarmé: The Poems*, trans. Keith Bosley (London, 1977).]

The faun cannot decide if his encounter was real or imagined, but his vivid and sensuous recollection of the experience transcends reality, and he happily goes to sleep again to seek new adventures.

The Symbolists looked with envy upon the art of music, which seemed to them most capable of eliciting a free play of emotions and associations. Musical imagery abounds in their poetry as a means of evoking realms of fantasy. They were especially drawn to Richard Wagner, in whose libretti they found a kindred symbolism and whose writings proclaim the same "total artwork" which was their aspiration. In fact, literary figures were the main contributors to a French journal devoted to the accomplishments of Wagner, the *Revue wagnérienne* (1885–88), which helped to provoke a flurry of interest in this composer among French amateurs and professional musicians alike.

Impressionism in French painting: Claude Monet, *Le pont japonais, Giverny.* (Oil on canvas, c. 1900, 35⅛" × 39½", Mr. and Mrs. Lewis L. Coburn Memorial Collection, Courtesy of the Art Institute of Chicago.)

Impressionism is a loosely defined style of French painting of the late nineteenth century associated with works by Edouard Manet (1832–83), Edgar Degas (1834–1917), Claude Monet (1840–1926), Pierre-Auguste Renoir (1841–1919), and others. Their subjects are usually unpretentious scenes from everyday life. Landscapes, which had a particular attraction for the Impressionists, were reproduced to capture the changing effects of light and the dynamic interplay of color. The artist's concentration upon spontaneous light often led to a blurring of the appearance of objects. Impressionism took on greater abstraction and

Art nouveau illustration: Aubrey Beardsley, illustration for Oscar Wilde's *Salome* (London, 1894).

emotion among painters such as Paul Gauguin (1848–1903) and Vincent Van Gogh (1853–90), and from these "post-Impressionists" there is a direct line to German Expressionism of the early twentieth century. The Impressionists were also forerunners of _art nouveau:_ a style of illustration and decoration characterized by fanciful organic shapes, often with grotesque or erotic overtones.

Certain composers active in France in the late nineteenth and early twentieth centuries—primarily Claude Debussy, and also Maurice Ravel, Paul Dukas, the Englishman Frederick Delius, and the American Charles Griffes—are commonly referred to as "Impressionists." Some aspects of their music indeed echo the style of the Impressionist painters: a fluidity of rhythm and meter suggestive of the hazy outlines of an Impressionist landscape, melodic arabesques reminiscent of _art nouveau_ illustration, a sensitivity to the play of instrumental and vocal color, and, in general, the use of a refined and evocative musical language that expresses the sensuousness of nature and the external world.

But the concept of an Impressionist movement in French music may also be misleading: composers such as Debussy and Ravel created their own independent styles rather than working within a single movement. Debussy strenuously objected to being termed an Impressionist—a word that was at first used pejoratively to describe his music. Regarding his orchestral pieces _Images,_ he wrote to his publisher, "What I am trying to do is something 'different'—an effect of reality, but what some fools call Impressionism."

The French Romantics

If French musical life of the later nineteenth century was not marked by the originality of German romanticism, it was nonetheless diverse and lively. César Franck (1822–90), Camille Saint-Saëns (1835–1921), and Ernest Chausson (1855–99) produced instrumental works of great tunefulness and color, marked by the cyclic return of themes in different movements. Operas by Emmanuel

Chabrier (1841–94) and Vincent d'Indy (1851–1931) reflected the influence of Wagner in their libretti and in certain musical formulas.

One of the most original of the late nineteenth-century French romantics was Gabriel Fauré (1845–1924). Although he worked in all of the major genres of his time, he is best known for his songs and Chopinesque piano music. His setting of Catulle Mendès "Dans la forêt de septembre" (1902, Anthology no. 10) will illustrate the restraint and subtle imagination that he brought to the composition of songs. The narrator of the poem beholds an aging forest that bears signs of long suffering. He gladly enters to escape from life, and a tree sends down a leaf as a brotherly token of approaching winter and, for the poet, death.

In phrasing and overall form, Fauré's setting is entirely regular. The music of the first four-line stanza returns in the third and sixth stanzas, and this principal melody is divided into four two-measure phrases. The tonality of G♭ major is clearly expressed in this stanza by motion from the tonic (mm. 1–3) to the dominant (mm. 6 ff.) and back to the tonic (m. 10). The music of the other stanzas emphasizes the relative minor E♭ (mm. 18–19 and 37–39). Fauré's harmonic palette is of great richness and ingenuity, capturing the bittersweet melancholy of the text. It derives in part from the harmonic idiom of Wagner. There is frequent use of the half-diminished seventh—one of Wagner's harmonic trademarks—to embellish the dominant, as in measures 6 and 9. Nondiatonic harmonies prolong chords with a diatonic function, as does the rich F♭ harmony of measure 5 on the words "troncs sonores" ("sonorous tree trunks"), which connects diatonic chords that prepare the dominant.

Debussy, Satie, and Ravel

The musician who rescued France from the dominance of German music was Claude Debussy (1862–1918). His works are monuments to the power of music to evoke an image or, to use his own words, "an effect of reality." Except for the early String Quartet and three late sonatas, he cultivated those genres that were suited to programmatic association: the character piece for piano, tone poem, and song. In a letter to Emile Baron of February 1887, he expressed "a profound disdain for music which has to follow a little story, which you are given when you arrive at the concert." Debussy's music is not literally programmatic, but seeks instead to capture the immaterial essence, poetry, or emotion of his subjects.

The themes of Debussy's works are sometimes drawn from exotic regions of the world or from fantastic visions of the mind. His most important subject is nature. In an article for the journal *Musica* (1903), he writes: "Music is a mysterious mathematical process whose elements are a part of Infinity. It is allied to the movement of the waters, to the play of curves described by the changing breezes. Nothing is more musical than a sunset!" *nature*

Nature is not only a recurrent subject of Debussy's instrumental works, it is also a metaphor for the true nature of music in general. Both are spontaneous, unconstrained, and asymmetrical. In an interview in 1902, Debussy used Baudelaire's notion of "correspondences" between objects, images, and artistic symbols to describe the function of nature in his works: "I should like for music a liberty that is proper to it—more to it, perhaps, than to any other art. It is not limited to a more or less exact reproduction of nature, but to the mysterious correspondences of nature and the imagination" (from Stefan Jarocinski, *Debussy: impressionnisme et symbolisme* [Paris, 1970], p. 122).

Debussy's style is consistently marked by refined understatement and simplicity of means: he rejected music that was formulaic, contrived, or grandiloquent. "Extreme complication is contrary to art," he writes. "Beauty must appeal to the senses, must provide us with immediate enjoyment, must impress us or insinuate itself into us without any effort on our part. Take Da Vinci or Mozart— these are the great artists!" In the *Revue musicale S.I.M.* (1912), he writes: "What one is meant to hear should be apparent at once. The rest is just a matter of environment and other extra-musical considerations."

Technical innovations in Debussy's music include a free use of dissonance where sevenths and ninths no longer require preparation or resolution, new methods of voice leading by which perfect intervals move in parallel, greater freedom in the expression of key, and passing use of nondi-

CLAUDE DEBUSSY

*(St. Germain-en-Laye, 1862—
Paris, 1918)*

Debussy was sent at the age of 10 to study at the Paris Conservatory in the hope that he would become a piano virtuoso. He
remained a student there for twelve years. During this time his
attention turned increasingly toward composition, which he
pursued with Ernest Guiraud. In 1884 he won the Grand Prix de
Rome, which made possible a three-year sojourn in Italy. He
resigned his stipend after two years and returned to Paris.

During the summers of 1888 and 1889, he traveled to Bay-
reuth to attend performances there of operas by Richard Wagner.
Debussy held a lifelong admiration for Wagner's music, although
he had a strong distaste for Wagnerian aesthetics and amateur
Wagnerites. At the Paris International Exhibition of 1889 he was
fascinated by Javanese gamelan ensembles and traditional Chinese theatrical music. He was closely associated with Symbolist
writers in the circle of Stéphane Mallarmé, and at least by 1891
he became a close friend of the eccentric musician Erik Satie.

Debussy's reputation as a composer was initially based upon
the great success of his opera *Pelléas et Mélisande* (1893–1902).
After 1907 he made several tours as a conductor of his own
music and worked sporadically on two operatic projects based on
tales of Edgar Allan Poe. He undertook several commissions by
the Russian impresario Sergei Diaghilev, including the score to
the ballet *Jeux*. Through Diaghilev he met Igor Stravinsky.

Selected Works

Dramatic Music. *Pelléas et Mélisande* (opera, 1893–1902), *Jeux*
(ballet, 1912), *Khamma* (ballet, 1912, mainly orchestrated by
Charles Koechlin).

Orchestral Music. *Prélude à l'après-midi d'un faune* (1894), *Nocturnes* (1899), *La mer* (1905), *Images* (1905–12).

Chamber Music. String Quartet (1893); Sonatas for cello (1915), flute, viola and harp (1915), and violin (1917); miscellaneous works for saxophone, clarinet, and flute.

Piano Music. Approximately 100 pieces including the collections *Pour le piano* (1894–1901), *Estampes* (1903), *Images* (two sets, 1905, 1907), *Children's Corner* (1908), Preludes (two books, 1910, 1913), Etudes, *Six épigraphes antiques* (four hands, 1914), *En blanc et noir* (two pianos, 1915).

Songs. Fifty-seven songs published during Debussy's lifetime, some with orchestral accompaniment. Eighteen are settings of poetry by Paul Verlaine.

---

atonic harmonies such as the whole-tone set. Although some of his later works are entirely atonal, he rejected the harmonic experimentation of his younger contemporaries. The triad and diatonic scale were his points of orientation. Most of the dissonances that lend a distinctive color to his music are triadic extensions such as seventh and ninth chords. Occasionally these harmonies are decorated by passing use of whole-tone, octatonic, or pentatonic scales and chordal formations, but, with only a few exceptions, these are ways of embellishing a diatonic framework.

Debussy's melodic lines are often spun into eccentric and flamboyant shapes, as in the Prelude to *The Afternoon of a Faun*. Or they may be flexible and chant-like, as in the song "En sourdine." Phrasing is also varied—some works, such as the Saraband from *Pour le piano*, are laid out primarily in multiples of two-measure units. But in pieces such as *Jeux*, periodic phrasing is little in evidence.

An example of Debussy's piano music in his early mature style is the Saraband from *Pour le piano* (Anthology no. 2). This work was composed in 1894 and provisionally titled "Image," but it was revised and retitled for its publication in 1901. It is superficially related to the Sarabands of Erik Satie, works that will be discussed shortly. Like all of Debussy's piano music, the Saraband is a character piece that creates a distinctive mood. The title comes from the work's rhythmic style, which suggests the slow, triple-time sarabands often found in works by seventeenth-century clavecinists whom Debussy admired. In the original version, the composer states that the work is to be played "in the tempo of a saraband, that is, with a slow and solemn elegance, a bit like an old portrait, a recollection from the Louvre."

The form of the work is ternary. The middle section (mm. 23–41) introduces new motives and contrasts with the outer sections by virtue of its quartal harmonies (mm. 23–28). Perhaps owing to its derivation from a baroque dance, the formal structure of the Saraband is regular: most motives span multiples of two measures, and phrases are built from simple repetitive patterns.

Motives in this work share similarities of interval and rhythm, but they are not developmentally linked as in music of the German and Austrian modernists. Debussy is reported to have rejected conventional exposition and development:

> I should like to attain a music which is truly released from motives or made from one continuous motive that is not interrupted and that never comes back upon itself. Then there will be logical development—compact and deductive. Between restatements of the same motive—typical and characteristic of the work—there will not be a superfluous and unimportant padding. Development will no longer be this amplification of material, this professional's rhetoric learned through excellent lessons. It will instead take on a more universal and ultimately psychic meaning. [From André Fontainas, *Mes souvenirs du symbolisme* (Paris, 1928), pp. 92–93.]

Harmonies of the Saraband do not project the tonic C♯ minor until the reprise at measure 42, and then only indistinctly. Their role instead is to enhance the melody by successions of parallel seventh chords (mm. 35–41), fourth chords (mm. 23–28, 67–70), or by combinations of seventh chords and triads that arise without reference to traditional resolutions of dissonances or harmonic functions within a key. "A chord is an edifice of sound," writes Debussy, "having merely the importance of a stone in a building. Its real value depends on the place it occupies and the support it lends to the flexible curve of the melodic line." Cadences completely avoid the strong dominant-to-tonic forms.

Pelléas et Mélisande, Debussy's first great success as a composer, was premiered in 1902 after a decade in the making. It is based on a Symbolist play by Maurice Maeterlinck in which the youthful lovers Pelléas and Mélisande are destroyed by the jealousy of Golaud, Mélisande's husband and half-brother of Pelléas. The play has a mythic and surrealistic atmosphere in which characters act out their roles as symbols of a morbid but all-powerful fate. It also has connections with Wagner's text to *Tristan und Isolde.* Both are studies of love that is frustrated by existential forces beyond the control of the lovers.

The orchestral part provides an unobtrusive backdrop to the singing, which is predominantly parlando in character, occasionally varied by song-like passages. A very subtle and unsystematic technique of leitmotifs may be discovered in the orchestral music, but the work's severe understatement is virtually the opposite of Wagnerian rhetoric. Toward the end of Act 4, for example, Pelléas and Mélisande declare their love in a scene that parallels the love duet of *Tristan,* Act 2. Wagner's lovers boldly vent their passions for more than a half hour, but Pelléas must confess that he could scarcely hear Mélisande's declaration of love, even though the orchestra had by then dwindled into complete silence.

In his two books of Piano *Préludes* (1910 and 1913), Debussy gives full rein to his musical imagination. The listener is transported to exotic locales in Spain, Greece, India, and Brittany; evocations of nature—mists, wind, dead leaves—give way to images of pure fantasy. These works are rivaled only by those of Robert Schumann in their subtle translation of diverse images into music for piano. At the same time these brief compositions are encyclopedic in their innovative structural resources. Some such as "La cathédrale engloutie" use diatonic scales but avoid the expression of a key; others rely on the whole-tone scale, as in "Voiles," and the octatonic scale, as in "Brouillards." But most retain an orientation to a key by ending with a triad and making at least passing references to diatonic chords and tonic and dominant pedal points.

Debussy's late style may be observed in the song "Placet futile" from the *Trois poèmes de Stéphane Mallarmé* of 1913. This text was also used in a song of the same year by Maurice Ravel, which allows a useful comparison of the works of these two composers. Debussy was a friend of

Mallarmé: he took part in literary discussions held weekly at Mallarmé's residence and, to Mallarmé's delight, composed an orchestral Prelude to his dramatic poem "The Afternoon of a Faun."

The text of "Placet futile" is an example of the Symbolists' sacrifice of clear meaning to suggestive metaphors and distorted syntax. The narrator of this sonnet makes his "futile petition" to be appointed "shepherd of the smiles" of the beloved; any more active participation in love must be sublimated beneath a flourish of pastoral metaphors. The central image of the poem is a Sevres teacup, whose naked goddesses are portrayed musically in a slow minuet with rococo ornamentation. As in most of Debussy's later works, tonality plays a minor role. The context is G major/minor, but most of the harmonies are nondiatonic seventh and ninth chords and whole-tone collections.

Debussy's last completed composition for orchestra is his score for the ballet *Jeux* (*Games*, 1912). This work was commissioned by Sergei Diaghilev for the Ballets Russes (see below), by whom it received its premier performance in 1913. The scenario of the ballet was devised by Vaslav Nijinsky (1890–1950), the leading dancer of Diaghilev's company. Debussy succinctly described the scenario in an article for *Le matin* written shortly after the first performance: "There was a park, a tennis court, and the chance meeting of two young girls with a young man in pursuit of a lost ball. A mysterious landscape with that slightly evil *je ne sais quoi* that always accompanies twilight. And a lot of leaping and turning in the air, and nimble footwork—all the necessary ingredients for real rhythms to be born."

In fact Nijinsky's scenario is considerably more risqué. A man encounters two ladies at a tennis court. He dances with one—even manages a kiss—which makes the other petulantly jealous. He dances next with the second lady, but the first leaves dejectedly. Now the three dance together a voluptuous waltz, ending in a triple kiss. A tennis ball bounds across the stage and the trio disappears. Nijinsky later wrote that the meaning of the story was that the two ladies represent two boys in a homosexual liason with Diaghilev, whom the man represents. Regardless, the work is known primarily for its musical setting, which is a masterpiece of motion and color.

The ballet is framed symmetrically by music to the

prelude (mm. 1–46), which returns in the epilogue (rehearsal 80). The body of the work consists of a through-composed succession of episodes, which are linked by rhythmic and motivic similarities. Some of the motives recur straightforwardly; others are developmentally linked. The harmonic content of *Jeux* is typical of Debussy's late music. The lines and chords are predominantly diatonic, although they do not dwell upon any single diatonic collection in a manner that defines a key. References to A at the beginning (rehearsal 1) and end, and to the tritone related region of E♭ at rehearsal 41, are brief and superficial. The harmonies that support Debussy's surging motivic arabesques are mainly seventh and ninth chords, occasionally varied by whole-tone formations (rehearsal 5, 61, 81), pentatonic sets and subsets (rehearsal 42), and bitriadic chords (rehearsal 10).

Debussy's wish to reestablish a distinctively French style of composition free of German influences was shared by his friend Erik Satie (1866–1925). Satie's music includes songs, piano pieces, and music for the stage. Most compositions are miniatures, and his works include imitations of the style of the music hall, certain farcical gestures, as well as music of considerable ambition and seriousness. The common threads running through it all are its melodiousness, simplicity, and complete lack of pretense.

An example of his early idiom is the first Saraband (1887, Anthology no. 1). This piece may be compared to Debussy's Saraband in its use of unresolved seventh and ninth chords. Such colorful harmonies are also found in passing in French opera of this time and in popular songs, which Satie accompanied as a cabaret pianist. On the large scale the Saraband expresses the key of A♭ major. But few chords occur diatonically in A♭ and most of them carry unresolved dissonances. The music is highly repetitive, simple in texture and rhythm, and—at least in comparison to Debussy's Saraband—curiously motionless.

Satie's later piano music adopts textures that are spartanly bare, usually consisting of a simple melody above a light accompaniment. The repetitiveness and freedom from diatonic harmony of the Sarabands are retained. Many pieces lack regular meter. Beginning with his first three *Gnossiennes* (1890), Satie's scores for piano contain witty marginalia which contribute a running commentary by the

ERIK SATIE
(Honfleur, 1866—Paris, 1925)

Satie spent his childhood alternately in Honfleur and Paris. He entered the Paris Conservatory in 1879, but his work there was found unpromising. His earliest compositions were published with assistance from his father in 1887. In the 1880s and 1890s he was active in various unorthodox Christian sects for which he composed music.

He earned his livelihood primarily as a pianist in Parisian cabarets, and he composed several music hall songs for the singers Vincent Hyspa and Paulette Darty. At the age of 40 he entered the Schola Cantorum to study counterpoint, which he did successfully with Albert Roussel. His career as a serious composer received encouragement from Ravel, who played some of his piano pieces in concerts, and from the writer Jean Cocteau. His collaboration with Cocteau on the ballet *Parade* (1917) produced his first major success as a composer. Toward the end of his life he and Cocteau became mentors to a group of younger French composers known as the Six.

Selected Works

Dramatic Works. Ballets: *Uspud* (1892), *Parade* (1917), *Mercure* (1924), *Relâche* (1924); incidental music: *Le piège de Méduse* (1913).

Piano Music. Approximately thirty collections including Sarabands (1887), *Gymnopédies* (1888), *Gnossiennes* (1890), Preludes, *Sports et divertissements* (1914), *Avant-dernières pensées* (1914), Nocturnes, *Trois morceaux en forme de poire* (four hands, 1890–1903), and arrangements.

Songs. Four collections for voice and piano, popular songs, *Socrate* for sopranos and orchestra (1918).

composer upon the work at hand. His collection *Sports et divertissements* (1914) is an especially charming series of fragments, each of which depicts in the space of a minute or less a particular sport or entertainment.

Two of his later works epitomize the different artistic stances that alternate in his music after the First World War. The symphonic drama *Socrate* (1918) is serious and poignantly expressive, while the ballet *Parade* (1917) is high spirited and tongue-in-cheek. The music to *Socrate* comprises solo songs for four sopranos and small orchestra. Its texts are drawn from Plato's *Dialogs*, concluded touchingly by Phaedo's description of Socrates' death. The vocal line is a tuneful recitation; the orchestra, a repetitive and unobtrusive backdrop. It is music that reveals Satie's debt to Debussy and *Pelléas*, where the largeness of sentiment and occasion expressed in the text is intentionally contrasted to the modesty and understatement of musical resources. This divergent relation of text and music was Satie's alternative to Wagnerian music drama and his solution to the question of how a truly French musical idiom should unfold in the modern age.

Parade was Satie's first real success as a composer. It was commissioned by Sergei Diaghilev, who brought Satie into collaboration with the writer Jean Cocteau and the painter Pablo Picasso. The setting is outside of a tent at a fair, where three managers, a juggler, acrobats, and an American girl try to coax the passersby to enter and see the show within. Satie's music is again modest: "a musical background," he said, "for certain noises which Cocteau considers indispensable in order to fix the atmosphere of his characters." The music for the Chaplinesque antics of the American girl includes gun shots and typewriter sounds in the orchestra as well as a ragtime dance.

The premiere of the ballet provoked a disturbance, which, since the scandalous first night of Stravinsky's *Rite of Spring*, had become increasingly obligatory among French audiences of new music. Satie was no doubt pleased with this mark of success, and he increasingly associated himself with the aesthetics of his collaborator Cocteau. The influence of Satie and Cocteau on French music after the First World War will be traced later in this chapter and in Chapter 10. After the death of Debussy in 1918, Satie became mentor to a new generation of French composers for whom the refined artistry of the Impressionists was

MAURICE RAVEL
(Ciboure, 1875—Paris, 1937)

Ravel's career is to an extent similar to that of the musician with whom he is most often mentioned, Claude Debussy. Both were sent as adolescents to the Paris Conservatory to study piano, and both later turned their attention mainly to composition. Ravel was in the composition class of Gabriel Fauré. Like Debussy, he was stimulated by the music and wit of Erik Satie, by Russian music, and by discussions with artists in other disciplines.

In 1912 Ravel completed *Daphnis et Chloé* for Sergei Diaghilev and the Ballets Russes; Diaghilev also brought Ravel and Stravinsky together to complete Musorgski's opera *Khovantchina,* thus beginning a lifelong friendship of these two musicians. In the 1920s and 1930s Ravel found himself outside of the circle of younger French composers who were actively renouncing the preciosity which they found in musical Impressionism. Ravel undertook numerous tours in the 1920s, including a lengthy visit to the United States in 1928. His work as a composer slowly came to a halt after 1933 due to a degenerative nervous disorder, which would cause his death in 1937.

Selected Works

Operas. *L'heure espagnole* (1909), *L'enfant et les sortilèges* (1920–25).

Ballets. *Daphnis et Chloé* (1909–12), *La valse* (1920), *Boléro* (1928).

Orchestral Music. Arrangements of piano music (see below).

Concertos. *Tzigane* (violin and piano or orchestra, 1924), Concerto for Left Hand (1930), Piano Concerto in G (1931).

Chamber Music. String Quartet (1903), Trio (piano, violin, cello, 1914), Sonata for Violin and Cello (1922), Violin Sonata (1923–27).

Piano Music. *Pavane pour une infante défunte** (1899), *Jeux d'eau*
(1901), *Sonatine* (1905), *Miroirs** (1905), *Rapsodie espagnole**
(four hands, 1908), *Gaspard de la nuit* (1908), *Ma mère l'oye**
(four hands, 1910), *Valses nobles et sentimentales** (1911), *Le
tombeau de Couperin** (1917). The asterisk (*) denotes works
transcribed—at least in part—for orchestra by Ravel.

Songs. *Histoires naturelles* (1906), *Trois poèmes de Stéphane
Mallarmé* (1913), *Chansons madécasses* (1926), *Don Quichotte
à Dulcinée* (1933).

---

disagreeable. Stravinsky, for example, credited Satie with
"opposing the vagueness of a decrepit Impressionism by a
precise and firm language stripped of all pictorial embellishments." Virtually all of the musicians who met Satie,
regardless of their artistic direction, were captivated by his
wit and generosity, and it was as much by the power of his
personality as by his musicianship that he exerted his
influence.

The rejuvenation of modern French music begun by
Debussy was continued by Maurice Ravel (1875–1937).
Ravel's early works reflect the style of Debussy: they are
vividly pictorial and expand the framework of diatonic
tonality in ways associated with Debussy. Ravel's piano
works, however, rely to a greater extent on virtuosity for
their expressiveness, and most are appropriate to orchestral
transcription, done with unparalleled brilliance by the
composer. He was also more inclined to experiment with
new stylistic directions, as in his Mallarmé songs and in
later works such as the *Tombeau de Couperin*, which is a
sympathetic reflection upon the idiom of the baroque
clavecinists.

Ravel's early style may be observed in his piano work
Jeux d'eau (1901, Anthology no. 3). This piece was probably
inspired by Liszt's "Les jeux d'eaux à la Villa d'Este" (1877)
from the third *Année de pèlerinage*. In both, the "play of
water" mentioned in the title is captured by an efferves-
cence of arpeggios and melodic arabesques. The spirit of
Ravel's piece is suggested by a line added to the score from
the poet Henri de Régnier: "River god laughing from the

water which tickles him." The work avails itself of the repertory of harmonies characteristic of both Debussy and
Liszt. It begins and ends in E major, but with all tonic triads
decorated by the major seventh D♯. The triads of the opening give way to a whole-tone passage in measures 4–6, and
the subsidiary theme (mm. 19 ff.) is pentatonic. A cadenza
near the end pits arpeggiated F♯-major triads in the left hand
against C-major triads in the right. This bitriadic passage
may well have been in Stravinsky's ear when he wrote the
very similar opening to the second tableau of *Petrushka*
(see below).

During a period of collaboration with Ravel in 1913,
Stravinsky introduced him to his *Trois poésies de la lyrique
japonaise* for voice and chamber orchestra. Stravinsky's
work for the medium of vocalist and diverse instruments
was stimulated by Schoenberg's *Pierrot lunaire*, which he
had heard in Berlin the previous year. Ravel now called
upon a similar ensemble in his *Trois poèmes de Stéphane
Mallarmé* (1913). At the very time that Ravel was completing these songs, he learned that Debussy was also at work
on three Mallarmé settings, and, by a remarkable coinci-
dence, two of them were the same texts that Ravel had
used. One of these two, "Placet futile," will show how far
Ravel had departed from the Impressionistic "Debussyism"
of his early music.

In a letter of 1913 to his student Roland-Manuel, Ravel
wrote about his objectives in this song:

> I fully realize the great audacity of having attempted
> to interpret this sonnet ["Placet futile"] in music. It
> was necessary that the melodic contour, the modu-
> lations, and the rhythms be as precious, as properly
> contoured as the sentiment and the images of the
> text. In spite of that, it was necessary to maintain
> the elegant deportment of the poem. Above all, it
> was necessary to maintain the profound and exqui-
> site tenderness which suffuses all of this. [Quoted in
> Arbie Orenstein, *Ravel* (New York: Columbia Uni-
> versity Press, 1975), pp. 128–29.]

In order to mirror the elegance and tenderness of the
poem, Ravel takes an entirely different approach from that
of Debussy. While Debussy casts the entire poem as an
ornate minuet, Ravel calls for the utmost variety in his

musical resources. The tempo is almost constantly in flux, there is little formal symmetry, and the accompanimental colors change kaleidoscopically. The harmonies, likewise, move back and forth from triads and triadically based dissonances to other dissonant collections without triadic suggestions. The dissonant chords at the beginning, such as the all-interval tetrachord on the downbeat of measure 2, give the work a distinctly German flavor. There is little sense of tonality, other than a hint of D minor near the beginning (mm. 4–6) and F major at the end. The Mallarmé songs are Ravel's most difficult and experimental works. They reflect both Mallarmé's euphuistic poetry and an openness to new directions which Ravel no doubt discovered in Stravinsky's music of this time.

Ravel composed relatively less after the end of the First World War. But from these years come such works as the opera *L'enfant et les sortilèges* (*The Child and the Magic Spells*) on a fairy-tale libretto by Colette. The music makes use of a ragtime dance, and Ravel's fascination with American popular music is also reflected in several later works such as the slow movement ("Blues") of his Violin Sonata (1927). The ever-popular *Boléro* (1928) was conceived as a ballet score for Ida Rubinstein. A simple bolero rhythm and folk-like tunes are repeated as an ostinato, sustaining a continual crescendo. The work was described by the composer as "wholly orchestral tissue without music." Ravel's two piano concertos mix different styles. The first, one of several concertos for left hand written for Paul Wittgenstein after he lost an arm in the war, uses jazz idioms in a somber way. The ensuing Concerto in G major is a lighter work, "in the same spirit," Ravel said, "as those of Mozart and Saint-Saëns."

Ravel considered his *Chansons madécasses* (*Madagascar* Songs, 1926) to be among his greatest works. These pieces, for soprano accompanied by flute, cello, and piano, use texts by Evariste Parny, who claimed that they were from folk songs that he had collected and translated. In fact they were written by Parny, expressing fanciful and evocative images of life among the Madagascans. Ravel's three texts dwell upon love, war, and blissful idleness. The second, "Méfiez-vous des blancs," narrates in prose the arrival of white men to the island, who, proving deceitful and treacherous, are finally slaughtered by the natives.

The music vividly traces the emotions of the narrator.

Lithograph by Luc-Albert Moreau for the first edition of Ravel's "Méfiez-vous des blancs" from *Chansons madécasses* (Paris, 1926). (Courtesy of Durand S.A. Editions musicales.)

He begins his tale with seething tension, builds to the frantic war cries at measure 35, and erupts with savage fury as he tells of the destruction of the second wave of settlers. In exhaustion he falls back at the end, confident that "they are no more and we shall live free." The setting is entirely atonal, with only passing reference to triadic harmonies. It is carefully unified by recurrent motives. The printed score makes novel use of conflicting key signatures in the various parts, but these do not reflect traditional tonality.

Among Ravel's contemporaries in France, Paul Dukas (1865–1935) and Albert Roussel (1869–1937) are especially notable. Dukas devoted himself to teaching at the Paris Conservatory; he left a relatively small number of compositions among which the tone poem *Sorcerer's Apprentice* is best known. His opera *Ariane et Barbe-bleue* (1907) on a play by Maurice Maeterlinck was highly regarded both in France and Austria, where it was performed in 1908. It is marked by whole-tone sonorities and a brilliant style of orchestration.

Roussel was a student of Vincent d'Indy and later his colleague on the faculty of the Schola Cantorum. His students there included Erik Satie and Edgard Varèse. Roussel's best-known music is for orchestra, for which he wrote in a powerfully direct manner. His symphonies use the technique of cyclic return of themes as do those of his teacher d'Indy, and they contain a rhythmic vigor and brilliant orchestral color reminiscent of Ravel and Prokofiev.

The Decline of the Avant-Garde

A significant musical avant-garde did not endure long after the end of World War I in France, despite the rambunctious high spirits of composers who were allied to the versatile Jean Cocteau (1889–1963). Cocteau was a writer who delved into cinema, the visual arts, and music and who catalyzed a generation of French artistic experiment. In a collection of aphorisms on music titled *Le Coq et l'arlequin* (1918), he decried "all music which has to be listened to through the hands. . . . What we need is a music of the earth, everyday music. . . . I want someone to build me music I can live in like a house." For Cocteau the ultimate in "hand music" was the work of Wagner, but Debussy's evocative Impressionism was also tainted in this way. "One cannot get lost in a Debussy mist as one can in a Wagner fog," he quipped, "but it is not good for one."

The antidote for Wagner and the Impressionists, according to Cocteau, was simplicity, an emphasis on straightforward melody, rejection of the colossal, and an art with the immediacy and accessibility of popular entertainment. "The music hall, the circus, and American negro bands: all these things fertilize an artist just as life does. . . . These entertainments are not art. [But] they stimulate in the same way as machinery, animals, natural scenery, or danger. . . . Do not derive art from art!"

Cocteau enunciated a new taste and direction in French music that was prefigured by Satie and realized between the world wars in different ways by the outstanding French composers of the following generation. This new idiom, which can generally be termed "neoclassicism," will be taken up again in Chapter 10.

The Russian Avant-Garde:
The Five and Scriabin

We turn now to the flowering of a distinguished musical culture in Russia and its remarkable influence on modern music in France. The development of music in Russia along Western lines was a by-product of liberalization in society and politics during the second half of the nineteenth century. Activities in music were largely centered in the capital St. Petersburg and Moscow. Conservatories were founded in both cities in the 1860s, and these institutions soon produced outstanding orchestras and opera companies. Throughout the nineteenth century Russia had been a center of classical ballet, thanks to the efforts there of the French ballet master Charles-Louis Didelot (1767–1837) and the choreographer Marius Petipa (1818–1910).

As the nineteenth century progressed, two distinct approaches to composition emerged. Figures associated with the Moscow Conservatory such as Nicholas Rubinstein (1835–81), Sergei Taneev (1856–1915), and Pëtr Ilich Tchaikovsky (1840–93) followed mainly Western models. A circle of composers who gathered around Mili Balakirev (1837–1910) in St. Petersburg, on the other hand, consisted of musical nationalists who felt less constrained by Western notions of musical structure. These composers came to be known as the "Russian Five" and they included, besides their mentor Balakirev, Alexander Borodin (1833–87), César Cui (1835–1918), Modest Musorgski (1839–81), and Nikolai Rimski-Korsakov (1844–1908).

Russian music was an important part of French musical life beginning in the last quarter of the nineteenth century. The orchestral works of Tchaikovsky were regularly performed by French orchestras beginning in the 1870s, and, at the International Exhibition of 1889, Rimski-Korsakov came to Paris to lead concerts of music by all of the "Five" in addition to music by several of his students.

French interest in Russian music at this time was also stimulated by close political ties between the two nations. In a great victory of diplomacy, France concluded an alliance with Russia that frustrated the plan of Prussia to isolate France politically and militarily. Tsar Nicholas II visited Paris in 1896 to seal this "Dual Alliance," setting off a burst of enthusiasm there for all things Russian. In that year the songs of Musorgski were heard in recitals by the soprano Marie d'Alheim, and these works greatly attracted Debussy and Ravel with their ingenuous spontaneity. It was only natural that younger Russian composers such as Stravinsky and Alexander Glazunov (1865–1936) should later adopt France as the center of their activities in the West.

Debussy was particularly admiring of the music of Modest Musorgski. "With Nurse" (1868), the first song from the cycle *Nursery*, shows Musorgski's gift for spontaneous and realistic narration with music. The text, written by Musorgski himself, is charmingly naive: a child at first wishes to hear the tale of the wolf who ate naughty children, but then decides that a story about an imaginary king and queen would be more congenial. The melodic line is recitational, moving almost entirely by quarter notes grouped into constantly changing meters according to the length and scansion of the poetic lines. Typical of many songs by Musorgski, the tonic harmony is not heard at the beginning. It is reached only at the end of the first section at measure 13. Before this point of orientation, various triads alternate with whole-tone harmonies, the latter brought in at the mention of the wolf. Throughout the nineteenth century, Russian composers commonly used whole-tone sets to depict images of fear or the unearthly. Musorgski's mentor Alexander Dargomyzhski used whole-tone sonorities to accompany the vivified statue in his opera *The Stone Guest*, an adaptation of the Don Juan legend. After the cadence on the tonic B♮ in measure 13 of "With Nurse," the music shifts directly to a D-major triad, a progression commonly encountered in operatic recitative. The second half of the song contains a comic musical picture of the hobbling king and his sneezing queen, turning finally to a codetta squarely in the tonic key.

About this cycle and its composer, Debussy wrote: "[Musorgski] is unique and will remain so, because his art is spontaneous and free from arid formulas. . . . It is like the art of an inquiring savage discovering music step by step through his emotions." Indeed, it was this model of unaffected simplicity more than any particular technical resources that became the primary influence of Musorgski upon Debussy.

The music of Rimski-Korsakov was also increasingly heard in Paris, especially his colorful orchestral works, which owed their general conception to the tone poems of Liszt. Rimski-Korsakov conducted *Antar, Capriccio espagnol*, and his Piano Concerto in Paris in 1889; in 1907 he returned to conduct selections from five other pieces. A feature of much of his music that proved especially important to composers in both France and Russia was the octatonic scale, a formation also prefigured in experimental works by Liszt. For example, the codetta to the third movement of the symphonic poem *Antar* (1868) (Example 8-1) begins upon a cadence in D major (rehearsal V), which is followed by octatonic movement in the upper strings and woodwinds. For Rimski-Korsakov the octatonic scale was an exotic embellishment to diatonic harmony. But it would later be used by Ravel, Debussy, Scriabin, Stravinsky, and Messiaen as a central harmonic resource in the atonal idiom.

From Moscow came one of the most prophetic figures in the transition from romantic to modern music, Alexander Scriabin (1872–1915). Like most of his fellow Muscovites, he did not outwardly adopt Russian folk materials, and he stayed closely in touch with modern developments in Western music. His evolution as a composer is unique among his countrymen at this time in the dispatch with which he moved toward complete atonality.

His music is almost wholly for orchestra or piano, on which instrument he performed as a virtuoso. The early piano works are based on the idiom of Chopin, and, by the turn of the century, his orchestral music was touched by the harmonic and orchestrational style of Wagner. Between this time and his complete break with tonality about 1908, his music increasingly reflected his devotion to cult and mystic notions of love. Several works are connected with his own poetry, the tone of which can be gathered from lines written to accompany his Fourth Symphony (*Poem of Ecstasy*): "The world is consumed in universal flame. The spirit is on the summit of being. . . . And the world resounds with the joyful cry: I am!" His scores from this time are peppered with exotic instructions suggesting their poetic

Example 8-1. Rimski-Korsakov, *Antar*, conclusion of third movement.

ALEXANDER SCRIABIN
(Moscow, 1872—Moscow, 1915)

Scriabin inherited his mother's gift as a prodigious pianist, and he later studied this instrument along with composition at the Conservatory in Moscow. From 1898 he was an instructor of piano at this institution, from which he resigned in 1903 to devote himself to composing. Scriabin enjoyed the support of two influential Russian patrons: the publisher Mitrofan Belyaev and the conductor and publisher Serge Koussevitsky. From 1904 until 1910 he lived in Western Europe, where he toured, composed, and refined an exotic philosophy in which theosophy, Nietzschean ideas, and Eastern religions mingled. He lived primarily in Moscow from 1910, and he continued to travel and perform as an interpreter of his own piano music.

Selected Works

Orchestral Music. Five symphonies (1900–10) (no. 3 is titled *Divine Poem* [1904]; no. 4, *Poem of Ecstasy* [1908]; no. 5, *Prometheus* [1908–10]); Piano Concerto (1896).

Piano Music. Collections of character piano pieces including études, preludes, *Albumblätter*, dances; ten sonatas (1892–1913).

content: "with profound and veiled ardor," "with a sad voluptuousness," "in a sweet intoxication"—these from the Tenth Piano Sonata. His symphony *Prometheus*, furthermore, calls for a "color organ," an instrument that would regulate colored lights which the composer associated with certain harmonies.

His works after about 1908 maintain the rhapsodic, improvisatory gestures of his earlier music, but they totally dispense with key and triadic harmony. In these pieces dissonance is emancipated as completely as in works by Schoenberg of the same era. But Scriabin favors a repertory of atonal sets quite unlike those embraced by Schoenberg. Most are symmetrical or nearly so. Whole-tone chords, for example, are frequently used before and after his break with tonality. After about 1908 his music is characterized by two other sets: the octatonic scale and the collection that was called the "nearly-whole-tone" hexachord in Chapter 2. Both whole-tone and octatonic collections had a long history in nineteenth-century Russian music, but there as exotically colorful embellishments to diatonic scales. In Scriabin's music these formations become central, creating a static harmony that corresponds to the motionless realm of the senses proclaimed in the composer's writings.

These features may be observed in Scriabin's Tenth Piano Sonata, op. 70 (1913). Like all of his later music, it is in one movement. Its surface is characterized by changes of mood in fits and starts, trills in all registers, little feeling of stable meter, and rhythm that changes suddenly from hymnic slowness to frenetic outbursts. These seemingly improvisatory gestures, however, are in contrast to the structure of the sonata, which is methodically planned and highly unified. Its form may be described as symmetrical: in the first 99 measures a number of distinct motives are introduced which are then varied by transposition and reharmonization. These are recapitulated in reverse order toward the end of the work, either at their original pitch or transposed.

The harmonic dimension is marked by recurrences of the nearly-whole-tone set, or, as it is more commonly known, the *Prometheus* or "mystic" chord. This set, as will be recalled from Chapter 2, is synonymous with a whole-tone scale in which any single pitch is raised or lowered a semitone. It occurs most often at structurally important junctures of the Sonata, articulating form just as tonic and dominant harmonies clarify the form of a tonal work. The motive first heard at measures 84–87 (Example 8-2) will illustrate the use of the *Prometheus* chord. This melodic

mm. 84-87
(also see mm.
103, 271, 290)

nearly-whole-tone hexachords

Example 8-2.   Scriabin, Piano Sonata no. 10. Used by permission of the original publisher Rob. Forberg-P. Jurgenson Musikverlag, Bonn.

idea is typical of lines in all of Scriabin's late music in its alternation of minor and major thirds. It is harmonized by forms of the basic hexachord, which occur most clearly on the downbeat of each of the last three measures. The chord of the first measure of this example is synonymous with a dominant seventh on the root E♭. This harmony does not suggest a tonicization of A♭ or any other such function. Instead, it is a familiar subset of the nearly-whole-tone hexachord, relating by inclusion to this controlling sonority.

Diaghilev, Stravinsky, Prokofiev, and Shostakovich

Connections between Russian and French music were greatly strengthened by the arrival in Paris of the impresario Sergei Diaghilev (1872–1929). As a young man in St. Petersburg, Diaghilev had briefly studied music with Rimski-Korsakov. But he realized that he would not have the career of a practicing artist; instead, he would become a promoter and propagandist of modern art and music. Supported by royal patronage and an impressive committee of sponsors, he brought a production of Musorgski's *Boris Godunov* to Paris in 1908. The following year he organized a company of dancers from the Maryinsky Theater in St. Petersburg, including the remarkable Vaslav Nijinsky, Anna Pavlova, and Tamara Karsavina, to perform in Paris. Thus began the "Ballets Russes," which continued under Diaghilev's leadership to perform around the world and which almost singlehandedly produced a revival of ballet as a central musical genre in the twentieth century.

Diaghilev favored ballets of a single act, several of which would constitute an evening's entertainment. He was particularly interested in the musical dimension of ballet, and he insisted on scores of high quality, whether orchestrations of preexistent works or new commissions. Increasingly Diaghilev wished to see innovation in all dimensions of his productions: "Surprise me!" was a common directive to the artists with whom he worked.

After their first few seasons in Paris, the Ballets Russes began to shed their connections to Russian art in favor of a more international image. Diaghilev eventually commissioned new ballet scores from most of the leading Western composers, including Debussy, Ravel, Satie, Milhaud, Poulenc, and Strauss. But Diaghilev's accomplishments are inevitably tied to his patronage of the young Russian composer Igor Stravinsky (1882–1971), whom he first brought to the attention of European audiences.

3. periods

For purposes of discussion, Stravinsky's music may be divided into three chronological periods, each with certain distinctive stylistic features. A period of experimentation extended to about 1920, in which his music had strong connections to Russian folk art and to the musical works of his Russian forebears. A period from about 1920 to the early 1950s is less experimental, more international than Russian, and more concerned with stylistic continuity and tradition. Finally, from the early 1950s to his last composition in 1966, he adopted serial methods associated with the music of Schoenberg and Webern. In this chapter we will deal with the first of these periods, returning to the middle period in Chapter 10 and the serial works in Chapter 12.

1. experimentation

2. stylistic continuity less experimental

3. serial

The centerpieces of Stravinsky's music during his first period are the first four of five ballet scores that he wrote for Diaghilev. All four are based on Russian tales and myths and make frequent use of Russian or Slavic folk melodies, but each is distinctive in its own way. The earliest, Firebird (1910), owes the most in style to Stravinsky's teacher Rimski-Korsakov, with its large, luminous orchestra, sensitivity to color, and passing references to whole-tone and octatonic passages within a tonal context. Stravinsky also uses a dramatic device associated with Rimski-Korsakov in which music depicting diabolical figures is chromatic and music for heroic figures, diatonic. Unlike

IGOR STRAVINSKY
*(Oranienbaum, 1882—
New York, 1971)*

As a young man in St. Petersburg, Stravinsky frequented performances of opera and ballet at the Maryinsky Theater, where his
father was a leading singer. His career as a composer was late
in developing, as he first pursued a degree in law. Subsequently,
he became the student of Rimski-Korsakov. His music came to
the attention of the impresario Sergei Diaghilev in 1909; this led
to a series of commissions through which he attracted international attention.

During World War I he lived in Switzerland, moving to
France in 1920, where he later became a citizen. After 1924 he
was increasingly active as a performer and conductor of his own
music, a capacity in which he toured throughout the world. In
September of 1939 he immigrated to the United States, settling
later in the Los Angeles area and becoming an American citizen.
In 1945 he began a series of revisions of many of his earlier
works, which were edited by his new publisher Boosey &
Hawkes. In 1962, with the assistance of the conductor Robert
Craft, he returned to the Soviet Union for a series of concerts. His
last years were spent alternately in Europe and New York City.
He is buried in Venice, near the grave of his friend and patron
Diaghilev.

Selected Works

Operas and Theater Pieces. *Nightingale* (1908–14), *Reynard* (1916),
    L'histoire du soldat (1918), *Mavra* (1922), *Oedipus rex* (1927),
    Rake's Progress (1948–51).

Ballets. *Firebird* (1910), *Petrushka* (1911), *Rite of Spring* (1911–13),
    Les noces (1914–23), *Pulcinella* (1920), *Apollon musagète*
    (1928), *Fairy's Kiss* (1928), *Perséphone* (1934), *Jeu de cartes*
    (1936), *Orpheus* (1947), *Agon* (1953–57).

Orchestral Music. Symphonies of Wind Instruments (1920), Symphony in C (1939–40), Symphony in Three Movements (1945), *Movements* for Piano and Orchestra (1959), Variations (1964).

Concertos. Concerto for piano and winds (1924), Capriccio for piano and orchestra (1929), Concerto in D for violin and orchestra (1931).

Chamber Music. Octet (1923), Concerto in E♭ (*Dumbarton Oaks,* 1937), Concerto in D (*Basle,* 1946), Septet (1953).

Piano Music. *Piano-Rag-Music* (1919), Sonata (1924), Serenade in A (1925).

Songs. *In Memoriam Dylan Thomas* (1954), numerous collections of Russian-language songs with diverse instrumental accompaniments.

Choral Music. *Zvezdoliki* (1912), *Symphony of Psalms* (1930), Mass (1944–48), Cantata (1952), *Threni* (1958), *Requiem Canticles* (1966).

most ballet music of the nineteenth century, the score is closely tied to the scenario by recurrent motives and passages accompanying pantomimed narrative rather than stock dancing numbers.

Petrushka (1911) makes greater use of folk song, and it prefigures Stravinsky's later music by dispensing with tonality as a principle of large-scale organization. The octatonic scale now takes on central importance, which it retains in Stravinsky's music throughout the first period. The story of the ballet was conceived by the composer in connection with a concerto-like work for piano and orchestra; it was elaborated at Diaghilev's urging as a ballet scenario, upon which Stravinsky collaborated with the painter Alexandre Benois (1870–1960).

The story is divided into four connected scenes. At a nineteenth-century Russian Shrovetide fair, a showman of a puppet theater brings to life his puppets: the little clown Petrushka, a Ballerina, and a Moor. In the second scene (Anthology no. 19) we encounter Petrushka in his cell, embittered by his fate. He cannot win the affections of the

Ballerina, and, in the final scene, he is "slain" by the brutish Moor. But, in the end, he elfishly thumbs his nose at the audience, having returned to life by the magic of the fairy tale. In his *Reminiscences of the Russian Ballet* (1941), Benois writes that Petrushka represents "the spiritual and suffering side of humanity." He indeed embodies the idea of the antihero, common to much twentieth-century art and literature.

Stravinsky's music integrates folk song and original material in an alternation of pentatonic, modal, and diatonic passages. The dance of the bear in the fourth scene (rehearsal 100) uses a whole-tone melody, typical of the earlier Russian musician's treatment of fearful objects. Stravinsky's first music for the ballet consisted of an elaboration of a bitriadic figure uniting major triads on C and F♯. This material was later placed in the second scene (rehearsal 49 ff.), where it represents Petrushka and his bitterness toward his lot. The bitriadic "Petrushka chord" has harmonic meaning as a six-note subset of the octatonic scale (Example 8-3), the latter of which plays a large integrative role in the music of the entire ballet.

Le sacre du printemps (*The Rite of Spring*, 1913) portrays scenes among prehistoric Slavonic tribes, gathered to celebrate the coming of spring. In the first of two parts, the choreography represents dances, games, and rituals. The second part focuses upon a single terrifying act: a maiden is chosen to dance herself to death to appease the gods. Stravinsky's music evokes the primitivism of the scenario in part by its quotations of folk melodies, ostinatos, and dissonant atonality. But the feature of *The Rite of Spring* that struck its early listeners as scandalously provocative was its rhythm and meter, whose free shapes were brazenly underscored by a massive orchestration. Sections such as the concluding "Sacrificial Dance," the maiden's frenzied dance of death, consist of rapidly pulsating small values gathered into constantly changing metric groups. Here Stravinsky gives full rein to the orchestra and its bitingly percussive effects in order to project the tumult and vi-

Example 8-3.   Derivation of the bitriadic "Petrushka" chord.

Example 8–4.   Stravinsky, *The Rite of Spring.* © copyright 1921 Edition Russe de Musique (Russischer Musikverlag). Copyright assigned 1947 to Booscy & Hawkes, Inc. for all countries. Reprinted by permission.

olence that were his recollections of the coming of spring to Russia.

The Rite of Spring is atonal despite the diatonic content of its folk tunes. The bassoon solo at the beginning of the work, for example, quotes a Lithuanian folk song suggesting A minor (Example 8-4). Other themes, whether of folk origin or not, are based typically on small segments of diatonic scales and treated in a repetitious manner.

The harmonic dimension of this ballet, as in *Petrushka*, makes use of the octatonic scale and its subsets. Bitriadic collections are also prominent, as in the seven-note chord underlying the "Augurs of Spring" section, where an F♭ triad is heard in the lower voices against an E♭ dominant seventh in the higher register (Example 8-5). This dark sonority is repeated as an ostinato, interrupted by irregular accents and by brief, undistinctive motives. The "Augurs of Spring" chord is also very similar to the octatonic collection: only its pitch class E♭ deviates from an octatonic arrangement of intervals.

Diaghilev referred to *The Rite of Spring* as the "Ninth Symphony" of the twentieth century. Like Beethoven's late music, it was widely imitated: to name a few instances, in Prokofiev's *Scythian* Suite, Samuel Barber's *Medea*, and numerous works by Latin American composers of the 1930s such as Silvestre Revueltas's *Sensemayá* (1938). It was not imitated by Stravinsky himself. His next ballet, *Les noces (The Wedding)*, was of a very different sort.

Les noces was composed between 1914 and 1917, but it was not definitively orchestrated until 1923. In its final

"Augurs of Spring" chord

Example 8–5.   The "Augurs of Spring" chord from Stravinsky's *Rite of Spring.*

shape it calls for a chorus and vocal soloists, four pianos, and percussion—an accompaniment that the composer described as "perfectly homogeneous, perfectly impersonal, perfectly mechanical." Although *Les noces* was first performed as a ballet, it is more akin to a cantata since there is no scenario beyond the text and since the voices sing from beginning to end. The words were drawn from wedding songs in a nineteenth-century collection of Russian popular poetry. In the first of two parts, the scene alternates between the houses of the bride and the bridegroom prior to their wedding. We hear their expressions of doubt, prayers, testaments, all embraced in busy preparations. Part 2 is the wedding feast. Drink loosens the guests' tongues, some bawdy remarks are heard, a couple is chosen to warm the wedding bed, and, finally, the couple is tucked away as wedding bells toll the happy occasion.

Although the chorus normally takes the role of the wedding party and soloists deliver the lines of the bride, groom, and other important individuals, there is no consistency in such a dramatic arrangement. For example, the groom's last expression of love to his bride is sung by the chorus, since by then the couple is tactfully out of sight in the bed chamber. This antioperatic detachment of drama from musical means characterizes much of Stravinsky's later vocal works; it represents, furthermore, a departure from the intimacy of text and music characteristic of both the romantics and the French Impressionists. "Music is, by its very nature, powerless to *express* anything at all," he wrote in his *Autobiography*. "Music is [instead] the sole domain in which man realizes the present. . . . The phenomenon of music is given to us with the sole purpose of establishing an order in things, including, and particularly, the coordination between *man* and *time*."

In addition to its unusual percussive orchestra, the music of *Les noces* is highly innovative in its treatment of the voices, which are declamatory and nonlyrical. Their patter-like rhythm is grouped in changing meters based upon the poetic structure of the Russian texts. During the wedding feast, the drunken revelers begin to blurt out their exhortations in a pitchless speaking voice—a technique also employed in the choruses of Milhaud's cantata *Les choéphores* (1915).

Toward the end of the First World War Stravinsky's

music began to leave behind the Russian influences of his early ballets and songs as well as the experimental directions that had allied him with the musical avant-garde. The first major work reflecting his new internationalism was *L'histoire du soldat* (1918). The story about a soldier's meeting with the devil was of Russian origin, but it was elaborated by his librettist Charles Ramuz in a more general and timeless way. The soldier trades his fiddle, symbolic of his soul, to the devil in return for untold wealth. But he finds that wealth is a curse and gladly rids himself of it. He is then able to cure an ailing princess by the power of his violin playing and claims her as his wife. But he loses all when he tries to return to the land of his childhood. The play is acted out by the devil and soldier, which are speaking roles, and by the princess, who is a dancer, with the story filled in by a narrator. A diverse band of seven musicians sits on stage adding musical commentary. The score contains virtuosic parts for violin, the soldier's instrument, and for the percussion, which represents the devil, who has the last word in both drama and music.

The music has an immediate accessibility. Some of it imitates popular or familiar genres: a march, tango, waltz, ragtime, and hymn. It is predominantly diatonic with the triad as the central sonority, but these elements are not used over large spans in the traditional expression of a key. Nevertheless, its tunefulness, clarity, and simplicity point to a new direction in Stravinsky's work.

This new direction is also apparent in his last ballet for Diaghilev, *Pulcinella* (1920). The music is a masterful arrangement of operatic excerpts by Giovanni Pergolesi (1710–36) and instrumental movements probably composed by Domenico Gallo, an obscure eighteenth-century composer whose music was passed off as Pergolesi's. It was in this ballet that Stravinsky revealed another important new direction—adapting the spirit, if not the music itself, of earlier composers whom he admired. Later he would pay similar homage to Tchaikovsky, Bach, Weber, Beethoven, Verdi, and others.

By 1922 with the completion of his Italianate comic opera *Mavra*, Stravinsky's transition to a new idiom was complete. Its traits were a cosmopolitan tone stripped of folk influence, frequent references to earlier styles of Western music, a predominantly diatonic harmony where

SERGEI PROKOFIEV

(Sontsovka, Ukraine, 1891—
Moscow, 1953)

Prokofiev's budding talent as a musician received every encouragement from his parents—especially from his mother, who was an amateur pianist. In addition to regular trips to Moscow and St. Petersburg to hear music, Prokofiev had Reinhold Glière as his private tutor in music for two summers at the family's provincial estate. At the age of 13 Prokofiev was enrolled at the St. Petersburg Conservatory where he studied with Rimski-Korsakov, Anatoli Liadov, and Nikolai Cherepnin. In 1914 he visited London to meet Diaghilev, hoping to interest him in his opera *The Gambler.* Instead, Diaghilev put him to work on a ballet score on a primitive subject inspired by Stravinsky's *Rite of Spring.* Although this commission was not completed, Prokofiev later composed three scores for Diaghilev's company.

After the Revolution, Prokofiev immigrated to Western Europe. He resided primarily in Germany from 1922, with many trips elsewhere in Europe and in America. After several visits to the Soviet Union, he returned there permanently in 1936 and settled in Moscow. His music became the object of repeated criticism for its tendencies toward "formalism" and lack of "Soviet realism." After the death of Stalin, however, it was recognized by Soviet authorities for its greatness.

Selected Works

Operas. *The Gambler* (1916), *Love for Three Oranges* (1919), *Flaming Angel* (1919–23), *War and Peace* (1943).

Ballets. *The Buffoon* (1915, revised 1920), *Le Pas d'acier* (1926), *The Prodigal Son* (1929), *Romeo and Juliet* (1936), *Cinderella* (1940–44).

Symphonies. Seven symphonies: 1917, 1924, 1928, 1930, 1944, 1947, 1952: *Scythian* Suite (1915).

Concertos. Five piano concertos (1912–32), two violin concertos (1917–35), cello concerto (1933–38), *Sinfonie concertante* for cello (1952).

Chamber Music. Two string quartets (1930–41), Sonata for violin and piano (1938–46), Cello Sonata (1949).

Piano Music. Numerous collections of short works, nine sonatas (1909–47).

Cantatas. *Seven, They Are Seven* (1918), *Alexander Nevsky* (1939).

Miscellaneous. *Lt. Kije* (film score, 1933), *Peter and the Wolf* (narration, 1936).

---

the triad was of central importance, and a lean and clear orchestration. In his *Autobiography* he made it plain that he wished to dissociate himself both from his immediate past—Russian music of the later nineteenth century and French Impressionism—and from the avant-garde. "It would be a great mistake to regard me as an adherent of *Zukunftsmusik*—the music of the future. Nothing could be more ridiculous. I live neither in the past nor in the future. I am in the present."

The other outstanding young Russian composer whom Diaghilev brought to the attention of Western Europe was Sergei Prokofiev (1891–1953). His three scores for the Ballets Russes (*The Buffoon*, 1915; *The Steel Step*, 1926; *The Prodigal Son*, 1929) were successful, but they have not had the longevity in the repertory of his later ballets *Romeo and Juliet* (1936) and *Cinderella* (1944). His seven mature operas are among his greatest works, but they are rarely performed in the West and only the symphonic suite from *Love for Three Oranges* is well known. However, his seven symphonies, nine piano sonatas, and five early piano concertos are among the most frequently performed works in their genres from the twentieth-century literature.

Prokofiev did not intend his music to be experimental. He carefully avoided association with any artistic movements, and his musical style did not follow a consistent line of evolution. In his *Autobiography* he defines four features, some of which characterize each of his works: classicism, innovation, toccata-like rhythm, and lyricism. These alternated freely throughout his entire career, and the only characteristics that he considered invariably present in all of his music were clarity and brevity.

Prokofiev's classicism occurs most clearly in works that are based on earlier models, such as his *Classical* Symphony (1917) in which he wrote as he thought Haydn would have had he lived into the twentieth century. Prokofiev rejected the neoclassical movement of many composers of the 1920s and 1930s. He considered such works as the *Classical* Symphony to be isolated within his music as a whole, and he was bitingly critical of Stravinsky's neoclassicism, calling it "Bach on the wrong notes."

Prokofiev said that his innovative contribution was seen mainly in harmony. Indeed, his harmonic idiom is entirely singular. It takes its departure from the triad and common-practice tonality, but it is also pungently dissonant and little constrained by triadic functions within a key or by normative voice leading. He also asserted his harmonic individuality by avoiding the repertory of dissonances that characterize works of the other French and Russian modernists, such as octatonic and pentatonic sets or the strings of seventh and ninth chords of the Impressionists.

Lyricism is the feature most consistently distinguishing Prokofiev's music. His melodic lines are often cast within a diatonic framework, but with chromatic turns of phrase and distinctively large and unexpected leaps. Prokofiev remarked that his many toccata-like piano works took their departure from Schumann's Toccata in C, op. 7, a technical showpiece that was often featured in Prokofiev's concerts as a pianist. An example of this type of music, which also illustrates his harmonic idiom at its most adventuresome, is the finale to the Seventh Piano Sonata (1939–42, Anthology no. 8). This fiery movement exploits asymmetrical divisions of 7/8 meter. Rhythm is nearly the sole point of focus: there are no important themes and the dissonant harmonies are limited in their variety and return in a highly repetitive fashion. The context of the piece, nevertheless, is the key of B♭. A B♭-major triad opens the movement and the end dwells on a B♭-major scale.

A musical avant-garde flourished in the Soviet Union for over a decade after the Revolution of 1917. For many, the ideals of liberation associated with the advent of communism were consistent with those of artistic experiment. Even before the Revolution there existed in Russia a distinctly experimental movement of which Scriabin was the guiding light. Music by Nikolai Rosslavetz and Yefim Golyscheff, for example, was not only entirely atonal, but systematically exploited the complete chromatic set. Western avant-garde composers were welcomed to the Soviet Union during its early years. Alban Berg, for example, traveled to Leningrad (formerly St. Petersburg) in 1927 to see *Wozzeck* performed. He was stunned by the great public involvement there in new music and gratified by the high quality of the production.

The ideals of the Revolution fired the imagination of a number of young Russians who experimented with new musical resources hoping to capture the spirit of the times. The tone poem *Iron Foundry* (1928) by the Moscow-trained Alexander Mosolov (1900–73), for example, depicted the glory of labor by using percussive imitations of the factory. Even Diaghilev, no friend of Bolshevism, hoped to capitalize on the artistic ferment in his homeland by commissioning Prokofiev's ballet *Le Pas d'acier* (*The Steel Step*), which extolled the factory and the machine.

The greatest of the younger Soviet composers whose careers were launched during the post-Revolutionary decade was Dimitri Shostakovich (1906–1975). Like Prokofiev he attended the conservatory in St. Petersburg, by then renamed Petrograd, where he was an outstanding pianist and prodigious composer. His First Symphony (1925), composed while he was still a student, brought him worldwide acclamation. In several works for orchestra or piano over the next five years, he experimented with highly dissonant textures and spare counterpoint, reflecting his knowledge of contemporary European developments. During the early 1930s he allied himself with the remarkably innovative Soviet theater by several ballets and operas in which he showed his gift for musical dramatization and witty parody.

But his meteoric rise as a composer was temporarily stayed in 1936 when his opera *Lady Macbeth of the*

DIMITRI SHOSTAKOVICH
(St. Petersburg, 1906—Moscow, 1975)

Shostakovich was one of numerous outstanding Russian musicians to attend the Conservatory in Petrograd, the name given to St. Petersburg after the Revolution. There he was a student of composition of Maximilian Steinberg, the son-in-law of Rimski-Korsakov. His First Symphony, composed as a graduation work from the Conservatory in 1925, gained him international attention.

His early works for stage emphasized revolutionary themes, but his opera *Lady Macbeth of the Mtsensk* was retracted after criticism by Soviet authorities in 1936. His Fifth Symphony (1937) was his initial attempt to conform to Stalinist guidelines for music, but Shostakovich remained an object of criticism in the Soviet Union for the remainder of Stalin's life. Toward the end of the Second World War he settled in Moscow.

Selected Works

Operas. *The Nose* (1928), *Lady Macbeth of the Mtsensk* (1932, revised and retitled *Katerina Izmailova* in 1963).

Ballets. *The Golden Age* (1930), *Bolt* (1931).

Orchestral Music. Fifteen symphonies, several of which use voices (1925–71).

Concertos. Concerto for piano, trumpet, and strings (1933), Piano Concerto no. 2 (1957), concertos for violin (2) and cello (2).

Chamber Music. Fifteen string quartets (1935–74), cello sonata (1934), violin sonata (1968).

Piano Music. Two sonatas (1926, 1942), *Aphorisms* (1927), 24 Preludes and Fugues (1951).

Songs. *From Jewish Poetry* (1948), *Song of the Forests* (with chorus and orchestra, 1949), *Satires* (1960), *The Execution of Stepan Razin* (with chorus and orchestra, 1964).

Mtsensk was chastised by the Soviet government. From this point, his career—as well as the careers of all Soviet composers—would be intertwined with political restraints to a degree unprecedented outside of Nazi Germany. Soviet criticism of free artistic expression will be taken up again shortly. But after 1936 Shostakovich almost completely avoided dramatic works in favor of instrumental composition, to which he eventually contributed fifteen symphonies and fifteen string quartets.

The opera *Lady Macbeth of the Mtsensk* (1932, revised and retitled *Katerina Izmailova* in 1963), like Hindemith's nearly contemporary *Mathis der Maler*, made its composer an international celebrity because of its suppression by a dictatorial regime. The work is freely based on a story of the same title by Nikolai Leskov (1831–95), which deals realistically with the lascivious and homicidal activities of one Katerina Izmailova. Her murderous nature and certain other themes led Leskov to the reference in the title to Shakespeare's character. Shostakovich's version of the story attempts to shed a sympathetic light on Katerina, showing her as the helpless victim of bourgeois society under the Tsars. In fact Shostakovich planned this as the first in a series of operas dealing with women, tracing their historical debasement by male-dominated society and their ultimate triumph in the Soviet utopia.

Katerina is unhappily married to Zinovy Izmailov, and the two are living with his father Boris, a wealthy merchant. She has an affair with the dashing serf Sergei, only to be discovered by Boris. Sergei is savagely beaten and saved only by Katerina, who poisons her father-in-law's food. Sergei later murders Zinovy. But Boris's body is found, and the nuptials of Katerina and Sergei are interrupted by the police. The two are condemned to march to a Siberian prison camp. Sergei now curses Katerina and takes up with another lady convict, but Katerina kills her rival and herself.

It is a little wonder that the opera was an instant success in both Leningrad and Moscow, as it had something for everyone: sentimentality, comedy, sex, violence, and clever caricature. The music is direct and eclectic, with touches of Wagner, Offenbach, Mozart, and Russian folk songs, mixed with grand orchestral production numbers and touching songs. Its style is primarily tonal and triadic, varied by scenes of brilliant orchestral dissonance and temporary suspension of key.

Such an area is the orchestral interlude between the fourth and fifth scenes, thus at the very center of the nine-scene opera (Anthology no. 21). Boris has just been murdered, and a priest has intoned an irreverent cavatina over his body. The orchestra then plunges into a dramatic passacaglia: eleven variations, that is, upon a ground bass first heard in measures 9 through 17 (Example 8-6). The ground has weak and conflicting tonal implications: D minor at the beginning and C♯ at the end. It is octatonic except for the pitch class C♮. The variations in the upper voices play upon the opening motive of the ground, but similarly avoid establishing a key even though they temporarily dwell upon various triads and diatonic scale segments.

The interlude is followed by Katerina's passionate love song to Sergei—a text that was rewritten by the composer for the 1963 revival to eliminate some of its frankness. It begins on a G-minor triad and the accompaniment continues the dotted figure from the end of the interlude. Although it is basically triadic, no key is established. By its touching lyricism—typical of all of Katerina's music in the opera—it invites the sympathy for her that Shostakovich intended.

Example 8-6.   Passacaglia theme from Shostakovich's *Lady Macbeth of the Mtsensk*, Interlude between scenes 4 and 5. Used by arrangement with G. Schirmer, Inc. U.S. agent for Musikverlag Hans Sikorski, Hamburg.

The friendly atmosphere for musical experimentation in the 1920s was clouded by the end of the decade in the Soviet Union by the rise of the Association of Proletarian Musicians (RAPM), who demanded a music geared in simplicity to the masses and who rejected works by the Western avant-garde. Although RAPM was disbanded in 1932 and superseded by the Union of Soviet Composers, its doctrines about the role of music in the Soviet state continued to gain importance. In 1934 the writer Maxim Gorky enunciated a doctrine of "socialist realism," by which works of art were to be models of optimism and propagation of communist values. The opposite of this realism was said to be "formalism," a catchall term describing works of art that appeared elitist and abstract.

Any hopes that Soviet musicians may have had for continuing the avant-garde movement were dashed once and for all in 1936. An article—perhaps dictated in part by Stalin himself—appeared in the newspaper *Pravda* at this time condemning Shostakovich's *Lady Macbeth* as "coarse, primitive, and vulgar." "Here is music turned deliberately inside out," the reviewer continued, "in order that nothing will be reminiscent of classical opera or have anything in common with symphonic music or with simple and popular musical language accessible to all." Not only was the subject deemed inappropriate, but the apparent "noise, wild rhythm, vocal shrieking, and deliberate dissonance" were henceforth unacceptable in the Soviet Union. Only at the height of World War II was there a measure of relaxation of governmental restraint over the arts, and it was during this time that works such as Prokofiev's Seventh Piano Sonata were composed.

After the war the charge of formalism was made all the more menacing against modernism in the arts. In a Decree on Music issued in 1948, Stalin's advisor Andrei Zhdanov castigated Prokofiev, Shostakovich, and others for their "errors" of atonality, dissonance, and lack of melody. In the years after the death of Stalin in 1953, a cautious measure of artistic freedom returned to the Soviet Union. But by then Stalin's repression had effectively removed Russian composers from their place in the evolution of musical style, a place that they had earlier occupied with great distinction.

Bibliography

The life and works of several composers treated in this chapter are concisely surveyed in The Master Musician Series (London: J. M. Dent). Especially commendable are books on Debussy by Edward Lockspeiser (1936) and on Musorgski by M. D. Calvocoressi (rev. G. Abraham, 1946). The Oxford Studies of Composers has excellent short books on the music of Debussy by Roger Nichols (1973), Scriabin by Hugh MacDonald (1978), and Shostakovich by Norman Kay (1971). A new series of longer analytic studies of the music of twentieth-century composers by the Yale University Press includes Pieter C. Van den Toorn's *Music of Igor Stravinsky* (1983), which emphasizes the octatonic content of Stravinsky's works.

The evolution of French avant-garde arts near the turn of the twentieth century is traced in a lively manner in Roger Shattuck's *The Banquet Years* (New York, 1968). The author focuses upon Satie among modern French musicians. The chapters on French composers in William W. Austin's *Music in the 20th Century* (New York, 1966) are especially informative; Austin's book is unparalleled in the thoroughness with which he presents composers' statements on modern music.

Debussy's life and relationships to contemporary artists are admirably recounted in Edward Lockspeiser's *Debussy: His Life and Mind* (London, 1962–65). Unless otherwise stated, all quotations in this chapter from the writings of Debussy are drawn from *Debussy on Music,* ed. François Lesure, trans. Richard Langham Smith (New York, 1977) or from Léon Vallas, *The Theories of Claude Debussy*, trans. Maire O'Brien (London, 1929). Lesure's *Debussy* (Geneva, 1980) contains a valuable collection of photographs and other documents. Two recent studies of Debussy are Robert Orledge's *Debussy and the Theatre* (Cambridge, 1982) and Arthur Wenk's *Claude Debussy and the Poets* (Berkeley, Los Angeles, and London, 1976).

Nijinski's remarks on the scenario of *Jeux* are found in his *Diary of Vaslav Nijinsky,* ed. Romola Nijinsky (New York, 1936). An extended analysis is made by Herbert Eimert in his article "Debussy's *Jeux," Die Reihe,* 5 (1959,

English translation 1961). Eimert seeks to derive all of the motives of the work from a single diatonic shape. Robert Orledge's *Debussy and the Theatre* contains historical background and an account of the autograph musical materials of this score.

Sympathetic portraits of the life and work of Satie are found in books by Pierre-Daniel Templier (1932, English translation 1969), Rollo H. Myers (London, 1948), and James Harding (London, 1975). Arbie Orenstein's *Ravel: Man and Musician* (New York, 1975) is highly recommended.

A survey of Russian music throughout history for the general reader is found in Richard A. Leonard's *History of Russian Music* (New York, 1956). Gerald Abraham's many contributions on the history of Russian music include *On Russian Music* (1939), *Eight Soviet Composers* (1944), and *Masters of Russian Music* (ed. with M. D. Calvocoressi, 1936). Victor Seroff has written popular biographies of Prokofiev (New York, 1968), Shostakovich (New York, 1943), Musorgski, and Rachmaninoff. His study of Prokofiev attempts to counterbalance the official Soviet account of this composer found in Izrail Nest'ev's *Sergei Prokofiev* (1946, later rev. and enlarged). Prokofiev's brief autobiography is available in English in his *Autobiography, Articles, Reminiscences* (Moscow, n.d.). Diaghilev and the Ballets Russes are studied in detail in books by Serge Lifar (New York, 1940) and Richard Buckle (New York, 1979, rev. 1984). The excerpt from Scriabin's *Poem of Ecstasy* is drawn from the translation by Hugh MacDonald in *The Musical Times*, 113 (1972).

It has long been known that Stravinsky solicited editorial assistance in his writings, which include the *Autobiography* (New York, 1936), *The Poetics of Music* (Harvard College, 1947), and six volumes of "conversations" with his assistant Robert Craft. It has recently come to light, however, that the *Poetics* was entirely written by Roland-Manuel (a student and biographer of Maurice Ravel), a revelation that casts doubt on the authenticity of all of Stravinsky's writings and vastly diminishes their importance. The literature on Stravinsky is immense. General studies by Eric Walter White (Berkeley, 1979) and Roman Vlad (London, 1967) are recommended; two books by Soviet musicologists recently available in English are Boris Asaf'yev's *Book about Stravinsky* (1929; Ann Arbor, 1982) and

Mikhail Druskin's *Igor Stravinsky* (Cambridge, 1983). Both emphasize Stravinsky's connections with music of his native land. Shostakovich's memoirs entitled *Testimony*, ed. Solomon Volkov (New York, 1979), paint a grim portrait of the Soviet artist's relationship with governmental authorities. The authenticity of these memoirs has been disputed. Documents that pertain to RAPM and to Zhdanov's criticism of Soviet composers in 1948 are found in the appendix to Nicolas Slonimsky's *Music Since 1900* (New York, 1971).

◆ *9* ◆
MUSICAL NATIONALISM

Nationalism, a major force in the evolution of modern music, exerted its greatest influence during the second half of the nineteenth century and early decades of the twentieth. National consciousness has had many forms of expression in music. Among the most direct is an awareness of the artistic value of folk song and its applicability to art music. Collections of folk texts and music began to appear in large numbers in the nineteenth century, some prepared by writers or amateur ethnologists, others by professional composers. Tunes in these collections were normally provided with harmonizations, as in the arrangements of Scottish, Welsh, and Irish songs made by Haydn and Beethoven for the collector George Thomson. In Russia, Rimski-Korsakov was active as an arranger and collector of folk music as was Brahms in Germany and Austria. The publication of anonymous German folk poetry by Achim von Arnim and Clemens Brentano under the title *Des Knaben Wunderhorn* (1806–1808) was especially influential upon German romantic poetry and was later an inspiration to Gustav Mahler among other musicians.

European composers of the nineteenth century also appropriated folk materials into their original works. Haydn and Beethoven occasionally quoted folk songs in their symphonies, and a folk element in piano works by Chopin

231

and Liszt betrays a nostalgia for their native lands. Many of
the strophic songs of Schubert have the foursquare simplicity of German folk music. Brahms was especially indebted
to German folk song, which was both a source of inspiration in its artless simplicity and economy of means and
also an object of his serious study. For most of these Europeans, folk song imparted spontaneity, color, and robust-
ness to their cosmopolitan musical language.

The widespread influence of German and Austrian
music during the later romantic period helped to provoke a
different and more intense form of nationalism among
composers working outside of Western Europe. The Czechs
Bedřich Smetana (1824–84) and Anton Dvořák (1841–1904),
the Russian Five, and the Norwegian Edvard Grieg (1843–
1907) infused their music with the spirit and substance of
their native cultures. They sought a deeper alliance with
their national history and art, and their music often echoed
the emotional struggle of their countrymen for national
identity. The use or assimilation of folk music was widespread among them. Their nationalism was in part a rebellion against romanticism, which increasingly was identified
with German culture.

The continuation of this last form of nationalism into
the early decades of the twentieth century will be the principal subject of this chapter. We will trace the work of several major composers who were active outside of France,
Italy, and Germany and who brought their national folklore
and history to bear on their music. Our survey will conclude with a discussion of the European composer's imitation of American ragtime and blues and Latin American
dance music.

Precursors of Twentieth-Century Musical Nationalism

Folk elements played a relatively minor role in works
of German and Austrian composers of the generation after
Brahms. Mahler had a great affinity for folk art, but his uses
of folk tunes, such as the quotation of "Bruder Martin"

("Frère Jacques") and the evocation of Jewish ghetto music in the third movement of his First Symphony, occur within an intensely autobiographical oeuvre as allusions to his musical past. Quotations of folk song by Schoenberg and Berg invariably had programmatic connotations. Schoenberg, for example, used the tune "Alles ist hin!" ("It's all over!") in his Second String Quartet, probably as a reference to the passing of tonality and to the temporary rupture of his marriage.

Debussy, Ravel, and Stravinsky, on the other hand, had a larger debt to folk music. These three composers were cited by Bartók as the founders of a new era in the enrichment of art music by folklore:

> In 1907 at the instigation of Kodály I became acquainted with Debussy's work, studied it thoroughly and was greatly surprised to find in his music pentatonic phrases similar in character to those contained in our peasant music. I was sure these could be attributed to influences of folk music from Eastern Europe, very likely from Russia. Similar influences can be traced in Igor Stravinsky's work. It seems, therefore, that, in our age, modern music has developed along similar lines in countries geographically far away from each other. It has become rejuvenated under the influence of a kind of peasant music that has remained untouched by the musical creations of the last centuries. [From the "Autobiography," 1921]

Strikingly different modes of national expression will be seen among the composers to be surveyed presently. Bartók and Aaron Copland readily quoted folk music in their original compositions, although their presentation of it differs markedly. Vaughan Williams and Manuel de Falla did not ordinarily quote folk tunes; instead, they assimilated certain features of their native music, which were then expressed in their own distinctive ways. The music of Jean Sibelius, on the other hand, has little connection with Finnish folk song, but he is nonetheless a nationalist by the immediacy with which his musical speech was understood and embraced by his countrymen.

BÉLA BARTÓK
(Nagyszentmiklós, 1881—
New York, 1945)

Bartók's parents were both amateur pianists who enthusiastically encouraged his first precocious steps as a musician. In 1894 he settled with his mother in Pozsony (also called Pressburg or Bratislava) where he studied piano with László Erkel and made the friendship of Erno Dohnányi. Like Dohnányi, Bartók later attended the Royal Academy of Music in Budapest to prepare for a career as a virtuoso pianist. His interest in composition was stimulated by a succession of composers whom he studied: Brahms, Wagner, Strauss, and Liszt. The last of these, according to Bartók, "revealed to me the true essence of composing."

His intense Hungarian nationalism drew his attention to folk music. Musical ethnology soon became a consuming passion, and, often in collaboration with Zoltán Kodály, he traveled in Eastern Europe, Asia Minor, and Northern Africa to collect peasant music. From 1907 until 1934 he taught piano at the Budapest Academy and concertized, but his work as a composer was several times put aside due to a lack of understanding for his music. From 1934 to 1940 he received a stipend from the Hungarian Academy of Sciences to pursue ethnographic work, and, by this time, he received several important commissions for new music. He immigrated to the United States in 1940, living impecuniously in New York until his death in 1945.

Selected Works

Dramatic Music. *Duke Bluebeard's Castle* (opera, 1911), *The Wooden Prince* (ballet, 1916), *The Miraculous Mandarin* (ballet, 1919).

Orchestral Music. Suites (1905, 1907), Four Pieces (1912), *Dance Suite* (1923), *Music for Strings, Percussion, and Celesta* (1936), *Divertimento* (1939), Concerto for Orchestra (1943).

Concertos. Two violin concertos (1908, 1938), three piano concertos (1926, 1931, 1945, the third unfinished), Viola Concerto (unfinished, 1945).

Chamber Music. Six string quartets (1909, 1917, 1927, 1928, 1934, 1939), Sonatas for violin and piano (1921, 1922), Sonata for solo violin (1944), Sonata for two pianos and percussion (1937), *Contrasts* (violin, clarinet, piano, 1938).

Piano Music. Bagatelles (1908); Dirges (1910); *Allegro barbaro* (1911); Sonatina (1915); Suite (1916); Studies, op. 18 (1918); *Improvisations on Hungarian Peasant Songs* (1920); *Out of Doors* (1926); *Mikrokosmos* (153 pieces, 1926–39).

Vocal Music. Choruses: *Cantata profana* (1930), *From Olden Times* (1935), Twenty-Seven Choruses (1935), folk song arrangements. Solo songs: two sets of five songs, op. 15 and op. 16 (both 1916); approximately ten collections of folk song arrangements.

Eastern Europe: Bartók, Kodály, Janáček, and Szymanowski

Folk art was a lifelong inspiration to Béla Bartók (1881–1945), which helped him to produce music of an originality and vitality unsurpassed in this century. Bartók's career was divided among three interests: musical ethnology, composition, and piano playing. The first of these was dominant. "The one thing which is as necessary to me as fresh air is to other people," he wrote to János Buşiţia in 1921, "is the possibility of going on with my studies of folk music in the countryside."

Folk music for Bartók was not only a self-contained study. It also offered the twentieth-century composer a model for natural expression:

> Pure folk music can be considered a natural phenomenon influencing higher art music just as bodily properties perceptible to the eye influence the fine arts or phenomena of life influence the poet. This

influence is most effective for the musician who acquaints himself with folk music in the form in which it lives, in unbridled strength, amid the lower classes. . . . If he surrenders himself to the impact of this living folk music and to all the circumstances which are conditions of this life, and if he reflects in his works the effects of these impressions, then we might say that he has portrayed therein a part of life. [From "The Influence of Folk Music on the Art Music of Today," 1920.]

Bartók considered the peasant song an epitome of artistic perfection, equaled only by the work of an individual genius. Both were marked by conciseness, inner life, and total lack of sentimentality and superfluity. "Artistic perfection can only be achieved by one of two extremes: on the one hand by peasant folk in the mass, completely devoid of the culture of the town-dweller; on the other, by creative power of an individual genius. The creative impulse of anyone who has the misfortune to be born somewhere between these two extremes leads only to barren, pointless, and misshapen works."

Many of Bartók's musical materials were absorbed from peasant music, which he put to a profoundly original use. His works also reveal an awareness of his contemporaries, especially of the music of Stravinsky, Schoenberg, and the French Impressionists. His mature style is relatively homogeneous: Bartók's music of the 1920s is experimental in comparison to his later works, which are clearer in texture and more consonant in sonority. But his music did not undergo the far-reaching evolution of Schoenberg or Scriabin nor the volte-face to neoclassicism of Strauss or Stravinsky.

His melodies usually adopt the tonal materials of peasant songs—especially pentatonic scales (pervasive elements in Bartók's music) or church modes. Rarely are they based upon major or minor scales. Bartók distinguished two rhythmic prototypes in Hungarian peasant tunes, both of which have analogies in his own music. The first is a chant-like "parlando-rubato" rhythm, as in the song quoted in his *Improvisation*, op. 20, no. 7 (see below). The other is derived from peasant dances: it is strict in tempo, but may contain changes of meter. The fast, driving rhythms with shifting accents of the *Allegro barbaro*, for example, are Bartók's adaptation of these dance rhythms. Bartók also found that certain dotted rhythms were common in peasant music, hence the "Scotch snap" so often heard in his works. In Bulgarian dance melodies he discovered a type of rhythm in rapid tempi in which the measure is asymmetrically divided. He used such meters, for example, in the last six *Mikrokosmos* and in the scherzo of the Fifth String Quartet.

Bartók considered all of his music to express a key. In fact, he saw atonality as impossible. "Perfect atonality does not exist," he said in a lecture at Harvard University in 1943, "even in Schoenberg's works, because of that unchangeable physical law concerning the interrelation of harmonics and, in turn, the relation of the harmonics to their fundamental tone." It is plain from his writings and music, however, that Bartók did not equate tonality in his music with common-practice techniques. Instead, tonality resides in the assertion of a pitch class—often at the very end of a piece or movement—as central or cadential. Such focus upon a principal pitch is normally conveyed by the melodic line.

Bartók's Fourteen Bagatelles for piano, op. 6 (1908), illustrate his novel interpretation of tonality as well as his methodic use of dissonant harmonies in his early works. The first of these pieces (Anthology no. 4) contains conflicting key signatures: four sharps in the right hand are pitted against four flats in the left. The melody of the upper part outlines a C♯-minor chord, with emphasis upon its third, E. The accompanimental left hand contains descending ostinato figures, which derive primarily from the Phrygian mode on C.

In the Introduction to *Béla Bartók Masterpieces for the Piano* (1945), the composer comments upon the implications of the conflicting key signatures:

> This half-serious, half-jesting procedure was used to demonstrate the absurdity of key signatures in certain kinds of contemporary music. After carrying the key signature principle *ad absurdum* in the first piece, I dropped its use in all the other Bagatelles and in most of my following works as well. The tonality of the first Bagatelle is, of course, not a mixture of C-sharp minor and F minor, but simply a Phrygian coloured C major.

Bartók's assignment of the piece to C major is presumably based upon the final cadence, which comes to a rest upon the notes C and E. The primary integrative element of the work is not a key, but a three-note set which underlies the melodic motion in the right hand. This element of pitch organization is first encountered at the beginning of the second phrase (measure 3) in the notes G♯ C♯ D♯; it gradually takes on more distinctive motivic shape, culminating in two related presentations in measure 16 (C♯ F♯ G♯) and measure 17 (A B E). The line in measures 12–14 (represented below) is almost entirely constructed from interlocking forms of this trichord, which is marked by brackets:

E A B C♯ F♯ | E B F♯ C♯ G♯ D♯ | A E B C♯ F♯ G♯

Bagatelle no. 8 (Anthology no. 4)—said by the composer to be in G minor—is in a ternary form whose three parts (mm. 1–15, 16–23, 24–32) are in progressively slower tempi. G-minor triads appear only in measure 10 and in the final bar, in the latter decorated by unresolved passing motion in an inner voice. The triadic tetrachords described in Chapter 3 play an especially large role in this piece.

The final two Bagatelles are given the titles "She is dead . . ." and "My dancing sweetheart. . . ." Both contain a melodic figure that Bartók had earlier adopted as a motto for his friend and confidante Stefi Geyer, who had broken off their relationship only weeks before the Bagatelles were written. The contrasting and sardonic character of these pieces reflects Bartók's bitterness at this turn of events. "She is dead" is a lugubrious study in which the left hand alternates between two tritone-related minor triads, while the right hand intones a chromatic plaint. After the appearance of Geyer's motive (the ascending triadic figure in mm. 22–23), the melody dwindles off into tritones and moves to a somber conclusion.

"My dancing sweetheart" (Anthology no. 4) places Geyer's motive (mm. 9–12) into a grotesque waltz, alternately banal, directionless, and misshapen in form. In the transition to the reprise (mm. 151–78), a search for Geyer's arpeggiated motto is launched. The motive is recovered at measure 179, but, despite great fanfare, its motion remains harmonically unresolved. It hangs upon the leading tone C♯ and, in the last four measures, tumbles broken and lifeless to the tonic note D in the lowest register of the instrument.

In his article "The Influence of Peasant Music on Modern Music" (1931), Bartók defines three ways in which folk melodies can be used by the modern composer. Preexistent melodies may first be quoted with the addition of incidental accompaniment or quoted as mottos amid more extensive elaborations. Bartók invariably signals the presence of a folk theme in his music by a footnote, an appropriate title, or by some other means. Original melodies can also be devised that imitate folk melodies, and, finally, folk elements may be evoked indirectly to capture the spirit and atmosphere of peasant music.

The fourth Bagatelle (Anthology no. 4) is a simple example of Bartók's first method of using folk song. Here the melody of the Magyar song "Mikor guláslegény voltam" is harmonized by parallel triads and seventh chords from Aeolian mode on D. More elaborate treatments of folk song are found, for example, in the *Improvisations on Hungarian Peasant Songs* for piano, op. 20 (1920). In the seventh *Improvisation* (a work dedicated to the memory of Claude Debussy), the preexistent melody "Belli, fiam, belli" is heard in octaves in measures 1–11 (Example 9-1). This tune, in Phrygian mode on C, returns varied and transposed a fifth higher in measures 15–21, and a final allusion to it at its original pitch is made in the last five measures. The melody illustrates the chant-like "parlando-rubato" rhythm that the composer found in the oldest Hungarian peasant songs.

Bartók's harmonization of the melody of this *Improvisation*—contrary to the fourth Bagatelle—is largely independent of the melody and of the mode upon which the tune is based. The chords consist of a small number of four- and five-note sets. Prominent among them is the major/minor tetrachord, a favorite harmony of Bartók which he attributed to "bimodality" or the simultaneous use of parallel major and minor modes. This chord punctuates the opening and closing statements of the melody (mm. 2–3, 11) with a bell-like sonority.

Example 9-1. Bartók, *Improvisations sur des chansons paysannes hongroises,* op. 20, no. 7, measures 1–11. Copyright 1922 by Universal-Edition. Renewal 1949. Copyright and renewal assigned to Boosey & Hawkes, Inc. Reprinted by permission.

Bartók's six string quartets are masterpieces of the modern quartet literature. They span his entire career as a composer and reveal a cross section of the various styles within his music as a whole. The First and Second Quartets (1909 and 1917) are each in three movements. The first adopts a post-Brahmsian style comparable to Schoenberg's First Quartet. The second is more closely related to Bartók's later music, especially in its absorption of folk elements. The Third and Fourth Quartets (1927 and 1928) are among his most advanced and difficult compositions in their recondite motivic work, dense counterpoint, and rhythmic energy. The Fourth and Fifth Quartets share a similar design in which five movements are laid out symmetrically: the first and fifth and second and fourth movements of each share similar material. The Fifth and Sixth Quartets (1934 and 1939) use a more relaxed texture and sonority compared to Bartók's works of the 1920s.

The Third Quartet illustrates Bartók's third method of applying folk material to art music. No folk songs are quoted or directly imitated, but essentials of peasant music

are assimilated nonetheless into an entirely original language. The quartet is in one movement, consisting of four
connected parts which have the relationship A B A′ B′. The
first of these four parts (pages 3 to 8 of the miniature score)
is intensely polyphonic and rigorously organized by the
development of motives from the first twelve measures.
There are no sectional repetitions within this part, and all
subdivisions are linked by common motives. The passage
from measures 35 to 42, a dialogue of disconnected chromatic fragments between the two violins, is a type of music
often heard in Bartók, the prototype of which is the "Night
Music" movement of the piano suite *Out of Doors* (1926).

In a lecture on "Chromaticism" given at Harvard University in 1943, Bartók described a type of melody that he
had begun to use twenty years earlier, in which the initial
pitches chromatically fill a boundary interval. He attributed this type of chromaticism to the conflation of several
diatonic modes. "This 'modal chromaticism' . . . is a main
characteristic of the new Hungarian art music," he remarked. "Another and different characteristic, as you will
probably remember, is the appearance of pentatonic melodic structures in our work, as a contrast, so to speak, to
the modal chromaticism, although both may be combined."

The opening theme of the Third Quartet (Example 9-2)
combines modal chromaticism and pentatonicism. The
head motive consists of pitches that chromatically fill the
interval from G to C (B♯). The accompaniment in the lower
strings is similarly a chromatic cluster D D♯ E. The theme
is continued, however, by pentatonic motion: F G B♭ G F C
(simplifying Bartók's curious enharmonic notation).

In his lecture at Harvard, the composer described how
a chromatic motive could be varied by splaying its intervals into a more diatonic shape. "This circumstance is very
good indeed," he concluded, "because we will get variety on
the one hand, but unity will remain undestroyed because of
the hidden relation between the two forms." This relation-

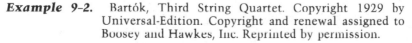

Example 9-2.   Bartók, Third String Quartet. Copyright 1929 by
Universal-Edition. Copyright and renewal assigned to
Boosey and Hawkes, Inc. Reprinted by permission.

ship between themes is clearly exploited in the first part of the Third Quartet, as the chromatic motive of measures 2–4 blossoms into diatonic (or, more precisely, pentatonic) forms (Example 9-3).

The pentatonic content of these variants is divided with some strictness between "black key" collections (as in mm. 27–32) and those among white keys (mm. 87–92, for example). The pentatonicism of motives is also apparent in chords. The final chord of the quartet (G♯ A♯ C♯ D♯) is a pentatonic subset, and the cadential succession of fourths and fifths in measure 33 states a complete pentatonic scale of the white-key type (Example 9-4).

Example 9-3. Bartók, Third String Quartet. Copyright 1929 by Universal-Edition. Copyright and renewal assigned to Boosey and Hawkes, Inc. Reprinted by permission.

Example 9-4.   Bartók, Third String Quartet. Copyright 1929 by Universal-Edition. Copyright and renewal assigned to Boosey and Hawkes, Inc. Reprinted by permission.

But Bartók does not excessively prolong these passages of pentatonic content. They appear and then quickly recede into the tissue of chromatically developing variations, by which we perceive the work as organically alive and devoid of the predictable or commonplace.

The second part of the quartet imitates the strict tempo and driving rhythms of a more modern stratum of Hungarian peasant music. It also displays Bartók's great resourcefulness in drawing diverse colors from the instruments of the string quartet. The final two parts (the last called a coda) are highly abbreviated and varied recapitulations of material from the first two.

Other Eastern European composers in the early twentieth century who used national idioms include Leoš Janáček (1854–1928), Zoltán Kodály (1882–1967), and Karol Szymanowski (1882–1937). Most of Janáček's music was composed in the twentieth century after the limited success of his opera *Jenůfa* (1904, later revised). His artistic outlook, however, was rooted in the nineteenth century and modeled on Smetana and Dvořák. His knowledge of folk music of his native Moravia helped him to develop a distinctively flexible and colorful lyric idiom which he used in his operas, including the starkly realistic *Jenůfa* and later in *The Cunning Little Vixen* (1923) and *The Makropoulos Affair* (1925). Among his instrumental works, the *Sinfonietta* is vividly orchestrated and direct in appeal.

Kodály's career was closely related to Bartók's from the time both studied composition with Hans Koessler at the Budapest Academy. They served subsequently on the faculty of the Academy, and they jointly undertook ethnomusicological research. Kodály's music is based almost exclusively on Hungarian peasant melodies, while Bartók availed himself of a wider variety of folk music. Kodály's adaptation of the folk idiom lacked Bartók's originality—he cleaved instead to a traditional harmonic and tonal style. Nevertheless, his music, steeped in the sounds and contours of folk song, is colorful and melodious. Among his best-known works are the opera *Háry János* (from which a popular orchestral suite was extracted), his orchestral *Dances of Galanta*, and oratorio *Psalmus hungaricus* (1923). Kodály is well known, especially in Hungary and America, for his innovative approach to teaching music to children.

The early music of the Pole Karol Szymanowski alternately reflected the influence of Chopin, Scriabin, and the German romanticists. During World War I his music became experimental, but it still followed lines of development associated with earlier French and German modernists. His music of the 1920s and 1930s reverted to a more traditional style, and it was during this time that he made his greatest use of folk music. Folk songs are often quoted outright, and the spirit of Polish folk dances is evoked in his mazurkas and other character pieces for piano.

Scandinavia: Sibelius and Nielsen

Finland during the nineteenth century was a duchy of Russia, although it was allowed considerable autonomy by the Tsars. A movement for Finnish nationalism waxed throughout the century, and, when Tsar Nicholas II attempted to reassert Russian sovereignty in 1899, rebellion was narrowly averted. Finnish nationalism, however, did not come immediately to Jean Sibelius (1865–1957). His native language was Swedish, which remained for most of the nineteenth century the language of government and of the upper classes in Finland. While a student in Vienna in 1890–91, he struggled through the Finnish heroic poem *Kalevala*. His imagination and patriotism were thus fired, and he shortly completed a choral symphony *Kullervo*, the first of many pieces inspired by this national epic.

The *Kalevala* is a saga of uncertain origin which deals with the exploits of three brothers inhabiting Kaleva, the land of heroes. It is divided into large sections or "runes," each line of which is in the distinctive trochaic quatrameter imitated by Longfellow in his poem *Hiawatha*. The *Kalevala* is closely associated with other Nordic myths such as the Icelandic *Eddas* and the German *Nibelungenlied*, the latter drawn upon by Richard Wagner in his texts for *The Ring of the Nibelung*. Each emphasizes man's closeness to nature, his heroic deeds, and his relationship with the gods. The *Kalevala* was preserved and transmitted among folk singers in the region of Karelia in eastern Finland (now part of the Soviet Union). Its texts were transcribed and edited by several nineteenth-century folk enthusiasts, and its chant-like music was recognized as the oldest type of Finnish folk song.

Although Sibelius did not have a great interest in studying folklore, he traveled to Karelia in 1892 to meet runic singers and to transcribe their melodies. These he found to be extremely simple, almost recitational formulas, by which poetry like that of the *Kalevala* was intoned in a series of varied repetitions. It was not an artistically sophisticated music which Sibelius could easily assimilate into his own work.

His national profile was revealed in other ways. The stories rather than the music of the *Kalevala* became for Sibelius a source of enduring inspiration. These tales would be celebrated in many of his tone poems. The four *Legends*, op. 22, relate the exploits of the hero Lemminkäinen as he woos the beautiful Kyllikki and recklessly shoots at the black swan that circles Tuonela, the land of the dead. *Pohjola's Daughter*, op. 49, recounts the tale of another hero, Väinämöinen, who tries to win the affection of a cunning maiden from the land of Pohjola. *Tapiola*, op. 112, Sibelius's last tone poem, depicts the brooding forests of the North, inhabited by the god Tapio.

Sibelius succeeded in translating the spirit of Finland and its people into a musical language without other recourse to folklore or to notable stylistic innovation. His works speak with great emotion to the Finns, capturing their love for their country and clarifying their national identity. Technical features of his music cannot alone

JEAN SIBELIUS
(Hämeenlinna, 1865—
Järvenpää, 1957)

Sibelius was born into a Swedish-speaking family and learned the Finnish language only as an adult. His early ambition as a musician was to be a virtuoso violinist, a goal he pursued at the Helsinki Conservatory from 1885 to 1889. There he met Ferruccio Busoni, who taught piano at the Conservatory, and he became a favorite student of the director of the school, Martin Wegelius. He subsequently studied for two years in Berlin and Vienna, where his interests turned decisively to composition under the tutelage of Robert Fuchs and Karl Goldmark.

From 1897 he received a stipend from the Finnish government in support of his work, and he was quickly recognized as the greatest modern composer of his nation. From 1904 until his death in 1957 he lived in Järvenpää near Helsinki; he traveled regularly in Europe and England and made one visit to America to receive an honorary doctorate from Yale University. He composed no major works after 1925.

Selected Works

Orchestral Music. Seven Symphonies (1899–1924; an Eighth Symphony was destroyed); tone poems: *En Saga* (1892, rev. 1901), *Four Legends (Lemminkäinen and the Maidens of Saari*, 1895; *The Swan of Tuonela*, 1893; *Lemminkäinen in Tuonela*, 1895; *Lemminkäinen's Homeward Journey*, 1895; all later revised), *Finlandia* (1899), *Pohjola's Daughter* (1906), *The Bard* (1913), *The Oceanides* (1914), *Tapiola* (1925); incidental music for theater: *Pelléas et Mélisande* (1905), *The Tempest* (1926).

Concertos. Violin Concerto (1903, rev. 1905).

Chamber Music. String Quartet in D minor (*Voces intimae*) (1909), collections of Pieces for Violin and Piano (five collections with opus numbers).

Vocal Music. Songs, choral music, part songs.

---

explain this attachment, but it rests in part upon certain recurrent features that mark his work: its dark sonority, sudden bursts of light leading to dramatic climaxes, archaic modal textures, ostinatos, and pedal points.

Many of these features are heard in one of his most cheerful works, the Seventh Symphony, op. 105 (1924). This piece was first designated a "Symphonic Fantasy" because of its unconventional one-movement form. In its unabashed lyricism, it owes much to the symphonies of Tchaikovsky; in its unusual form, cautious pace, and epic climaxes, it is indebted to those of Mahler; and in its dense texture and motivic unity, it is connected to the works of Brahms.

The Seventh Symphony is not in any conventional instrumental form. Several lines of thought run through it and emerge alternately. It can be viewed in three large parts: an introductory exposition (mm. 1–93), development of a new theme (mm. 94–474), and epilogue (mm. 475 to the end). The development concerns a scherzando theme (Example 9-5) introduced at measure 94. Its motives are spun into endlessly varied shapes, borne along by ever greater rhythmic motion. A familiar device in Sibelius's orchestral music may be observed in measures 96–97 of this theme: the same motive is stated in octaves by the high and low strings, but the lower voices are slightly out of phase with the upper ones. The effect is to make the polyphonic texture denser and to blur the sense of pulse.

The development section is interrupted by two important episodes: first, the return at measure 222 (rehearsal L) of a theme in the brass heard earlier at measure 60; and, second, an exposition of new themes beginning at measure 261. The development resumes at measure 322, now involving the new themes as well as the older one. A climactic epilogue begins at measure 475, recapitulating the brass

Example 9-5.   Sibelius, Symphony no. 7. Copyright 1926 by Wilhelm Hansen, Copenhagen. Reprinted by permission.

episode from measures 60 and 222 and touching at the end upon a flute motive from measure 11.

The large quantity of melodic material in the Seventh Symphony can be reduced to three developmentally inter-related families of themes: those with stepwise diatonic motion (the opening of the work is a prototype), those out-lining a triad (for example, the theme in the woodwinds and horns at measure 261), and themes that contain a turn fig-ure. The last of these is the most important. Eight themes of this type are shown in Example 9-6 (the turn figure is bracketed in each). These turn figures are brought to a tri-umphant peroration near the end in a unison passage in the high strings (Example 9-7).

The harmonic language of the Seventh Symphony is influenced by the modal content of its lines. A resonant polyphony from measures 22 to 50, for example, is based upon the Mixolydian mode on G. The tonal plan of the work alternates between regions emphasizing G and C, with C emerging as the central tonality. Secondary areas a third away (such as the region in E♭ major at rehearsal T) are also prominent.

Carl Nielsen (1865–1931) occupies a position in his native Denmark comparable to that of Sibelius in Finland, although Nielsen's music is not overtly nationalistic in theme or substance. His six symphonies exhibit several of

Example 9-6.   Sibelius, Symphony no. 7. Copyright 1926 by Wilhelm Hansen Copenhagen. Reprinted by permission.

Example 9-7.   Sibelius, Symphony no. 7. Copyright 1926 by Wilhelm Hansen, Copenhagen. Reprinted by permission.

RALPH VAUGHAN WILLIAMS
(Down Ampney, 1872—London, 1958)

Vaughan Williams's education as a composer was pursued alternately at the Royal College of Music in London under Hubert Parry and Charles Stanford and at Trinity College, Cambridge, from which university he received the degree of Doctor of Music in 1901. He also studied briefly in 1897 with Max Bruch in Berlin and in 1908 in Paris with Ravel, with whom he formed a warm friendship.

During the first decade of the new century, he devoted himself to folk song collecting and to editorial work on the *English Hymnal.* After four years of wartime service on the Continent he returned to London and was appointed to the faculty of the Royal College of Music and conductor of the London Bach Choir. He devoted himself unflaggingly to teaching and to his work as a composer until his death in 1958.

Selected Works

Operas. *Hugh the Drover* (1914), *Sir John in Love* (1928), *The Poisoned Kiss* (1929), *Riders to the Sea* (1932), *Pilgrim's Progress* (1936–49).

Ballets. *Old King Cole* (1923), *Job* (1930).

Orchestral Music. Nine symphonies (1909–57), *Fantasia on a Theme by Thomas Tallis* (1910).

Concertos. *The Lark Ascending* (violin and orchestra, 1914, rev. 1920), violin (1925), piano (1931), and oboe (1944).

Chamber Music. Sonata for violin (1954), three string quartets, three piano quintets.

Songs. Numerous songs and cycles, including arrangements of folk songs.

Choral Music. *Toward the Unknown Region* (1906), *Five Mystical Songs* (1911), Mass in G (unaccompanied, 1922), *Sancta civitas* (1925), Magnificat (1932), *Five Tudor Portraits* (1935), *Dona nobis pacem* (1936), *Old Hundredth Psalm Tune* (1953), *Hodie* (1954), *Epithalamion* (1957).

Sibelius's trademarks: dense modal counterpoint, motivic interconnection of themes, and free handling of dissonance within a tonal context. They are also marked by a dramatic rivalry between key areas, often producing a highly chromatic and dissonant texture. In the end, one key will emerge victorious over its rivals.

England: Vaughan Williams and Holst

Serious attempts to record and preserve English folk song began early in the nineteenth century. They reached an apogee at the turn of the century in the work of Cecil Sharp (1859–1924). This indefatigable collector pursued authentic examples of folk music throughout England, and he then came to America in the hope of finding more primitive versions of songs and dances among descendants of English settlers. His work was an inspiration to English composers of the early decades of the century.

Foremost among England's musical nationalists was Ralph Vaughan Williams (1872–1958). Between 1903 and 1913 he was active as a collector of folk songs and English carols, which he arranged and published in several volumes. Like Bartók, he considered the folk song to be a model of artistic perfection. He demanded that national traits be evident in art music: "Art, like charity, should begin at home," he wrote. "If [a composer's work] is to be of any value it must grow out of the very life of himself, the community in which he lives, and the nation to which he belongs." He rejected aestheticism and contrived universality, preaching instead a utilitarian element in music that should grow from a diverse culture and human experience. Like his contemporary neoclassicists, he embraced traditional idioms, especially folk song, the Anglican hymn, and English music of the sixteenth and seventeenth centuries. "Why should music be original?" he queried. "The object of art is to stretch out to the ultimate realities through the medium of beauty. The duty of the composer is to find the *mot juste.* It does not matter if this word has been said a thousand times before as long as it is the right thing to say at that moment."

Vaughan Williams's assimilation of English folk music is revealed in his nine symphonies. The *Pastoral* Symphony (Symphony no. 3, 1916–21) is an especially important example of the applicability of modality and folk-like pentatonicism to the symphonic genre in the twentieth century. This work is in four movements. A serene sonata form in the first suggests the gentle melancholy of the countryside. Its pentatonic themes are accompanied by parallel root position triads. Several such streams of "enhanced melody" frequently overlap. The second movement is slow and elegiac, making use of an unmeasured pentatonic melody, first on natural trumpet, then natural horn. The pungent intonation of valveless brass instruments was influential on Benjamin Britten, who called for similar effects in his Serenade and *Noye's Fludde.* The third movement is a scherzo with folk-like tunes heard in the two trios.

An unmeasured soprano or tenor vocalization introduces and concludes the finale of the *Pastoral* Symphony. This melody touches upon all notes of the C-major scale, but it focuses on A and E and otherwise emphasizes pentatonic segments. The first theme of the free sonata form that follows is also pentatonic, accompanied by root position major triads descending in whole steps. The second theme, in Dorian mode, is accompanied at first by a diatonic polyphony (Example 9-8). A development begins at measure 56 and a majestic recapitulation is heard at measure 110.

The symphony is distinguished by its unaffected melodiousness and simplicity. It avoids clear expression of a major or minor tonality—none is indicated in the title—

First theme

Strings   (and 8va)-

m. 5

Second theme

Ob.

m. 21

Example 9-8.   Vaughan Williams, *Pastoral* Symphony, fourth move-
ment, finale. Copyright 1924 by J. Curwen & Sons Ltd.
U.S. copyright renewed 1952. Used by arrangement with
G. Schirmer, Inc., U.S. agent for J. Curwen & Sons, Ltd.,
London.

but the melodic assertion of local tonics within a pentatonic or modal framework creates a fluctuating sense of
key. Triads reign unchallenged among the accompanimental harmonies. They are applied almost solely to
enhance the resonance of the melodic line; their content of
pitches is not confined to any prevailing diatonic scale, nor
do they suggest a key in a traditional way.

Gustav Holst (1874–1934) met Vaughan Williams in
1895, while both were students at the Royal College of
Music. They formed a lifelong friendship and proceeded
along similar paths as composers. Holst's music, like that of
Vaughan Williams, reflects his interest in folk song and
earlier English polyphony, the former seen in his popular
Suites for military band. His fascination with Sanskrit
literature is revealed in the texts of several early works. He
is best known for the orchestral suite *Planets* (1917), which
is skillfully orchestrated and powerful in its driving five-
and seven-beat meters.

Spain: Manuel de Falla

Spain in the 1500s—its "golden century"—was a center of European wealth and political power and a rival to Italy and France in the arts. She produced masters of sacred music, among them Tomás Luis de Victoria and Cristóbal Morales, and great instrumentalists such as the lutenist Luis Milán. But by the nineteenth century, Spain had become a musical province. Its artistic life had long been dominated by foreigners, especially Italians since Spain had close political ties with Italy. The Italian composer Domenico Scarlatti spent his last twenty-eight years in Madrid in the service of the Spanish royal family, and Italian opera gained a firm grasp on Spanish taste later in the eighteenth century. Native music dwindled into the confines of vigorous folk songs and dance, a brilliant school of guitar playing, and an Italianate genre of operetta called *zarzuela*.

The modern renaissance of Spanish music was brought about largely through the influence of Felipe Pedrell (1841–1922). This composer, pedagogue, and musicologist almost singlehandedly revived knowledge and appreciation of sixteenth-century Spanish art music and of his nation's vibrant musical folklore. He was also closely in touch with contemporary developments in European music, and he helped to launch the careers of three young protégés who became the outstanding figures in Spanish music of the early twentieth century: Isaac Albéniz (1860–1909), Enrique Granados (1867–1916), and Manuel de Falla (1876–1946).

Albéniz, a student of Liszt, was a virtuoso pianist whose cycle of Spanish character pieces *Iberia* (1906–1908) was widely admired. Granados wrote a comparable set of piano works entitled *Goyescas*, in which he sought to translate into music the dramatic images of life portrayed by the eighteenth-century Spanish painter Goya. Granados later refitted this music as an opera of the same title.

By the turn of the century, Paris had emerged as a proving ground for the Spanish musical renaissance. Both Albéniz and Granados were active in France, where audiences relished their stylized portraits of their homeland. Bizet's *Carmen* and Chabrier's *España* initiated a series of works by French composers imitating Spanish life and customs. Spain was of particular fascination to Debussy, who

MANUEL DE FALLA
(Cádiz, 1876—
Alta Gracia [Argentina], 1946)

Falla's native city of Cádiz is in the Andalusian region of southern Spain, a melting pot of Eastern and Western cultures whose folk music he would later celebrate. His family moved to Madrid in 1896, where he continued preparation as a concert pianist. He tried his hand at composing popular operettas or *zarzuelas*, at which he was largely unsuccessful. His studies with Felipe Pedrell were a great encouragement to his career as a serious composer.

From 1907 to 1914 he lived in Paris where he made the acquaintance of most of the leading French composers of that time. He returned to Madrid in 1914, moving to Granada in 1919. There he was active in efforts to preserve the authentic *cante jondo*. He formed a close friendship with the poet and musical amateur Federico García Lorca. After the end of the Spanish Civil War he immigrated to Argentina.

Selected Works

Dramatic Music. *La vida breve* (opera, 1913), *El amor brujo* (ballet, 1915), *Three-Cornered Hat* (ballet, 1916–19), *El retablo de Maese Pedro* (for puppet theater, 1919–22), *Atlántida* (opera, incomplete, 1926–).

Orchestral Music. *Nights in the Gardens of Spain* (1911–15), Concerto for harpsichord and five instruments (1926).

Piano Music, *Pièces espagnoles* (1908), *Fantasía baetica* (1919), *Pour le tombeau de Paul Dukas* (1935).

Guitar Music. *Homenaje "le Tombeau de Claude Debussy"* (1920, also a version for piano solo).

Vocal Music. *Trois mélodies* (1909), *Seven Spanish Folk Songs* (1915), *Psyché* (1924), *Soneto a Córdoba* (1927).

translated the impressions that he garnered from pictures and literature into numerous piano works. These pieces and others by Ravel were played with fiery conviction in Paris by the Spanish virtuoso Ricardo Viñes.

Manuel de Falla also came under the wing of Pedrell, and he later followed Albéniz and Granados to Paris. There he made the friendship of Dukas, Ravel, and Debussy, who supported his efforts to meld impressionistic imagery with rhythms and accents of his native Andalusia. Falla particularly admired the Spanish character pieces of Debussy. "Here we are actually given Andalusia," he wrote regarding Debussy's *Soirée dans Grenade*. "The truth without the authenticity, as it were, for although not a single measure is taken from Spanish folklore, the whole piece, down to its smallest details, brings Spain to us."

Debussy's method of evoking Spanish colors without overt references to folk songs was Falla's model for most of his early works. These included sets of character pieces for piano, the opera *La vida breve*, the ballets *Three Cornered Hat* and *El amor brujo*, and the orchestral *Nights in the Gardens of Spain*. In all of them he sought the "truth" about his homeland without directly quoting folk tunes, a practice he deemed provincial. "The essential elements of music, the sources of inspiration, are nations and people," he wrote. "I am against music resting on authentic folklore documents. I believe, on the contrary, that one must start from the natural living fountainheads and use the substance of sonority and rhythm, not their outward appearance."

In his *Fantasía baetica* (1919), Falla educes the sonorous and rhythmic outlines of his native Andalusia, the region of southern Spain called Baetica by the Romans. In this virtuosic work for piano, Falla imitates the traditional

m. 9

Example 9-9.   Falla, *Fantasía baetica*, measures 9-11. Reprinted by kind permission of J & W Chester/Edition Wilhelm Hansen London Limited.

m. 115
Tranquillamente mosso ($\downarrow$.= 60)

Example 9-10.   Falla, *Fantasía baetica,* measures 115–118. Reprinted by kind permission of J & W Chester/Edition Wilhelm Hansen London Limited.

Andalusian *cante jondo,* a genre sometimes called "flamenco." The *cante jondo* is a song accompanied by guitar in which the voice is metrically free, highly ornamented, limited in range, and often unfixed of intonation. These songs are tragic in mood and usually peppered by shouts from the audience and the chatter of castanets and clicking of heels.

All of these features are evoked in the *Fantasía.* It is a ternary work in which the middle "intermezzo" is a lyrical interlude between sections of vivid dissonance, driving dance rhythms, melodic ostinatos, and flamboyant accompanimental figuration. The piece has no central key, although most of the themes focus in modal fashion on some pitch, most often A or E. The sound of castanets and tambourins is captured by pointed dissonances on strong beats, as in Example 9-9. A passage from measures 115 to 149 imitates the traditional flamenco guitar prelude and tragic song or "copla." Guitar figuration is suggested here by a motive in fourths, which could be played on open strings if the instrument were tuned—as it often was by the native player—higher than usual (Example 9-10). The bitter and nasal plaint of the folk singer is evoked by dissonant grace notes, as in Example 9-11.

m. 134
Lento ($\downarrow$ = 72, *ma libero*)

Example 9-11.   Falla, *Fantasía baetica,* measures 134–136. Reprinted by kind permission of J & W Chester/Edition Wilhelm Hansen London Limited.

Fantasía baetica was one of Falla's last works of an overtly Spanish type. In the mid-1920s he turned toward a more abstract musical style, perhaps following the example of Stravinsky, who in these years was outspoken in his rejection of the regionalism that pervaded his own earlier music. In this new idiom, Falla composed *El retablo de Maese Pedro*, a work for puppets dramatizing a scene from Cervantes's *Don Quixote;* a chamber concerto for harpsichord, strings, and winds; vocal music; and laments for several departed friends. His "Homages" to Dukas and Debussy—the former for piano and the latter for guitar— quote from music by these two composers whom Falla so greatly admired.

The New World: Copland and Other Composers in the Americas

New music in the United States in the late nineteenth century was dominated by composers who hewed to European models. Horatio Parker (1863–1919), George Chadwick (1854–1931), Edward MacDowell (1861–1908), and Charles Griffes (1884–1920) all studied in Germany, and their music later developed styles that they had discovered toward the end of the century on the Continent. Mac-Dowell, the possessor of a great lyric gift, was influenced by programmatic trends in German music, and Griffes adopted the idiom of the French Impressionists and a stylized orientalism. Parker composed mainly choral works, among which his Latin oratorio *Hora novissima* (1892) is best known. Chadwick worked in both instrumental and vocal genres, and his symphonic and chamber music is occasionally touched by elements from American folk music.

Coexistent with serious music in America at this time was an unusually diverse and lively popular music. Many interrelated popular song repertories developed in the course of the nineteenth century, including secular songs, Negro spirituals, religious songs set to folk melodies, and revival or gospel hymns. Two important forerunners of jazz were heard in the broadly appealing ragtime and the more obscure early blues. We shall return later in this chapter to early jazz and its imitation by European musicians.

Idealized visions of rural America: Grant Wood, *Young Corn* (Courtesy of the Cedar Rapids Museum of Art, Cedar Rapids School District Collection.)

A common goal uniting American composers of the early twentieth century—one shared by many of their fellow writers and painters—was to forge a language different from that of Europe and to root it instead in native culture. The first important American composer who was unfettered by European traditions was Charles Ives, whose prophetic experimentalism accommodated an intensely American musical speech. He will be discussed in Chapter 11. Ives's music was scarcely known until the 1930s, and he was not especially influential in the United States until that time. To the younger composers in this country, the only models at hand seemed to be those that would submit them to the hegemony of Western Europe.

Aaron Copland (1900–) rejected the polite Europeanisms of composers like Horatio Parker as well as the aes-

AARON COPLAND
(Brooklyn, 1900—)

Copland's youth in Brooklyn was spent, in his words, "in an environment that had little or no connection with serious music." His discovery of this art and of his own ability in it was at first self-guided. He received his musical education in France from 1920 to 1924, mainly at the hands of Nadia Boulanger. His Symphony for Organ and Orchestra, commissioned by Mme. Boulanger, brought him to the attention of several influential American conductors.

Copland's music from the mid-1920s reflected an imitation of jazz idioms, which was widespread at this time among many composers in Europe and America. He dispensed with this influence at about the same time as did the Europeans, but he continued to forge a distinctive American dialect in works that were alternately abstract or popular.

He lived abroad for much of the period before the Second World War, including several sojourns in Mexico arranged by his friend Carlos Chávez. He has been associated as a teacher with the Berkshire Music Center and Harvard University, and he was active in the founding of the League of Composers and the American Composers Alliance. He continues to compose and remains active as a conductor of his own music.

Selected Works

Opera. *The Tender Land* (1954). Also film scores.

Ballets. *Billy the Kid* (1938), *Rodeo* (1942), *Appalachian Spring* (1944).

Orchestral Music. Three symphonies (1924, 1933, 1946), *Music for the Theater* (1925), *Statements* (1934), *El Salón México* (1936), *Outdoor* Overture (1938), *Quiet City* (1940, with obbligato trumpet and English horn), *Lincoln Portrait* (1942, with narrator), Variations (1957), *Connotations* (1962), *Emblems* (1964, for band), *Inscape* (1967).

Chamber Music. *Vitebsk* (1929), Sextet (1937), *Fanfare for the Common Man* (1942, brass), Violin Sonata (1943), Piano Quartet (1950), Nonet (1960).

Piano Music. Piano Variations (1930), Sonata (1941), Piano Fantasy (1957).

Vocal Music. *Old American Songs* (1952), *Twelve Poems of Emily Dickinson* (1950), *Canticle of Freedom* (1955, chorus and orchestra).

---

theticism of Charles Griffes. Music that simply quoted folk tunes seemed provincial to him. Instead, he sought "a music that would speak of universal things in a vernacular of American speech rhythms." He wrote in *Music and Imagination:*

> In order to create an indigenous music of universal significance, three conditions are imperative. First, the composer must be part of a nation that has a profile of its own—that is the most important; second, the composer must have in his background some sense of musical culture, and, if possible, a basis in folk or popular art; and third, a superstructure of organized music activities must exist.

For Copland, rhythm was the most distinctive part of America's musical profile. "What is the nature of this gift?" he asked.

> First, a conception of rhythm not as a mental exercise, but as something basic to the body's rhythmic impulse. This basic impulse is exteriorized with an insistence that knows no measure, ranging from a self-hypnotic monotony to a riotous frenzy of subconsciously controlled pounding. Second, an unparalleled ingenuity in the spinning out of un-

equal metrical units in the unadorned rhythmic line. And lastly, and most significant, a polyrhythmic structure arrived at through the combining of strongly independent blocks of sound. [*Music and Imagination.*]

After returning from France, where he pursued his musical education in the early 1920s, Copland used jazz to capture this rhythmic vitality. But after about 1930 he turned to an abstract style in which Americanisms were temporarily banished. In 1936 he completed *El Salón México,* his first work in an entirely different vein. Music of its type was intended to be accessible to the larger audiences created in America by the media of radio and film. It embodied a simpler and more straightforward style that was once again intensely American.

What I was trying for in the simpler works was only partly the writing of compositions that might speak to a broader audience. More than that they gave me an opportunity to try for a more homespun musical idiom. . . . This musical vernacular . . . was perhaps nothing more than a recrudescence of my old interest in making a connection between music and life about me. [*Music and Imagination.*]

Copland's works in his "simpler" style include three ballets—*Billy the Kid, Rodeo,* and *Appalachian Spring*—several film scores and operas, and the recitation *Lincoln Portrait. Appalachian Spring* (1944) shows Copland's gift for a musical expression whose direct appeal is devoid of banality. Its apparent simplicity is belied by the depth and ingenuity of its structural relationships.

The choreography presents a young bride and groom beginning their married life in rural Pennsylvania in the nineteenth century. They are greeted by a helpful neighbor and a revivalist minister and his following, with whom they share moments of tenderness alternating with rousing country dances. They pantomime their everyday activities, and, at the end, the bride willingly takes her place among her neighbors. The scenario speaks of values widespread among Americans in the 1930s and 1940s: a desire to be isolated from the complications of life, a wish to be close to the earth and frank in the expression of emotion, and a readiness to accept conventional social roles.

The music is perfectly suited to this story. It is best known in an orchestral suite, which is a slightly shortened version of the original score written for thirteen instruments. The music is predominantly diatonic; its tonal plan progresses from A major at the beginning through the dominant E major near the middle to C major at the end. Many passages vividly illustrate the rhythmic characteristics that Copland found in the American musical imagination. The bride's dance at rehearsal 35 (1945 orchestral score) contains asymmetrical changes of meter governing a motoric eighth-note rhythm reminiscent of passages from Stravinsky's *Rite of Spring*. A polyrhythm created by "strongly opposing blocks of sound" is heard at rehearsal 31 (Example 9-12). The opposition of these two strata is enhanced by harmony, as the top strand dwells on the tonic A-major chord, the bottom on F major.

To accompany a pantomine near the end of the ballet, Copland quotes a Shaker hymn "The Gift to be Simple," which is then used as a subject for variations. Both text and music of the hymn project the unadorned directness that reigns over the whole ballet. The beginning of the hymn is shown in Example 9-13. Regarding the use of preexistent melodies, the composer writes in *Music and Imagination:* "A hymn tune represents a certain order of feeling: simplicity, plainness, sincerity, directness. It is the reflection of those qualities in a stylistically appropriate setting, imaginative and unconventional and not mere quotation, that gives the use of folk tunes reality and importance."

The full-blown appearance of the tune in the penultimate scene is prefigured by triadic shapes underlying most of the earlier themes and motives. Those that unfold a triad in second inversion, beginning, that is, with an ascending fourth followed by a major third, are all the more closely

(rehearsal 31)

Example 9-12.   Polyrhythm in Copland's *Appalachian Spring.*

'Tis the gift to be sim-ple, 'tis the gift to be free, 'tis the

gift to come down where we ought to be, and when we find our-selves in the

place just right, 'twill be in the val-ley of love and de-light.

Example 9-13. "'Tis the Gift to be Simple," from Edward D. Andrews's *The Gift to be Simple* (New York: J. H. Augustin, 1940). Used by permission of Dover Publications, Inc.

related to the head motive of the hymn. The interval of the fourth alone has great importance in the contour of lines, as in a flute solo near the end (Example 9-14)—a melody that is developmentally related to numerous other themes and motives. Here the head motive of the hymn is varied by a concatenation of intervals of the fourth.

The Shaker hymn is also subtly related to the work's harmonic organization. The tune outlines only two harmonies, tonic and dominant. Copland superimposes these to form a bitriadic chord that is central to the entire work. It is first heard as a conflation of tonic A major and dominant E major in the strings in measures 4–6 (Example 9-15). Later it appears in various reorderings and transpositions, as at the end of the piece where the tonic C major is joined to its dominant G major. Some of the ways this set is manipulated are illustrated by the first scene (mm. 1–50). It is "inverted" in measures 34–38 so that the A-major triad is

Example 9-14. Copland, *Appalachian Spring.* Copyright 1945 by Aaron Copland. Renewed 1972. Reprinted by permission of Aaron Copland and Boosey & Hawkes, Inc., sole licensees.

mm. 4-6

Example 9-15.   Copland, *Appalachian Spring.* Copyright 1945 by
Aaron Copland. Renewed 1972. Reprinted by permis-
sion of Aaron Copland and Boosey & Hawkes, Inc., sole
licensees.

combined with its subdominant D major (Example 9-16).
The oboe melody in measures 40-44 (Example 9-17) is a
linear representation of this form of the set.

Quotation of traditional American materials was practiced by many of Copland's contemporaries. Henry Cowell
(1897-1965) at first followed the experimental vein which
has been an important part of music in America throughout the century (see Chapter 11). But in the 1940s he began a series of more conventional *Hymns and Fuguing
Tunes,* using music by the eighteenth-century American
composer William Billings. Virgil Thomson (1896-   ) also
wrote music based on colonial hymn tunes, but he is best
known for his two operas in collaboration with Gertrude
Stein, *Four Saints in Three Acts* (1928) and *The Mother
of Us All* (1947). These recall the simplicity, wit, and
eclecticism of Erik Satie and, according to Aaron Copland,
"give us the musical counterpart of a [midwestern] regionalism that is familiar in our literature and painting
but is seldom found in our symphonies and concertos." Roy
Harris (1898-1979) regularly appropriated American patriotic, religious, and folk melodies in his music. Other works,
such as his much-admired Third Symphony (1938), share

m. 35

Example 9-16.   Copland, *Appalachian Spring.* Copyright 1945 by
Aaron Copland. Renewed 1972. Reprinted by permis-
sion of Aaron Copland and Boosey & Hawkes, Inc., sole
licensees.

Example 9-17.   Copland, *Appalachian Spring.* Copyright 1945 by Aaron Copland. Renewed 1972. Reprinted by permission of Aaron Copland and Boosey & Hawkes, Inc., sole licensees.

the "noisy ribaldry, the sadness, and groping earnestness" which he found in the American spirit.

Music by Latin American composers in the early decades of the century was strongly national in character, although it sometimes mixed folk styles with modern harmonic techniques. Heitor Villa-Lobos (1887–1959) joined Brazilian folk music to a mixture of conventional and modernistic accompaniments in his series of nine *Bachianas brasileiras* and sixteen *Chôros.* The music of Alberto Ginastera (1916–83) in the 1930s and 1940s was based upon the style of Argentinian dances and folk songs. In the 1950s and later, his works took on a more international and avant-garde character, as they used elements of serialism, aleatory techniques, and manipulation of textural masses.

The music of Carlos Chávez (1899–1978) reveals the profile of Indian culture in Mexico. His orchestral works are marked by a powerful use of percussion and other coloristic devices. His Mexican colleague Silvestre Revueltas (1899–1940) was fascinated by the rhythmic and orchestrational style of Stravinsky's *Rite of Spring,* which he imitated in his fancifully barbaric tone poem *Sensemayá* (1938).

Popular Music of the New World and the European Composer

Dance music from the United States and Latin America flooded Europe after World War I. In Paris jazz was heard from visiting American bands, who were eagerly joined by native musicians. The resourceful French pianist Jean Wiéner played jazz with the American Vance Lowry at the bar La Gaya, patronized regularly by French composers. Wiéner later founded an important series of concerts in Paris where jazz was performed on concerts of contemporary music.

Ragtime and blues were the most important forms of American popular music heard in Europe after the war. Ragtime is a slow march, usually played on piano, which enjoyed great popularity in America between about 1890 and 1915. Unlike early jazz it was not improvised; rather, it was composed, notated, and often published. It shared with the march its duple meter and form; the walking rhythms in the left hand and repetitive harmonic patterns of ragtime are also typical of march accompaniments. Ragtime was distinctive in its syncopated or "ragged" rhythms of the melodic line. These figures often resembled the syncopations of the "cakewalk," a popular American dance and march genre of the later nineteenth century.

Music of the blues was not at first notated, and, accordingly, it was slower to be absorbed into the language of serious music. Unlike ragtime, blues was originally limited to the social and artistic milieu of American blacks, and its distinctive manner of performance was passed on solely by musicians listening to and imitating one another. Like any improvised art, its musical features were varied. Originally, blues were vocal pieces. Their texts were strophic, each stanza consisting of three lines, of which the first two were identical and the third resolved some dilemma that the earlier lines posed. The words typically dealt with the downtrodden condition of the singer or the miseries of love and often contained earthy erotic allusions.

The music was a continuously improvised variation on a harmonic formula. Most simply, this harmonic pattern extended over twelve measures (equivalent to one stanza of text) and dwelled in turn upon the tonic harmony (four bars), subdominant (two bars), tonic (two bars), dominant (two bars), and tonic (two bars). The original accompaniments may have been performed on guitar or banjo by the singer, but they were later taken over by jazz bands.

In the 1920s some blues dispensed with the singer, for whom one or more instrumentalists were substituted. In instrumental blues, the vocalist's characteristic sliding between tones was imitated by lowering certain scale degrees, especially the third and seventh, which are sometimes called "blue notes." The typical jazz band of the 1920s had two distinct groups of instruments, one marking the rhythm (for example, piano, drums, and banjo) and the other (consisting, for example, of cornet, clarinet, and trombone) taking the melody. This ensemble was clearly different from the "big band" dance orchestra of the 1930s and 1940s, which had a much greater resonance by virtue of its full complement of saxophones, trumpets, and trombones.

The influence of popular music from the New World was especially strong on French composers after the war. Satie wrote a ragtime in his ballet *Parade* in 1917; Stravinsky included both a ragtime and a tango (an Argentinian dance) in *L'histoire du soldat* (1918), which was shortly followed by his *Rag-Time* (for chamber orchestra, 1918) and *Piano-Rag-Music* (1919). Ravel imitated blues and ragtime in several works, as did the younger composers Arthur Honegger, Francis Poulenc, Georges Auric, and the Czech expatriate Bohuslav Martinů (1890–1959).

Musicians in Germany and Austria also adapted jazz idioms, although not always as ingenuously as their French counterparts. Ernst Křenek caused a sensation with his jazz opera *Jonny spielt auf* (1926), and the jazz band was imitated by onstage musicians in Berg's *Lulu*. The finale of Paul Hindemith's Piano Suite "1922" is a ragtime, where the composer instructs the player, "Pay no heed to what you learned in your piano lessons; don't worry whether the D♭ is played with the fourth or sixth finger. Play this piece wildly, but always strictly in tempo, like a machine. Consider the piano as a kind of percussion instrument and treat it accordingly." Hindemith wittily manipulates the percussive style of American ragtime, its syncopated sixteenth-note rhythms, and its form (the customary trio enters at measures 51, a reprise at measure 80). But his treatment is otherwise a heavy parody—it is dense in texture and alternates ponderously between fourth chords and bitriadic formations. His ragtime in fact gives ample testimony to his distaste for popular music as art. In 1920 he wrote to his publisher Willi Strecker, "Would you be interested in publishing foxtrots, Bostons, ragtimes and other junk? When I run out of any decent ideas I always write such things."

Darius Milhaud (1892–1974) was the European composer who made the most sympathetic adaptations of American jazz and Latin American popular dances. His fascination for the music of Latin America was born in 1917 and 1918, when he served as an aide to the writer and diplomat Paul Claudel in Rio de Janeiro. "I was fascinated by the rhythms of this popular Brazilian music," he wrote in his autobiography *Notes Without Music.* "There was an imperceptible pause in the syncopation, a careless catch in the breath, a slight hiatus that I found very difficult to grasp. So I bought a lot of maxixes and tangos and tried to play them with their syncopated rhythms, which run from one hand to the other. At last my efforts were rewarded and I could both play and analyze this typically Brazilian subtlety."

The rhythms of the *maxixe,* samba, and the Argentinian tango are captured in his piano dances *Saudades do Brazil* (*Longing for Brazil,* 1920). Each of these is named for a place near Rio, and, in addition to their allusions to Latin American dance rhythms, each is an example of polytonality (see Chapter 3). "Botafogo" (Anthology no. 5) illustrates the unmannered spontaneity that Milhaud derived from Brazilian dances. The piece has the slow and lyrical quality of the *maxixe* or *lundú.* It is divided harmonically into two strata corresponding to the two hands, of which the right hand carries the melody. The middle section (mm. 27–42) contrasts with the outer ones by a change of tempo, figuration, and harmony. Here the two hands each state different pentatonic collections, the left hand confined to the black keys and the right hand mainly on the white. The outer sections, on the contrary, superimpose different diatonic scales (F minor and F♯ minor).

After the war Milhaud became familiar with ragtime and other popular American dance music, which he imitated in his "Caramel mou" for voice, dancer, and jazz ensemble. He did not experience true jazz until he visited Harlem in 1922. "The music I heard was absolutely different from anything I had ever heard before, and it was a revelation to me," he wrote in his autobiography. "Against the beat of the drums the melodic line criss-crossed in a breathless pattern of broken and twisted rhythms."

His recollections of improvised jazz were put to use in

DARIUS MILHAUD
(Aix-en-Provence, 1892—
Geneva, 1974)

A youthful enthusiasm for the music of Debussy led Milhaud to embark upon the career of a musician. He studied at the Conservatory in Paris from 1909 to 1912, where he was in the counterpoint class of André Gédalge and the composition class of Charles Widor. He was secretary to the French writer and diplomat Paul Claudel, in whose service he sojourned in Brazil from 1917 to 1918 and later traveled to Scandinavia and England. He collaborated with Claudel on the ballet *L'homme et son désir* and other dramatic or vocal works.

In the early 1920s he was active with a group of young Parisian composers who had been dubbed the Six. His music was the most experimental of this group, as it delved into polytonality, adaptations of jazz, and other modernistic directions. He later collaborated with Paul Hindemith in the organization of music festivals in Baden-Baden and Berlin.

He immigrated to the United States in 1940 and taught at Mills College; in 1947 he returned to France to accept an appointment to the faculty of the Conservatory. Despite crippling arthritis, he frequently returned to America, where he taught at Tanglewood, Music Academy of the West, and Aspen.

Selected Works

Operas. *Le pauvre matelot* (1926), *Christophe Colomb* (1928), *Médée* (1938), *Maximilien* (1932), *Bolivar* (1943), *La mère coupable* (1964).

Ballets. *L'homme et son désir* (1917), *La création du monde* (1923), *Le train bleu* (1924).

Orchestral Music. Thirteen symphonies (1940–65), *Suite provençale* (1937), *Suite française* (band, 1945); concertos for diverse instruments.

Chamber Music. Eighteen string quartets, sonatas for diverse instruments.

Piano Music. *Le boeuf sur le toit* (piano duet, 1919, later rev. as ballet music), *Saudades do Brazil* (two books, 1920), *Scaramouche* (1939, two pianos).

Choral Music. *The Orestes Trilogy of Aeschylus: Agamemnon* (1913), *Les choéphores* (1915), *Euménides* (1916); *La sagesse* (1935), *Jewish Sacred Service* (1947), *Pacem in terris* (1963).

---

his ballet *La création du monde* (*Creation of the World*, 1923), written for the Swedish Ballet to a scenario by Blaise Cendrars. The story has obvious connections with Stravinsky's ballet *Rite of Spring*, which had caused a sensation in Paris a decade earlier. The setting is Africa, which for Milhaud made the use of jazz all the more appropriate. "There can be no doubt that the origin of jazz music is to be sought among the Negroes," he wrote in the article "The Jazz Band and Negro Music." "Primitive African qualities have kept their place deep in the nature of the American Negro and it is here that we find the origin of the tremendous rhythmic force as well as the expressive melodies born of inspiration which oppressed races alone can produce."

By the later 1920s, jazz had lost its appeal for Milhaud, as it had for many of the French composers who had earlier relished its vitality. Milhaud himself set out in several new directions. After this time his music often fell back upon a pleasant tune and comfortable rhythm suggestive of popular music, but lacking the "broken and twisted rhythms" that gave works such as *Création du monde* their distinctive power.

The national movements that promised to reinvigorate music early in the twentieth century began to wane by the latter 1920s and 1930s. Stravinsky—whom Bartók had earlier identified as one of the most outstanding folklorists— now dismissed this movement: "What is so obvious in [the Five]," he wrote in his *Autobiography*, "as indeed in the modern Spanish 'folklorists,' whether painters or musicians, is that naive but dangerous tendency which prompts them to remake an art that has already been created instinctively by the genius of the people. It is a sterile tendency and an evil from which many talented artists suffer."

Stravinsky thus joined with Schoenberg, who had never considered folk music applicable to original composition. In an article "Folkloristic Symphonies," Schoenberg wrote: "The discrepancy between requirements of larger forms and the simple construction of folk tunes has never been solved and cannot be solved. A simple idea must not use the language of profundity.... Structurally, there never remains in popular tunes an unsolved problem, the consequences of which will show up only later.... There is nothing in them that asks for expansion."

Musical nationalism endured outside of Western Europe until after World War II, but in France and Germany it was outshone by a new mode of expression that was purged of regional color. We turn to this development in the next chapter on neoclassicism.

Bibliography

Important statements by composers concerning musical nationalism may be found in *Béla Bartók Essays*, ed. Benjamin Suchoff (New York, 1976), Stravinsky's *Autobiography* (New York, 1936), Schoenberg's essay "Folkloristic Symphonies" in *Style and Idea*, ed. Leonard Stein (London, 1975), Falla's *On Music and Musicians* (London, 1979), Vaughan Williams's *National Music* (London, 1934), Copland's *Music and Imagination* (Cambridge, 1952), Ravel's "Contemporary Music," *Revue de musicologie*, 50 (1964), 208-21, and Milhaud's *Notes Without Music* (New York, 1953). Milhaud's article "The Jazz Band and Negro Music" is found in *Living Age*, 1924, 169-73.

Halsey Stevens's *Life and Music of Béla Bartók* (London, 1964) is authoritative and powerfully written. Elliott Antokoletz emphasizes Bartók's use of symmetric sets in his analytic study, *The Music of Béla Bartók: A Study of Tonality and Progression in Twentieth-Century Music* (Berkeley, 1984). *The Music of Szymanowski* by Jim Samson (New York, 1981) is an authoritative analytic survey.

Erik Tawaststjerna's multivolume study of Sibelius is available in English only in one volume, covering this musician's life and works through 1905. Michael Kennedy's *Works of Ralph Vaughan Williams* (London, 1964) deals with both the life and music of his subject. Suzanne Demarquez's *Manuel de Falla,* trans. Salvator Attanasio (Philadelphia, 1968) surveys this composer's life and works. Julia Smith's study of Copland (New York, 1955) is thorough, but it is now somewhat out of date. Copland's *Music and Imagination* is based upon his Charles Eliot Norton Lectures at Harvard University in 1951–52. Also see the autobiographical *Copland 1900 through 1942* (with Vivian Perlis, New York, 1984).

• 10 •

NEOCLASSICISM IN FRANCE, GERMANY, AND ENGLAND

Rapid changes in musical style of the late nineteenth and early twentieth centuries were temporarily stayed by the First World War. The years after the war were a time of questioning and reevaluation in the arts in general. Had artistic expression progressed too far too fast? Were the war and its aftermath the results of an unhinged civilization to which artistic experimentation had unwittingly contributed?

For many observers, the issues that fueled the war could be overcome by artistic communication. According to their view, music had to seek a new universality. Such thoughts came to Paul Hindemith when he recalled a poignant moment during his wartime service, as he performed Debussy's String Quartet for his German commanding officer:

> When we had finished the slow movement, the officer who led the communications division came in with dismay and reported that just then news of Debussy's death had been received over the wire.

music after the war?

274

We did not continue. It was as though life had been
taken from our playing. We felt then for the first
time that music is more than style, technique, and
expression of personal feeling. Music then went
beyond political boundaries, beyond national hatred
and beyond the horror of war. At no other time has
it appeared so clearly to me in which direction
music had to unfold. [*Paul Hindemith: Zeugnis in
Bildern* (Mainz, 1955), p. 8.]

music at time of debussy's death Paul Hindemith

Hindemith implies that music cannot be allowed to
evolve beyond the understanding of the public. His words
suggest that a damaging esotericism had already diminished the broad communicative role of music and that this
art had to be called back to a simpler and more natural
order.

In fact, most of the outstanding European composers
after the war entered a phase of retrenchment or consolidation of their stylistic advances of the pre-war decade. Clarity and accessibility were the order of the day. Experimentation became much less important to the mainstream of
musical development and was confined instead to outlying
regions such as the United States or to the dilettantish
activities of Dadaism or Futurism.

clarity & accessibility

This desire to communicate directly to a larger audience was shared by contemporary painters and writers,
whose message was often one of social or political satire.
Several German painters of the 1920s such as George Grosz
(1893–1959) and Otto Dix (1891–1969) put aside the abstractions of Expressionism and adopted instead a realistic
manner dubbed "The New Objectivity." Their themes were
often bitter social criticisms. German writers such as
Bertolt Brecht (1898–1956) held similarly that social reform
was a goal of art, and the musicians with whom he
collaborated—Kurt Weill (1900–1950) and Hanns Eisler
(1898–1962)—used a direct and popular style to facilitate
the comprehension of their works.

Writings by Ferruccio Busoni after the war enunciated
the new conservatism among musicians as emphatically as
his earlier *Sketch of a New Esthetic of Music* (1907) had
informed the pre-war avant-garde. In a letter of 1920 to the
critic Paul Bekker, Busoni called for an era of "Young
Classicism." "By Young Classicism I mean the mastery, the

The "New Objectivity": Otto Dix, *Two Victims of Capitalism* (Courtesy of the Otto Dix Stiftung, Vaduz.)

sifting and turning to account of all the gains of previous experiments and their inclusion in strong and beautiful forms." Young Classicism, Busoni predicted, would be marked by a renewed melodic emphasis, renunciation of subjectivity, and the "reconquest of serenity."

These and other classicizing directions were adopted by a large number of composers in Europe and America between the world wars. Their music assimilated and reinterpreted the forms, genres, and styles of European music of the eighteenth and nineteenth centuries. Triads and diatonic collections of pitches gained favor, and straightforward melody and homophonic textures were reasserted.

neo-classicism

Traditional instrumental and vocal types were emphasized, and compositional techniques of earlier times were revived in a modern guise. The particular musical language of an earlier composer was often imitated, and artistic arrangements of earlier masterworks won a new respect. These features collectively point to a style to be termed *neoclassicism*, and its appearance in the works of leading composers in France, Germany, and England in the 1920s, 1930s, and 1940s will be the subject of this chapter. Like most other collective styles of this century, however, neoclassicism will be found to include diverse artistic manifestations.

French Neoclassicism:
Stravinsky and the Six

The leading neoclassicist in France between the world wars was the Russian émigré Igor Stravinsky. The power and originality of his music in this new idiom carried the younger generation of French composers in its wake, much as the experimental style of the *Rite of Spring* had proved so compelling to European and American composers prior to the First World War. Stravinsky's neoclassicism endured from the early 1920s until the early 1950s, at which time he embraced chromatic serialism (to be discussed in Chapter 12).

During this period between the world wars, Stravinsky spoke emphatically of the necessity of tradition in music:

> Tradition is entirely different from habit, even from an excellent habit, for habit is by definition an unconscious acquisition and tends to become mechanical, whereas tradition results from a conscious and deliberate acceptance. A real tradition is not the relic of a past irretrievably gone; it is a living force that animates and informs the present. In this sense the paradox which banteringly maintains that everything which is not tradition is plagiarism is true. . . .
>
> Far from implying the repetition of what has been, tradition presupposes the reality of what endures. It appears as an heirloom, a heritage that

one receives on condition of making it bear fruit
before passing it on to one's descendants. [From the
Poetics of Music. See the Bibliography to Chapter 8
concerning the authenticity of this book.]

Stravinsky made many traditions bear fruit during his
neoclassical period, including the Russo-Italian operatic
style of the nineteenth century, the instrumental idiom
of Bach, and the nineteenth-century lyric tradition of
Rossini, Verdi, and Weber. But for other traditions—especially that of Wagner—he had disdain, and his neoclassical works stand as a rejection of ultraromantic progressivism among German composers as well as a reaction
against his own earlier milieu: French Impressionism and
Russian nationalism.

Stravinsky's Octet (1922–23) was one of his earliest
masterpieces in this new style. It will illustrate that neoclassicism was at first primarily a rebellion against turn-of-
the-century romanticism, rather than an attempt to revive
earlier musical traditions. This three-movement work is
scored for flute, clarinet, and pairs of bassoons, trumpets,
and trombones, a medium that reflects Stravinsky's predilection at this time for small ensembles. His choice of
woodwinds and brass rather than strings is also typical of
his early neoclassical music. The winds provide Stravinsky
with a clear, hard, and objective sonority, which conformed
to the image he intended his music to convey. "My Octuor
is made for an ensemble of wind instruments," he writes in
the article "Some Ideas about my Octuor [Octet]" (1924).
"Wind instruments seem to me to be more apt to render a
certain rigidity of the form I had in mind than other
instruments—the string instruments, for example, which
are less cold and more vague."

In its linearity and rhythmic clarity, the Octet forms a
marked contrast to the hyperemotive music of German and
Austrian composers at the turn of the century as well as to
the refined and evocative textures of the French Impressionists. "My Octuor is not an 'emotive' work, but a musical
composition based on objective elements which are sufficient in themselves," he writes.

In order to dispel more completely the mists of romanticism, Stravinsky applies classical forms of absolute music:

sonata form in the first movement, theme and variations in the second, rondo in the third, fugue in part of the second movement, and, in general, a terse and economic polyphony.

The centerpiece of the composition is the theme and variations. The theme (rehearsal 24–26) is entirely octatonic, and it does not have a strongly asserted keynote. The underlying chords, on the contrary, begin and end with triads on D, and the theme concludes with a cadential progression from dominant to tonic in D major. Throughout the Octet, such dominant–tonic progressions serve to connect structural elements and to mark cadences, but they do not create traditional tonality nor do they organize large spans of the music.

The variations that follow all contain the theme in a recognizable though varied form. The first accompanies the theme by what the composer called "ribbons of scales"—a flurry of diatonic scales departing from different tonics. This variation returns as a refrain before the third and fifth variations. Each of the other variations takes on a different character: the second is a march, the third a waltz, the fourth a cancan, and the last a solemn fugue.

Beginning with the opera-oratorio *Oedipus rex* (1926–27), Stravinsky returned to a larger orchestra and a more conventional style of orchestration in which the string ensemble is again prominent. His music from this time emphasizes symphonic and dramatic genres.

The Mass (1944–48), however, reverts to a small wind orchestra, which accompanies a mixed chorus using children's voices on the higher parts. Although Stravinsky was a communicant of the Russian Orthodox Church from 1926, the music of his neoclassical years is overwhelmingly secular. He was provoked to write a concerted Latin Mass, as he relates in *Expositions and Developments*, by his desire to provide music for use in the Christian liturgy which would be untainted by theatricality:

> Why, then, did I compose a Roman Catholic Mass? Because I wanted my *Mass* to be used liturgically, an outright impossibility so far as the Russian Church was concerned, as Orthodox tradition proscribes musical instruments in its services—and as I can endure unaccompanied singing in only the most harmonically primitive music.... My *Mass* was

partly provoked by some Masses of Mozart that I found in a second-hand music store in Los Angeles in 1942 or 1943. As I played through these rococo-operatic sweets-of-sin, I knew I had to write a Mass of my own, but a real one. Incidentally, I heard Machaut's *Mass* for the first time a year after mine was composed, and I was not influenced in my *Mass* by any "old" music whatever, or guided by any example.

Although Stravinsky denies having adopted any models of earlier music, the treatment of voices is highly reminiscent of medieval and Renaissance polyphony. An alternation of imitative and homophonic textures suggests the Renaissance Mass, and the pungent alternation of perfect and imperfect consonances between the solo voices in the Gloria is comparable to medieval organum.

The Credo (Anthology no. 23) stands as the centerpiece of this work. Its lengthy text is set as choral declamation where cadences and rests closely follow the punctuation and meaning of the words. Its declamatory rhythm conforms to the rhythm of the Latin words as they might be spoken. The composer remarked, "In making the musical setting of the Credo, I wished only to preserve the text in a special way. One composes a march to facilitate marching men; so with my Credo I hope to provide an aid to the text. The Credo is the longest movement. There is much to believe."

In the traditional manner of polyphonic Credos, the initial phrase "Credo in unum deum" ("I believe in one God") is sung in Gregorian chant by the celebrant. The composer specified the so-called "authentic" Credo melody (*Liber usualis*, p. 64, no. 1) for this purpose. The music that follows is unified by the recurrence of two prominent tetrachords, both of which are subsets of diatonic scales

E G A B   C♯ D F♯ A

Example 10-1.   Cadential tetrachords in the Credo of Stravinsky's Mass.

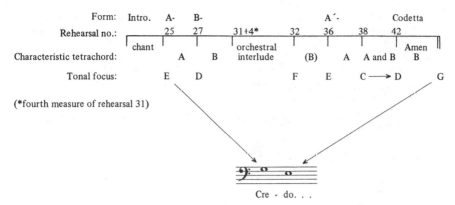

Example 10-2.   Form and harmonic recurrence in the Credo of Stravinsky's Mass.

and which themselves contain triads. The first, designated in Example 10-1 as tetrachord A, is heard as the initial chord. It is scored so as to emphasize the root-position triad (E minor) which it contains. This chord is most prominent at the beginning and end of the movement.

The second tetrachord (tetrachord B in Example 10-1) is the familiar major seventh, based upon the root D in most occurrences. It characterizes the middle of the Credo, where it is heard at virtually all cadences. It is introduced in the bar before rehearsal 27.

The contrast of these two sonorities and the concentric tonal motion about E give the Credo a freely ternary form, which is diagrammed in Example 10-2. The *a cappella* fugato of the Amen relates subtly to tetrachord B, which is equivalent to the set of pitches upon which the voices enter: F A C E. The music comes to a rest on the bass note G so that the tonal motion of the entire movement spans the same interval (E to G) heard in reverse order at the opening of the celebrant's chant.

An article published in 1920 by the critic Henri Collet refers to a group of younger French composers as the "Six" and relates their music to the influence of Erik Satie. The composers whom Collet cites are Darius Milhaud, Francis Poulenc, Georges Auric, Arthur Honegger, Germaine Tailleferre, and Louis Durey. Despite considerable differences in their music, they accepted this common designation and collaborated for several years. Their mentors were Satie and Cocteau, with whom they shared the ideal of a simplified, anti-Wagnerian, and anti-Impressionistic music. The Six were not modernists. In fact, modernism was decried in their broadsheet *Le Coq* as a danger second only to the overrefinement of Impressionism. As these composers increasingly asserted their own artistic personalities, their music generally remained in the neoclassical vein with an emphasis on melody, clear lines and textures, conventional forms, and diatonic or triadic sonorities. The music of Durey and Tailleferre remains relatively obscure, and Auric soon devoted himself to composing for film. Milhaud was the most innovative figure in the group; his application of polytonality and of jazz and Latin rhythms has been described in Chapter 9. Although different in background and artistic personality, Poulenc and Honegger best exemplify the spirit of neoclassicism among native French composers between the world wars.

The music of Francis Poulenc (1899–1963) during the 1920s was closely allied to the direction of Satie and Cocteau in its eclecticism, witty simplicity, and spirit of the music hall. But in the later 1920s his mature style emerged in a succession of songs for voice and piano, a medium in which he was also active as accompanist to the singer Pierre Bernac. Poulenc's songs are among the most distinguished twentieth-century contributions to this genre. They continue the tradition of the nineteenth-century French *mélodie*, a genre inspired by the lieder of Schubert and Schumann. Although they occasionally delve into modern dissonant harmonies and liberated tonal plans, their style conforms primarily to the romantic song.

Tel jour, telle nuit (1936–37), a cycle of nine songs drawing upon verse by Paul Eluard (1895–1952), shows Poulenc's great ability to elucidate modern poetry by musical means. Eluard's surrealistic writings were a continuing inspiration to Poulenc during the last thirty years of his life. The nine works selected by Poulenc for *Tel jour, telle nuit* forgo logical narrative in favor of free expression of the poet's thought and emotion. Poems celebrating love ("Je n'ai envie que t'aimer" and "Nous avons fait la nuit") alternate with verses depicting loneliness ("Le front comme un drapeau perdu"), joy ("Bonne journée"), violence ("Figure de force brûlante et farouche"), and dreams ("Une ruine coquille vide"). Although these texts are not unified by a common theme, Poulenc shapes them into a cycle by returning in the last song to the key and accompanimental figuration of the first.

FRANCIS POULENC
(Paris, 1899—Paris, 1963)

Poulenc has written that his greatest childhood experiences in music were first hearings of works by Debussy and Schubert. Both composers would later provide models for his own work. He did not attend a conservatory; instead, he studied piano privately with Ricardo Viñes and, after his initial successes as a composer, composition with Charles Koechlin (1921–24). His early works are modeled on those of Erik Satie, but in the 1920s, and 1930s his interest turned increasingly to the composition of songs, which were allied in style to French and German models of the nineteenth century.

He lived primarily in Paris, and he toured throughout Europe as accompanist to the singer Pierre Bernac. His later works include larger genres such as opera and dramatic monologues.

Selected Works

Operas. *Les mamelles de Tirésias* (1944), *Dialogues des carmélites* (1955), *La voix humaine* (1958).

Ballets. *Les biches* (1923), *Aubade* (1929).

Concertos. *Concert champêtre* (harpsichord, 1928), two pianos (1932), organ (1938), piano (1949).

Chamber Music. Sonatas for clarinet and bassoon (1922); horn, trombone, and trumpet (1922), violin (1943), cello (1948), two pianos (1953), flute (1956), oboe (1962), clarinet (1962).

Songs. Over 100 songs on texts by Max Jacob, Paul Eluard, Guillaume Apollinaire, and others.

Choral Music. Mass in G (1937), Motets (1939), *La figure humaine* (1943), Stabat mater (1950), Gloria (1959).

The music in this cycle is unusually free in its handling of both tonality and dissonance. As in most of Poulenc's vocal music, an underlying sadness and nostalgia well up beneath its surface. His settings are finely tailored to the poetic structures and images. To his collaborator Pierre Bernac he said, "I recite the poem to myself many times. I listen, I search for the traps, at times I underline the text in red at the difficult spots. I note the breathing places, I try to discover the inner rhythm from a line which is not necessarily the first. Next I try to set it to music, bearing in mind the different densities of the piano accompaniment" (from Pierre Bernac, *Francis Poulenc*, trans. Winifred Radford [New York, 1977], p. 39).

Arthur Honegger (1892–1955) was of a different artistic temperament from any of the other figures of the Six. His parents were Swiss and he proudly maintained Swiss citizenship throughout his life. He was educated in Zurich, where he developed a great admiration for Wagner and other German modernists. He saw no need for French composers to reject German music, as did Satie and Cocteau. In fact, he had little affinity for Satie, whose irreverent jesting was far from his own serious approach.

Among his better known compositions is the orchestral portrait *Pacific 231*. This work—one of many "mechanistic" pieces of music composed in France in the 1920s—is intended to capture the energy and dynamism of a steam locomotive. His operas and oratorios are his most ambitious works. The oratorio *King David* (1921) was his first success as a composer, and the oratorio *Joan of Arc at the Stake* (1935) enjoyed a huge popularity in France during the 1940s.

Joan of Arc was commissioned by Ida Rubinstein, a Russian expatriate who organized her own ballet company in Paris in 1927. Her commissions also led to Ravel's *Boléro* and Stravinsky's *Baiser de la fée* and *Perséphone*, the last of which shares with *Joan of Arc* a principal role for speaker and mime. *Joan of Arc* was written to a libretto by Paul Claudel, who also took an active part in its musical setting. Claudel's text recounts the life and death of the fifteenth-century heroine Joan of Arc, who resisted English domination of parts of France that had resulted from the Hundred Years War and who promoted the restoration of Charles VII

ARTHUR HONEGGER
(Le Havre, 1892—Paris, 1955)

Honegger was born to a German-Swiss family living in France, and he maintained lifelong contact with musical developments in both nations. He attended the Zurich Conservatory from 1909 to 1911, where his fondness for the music of Bach and German moderns was strengthened. During the, next two years, he was enrolled at the Paris Conservatory, after which he continued to study composition with Charles-Marie Widor and Vincent d'Indy.

In 1920 he became associated with the young French composers called the Six, a group with whom he had little in common. He frequently traveled to Switzerland to promote performances of his music, although he resided primarily in Paris.

Selected Works

Operas. *Judith* (opera or oratorio, 1925), *Antigone* (1927), *La belle de Moudon* (1933).

Oratorios. *King David* (1921), *Cris du monde* (1931), *Jean d'Arc au bûcher* (1935).

Orchestral Music. Five Symphonies (1930–50), *Pastorale d'été* (1920), *Pacific 231* (1923), *Rugby* (1928).

Chamber Music. Three String Quartets (1917–37); Sonatinas for clarinet and piano (1922), violin and cello (1932); Sonata for solo violin (1940), *Le cahier romand* (solo piano, 1922).

Miscellaneous. Songs, ballet scores, incidental music, popular songs, film scores.

to the French throne. Joan was captured by forces allied to England and turned over to an ecclesiastical court in Rouen to be tried on a charge of witchcraft and heresy. She was burned at the stake in 1431. Joan's legendary bravery and patriotism had a special meaning to the French during the period of German occupation from 1940 to 1944.

Claudel's poem takes the form of a flashback at the moment of Joan's death. At the beginning of the oratorio, she is shown chained to the stake, and her life is recounted by her confessor Brother Dominic. In the final scene she is comforted by the Virgin Mary as she breaks loose from her fetters and ascends into heaven. Honegger's music is intensely dramatic; indeed, its range of expressive media is more akin to opera than to oratorio. The musical language is likewise diverse: polytriadic effects depict the chaos of the Prologue (added by the composer in 1945 to celebrate France's delivery from the Germans), and a free, colorful dissonance alternates with simple triadic passages. Joan's child-like purity is captured by the use of folk song. The polyphonic choruses take their departure from those of Bach's *Passion According to St. John* as they depict the frenzied mob accusing Joan of heresy.

In the fourth scene Joan is turned over to a court populated by barnyard animals, playing upon the name of her judge Cauchon and the French word for pig, *cochon.* The use here of coarse French and corrupt Latin underscores the hypocrisy of the proceedings, as does Honegger's jazzy, commercial music. The work reaches its dramatic climax in the final scene, "The Burning of Joan of Arc." The chorus at first represents the crowd, denouncing Joan and praising the flames by which she is engulfed. The chorus then becomes an ensemble of angels celebrating her triumph. Joan's role is spoken and mimed, and she is accompanied by the singing of the Virgin Mary, who provides comfort and consolation. The music ends serenely on a D major/minor tetrachord.

German Neoclassicism: Strauss and Hindemith

Just as Richard Strauss prefigured Expressionist opera in his *Salome* in 1905, he became a forerunner of postwar

German neoclassicism with his opera *Der Rosenkavalier* in 1910. In this work he put behind his foray with the avant-garde and returned to a style combining Mozartean clarity with his innate romantic lyricism.

The libretto of *Der Rosenkavalier* by Hugo von Hof-mannsthal is based upon conventions of the seventeenth- and eighteenth-century French farce. Thus it has much in common with Mozart's *Marriage of Figaro,* a work that served both Strauss and Hofmannsthal as a model. The characters and comic situations of both are cut from the same cloth: youthful lovers thwarted at first by lecherous older men, intrigues complicated by disguises, and, in the end, young love winning out over all. Hofmannsthal weaves into this predictable comedy a more profound and touching story: the "Marschallin," Princess of Werdenberg, must endure the passing of her youth and innocence, symbolized by the loss of her lover Octavian to a younger rival.

After the success of *Der Rosenkavalier,* Strauss and Hofmannsthal began work on *Ariadne auf Naxos* (1911–12). Their original conception was most unusual—to interpolate an operatic divertissement dealing with the Greek myth of Ariadne and Theseus into a version of Molière's farce *Le bourgeois gentilhomme.* Strauss composed music for the opera and incidental music for the play. Later the opera was revised as an independent work (1916), and the incidental music was reshaped into an orchestral suite, *Der Bürger als Edelmann* (1920). Strauss's music evokes the atmosphere of the seventeenth century in numerous ways: the orchestra is reduced to chamber proportions, and a piano is used to imitate the harpsichord in accompaniment of recitatives. Strauss also quotes several melodies from the works of Jean-Baptiste Lully (1632–87), who had composed the original incidental music for *Le bourgeois gentilhomme.*

Paul Hindemith (1895–1963) is the greatest German neoclassicist of the years between the world wars. His career is typical of his generation: a youthful period of experimentation gave way shortly after the First World War to a more traditional artistic orientation. In his early music, Hindemith dabbled in many of the experimental approaches to composition of his day: atonality, Expressionism, jazz, parody, and satire. None of these, however, was true to his deeply serious and philosophical nature, which emerged in his music by the mid-1920s.

PAUL HINDEMITH
(Hanau, 1895—Frankfurt, 1963)

Hindemith began his musical career as a violinist at the Hoch Konservatorium in Frankfurt. He also received instruction there in composition from Arnold Mendelssohn and Bernhard Sekles. He was concertmaster of the orchestra of the Frankfurt Opera from 1915 to 1923. Between 1921 and 1929 he played viola in the Amar Quartet, an ensemble that he founded and that was devoted to the performance of modern music. He was brought to international attention as a composer by performances of his music at the Donaueschingen Festival (1921–   ).

From 1927 to 1937 he served on the faculty of the Staatliche Hochschule für Musik in Berlin. Here he discovered his great talent for teaching, and his interests broadened to include musical theory and performance of early music. From 1934 until his departure from Europe in 1940, his music was increasingly opposed by Nazi authorities, and, after several trips to Turkey as a musical consultant and a period of exile in Switzerland, he accepted an appointment at Yale University. In 1951 he began teaching at the University of Zurich and attempted a new career as an orchestral conductor.

Selected Works

Dramatic Music. Operas: *Cardillac* (1926, rev. 1952), *Mathis der Maler* (1934–35), *Die Harmonie der Welt* (1956–57); ballet: *Nobilissima visione* (1938).

Orchestral Music and Concertos. *Kammermusik* (1921–27: seven works of which the first is for chamber orchestra and the others a cycle of concertos); *Konzertmusik*, opp. 48–50 (1930, three works), *Concerto for Orchestra* (1925); *Philharmonic Concerto* (1932); Symphony *Mathis der Maler* (1934); *Der*

Schwanendreher (viola concerto, 1935); Suite *Nobilissima visione* (1938); Concertos for violin (1939), cello (1940), piano (1945), clarinet (1947), horn (1949), organ (1962); *Symphonic Metamorphoses on Themes of Carl Maria von Weber* (1943).

Chamber Music. Six string quartets (1918–45), two string trios (1924–33), *Ludus tonalis* for piano (1942), solo sonatas for orchestral instruments and piano, three piano Sonatas, Suite "1922."

Songs and Choral Music. *Das Marienleben* (1923, rev. 1936–48), Mass (1963), Madrigals for unaccompanied chorus (1958), *Das Unaufhörliche* (oratorio, 1931), Six chansons for chorus (1939).

Theoretical Writings. *Unterweisung im Tonsatz*, three vols. 1937, 1939, 1970; vols. 1 and 2 translated as *The Craft of Musical Composition*.

Hindemith held that music was functional and ethical. Its purpose was to communicate to the musically literate public and play a salutary role in society and culture. It was a composer's moral obligation to defend music's comprehensibility, which in the twentieth century seemed under attack by unrestrained modernity and unnatural abstraction. He was highly critical of atonal or twelve-tone composers, who, "attempting to replace with an apparent rationality what is lacking morally, develop an oversublimated technique which produces images of emotions that are far removed from any emotional experiences a relatively normal human being ever has. In doing so they advocate an esoteric *art pour l'art*, the followers of which can only be emotional imps, monsters, or snobs."

An outcome of his functional conception of art was the composition of what he termed *Gebrauchsmusik* or "useful" music. Such works were intended for students or amateurs, comparable in type to the keyboard sonatas of C. P. E. Bach written for dilettantes or for purposes of teaching. Several of Hindemith's early examples in this genre were published under the title *Music to Sing and to Play: For Amateurs and Music Lovers* (1928). His last major essay in *Gebrauchsmusik* was the *Plöner Musiktag* (1932), which consisted of a cycle of vocal and instrumental pieces to accompany daily student activities at a private school in the town of Plön. Hindemith considered them facile enough for student players and singers, but most are of considerable difficulty, as is virtually all of his music for "amateurs."

Hindemith's song cycle *Das Marienleben* (*The Life of Mary*, 1923, rev. 1936–48) was the first important work in his mature or neoclassical style. The text is a cycle of fifteen poems by Rainer Maria Rilke (1875–1926) of the same title. It elaborates major events in the life of the Virgin Mary as they are told in Scripture and traditional Christian lore. Rilke fluctuates between simple lyrics and flamboyant images. His Marian poems delve intensely into human emotions, ranging from suppressed joy in "Birth of Mary" to anger and remorse in "Joseph's Suspicion" to self-pity in "Before the Passion."

The cycle is concluded by three poems "On the Death of Mary." Hindemith's setting of the first of these three (Anthology no. 13) is an example of the touching simplicity that he allied to Rilke's poetry. The lengthy text is an account in free verse of Mary's last moments on earth: her encounter with an angelic messenger, her final meeting with the Apostles, and the legendary giving away of her two cloaks.

The music is placidly detached from this dramatic text. The composer made no attempt at word painting or other graphic musical expressions of the miraculous events of Mary's assumption. By its very lack of graphic realism, the song captures the abstract unearthliness of this phase of Mary's existence. The musical form is that of the baroque passacaglia—continuous variations upon a five-measure ground bass. The ground was intended by the composer to suggest the majesty of Mary's departure. Other neoclassical elements of the setting reside in its rigidly contrapuntal texture, triadic points of arrival and departure, and regularity of rhythm and phrasing. The continuous motor rhythms, especially apparent in the right hand of the piano, enhance its relation to baroque music.

The song is a ternary design, the outer parts variations upon the ground. This ostinato line moves deliberately through intervals of the fourth and fifth, typical of the ground bass in baroque music. Its harmonic implications, however, are not realized in the chords of the upper voices

a)   m. 27   b)   m. 28

Example 10-3.   Hindemith, "Vom Tode Mariä I" from *Das Marienleben*
(1924 version). © B. Schott's Soehne, Mainz, 1924; ©
renewed. All rights reserved. Used by permission of
European American Music Distributors Corp., sole U.S.
agent for B. Schott's Soehne.

except at cadences. The upper voices move instead in
rapidly changing diatonic patterns. The ground ends on the
pitch class G, which functions throughout the song as the
main goal of tonal motion.

The contrasting middle section (mm. 27–58), typical of
many baroque passacaglias, dispenses with the ground,
although it continues in the form of continuous variations,
now upon two motives in the right hand of the piano
shown in Example 10-3. These figures are varied by changing harmonizations in the piano and by a through-composed vocal line which focuses on the note G. The "tonality" of G is reaffirmed at the end of the song by motion to
a concluding G-major triad.

In 1948 Hindemith completed a revision of *Das Marienleben* in which he sought to improve its vocal line and
large-scale structure. The opening of the new version of
"On the Death of Mary I" shows that the vocal line was
completely rewritten to make it more diatonic and to bring
its phrasing into agreement with the bass (Example 10-4).
The middle section was simplified harmonically as well as
being fitted with a new vocal melody.

In the Introduction to the revised edition, Hindemith
explains a symbolism of keys that guided him in revising
the harmonic vocabulary of the entire cycle. Keys (or triadic areas) are used in the revised version to represent characters or spiritual qualities found in Rilke's poetry. These
are based upon a central tonality of E, which represents
Jesus. The remaining tonal centers are assembled into a series of increasingly distant relationships to E, corresponding
to the diminishing importance of the characters or qualities that these keys represent. Closest to E is its dominant
B, the symbol of Mary; next is the subdominant A, representing angels; C symbolizes eternity, and so forth through
all twelve pitch classes. The G tonality of "On the Death of
Mary I" points to idyllic contentment, bringing with it, as

each key center representing characters or events

Example 10-4.   Hindemith, "Vom Tode Mariä I" from *Das Marienleben* (1948 version). © by Schott & Co. Ltd. London 1948. All rights reserved. Used by permission of European American Music Distributors Corp., sole U.S. agent for B. Schott's Soehne.

the composer writes in the Introduction, "a shimmer of lyric softness."

The opera *Mathis der Maler* (*Mathis the Painter*, 1934–35) is Hindemith's masterpiece and the work that vaulted him to international recognition after its suppression by the Third Reich. The text, written by the composer, is a fictionalized account of the life of the painter Matthias (or Mathis) Grünewald (fl. 1500–1530). Using Grünewald's life as a pretext, Hindemith explored a subject of lifelong fascination to him: the role of the artist in culture and society. His work on the score came at the time of his greatest mastery. It was also the beginning of a period of intense concern with a theory of harmony and tonality, which would be formulated in the first volume of his *Unterweisung im Tonsatz* (*Craft of Musical Composition*, 1937) and have a profound influence on his music of the 1940s and 1950s.

The action takes place in Germany at the time of the *opera's* Peasants' War (1524–25). Mathis is a painter in the ser- *libretto* vice of Albrecht, Cardinal Archbishop of Mainz. He has taken a leave-of-absence from Mainz to work at a convent of the Order of St. Anthony; there he meets the rebel leader Hans Schwalb and his daughter Regina. Mathis joins the revolution in order to make a greater contribution to the people. But he is revulsed by their excesses and narrowly escapes execution after the rebels are put to rout.

In the sixth tableau, Mathis has fled into the forest with Regina, whose father, Schwalb, is dead. After reassuring her about the joys of heaven now partaken of by her father, Mathis has a dream in which he is the legendary hermit St. Anthony. Mathis relives through Anthony the temptations which, according to legend, the saint endured in the desert. He also witnesses the legendary meeting of Anthony with St. Paul the Hermit, the latter represented in the dream by his patron Albrecht. Paul advises him to put aside his other interests and return to his work as artist, by which he can best serve God and man. The seventh tableau is a denoucment in which the elderly artist puts away his painting tools and prepares to die.

Hindemith's characterization of Mathis is in part autobiographical. Mathis, like Hindemith, comes to learn the truly social and ethical purpose of art, which, far from being a diversion, is fundamental to man's higher nature.

Much of the scenery, text, and music of this opera was inspired by Grünewald's masterpiece: a series of nine altar paintings for the Order of St. Anthony in Isenheim, where the painter worked for a period early in the sixteenth century. Grünewald's polyptych portrays events in the lives of Christ and St. Anthony and a mannered "Concert of Angels" which lends its name to the overture of the opera. The paintings are now found in the Musée d'Unterlinden in Colmar, France, where they were studied by Hindemith during his work on the libretto.

In the panel depicting the meeting of Anthony and Paul (see figure), the artist may have modeled the figure of St. Anthony upon his patron at the convent, Guido Guesi. The figure of St. Paul may be a self-portrait of Grünewald. Hindemith dramatized this iconography in the third

Models for *Mathis der Maler:* Matthias Grünewald, *Meeting of St. Anthony and St. Paul the Hermit,* from the Isenheim Altarpiece. (Courtesy of the Musée d'Unterlinden, Colmar.)

scene of the sixth tableau, but with a reversal of roles, as he has Mathis imagine that he is Anthony, and his patron Albrecht appears as St. Paul. The symbolism is carried to a still higher level since Anthony (Mathis) also represents the composer Hindemith and, by implication, all artists.

The third scene of the sixth tableau is the climax of the opera, as Anthony, under the tutelage of St. Paul, comes to accept the importance of his creative work. Hindemith notes in the score that the scenery is to resemble Grünewald's painting of this legendary meeting. The scene is divided into four sections with an introduction:

> Introduction: dialogue in recitative. Anthony tells Paul of the depths of his despair;
> 1. Paul's homily: arioso with refrain (six measures before rehearsal 85 to rehearsal G). Paul advises Anthony to return to his former profession;
> 2. Paul's peroration: aria in bar form and codetta (rehearsal G to rehearsal 97). Through artistic creativity, the individual is subsumed by service to God and man.
> 3. Epilogue: duet (four measures before rehearsal 98 to two measures before rehearsal 102). Man cannot escape his earthly calling, through which he best recognizes and appreciates heavenly power.
> 4. Coda: duet. Alleluia (a quotation of the Alleluia for the Feast of Corpus Christi).

The aria (rehearsal G) makes use of the traditional German "bar" form A A' B, thus accenting certain nationalistic overtones in the libretto; elsewhere in the opera the bar form is associated with German folk music. The following diagram of the aria also shows Hindemith's use of focal triads to articulate the aria's closed form:

Paul's Aria:	A-	A'-	B-	Codetta
Rehearsal:	G	95–2*	96–2	97
Triadic Focus:	D♭	D♭	E	(D♭)

(* two measures before rehearsal 95)

The key of D♭ is the central tonality of the entire opera, heard at the beginning of the first tableau and at the conclusion of the seventh. But in the sixth tableau it has a secondary role as lower neighbor to the triadic area of D, to which the music turns without break at the beginning of the duet. The magnificent coda of the duet, which paraphrases the Gregorian Alleluia for the Feast of Corpus Christi, ends on a luminous D-major triad (Example 10-5).

Hindemith's first compositional work on *Mathis der Maler* took the form of an orchestral suite, the Symphony *Mathis der Maler*. This piece received its premier performance in 1934 and served to prepare for a staging of the entire opera that was blocked at the eleventh hour by Nazi opposition. The three movements of the Symphony are titled "Concert of Angels" (later used as prelude to the opera and in music of the first scene of the sixth tableau), "Entombment" (used as an interlude in the seventh tableau), and "Temptation of St. Anthony" (used in the second scene of the sixth tableau). The music of the "Alleluia" at the end

Example 10-5. Hindemith, *Mathis der Maler*, sixth tableau. © B. Schott's Soehne, Mainz, 1935; renewed 1963. Used by permission of European American Music Distributors Corp., sole U.S. agents for B. Schott's Soehne.

of the sixth tableau is added to form the conclusion of the Symphony.

Neoclassicism in England: Britten and Tippett

English composers did not in general participate in the European avant-garde of the first two decades of the century. The conservatively classical language popular there during the interwar period was an uninterrupted continuation of the romantic tradition brought into the twentieth century by composers such as Edward Elgar and Frederick Delius. Their musical idiom was carried on by William Walton, Gustav Holst, and Ralph Vaughan Williams, none of whom placed primary emphasis on innovation or stylistic experiment.

The classical-romantic tradition of English music was carried to its greatest heights in the twentieth century by Benjamin Britten (1913–76). His music grew from the same soil as that of Vaughan Williams. Both used English folk song and both found inspiration in the music of Purcell and his English predecessors. Neither composer dispensed completely with traditional harmony, tonality, or concepts of form. But Britten went far beyond Vaughan Williams in establishing an original musical language within an essentially traditional framework.

Britten's music is primarily vocal and dramatic. His eleven operas are the greatest contributions to English-language opera since Handel, and their number is augmented by several dramatic pieces for churches, numerous collections of songs, and a repertory of choral music that is among the greatest of this century. His choice of texts was exceedingly broad, including poetry in Italian, French, and German as well as English verse from all eras. His religious music draws upon biblical stories, English carols and hymns, medieval lyrics, and Latin texts.

Britten's music before the 1950s continued the classicizing directions of Vaughan Williams. It was largely diatonic, triadic, and it expressed key in novel ways. His works created easily recognizable forms by refrains, strophic

BENJAMIN BRITTEN
(Lowestoft, Suffolk, 1913—
Aldeburgh, 1976)

Britten began the study of composition with Frank Bridge, and he continued with John Ireland at the Royal College of Music in London from 1930 to 1934. Dismayed by the prospect of European hostilities, he immigrated in 1939 to Canada, later moving to the United States, where he remained until 1942.

After the end of World War II, he settled permanently in his native Suffolk. In 1948 he collaborated with the singer Peter Pears and writer Eric Crozier to found the Aldeburgh Festival, at which many of his works subsequently received their first performance. Until he was prevented by illness, Britten was active as a pianist and conductor, specializing in performances of his own music.

Selected Works

Operas and Other Dramatic Works. Operas: *Paul Bunyan* (1941, rev. 1976), *Peter Grimes* (1944–45), *Rape of Lucretia* (1946), *Albert Herring* (1947), *Let's Make an Opera* (including the opera *The Little Sweep*, 1949), *Billy Budd* (1951), *Gloriana* (1953), *Turn of the Screw* (1954), *A Midsummer Night's Dream* (1960), *Owen Wingrave* (1970), *Death in Venice* (1973). Dramatic works intended for performance in churches: *Noye's Fludde* (1957), *Curlew River* (1964), *Burning Fiery Furnace* (1966), *Prodigal Son* (1968).

Orchestral Music. *Sinfonietta* (1933), *Sinfonia da requiem* (1940), *Young Person's Guide to the Orchestra* (1946).

Concertos. Piano Concerto (1938, rev. 1945), Violin Concerto (1939, rev. 1958), Symphony for Cello and Orchestra (1963).

Chamber Music. Three string quartets (1941, 1945, 1975; also an early string quartet in D, 1931), Cello Sonata in C (1961), Suites for Cello (1964, 1967, 1972).

Songs and Song Cycles. *Our Hunting Fathers* (1936), *Les illuminations* (1939), *Seven Sonnets of Michelangelo* (1940), *Serenade* (1943), *Holy Sonnets of John Donne* (1945), *Songs and Proverbs of William Blake* (1965), *A Birthday Hansel* (1975).

Choral Music. *A Boy Was Born* (1933), *Ceremony of Carols* (1942), *Rejoice in the Lamb* (1943), *Saint Nicolas* (1948), *Spring Symphony* (1949), *Missa brevis* in D (1959), *War Requiem* (1961).

---

recurrences, and other repetitive patterns. Beginning with the opera *Billy Budd* (1951), Britten spoke with a more dissonant, nontriadic vocabulary and in more concentrated forms. His opera *Turn of the Screw* (1954) and most of his later works reflect a singular adaptation of aspects of the twelve-tone method.

Britten's early style is exemplified by the *Serenade for Tenor, Horn and Strings*, op. 31 (1943). The six songs of this cycle are framed by a Prologue for valveless French horn, repeated offstage as a concluding Epilogue. The poetry ranges from an anonymous medieval lyric to verses by Charles Cotton, Tennyson, Blake, Ben Jonson, and Keats. These texts are linked by references to night, death, love, and evil—all recurrent themes and images in Britten's music. Each of the songs utilizes a repetitive form and each focuses upon some triadic goal which acts as a tonic key.

The Dirge found as the fourth song of the Serenade (Anthology no. 14) sets a chillingly realistic poem of the fifteenth century in Scottish dialect (also used by Stravinsky in his Cantata of 1952). It tells of the horrors of hell that await those who have lacked Christian charity. Its nine stanzas are set vocally by a recurrent ostinato which outlines a G-minor triad. Just as the last judgment will be inexorable and pitiless, the ostinato relentlessly disregards the tortured plaint of the accompanying orchestral fugue.

Voice and orchestra are, however, interrelated by the principal motive of the ostinato—a rising and falling semitone shown in brackets in Example 10-6. The semitone figure is duplicated over a longer span of time by tonal motion underpinning the orchestral music. The orchestra begins on an E♭ triad; at the climax of the movement (rehearsal 17) it arrives on E, and it returns to E♭ for the concluding verse (rehearsal 20).

Britten's first important opera was *Peter Grimes* (1944–45). Its central character, Peter Grimes, is a maladjusted loner who cannot adapt to society and who is finally destroyed by his environment. Like Wozzeck, Petrushka, and Schoenberg's Pierrot, he embodies the recurrent twentieth-century dramatic image of the antihero. The libretto of *Peter Grimes* was written by Montagu Slater, based on the poem *Borough* (1810) by George Crabbe. Grimes is a fisherman in a coastal village in England about 1830. He seeks respect from the townspeople and is distracted by their gossip. As the Prologue opens he is facing an inquest regarding the death of an apprentice who perished during a fishing expedition. Although the death is ruled accidental, Grimes is warned to take no other boys as apprentices.

Peter is supported by Ellen Orford, a widow and former schoolteacher, and by Balstrode, a retired fisherman. Ellen arranges for Grimes to obtain another apprentice, as she believes that only with such assistance can he be successful in his trade and establish a normal existence. But the townsfolk suspect that he is abusing his new assistant, and the men menacingly approach his cottage atop a cliff. Grimes forces the boy out a back door and down the steep cliff to his boat, but the apprentice loses his step and falls to his death.

After several days Grimes returns, totally deranged. He is met by Ellen and Balstrode; the latter tells him that he must take his boat to sea and scuttle it, committing

Example 10-6.   Britten, Serenade for Tenor, Horn and Strings, op. 31, Dirge. Copyright 1944 in U.S.A. by Hawkes & Son (London) Ltd. Renewed 1981. Reprinted by permission of Boosey & Hawkes, Inc.

suicide. Ellen is horrified, but Grimes does as Balstrode commands. As Grimes perishes, the townspeople are seen once again about their daily activities.

The story can be understood on several levels. Most obvious among them is Grimes's implicit homosexuality, a theme addressed many times by Britten, most explicitly in his operatic adaptation of Thomas Mann's *Death in Venice* (1973). In this interpretation Ellen represents a "legitimate" heterosexual alliance, which Grimes desires alternately with a compulsion for boys, the latter invariably proving destructive. Balstrode is his conscience. He tries to put Grimes's aberrations in the best light until Grimes's split personality makes suicide appear the only alternative.

On a more abstract level, Grimes represents a twentieth-century everyman, torn between good and evil, compassion and brutality, acceptance and rebellion, society and isolation. He is destroyed by the conflicting, schizophrenic forces within his very nature and within society.

The opera is divided into a Prologue and three acts, each of two scenes. Orchestral interludes link these seven parts. The acts and scenes are made up from distinct (though connected) subsections or numbers, which include recitatives, arias, large ensembles, and choruses. The music within a number may be a concise closed form (as in the duet of the nieces, Act 1, rehearsal 67) or a through-composed *scena*.

Although Britten generally eschewed Wagnerian through composition, he makes important use of recurrent motives and recurrent sections to underscore parallelisms in the drama. A striking example is the return of the "dawn music" of Act 1, scene 1, at the end of the opera (from rehearsal 53), as Grimes's boat is seen sinking far at sea while the townspeople go about their daily routines.

The music is predominantly diatonic and triadic, which freely creates keys or areas of triadic focus. These tonalities have dramatic functions. The opposition of keys in sharps and those in flats depicts the dichotomies that Grimes represents. This juxtaposition of flats and sharps is presented in the opening phrase of the opera (Example 10-7), which begins on a B♭ triad but moves to an E-major collection at its end. The duet of Ellen and Peter at the end of the Prologue (rehearsal 9) pits Ellen's optimism (four sharps: E major) against Peter's resentment (four flats: F minor). At

interpretation

Woodwinds

the end of the duet, however, he accepts her friendship and
moves into her key of E.

At the beginning of the climactic second scene of Act
3 (rehearsal 47), Grimes's derangement is depicted by the
bitriadic conjunction of D-seventh chords in the chorus
with the E♭ by which the tuba evokes a fog horn. Peter's
music wanders between elements of both chords, showing
that his schizophrenia is by then complete.

Michael Tippett (1905–   ) worked along the same
general lines as Britten during the earlier part of his career.
His music prior to about 1945 was vigorously rhythmic and
contrapuntal with an extended triadic tonality organizing
large passages. He made poignant use of Negro spirituals in
his oratorio *Child of Our Time* (1941). His works of the
1960s reflect more innovative trends in music after the
Second World War in their greater chromaticism, dissonance, and conciseness. Several of these more recent
pieces imitate jazz, and others (such as his *Songs for Dov*)
are quotation collages.

Neoclassicism did not become an enduring common
practice of the twentieth century, which some observers
between the world wars had anticipated. Just as the First
World War had turned many artists away from experimentation, the Second World War made them question the
truthfulness of an artistic language that emphasized classical proportion and serenity. The years after the Second
World War brought a resurgence of the avant-garde, which
we shall discuss in Chapter 12. In the next chapter we
turn to experimental composition in the United States,

which to a large extent laid the groundwork for the postwar revival of the avant-garde.

Bibliography

Paul Hindemith's *A Composer's World* (Garden City, NY, 1961)—based on lectures given in 1949 and 1950—is a detailed statement of his aesthetics; it is the source of all quotations attributed to Hindemith in this chapter, unless otherwise indicated. Hindemith's music is discussed in concise but informative fashion in Ian Kemp's *Hindemith* (London, 1970), and his life is traced by Geoffrey Skelton in *Paul Hindemith: The Man Behind the Music* (New York, 1975).

The Bibliography to Chapter 8 recounts representative writings by and about Stravinsky. Stravinsky's essay "Some Ideas about my Octuor" (1924) is reprinted in Eric Walter White, *Stravinsky: The Composer and his Works* (Berkeley and Los Angeles, 1979), Appendix A. Henri Hell's biography of Poulenc (New York, 1959) outlines this composer's life and works up to 1958; Keith W. Daniel's *Francis Poulenc: His Artistic Development and Musical Style* (Ann Arbor, 1982) is an excellent and thoroughly documented study. Arthur Honegger's *I Am a Composer* (London, 1966) is mainly a polemic on the lack of interest shown in modern music. There is no significant study of his music in English, but Pierre Meylan's *Arthur Honegger* (Frauenfeld and Stuttgart, 1970) gives untechnical descriptions of his works which will be useful to readers of German.

Detailed studies of the music of Benjamin Britten are found in Peter Evans's *The Music of Benjamin Britten* (London, 1979) and Arnold Whittall's *Music of Britten and Tippett* (Cambridge, 1982). A concise account of his life is found in Michael Kennedy's *Britten* (London, 1981). Also see Ian Kemp's *Tippett: The Composer and his Music* (London and New York, 1984).

• 11 •

EXPERIMENTAL MUSIC IN AMERICA

"America," wrote John Cage, "has an intellectual climate suitable for radical experimentation." This was a climate produced in part by America's distance from European traditions and her self-conscious participation in the social and political experiment of democracy. Original expression in the arts and letters in America began in the nineteenth century. The Transcendentalists Ralph Waldo Emerson (1803–82) and his disciple Henry David Thoreau (1817–62) preached an individualism and self-reliance that later contributed to social reform and experiments in cooperative living. The poetry of Walt Whitman (1819–92) used bold and unconventional free verse to celebrate the common man and spirit of democracy. The pragmatic philosophy of Charles Peirce (1839–1914) was influential in both America and Europe, as were the painting of seascapes by Winslow Homer (1836–1910) and abstract techniques of James Whistler (1834–1903).

In American music of the early twentieth century, experimentation was only one of numerous stylistic directions. Composers such as Horatio Parker continued European nineteenth-century traditions, and a younger generation of European-trained composers such as Aaron Copland,

Abstraction in nineteenth-century American painting: James Whistler, *The Angry Sea*. (Courtesy of the Freer Gallery of Art, Smithsonian Institution, Washington, D.C.)

Roy Harris, and Walter Piston (1894–1976), increasingly turned to neoclassicism to seek broader appeal and a distinctively American style. All serious idioms were stimulated by America's energetic popular music.

During the 1920s and 1930s, the musical avant-garde in America became clearly distinct from the neoclassical populism of composers such as Copland. The split between these camps was brought into focus by two important organizations of composers. The modernists were generally allied to the International Composers' Guild (1921–27) and its successor, the Pan-American Association of Composers (1928–34). Both organizations were founded by Edgard Varèse, and Charles Ives, Wallingford Riegger (1885–1961), Carl Ruggles, and Henry Cowell were represented in their concerts. The League of Composers (1923–ca. 1946), on the other hand, was dominated by French-trained musicians of more conservative tastes. Aaron Copland was among its leaders and most notable composers.

While both groups made important contributions to American music between the world wars, the experimentalists laid the groundwork for developments in music in the United States after the Second World War, when the avant

CHARLES E. IVES
(Danbury, Conn., 1874—
New York, 1954)

father=
greatest
influence

The greatest influence upon Ives's career as a musician was his father, George Ives, a municipal band leader and free-thinking experimentalist. The musical impressions of his childhood—his father's experiments, traditional European music, and varieties of American popular music—would be a font of inspiration for all of his later work.

Ives attended Yale University from 1894 to 1898, where he studied music with Horatio Parker. Upon graduation he entered an insurance firm in New York City, beginning a career at which he was immediately successful. In 1907 he opened his own agency, which, by his retirement in 1930, had become the largest life insurance firm in the country.

From his college days until he suffered a heart attack in 1918, he worked with furious dedication as a part-time composer. From 1918 to 1922 he published at his own expense his *Concord* Piano Sonata, the rambling *Essays Before a Sonata,* and a collection of *114 Songs.* After completing work on the contents of this songbook in 1921, he virtually ceased composing. Ives's reputation grew steadily from this time, largely due to efforts of his friend Henry Cowell, who printed Ives's works in his periodical *New Music* and arranged for performances in Europe and America. Performances of the *Concord* Sonata in New York in 1939 by John Kirkpatrick brought additional attention to Ives's music. Ives was awarded the Pulitzer Prize in music in 1947 for his Third Symphony.

Selected Works

Orchestral Music. Four symphonies; fragmentary *Universe* Symphony; *Holidays* Symphony; *Robert Browning* Overture (1912); three orchestral suites ("sets"), the first subtitled *Three Places in New England;* band marches.

Chamber Music. Two piano sonatas (no. 2 subtitled *Concord, Mass., 1840–60*), miscellaneous works for organ including *Variations on America*, two string quartets, four sonatas for violin and piano, experimental music for chamber ensembles including *Central Park in the Dark* (1906), *The Unanswered Question* (ca. 1906), *From the Steeples and the Mountains* (1901), and *Over the Pavements* (ca. 1906–13).

Songs. Approximately 200 songs, ca. 1886–1929. A collection of *114 Songs* was published privately by Ives in 1922.

Choral Music. *67th Psalm* (ca. 1894), *Three Harvest Home Chorales* (ca. 1898–1901), *The Celestial Country* (1898–99), *Let There Be Light* (1901).

garde returned to a position of leadership. Thus we turn in this chapter to the work of outstanding experimentalists in America prior to about 1945.

Composers in New England: Ives and Ruggles

Charles E. Ives (1874–1954) was the first important American modernist of the twentieth century. Although he possessed a good musical education and a respectable knowledge of European music, his culture and aesthetic were self-made. Working in nearly complete isolation from traditional musical institutions and bolstered by great independence of thought, he forged a remarkably advanced musical style.

Music for Ives was an art that expressed spiritual and ethical qualities. Its sources were in the human character rather than in abstract laws of sound and time. There was music to be found in human affairs and in people whom Ives admired. "Thoreau was a great musician," he wrote in *Essays Before a Sonata*, "not because he played the flute but because he did not have to go to Boston to hear 'the Symphony.'" Later in these *Essays* he exclaimed, "My God! What has sound got to do with music!"

Music that spoke from the soul with truth, sincerity, and universality was said by Ives to possess "substance." It was very different, he wrote, from the shallow "manner" of composers such as Wagner and Debussy, which too greatly emphasized form, technique, and aural sensuality. An assertive individualism aimed at financial or material advancement in music also diminished substance. For Ives the great artists of substance were Bach, Beethoven, and writers such as Emerson and Thoreau. Like Jean Cocteau, he proclaimed that art should be drawn from life, not from other works of art. Cocteau might also have envied Ives's assessment of Debussy: "Debussy's content would have been worthier his manner if he had hoed corn or sold newspapers for a living."

In order to imbue his own music with substance, Ives makes it depict the musical landscapes of his memory. Quotations of marches, patriotic tunes, and revival hymns punctuate his works. These tunes were part of his background and soul, and they had to be expressed in his music if it was to be sincere and truthful. "If a man finds that the cadences of an Apache war dance come nearest to his soul," he wrote, "let him assimilate whatever he finds highest of the Indian ideal so that he can use it with the cadences, fervently, transcendentally, inevitably, furiously, in his symphonies, in his operas, in his whistlings on the way to work, so that he can paint his house with them." Ives sometimes tries to capture the powerful but unpolished renditions of country bands or revival singers. Other works are evocative musical impressions of scenes welling up in his memory—Central Park after dark, the Housatonic River at Stockbridge, or the sounds of church bells echoing through the mountains of New England.

His music achieved an emancipation of dissonance far in advance of its time. Dissonance was especially valuable to Ives as it matted the shallow surface of music. "Beauty in music," he writes, "is too often confused with something that lets the ears lie back in an easy chair." Ives's dissonant harmony is sometimes systematically constructed: it may draw upon collections of pitches such as whole-tone or pentatonic scales and use them in ways that preserve intervallic unity. In some works, on the contrary, Ives is not systematic in selecting pitches. In these pieces the musical element resides alternately in a vigorous manner of performance or innovative manipulations of rhythm, space, color, and texture.

Ives was indeed chary of conventional notions of musical unity. "The 'unity of dress' for a man at a ball requires a collar; yet he could dance better without it," he writes. In works such as *The Unanswered Question*, superficial unity is dispelled by a texture consisting of several nonsynchronous streams of sound.

By the end of his apprenticeship at Yale University with Horatio Parker in 1898, Ives had mastered his own highly original musical language. Most of his compositions were written during the next two decades, after which he devoted himself to revising his earlier works and attempting to make them better known. Many pieces were left incomplete or in versions for different media, as Ives rarely composed for a specific performance.

His songs are among his finest music. They reveal the eclectic diversity of his work and contain a cross section of his many styles. The songs belong to three general types. First are those that are tonal, largely triadic, and often in simple repetitive forms. These include early pieces such as "Christmas Carol" and "Memories," settings of German, French, and Italian texts ("Feldeinsamkeit" is an especially handsome example), folk-like tunes ("Side Show" and "Charlie Rutlage"), marching songs ("Circus Band," "Son of Gambolier"), arrangements ("Watchman," "At the River"), and nostalgic narratives ("The Greatest Man"). Except for the earliest songs written under the eye of Horatio Parker, most of these works contain passages of unconventional harmony, melody, or rhythm.

The second type of song is slow, static, mildly dissonant, and atonal. In this category are such examples as "The Innate," "Serenity," "Thoreau," "Indians," and "Afterglow." Third is a more bombastic, aggressively dissonant type, such as "Majority," "From *Paracelsus*," and "From *Swimmers*." These atonal songs make frequent use of whole-tone sets (as in "White Gulls"), tone clusters ("Majority"), and fourth chords ("The Cage").

Quotations from preexistent tunes may appear in any of the three types; they normally occur when the text of the preexistent melody is appropriate to the sentiments of the song in which it is used. Many of the songs freely combine features of two or more types.

An example of a work combining all three types is "From *Paracelsus*" (1921, Anthology no. 12). This song—a reworking of passages from the *Robert Browning* Overture (1912)—sets lines from Browning's closet drama *Paracelsus* (1835). The play fictionalizes thoughts of the sixteenth-century Swiss physician and mystic Philippus Aureolus Paracelsus, and it emphasizes Browning's philosophy of the proper relation of love and knowledge among mankind. Browning was greatly admired by Ives. An interest in transcendental philosophy and a belief that great art sprang from life and experience were shared by both men.

Ives's setting includes passages in each of the three styles described above. It begins with an energetic, dissonant flurry in the piano, settles into a progression in G major in the middle, and ends in dreamy, static atonality. This threefold division corresponds to the three stages in Paracelsus' enlightenment: he is first devoted to power (mm. 1–15), then he perceives its limitations (mm. 16–17), and finally he understands that power must be preceded by love (mm. 17–20).

The opening is bombastically dissonant, marked by busy chromatic lines, chords moving in parallel by semitone, and abrupt disjunctions in register. The song has no stable meter, and its division into measures is free. Whole-tone or nearly-whole-tone harmonies are emphasized as well as pentatonic chords and diatonic sets (triads, seventh chords, and "white key" clusters). All of these harmonies may be observed in Example 11-1 (mm. 10–12). The transition to a passage in G major is accomplished by bitriadic harmonies in measure 15, and the conclusion ("always preceding power . . .") uses whole-tone chords which finally resolve upon the note D.

"Charlie Rutlage" (before 1921, Anthology no. 12) is a predominantly tonal and diatonic song with an atonal middle section. The text, by the Montana rhymester D. J. O'Malley, was drawn from a collection of cowboy ballads. It narrates the passing of the "good cowpuncher" Charlie Rutlage, one of several cowboys who came to nought at roundup time at the X I T Ranch. The outer sections of the song are in a quirky folk-song style; the piece begins in F major and passes quickly through C (measure 6), D (suggested by its dominant, 8–12), B♭ (13–16), and A (16–17). The vocal melody begins with pentatonic motion (mm. 1–7),

Example 11-1. Ives, *Charlie Rutlage.*

which not only enhances its flavor as folk song, but also connects it to pentatonic harmonics later in the piece.

The middle part begins at measure 21 as the voice changes from song to rhythmic narration. The piano spins out a static ostinato figure while the accompanist takes the part of Charlie, calling out "Whoopee ti yi yo, git along little dogies!" to a variant of the opening pentatonic melody. Whole-tone chords and tone clusters bring the music to a frantic climax as Charlie is killed by his falling horse. Solemn pentatonic chords shown in Example 11-2 lead back to the music of the beginning.

Ives's works for instruments include string quartets, violin sonatas, and piano sonatas as well as experimental chamber music, symphonies, and a fragmentary *Universe Symphony* in which creation, evolution, and heaven were to be depicted. Virtually all of his instrumental music is programmatically linked to his philosophical or historical interests.

CDEGA
(pentatonic)

m. 40

F D♯ C♯ B A♯ G♯   D E F♯ A B
(pentatonic   (pentatonic)
superset)

Example 11-2.   Ives, *Charlie Rutlage,* © copyright 1939 by Arrow
Music Press, Inc. Copyright assigned 1957 to Associated
Music Publishers, Inc.

One of his most original orchestral works is *The Unanswered Question* (ca. 1906). This piece is for a chamber ensemble of trumpet, four flutes, and strings, although the instrumentation was intended to be flexible. It was at first subtitled "A Contemplation of a Serious Matter" and was intended to be paired with *Central Park in the Dark*, the latter "A Contemplation of Nothing Serious." *Central Park in the Dark* is a lively orchestral work described by the composer as a "picture-in-sound." It contains several quotations of American tunes. *The Unanswered Question* does not contain quotations, but it exemplifies the contemplative, impressionistic sonority of much of Ives's best music, his adaptation of a philosophical program, and his technique of layering several loosely coordinated musical strata.

In the Foreword to the score, the composer outlines the program of the work, which has to do with the "perennial question of existence" by which mankind is eternally confronted but to which no satisfactory answer can be found. The strings provide the backdrop of the continuum of time. They play serenely and continuously in G major with little definition of beat or meter. The other strata are not precisely coordinated: they react to one another in the free manner of a dialogue. The trumpet states a five-note non-triadic motive which poses the question of life's meaning. The flutes, which represent mankind, seek an answer, beginning softly and slowly, but becoming progressively louder and more animated. As their answers are frustratingly inadequate, they become increasingly shrill and densely chromatic. Example 11-3 shows the final chords of each of their first five statements, which move gradually from a diminished triad to a semitonal cluster. The flutes then gather for a "secret conference" (to quote the composer) and, realizing the futility of their quest, they mock the question derisively (Example 11-4). But their noisy argument is to no avail as the trumpet returns with the unanswered question and the strings continue their endless melody.

Carl Ruggles (1876–1971) shared with his friend Charles Ives a stubborn Yankee individualism, an openness to experimental ideas, and an untiring fondness for dissonance. But their differences in style far outweigh their similarities. Ruggles was not an eclectic like Ives: he hewed to a unified language that banished diatonic structures and strove instead toward chromatic saturation. Ruggles did not use quotations of preexistent music nor was his music as graphically programmatic as Ives's. Much of Ives's music

Thomas Hart Benton, *The Sun-Treader—Portrait of Carl Ruggles.* (Courtesy of The Nelson-Atkins Museum of Art, Kansas City, Missouri.)

depended upon a spirited performance rather than a precise rendition of notated pitches. But Ruggles's music is more consistently organized in pitch, making an accurate reading crucial to its effect.

Ruggles was an exceedingly meticulous worker. His first mature composition was the song "Toys," which he completed at the age 43. His oeuvre remained small, as he devoted himself increasingly in his later years to painting as well as to music. He is best known for a few orchestral works (of which *Sun-Treader*, 1932, is outstanding), the brass ensemble *Angels* (1921), songs, and four *Evocations* (1935–44, rev. 1954) for piano.

Evocation no. 4 will illustrate the austere simplicity, uncompromising dissonance, and strict pitch organization of all of his music. The revised version is dedicated to Charles Ives, a supporter of Ruggles, who died in the year that the revision was made. It shares with much of Ives's music a slow, wistful contemplativeness. The piece is in ternary form with an animated middle section beginning at measure 11 and a varied reprise at measure 25. Constantly

Example 11-5. Ruggles, *Evocation* no. 4 for piano. Revision of 1954, edited by John Kirkpatrick. Original version copyright 1943 by Carl Ruggles. Revised version copyright 1956 by American Music Edition. Reprinted by permission of Theodore Presser Co.

changing tempi and meters and irregular divisions of the beat—characteristics of all of his music—create a "musical prose" akin to the work of Schoenberg. The piece is also Schoenbergian in its chromatic density, avoidance of triadic structures, and certain harmonic relations, but its spare texture and motivic sequences are unlike most of Schoenberg's music.

The texture of the work emphasizes line, which, the composer remarked, "is the basis of all music." Harmonies are built by sustaining melodic notes through a pedaling effect, which is also imitated in orchestral works such as *Sun-Treader*. The line that opens this *Evocation* (Example 11-5) illustrates a guiding melodic principle for Ruggles, by which a pitch class was usually not repeated until the tenth or eleventh note. He rarely constructed lines containing all twelve pitch classes in succession, as in the twelve-tone method, since this would amount, in his words, to "a dog chasing its tail." The opening motive (D G F♯C♯F C) is made so that its sequential repetition in the second measure (B E D♯A♯D A) will produce a recurrence of the first pitch class D as the eleventh note of the line. The chromatic aggregate is then completed by the next two notes, A and A♭.

The *Evocations* use a rudimentary serialism, suggesting that Ruggles was aware of Schoenberg's twelve-tone method. An example in *Evocation* no. 4 is the thirteen-note series of pitches in measures 15–18: G C F♯F B♭E E♭A♭ D D♭G♭C B. This series is a concatenation of forms of its initial trichord (G C F♯), which is spun out by sequential repetitions. The series recurs in retrograde and with an inverted contour in measures 21–23, beginning with the note B-natural.

Composers on the West Coast: Cowell, Cage, Harrison, and Partch

The early works of Henry Cowell (1897–1965) were experimental studies in new musical resources. These include early applications of tone clusters on the piano, noise, and open or "elastic" forms. In the 1940s and 1950s, he produced most of his twenty symphonies, eighteen

Hymns and Fuguing Tunes, music for Asian instruments, and numerous works in other genres, most of which adopt a more conventional style. Cowell was an active supporter of the music of Charles Ives, and Ives generously contributed to Cowell's periodical *New Music Quarterly* (1927–58), in which the scores of several major American composers were first published.

One of Cowell's most resourceful works of the experimental type is "The Banshee" (1925, Anthology no. 7). In this piece the performer produces both fixed and sliding pitches by manipulating strings inside the piano. These sounds suggest the cry of the banshee, a mythical creature in Irish folklore whose unearthly wail forecast death. Fixed pitches establish two recurrent motives. The first, heard in long values at the outset, imitates the funeral chant "Dies irae." The second (mm. 8, 20, 33) is a short motive made from plucking the strings.

"The Banshee" illustrates the expansion of sources of sound that underlies the work of several other American experimentalists. Noise—sounds, that is, of unfixed pitch—had been used earlier by the Italian Futurist Luigi Russolo (1885–1947), but his music was never more than an obscure curiosity. The liberation of sound by Americans such as Cowell, John Cage, and Edgard Varèse, on the contrary, had a lasting impact on the history of musical style, as it laid the foundation for electronic and taped media of the 1950s and led to significant and widespread changes in musical structure.

Cowell referred to music made of noise and sliding pitch in his book *New Musical Resources* (1917–19, rev. ca. 1930):

> Natural sounds, such as the wind playing through trees or grasses, or whistling in the chimney, or the sound of the sea, or thunder, all make use of sliding tones. It is not impossible that such tones may be made the foundation of an art of composition by some composer who would reverse the programmatic concept. . . . Such a composer would build perhaps abstract music out of sounds of the same category as natural sound—that is, sliding pitches—not with the idea of trying to imitate nature, but as a new tonal foundation.

[handwritten margin note: natural noise: nature / sliding tones]

JOHN CAGE
(Los Angeles, 1912-   )

Cage's teachers of music included Richard Buhlig, Adolph Weiss, Henry Cowell, and Arnold Schoenberg. Beginning in 1937 he was active as an accompanist and composer for modern dance groups, and he later toured throughout the world as composer for the Merce Cunningham Dance Company. In 1942 he moved to New York where he quickly established a reputation as a leader of the avant-garde. His study of Zen with Dr. Daisetz Suzuki led to his "chance" music of the early 1950s, work that soon exerted an influence on both European and American composition.

Cage's interests are broad, extending not only to the modern arts but to other fields such as the study of mushrooms. He has been associated with several American universities, including Wesleyan University, the University of Illinois, and the University of California, Davis.

Selected Works

Music for Prepared Piano. *Bacchanale* (1940), *Tossed as it Is Untroubled* (1943), *Perilous Night* (1943–44), *A Book of Music* (two prepared pianos, 1944), Three Dances (two prepared pianos, 1944–45), *Sonatas and Interludes* (1946–48).

Percussion Ensembles. *Imaginary Landscape* nos. 1–5 (1939–52), *Construction* nos. 1–3 (1939–41), *Double Music* (with Lou Harrison, 1941), *Credo in Us* (1942), *Amores* (1936–43 [movements 1 and 4 for solo prepared piano]).

Music for Other Conventional Media. *Seasons* (piano or orchestra, 1947), String Quartet in Four Parts (1949–50), Concerto for Prepared Piano and Chamber Orchestra (1950–51), *Music of Changes* (piano, 1951), *Music for Piano* (nos. 1–84, 1952–56), *Aria* (solo voice, 1958), *Cheap Imitation* (piano, 1969).

Music with Tape or with Live Electronic Manipulation. *Williams Mix* (1952), *Fontana Mix* (1958–59), *Cartridge Music* (1960), *HPSCHD* (1967–69).

Aleatoric Music of Unfixed Medium. 4′ 33″ (1952) (followed by a series of works with durational titles), Variations (1–8, 1958–78), *Theater Piece* (1960), Improvisations (1–4, 1975–80), Quartets 1–8 (1976–77).

This "new tonal foundation"—which would be explored more by Cowell's student John Cage than by Cowell himself—had momentous significance. Not only did it admit to music a new and intriguing palette of sounds, but, more important, it diminished the importance of pitch and interval as the structural bases of music. Cowell helped to set in motion a new understanding of musical form, the ramifications of which would be worked out by major composers in Europe and America after the Second World War.

Cowell's experiments with sounds of variable pitch and noise were carried on by his student John Cage (1912–   ). Cage's works of the early 1930s were chromatic contrapuntal studies, some of which used a type of serialism learned from the music of another of his teachers, Arnold Schoenberg. Cage's music from 1939 through the 1940s dwelled upon new sonorities and innovative ways of organizing them. He was a pioneer in the use of electronic gadgetry to produce musical sounds, and he refined Cowell's methods of manipulating strings within the piano. Several works for percussion ensemble emphasize metallic sonorities reminiscent of oriental music. In pieces such as *Living Room Music* (1940), Cage instructs the percussionists to choose everyday household objects upon which to produce musical sounds.

His most resourceful new musical instrument was the "prepared" piano, which he first used as a solo medium in *Bacchanale* (ca. 1938–40). Objects such as screws, bolts, erasers, and bits of plastic and rubber were placed between the strings of the instrument according to instructions of the composer. The piano was thus transformed into a percussion ensemble which could produce tones of fixed pitch as well as colorful noises. Cage's prepared instrument often approximated the sound of Balinese gamelans, which he had earlier imitated in such percussion ensembles as his three *Constructions* (1939–41).

He matched these innovations in musical timbre with new structural principles. Increasingly, these were determined by rhythmic or durational considerations rather than by harmony, motive, or other configurations of pitches. In an article in *Modern Music* of 1942, Cage states:

> In writing for these sounds, as in writing for percussion instruments alone, the composer is dealing with material that does not fit into the orthodox scales and harmonies. It is therefore necessary to find some other organizing means than those in use for symphonic instruments. The sounds cannot be organized through reference to an underlying fundamental tone since such a tone does not exist. Each sound must be considered as essentially different from and independent of every other sound. . . . Because of the nature of the materials involved, and because their duration characteristics can be easily controlled and related, it is more than likely that the unifying means will be rhythmic.

In a lecture at Black Mountain College in 1948 on Erik Satie, he pointed to the music of Webern and Satie as the earliest in which duration rather than pitch created basic formal patterns. He continued:

> If you consider that sound is characterized by its pitch, its loudness, its timbre, and its duration, and that silence, which is the opposite and, therefore, the necessary partner of sound, is characterized only by its duration, you will be drawn to the conclusion that of these four characteristics of the material of music, duration, that is, time length, is the most fundamental.

Beginning with *Imaginary Landscape* no. 1 (1939), the basic designs of his music were prearranged successions of durations following simple numerical ratios. The *First*

Construction (in Metal) (1939), for example, consisted of sixteen sections that were grouped according to the ratios 4:3:2:3:4. Such durational plans may have been suggested to Cage by the theories of Cowell, who speculated in *New Musical Resources* about the extension of simple integral ratios of the overtone series to all musical parameters.

In his earlier works using predetermined patterns of duration, the ratios that controlled large-scale form were duplicated on the small scale as well. In the *First Construction (in Metal)*, for example, each of the sixteen sections contains sixteen measures. These were grouped by similar instrumentation into a succession of four, three, two, three, and four measures, thus duplicating the large structure. In later works of the 1940s, however, Cage often dispensed with any logical preplanning of small-scale durations. He was content instead to lay out a strictly planned large structure and freely allow these durations to be filled by conventional musical sounds, noise, or silence.

Cage's most substantial work for prepared piano is *Sonatas and Interludes* (1946–48). This 70-minute cycle consists of sixteen sonatas, each in binary form A A B B, and four through-composed interludes. The composer sought to convey in them a panorama of emotions. "After reading the work of Ananda K. Coomaraswamy," he wrote, "I decided to attempt the expression in music of the 'permanent emotions' of Indian tradition: the heroic, the erotic, the wondrous, the mirthful, sorrow, fear, anger, the odious, and their common tendency toward tranquility."

Among these slow and quiet pieces, Sonata no. 5 (Anthology no. 9) is perhaps the most mirthful. Its large form is determined by a prearranged sequence of durations, which may be expressed in numbers of half notes:

As in the *First Construction (in Metal)*, these durations are reduceable to simple numerical ratios, here 4:4:5:5 (equivalent to 36:36:45:45).

The content of each subsection is not so precisely structured; indeed, it is improvisational in character. The pitches in both hands wander chromatically between the notes B and E♭. The sonorous image of this sonata—which is not directly revealed by its notation—resembles a duet between a drum-like left hand and bell sounds in the right. It is thus closely related to the sound of the gamelan.

Cage's music of the 1950s underwent a radical change, as he brought elements of chance into the compositional process and, under the influence of oriental philosophy, questioned the conventional acceptance of art as a form of communication. Both his ideas and music proved immensely influential in the decade after the Second World War, and his work of these years will be taken up again in Chapter 13.

Lou Harrison (1917–) shared much of the background of John Cage, with whom he was closely associated in the 1930s. Like Cage he was a student of Cowell and Schoenberg and active as a composer for dance. He collaborated with Cage in organizing and composing for percussion ensembles, and, like Cage, he was inspired by the sonorities of oriental music. His works contain innovative sources of sound (such as the tin cans so congenial to Cage) and a type of prepared piano in which tacks are inserted into the hammers of the instrument. He composed in conventional genres such as the symphony and concerto, music for percussion ensembles, and works imitating oriental media such as the gamelan.

Harry Partch (1901–74) was an entirely self-made musician. By 1928 he developed a unique technique and philosophy that is described in his book *Genesis of a Music.* The basis of his system is a microtonal scale that divides the octave into forty-three pitches, tones that can be realized on a variety of string, wind, and percussion instruments of his own making. Most of these are based on non-Western or ancient models, and they include devices that he dubbed with exotic names such as the "spoils of war" and the "eucal blossom." Performances of his works are often multimedia events in which dance and recitation play a role.

Edgard Varèse

The French-born Edgard Varèse (1883–1965) may be considered an American composer not only because he spent most of his adult life in this country, but also because his experimental temperament and his eagerness to bring new sounds and formal procedures to music closely allied him to developments among native-born musicians. Varèse, like his mentor Ferruccio Busoni, was a cosmopolitan. He resided alternately in France, Italy, Germany, and America, and he was sympathetic to the culture and musical traditions of all four nations. He was personally acquainted with many of the founders of modernism in France and Germany.

In 1921 Varèse and the harpist Carlos Salzedo founded the International Composers' Guild, which for six years sponsored concerts of modern music in New York City. The Guild was comparable in aim to the Society for Private Musical Performances, which had been organized by Arnold Schoenberg in Vienna three years earlier. Both groups were devoted to performing modern music by composers of all nationalities and styles. In his prospectus for the Guild, Varèse wrote, "The International Composers' Guild refuses to admit any limitation, either of volition or action. The International Composers' Guild disapproves of all 'isms'; denies the existence of schools; recognizes only the individual." Although their programs included works by several European neoclassicists (a movement opposed by Varèse), the Guild was associated primarily with music of the avant-garde. They brought to New York the first American performances of works by Schoenberg, Bartók, Stravinsky, and Varèse himself. In 1928 the Guild was superseded by the Pan-American Association of Composers, in which experimental directions were reinforced by the participation of Henry Cowell, Charles Ives, and the composer-conductor Nicolas Slonimsky.

Varèse's music falls into three chronological and stylistic areas. His works before 1914 consist of pieces for orchestra and an uncompleted opera, all of which were either lost or destroyed. Between 1918 and 1936, after his

EDGARD VARÈSE
(Paris, 1883—New York, 1965)

Varèse's youth was spent in Burgundy—a region to which he was greatly attached—in Turin, where he attended a scientific and technical school, and in Paris where he pursued his musical education at the Schola Cantorum and Conservatory. In 1907 he moved to Berlin, attracted there by opportunities for modern music. His early compositions—all of which were subsequently lost or destroyed—were praised by Richard Strauss, Busoni, and Hugo von Hofmannsthal. He also began his career as an orchestral and choral conductor.

After wartime service in the French army, he immigrated in 1915 to America; he lived in New York for the remainder of his life except for frequent sojourns in France and Germany. He was co-founder of the International Composers' Guild (1921–27) and Pan-American Association of Composers (1928–34), both societies devoted to performances of modern music. In addition to private teaching in New York, he was temporarily associated with the faculties of Columbia University and the International Summer Courses for New Music in Darmstadt.

Selected Works

Orchestral Music. *Amériques* (1918–22), *Arcana* (1925–27).

Chamber Ensembles. *Offrandes* (with voice, 1921), *Hyperprism* (1923), *Octandre* (1923), *Intégrales* (1924), *Ionisation* (percussion ensemble, 1931), *Ecuatorial* (with voice, 1934), *Density 21.5* (solo flute, 1936), *Nocturnal* (with soprano and chorus, unfinished, 1961).

Works with Tape. *Déserts* (tape alternating with instruments, 1954), "Good Friday Procession in Verges" (for the film *Around and About Joan Miró*, 1956), *Poème électronique* (1958).

immigration to the United States, he completed nine works for orchestra or chamber ensemble which realize in conventional media his visionary ideas on musical form and content. After a period of almost two decades when no new works were completed, he pioneered the compositional use of taped electronic sounds.

Varèse emphasizes sound and rhythm, and he dispenses with conventional principles of meter, harmony, texture, and form. He was a crusader for new musical instruments: "I dream of instruments obedient to my thought," he wrote in the journal *391* in 1917, "which, with their contribution of a whole new world of unsuspected sounds, will lend themselves to the exigencies of my inner rhythm."

He hoped to replace conventional textures with mobile interplay among masses of sound. In a lecture in Santa Fe in 1936 he remarked:

> Music as I conceive it [consists in] the movement of sound-masses, of shifting planes. . . . When these sound-masses collide the phenomena of penetration or repulsion will seem to occur. Certain transmutations taking place on certain planes will seem to be projected onto other planes, moving at different speeds and at different angles. There will no longer be the old conception of melody or interplay of melodies. The entire work will be a melodic totality. The entire work will flow as a river flows.

Rhythm was also to be liberated from its confinement to regular pulse and metric organization: "In my own works," he remarked in a lecture in 1959 at Princeton University, "rhythm derives from the simultaneous interplay of unrelated elements that intervene at calculated, but not regular time lapses." Varèse was inspired by science and technology, which is reflected in his choice of musical titles. But his works are written in a nonprogrammatic, nonreferential language:

> There is more musical fertility in the contemplation of the stars—preferably through a telescope—and the high poetry of certain mathematical expositions than in the most sublime gossip of human passions.

> However, there are no planets or theorems to be looked for in my music. Music being a special form of thought can, I believe, express nothing but itself. [From program notes to the first performance of *Intégrales*, 1925.]

The forms of Varèse's music are largely through composed, although most of his works contain localized repetitions and occasional recurrence of harmonies or motives on a larger scale. He rejected the notion that music should be shaped into a preestablished form or composed according to a formal system. Instead, each work establishes its own form, which results from a "process" by which an initial idea is spun into a unique shape by the motor of rhythm and other unspecified forces. "Form is a result—the result of a process," he stated in his Princeton lecture. "Each of my works discovers its own form. . . . There is an idea, the basis of an internal structure, expanded and split into different shapes or groups of sound constantly changing in shape, direction, and speed, attracted and repulsed by various forces. The form of the work is the consequence of this interaction. Possible musical forms are as limitless as the exterior forms of crystals."

The first movement of *Octandre* (1923, Anthology no. 24) illustrates several of these formal characteristics. This work, which is in three short movements, is for a chamber ensemble of eight different instruments. The medium shows Varèse's fondness for the small heterogeneous ensemble that emphasizes woodwinds and brass, but it is untypical in its lack of percussion instruments. The work is freely atonal and chromatic, and it does not consistently project any standard harmonic elements. The composer later stated in notes to *Déserts* (1954) that his music "was not based on any fixed set of intervals such as a scale or series, or any existing principle of musical measurement."

The movement is tied together by varied recurrences of a descending chromatic motive heard in the oboe in the first measure. The motive in its original contour returns at the end of the movement. This figure constitutes the "idea" of internal structure, about which Varèse spoke in his lecture at Princeton. It is freely transformed into blocks of sound—largely of chromatic content—which are juxtaposed, overlapped, or intersected. Typical of Varèse's instrumental music, the parts are often driven to extremes of register; they do not project a stable beat or meter, and their figures are repeated locally before moving on to a new "mass" of sound.

Varèse's music forms a bridge between the European avant-garde of the first two decades of the century and music after World War II. He helped to preserve the spirit of the avant-garde in a period when this movement was abandoned by many. His understanding of musical space as "open rather than bounded" became widespread after the Second World War, even if particulars of his style of "organized sound" were superseded by new musical ideas.

Bibliography

Three excellent surveys of music in the United States are Gilbert Chase, *America's Music*, 2nd ed. (New York, 1966); Wilfrid Mellers, *Music in a New Found Land* (London, 1964); and H. Wiley Hitchcock, *Music in the United States: A Historical Introduction*, 2nd ed. (Englewood Cliffs, N.J., 1974). The symposium *American Composers on American Music*, ed. Henry Cowell (1933), is also of interest.

Frank Rossiter's *Charles Ives and his America* (New York, 1975) is an outstanding study of the composer's life and cultural milieu, but it does not deal in detail with the music. H. Wiley Hitchcock's *Ives* (London, 1977) is a short analytic survey. Ives's own reminiscences or *Memos*, written in 1931 and 1932, have been edited with copious annotations by John Kirkpatrick (New York, 1972); this document served as the basis of the pioneering study of Ives by his friends Henry and Sidney Cowell (1955). Ives's writings are collected by Howard Boatwright in the volume *Essays Before a Sonata, The Majority, and Other Writings* (New York, 1962). The Epilogue to his *Essays* is Ives's most important statement of his musical outlook. An informative and amusing study of Ruggles is John Kirkpatrick's "Evolution of Carl Ruggles: A Chronicle Largely in His Own Words," *Perspectives of New Music*, 6 (1968).

A general survey of the music of Henry Cowell is found in Hugo Weisgall's "Music of Henry Cowell," *Musical*

Quarterly, 45 (1959). Cowell's *New Musical Resources* (New York, 1969) was written in 1919, before he had developed his mature musical style, but it reveals his experimental spirit. Articles and lectures by Cage are collected in *Silence* (1961), *A Year from Monday* (1967), *M* (1973), and *Empty Words* (1979), and other statements by and about Cage are in Richard Kostelanetz, ed., *John Cage* (New York, 1970). A concise study of his music is by Paul Griffiths, *Cage* (London, 1981).

Louise Norton Varèse's engagingly written biography *Varèse: A Looking-Glass Diary*, vol. 1 (New York, 1972) traces her husband's life and career to 1928. It is supplemented by several articles by his student Chou Wen-Chung: "Varèse: A Sketch of the Man and His Music," *Musical Quarterly*, 52 (1966) and "Open Rather Than Bounded," *Perspectives of New Music*, 5 (1966). Varèse's lectures at Santa Fe (1936), the University of Southern California (1939), Princeton (1959), and Yale (1962) are summarized in the article "Liberation of Sound," *Perspectives of New Music*, 5 (1966), and his illuminating "Conversation" with Gunther Schuller is recorded in the same journal, 3 (1965).

◆

Music from 1945 to the Present

◆

◆ *12* ◆

THE REVIVAL OF THE AVANT-GARDE

As Europe emerged from the chaotic aftermath of World War II, it appeared likely that neoclassicism would remain in the dominant position that it occupied before the war. Many of the leaders of modernism earlier in the century were now in retirement or in exile: Berg and Webern were dead, and Schoenberg had not established a following in America as he earlier had in Europe. Works by Hindemith and Stravinsky seemed destined to become the models for musical developments in the postwar years.

But the decade after the Second World War was instead a period of dramatic and far-reaching innovations in style which pushed neoclassicism far from the center of attention. The war thus had the opposite effect of the First World War, which had temporarily halted progressivism as an important trend in music. For many artists the legacy of the Second World War was a cynical view of the human condition and psyche that called for a clean slate. Elliott Carter remarked that his conversion from neoclassicism was provoked by his realization that violence was an unavoidable part of human nature. He says in *Flawed Words and Stubborn Sounds:*

> Before the end of the Second World War, it became
> clear to me, partly as a result of rereading Freud and
> others and thinking about psychoanalysis, that we
> were living in a world where this physical and intel-
> lectual violence would always be a problem and that
> the whole conception of human nature underlying
> the neoclassic esthetic amounted to a sweeping
> under the rug of things that, it seemed to me, we
> had to deal with in a less oblique and resigned way.

Similarly in Europe the leading younger composers
ruthlessly dismissed the musical language of their forebears. Pierre Boulez, for example, proclaimed serialism to be
the only path for future development. "I . . . assert that
any musician who has not experienced—I do not say
understood, but, in all exactness, experienced—the necessity for the dodecaphonic language is USELESS. For his whole
work is irrelevant to the needs of his epoch" (from "Even-
tuellement," 1952).

In this and the following two chapters, we shall trace
several major developments in music during the postwar
decades. The two principal innovations of this period—
indeterminacy and electronic composition—will be surveyed in Chapters 13 and 14. In this chapter we focus upon
the revival of atonality and extension of serialism. Prior to
the Second World War serialism was largely restricted to
the music of Schoenberg and his circle. But after the war it
underwent a great expansion, both in its modes of application and in the number of composers who used at least
some of its principles. Numerous neoclassicists of the
1930s and 1940s now became serialists of some description:
in America the conversion of Igor Stravinsky to serial composition was a major historical development, and Roger
Sessions and Aaron Copland also devised their own free
serial procedures. In Europe Benjamin Britten used serial
methods in his opera *The Turn of the Screw* and in later
works, and the Italian composer Luigi Dallapiccola became a
devoted adherent to this technique.

Atonality and Serialism in America: Carter, Stravinsky, and Babbitt

The evolution of style in music by Elliott Carter (1908–   ) mirrors the general transformation in American musical culture from cautious experimentation in the 1920s to neoclassicism in the 1930s to avant-garde innovations in the decades following the Second World War. Carter's mature style was formed in the late 1940s, when he dispensed with his earlier neoclassical populism—an idiom that he then dismissed as "music for a masquerade in a bomb shelter." Yet Carter also kept his distance from the experimental directions of American and European composers of the postwar era. He writes in traditional genres for conventional media, and he has not adopted techniques of serialism. He is especially chary of the emancipation of sound so congenial to American experimentalists since Varèse. "I don't believe in novelty of sound for its own sake," he said in *Flawed Words and Stubborn Sounds.*

Carter has been most resourceful in his attempts to establish a new temporal organization in music:

> The flow of the music [is] the most important thing; the "now" of any given point to me is only as significant as how it came to be "now" and what happens afterward. Therefore to me composing consists in dealing with the flow of music rather than with particular instants of sound, which is why I've never been so interested in remarkable sounds or effects of any kind for themselves alone, because they seem to evoke a very elementary past or future. [From *Flawed Words.*]

To explore the flow of music, he first dispensed with traditional temporal processes such as regular meter, a single common pulse in all parts, and regular divisions of the beat. He also eliminated the demarcation of time brought about by a thematic or motivic statement followed by its development. In place of these conventional ways of organizing time, Carter erected intricate contrapuntal textures con-

ELLIOTT CARTER
(New York, 1908—)

A fascination with the avant-garde compositions of Stravinsky, Scriabin, and Varèse led Elliott Carter toward the career of a professional composer. He was introduced to Charles Ives in 1924, with whom he maintained personal contact until the early 1930s. Carter attended Harvard University from 1926 to 1932, dividing his interests in music with the study of other arts and letters. On advice of his teacher Walter Piston, he traveled to France in 1932 to study with Nadia Boulanger.

He returned to America in 1935 and became musical director of the newly formed Ballet Caravan. Subsequently, he held teaching positions in music and in the humanities at several American universities and conservatories. Among his many awards and honors is the Pulitzer Prize, which he received in 1960 for his Second String Quartet.

Selected Works

Orchestral Music and Concertos. *Holiday* Overture (1944); Variations for Orchestra (1953–55); Piano Concerto (1963–65); Concerto for Orchestra (1970); Double Concerto for Harpsichord and Piano and Two Chamber Orchestras (1961); Symphony of Three Orchestras (1976–77).

Chamber Music. 3 String Quartets (1951, 1960, 1971); Brass Quintet (1974); Sonata for Cello and Piano (1948); Piano Sonata (1945–46); Eight Pieces for Four Timpani (1950–1968); Eight Etudes and a Fantasy for Woodwind Quartet (1950); Sonata for Flute, Oboe, Cello, and Harpsichord (1952–53); Duo for Violin and Piano (1974); *Night Fantasies* for piano (1979–80).

Songs and Vocal Ensembles. *A Mirror on Which to Dwell*
(soprano, instruments) (1976); *Syringa* (mezzo-soprano, bass,
instruments) (1978).

---

sisting of distinct strata which progressively interchange
features. Such compositions become, in his words, "large,
unified musical actions or gestures."

Each line or stratum in a work by Carter normally begins with its own "personality," created by a unique combination of tempo, rhythmic figures, intervals, and expressive
gestures. These personalities subsequently interact as characters in an inarticulate drama: they dominate momentar-
ily or recede into the background, they take on the features
of other characters, and they evolve within themselves.

The First String Quartet (1951) is one of Carter's earliest works in this mature style. It combines a three-
movement and a four-movement shape. The more essential
form consists of four connected parts: fantasia, allegro
scorrevole, adagio, and variations. But the traditional pauses
between movements occur, first, within the allegro section
and then within the variations, thus creating an apparent
three-movement cycle. The composer wished to avoid a
pause at a major change of tempo since these are climactic
moments in a work with almost constant changes of speed.

The First String Quartet is unusual among Carter's
works after 1950 in its substantial amount of motivic
development and recurrence. A large number of motives are
introduced throughout the fantasia, for example, and these
recur freely in different shapes in a through-composed continuum. The ongoing development is broken only by a brief
reprise at measure 138 and by a climactic stretto beginning
at measure 213, where several earlier themes are brought
back simultaneously. This latter passage also functions as a
transition to the second of four movements (allegro scorrevole) beginning at measure 356.

Important themes and motives are often presented
simultaneously, each establishing a character of its own by
intervallic contour as well as by its own tempo, dynamic

level, playing technique, and expression. The passage beginning at measure 22 is an example of such a simultaneous exposition. Here, five important themes are heard (the one in the second violin had been introduced in measure 12). Each theme is extremely simple in rhythm, moving almost entirely by equal values. But each moves at a different pace with different expressive gestures. These are summarized in Example 12-1, where the rhythm of each theme is renotated in quarter notes.

After this expository passage, the pacing in each part begins a continuous process of change, which is carried on by metric modulations (see Chapter 5). Each of the five themes occasionally darts out in new guises and, having had its brief moment in the spotlight, recedes into the "flow" of passing time.

The main antecedent of Carter's temporal and polyphonic idiom is the music of Charles Ives. Carter was acquainted with Ives in the 1920s in New York City, but he was later critical of the untutored quality of much of Ives's work. Ives's innovations in texture nevertheless became Carter's point of departure for all of his mature music. Perhaps in homage to this influence, Carter quotes the bass line of the opening of Ives's First Sonata for Violin and Piano as the cello theme in measure 27 of the First String Quartet.

Ives's *Unanswered Question* (discussed in Chapter 11) is an example of polyphonic stratification of distinct but interactive lines—a concept that reappears with greater abstraction in Carter's First String Quartet. Each of the three strata of *The Unanswered Question* has its own tempo and dramatic character. Like the lines of the First String Quartet, strata of *The Unanswered Question* reflect upon one another, for example, when the woodwinds sneeringly imitate the line of the trumpet. Ives's use of metric modulation in the *Robert Browning* Overture (see Chapter 5) prefigures its appearance in Carter's music.

Carter organizes his music to a considerable extent by recurring pitch-class sets. Usually one or more sets will emerge as central, made especially evident at important structural junctures. In the First String Quartet these focal harmonies are the two all-interval tetrachords equivalent to those shown in Example 2-21. These sets are prominent in the opening cello cadenza (Example 12-2). All-interval

1. Violin 2

♩ = 120

pizz.

m. 22 *f marc.*

(♩ = 96)

2. Cello

♩ = 120

m. 22

(♩ = 120)

3. Violin 1

♩ = 120

m. 22 *mp tranquillo*

(♩ = 36)

4. Viola

♩ = 120

m. 25 *f marc., détaché*

(♩ = 180)

3. Cello

♩ = 120

in fuori

m. 27 *f sost. e cant.*

(♩ = 48)

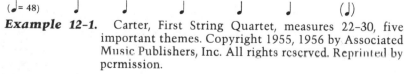

Example 12-1. Carter, First String Quartet, measures 22–30, five important themes. Copyright 1955, 1956 by Associated Music Publishers, Inc. All rights reserved. Reprinted by permission.

337

Example 12-2.   Carter, First String Quartet, first movement, measures 1–12 (cello), rhythm omitted. Copyright 1955, 1956 by Associated Music Publishers, Inc. All rights reserved. Reprinted by permission.

tetrachords were attractive to Carter as unifying sonorities precisely because they contain all of the interval classes. Each interval is subsequently assigned to one of the lines, helping to mold its distinctive personality. Just as the lines occasionally merge into a single stratum, the intervallic repertories of the lines occasionally come together in these focal harmonies.

In later music Carter availed himself of other sets with similarly comprehensive arrays of subsets. In the Piano Concerto, for example, he uses a hexachord as a referential harmony which has the unique property of containing all the possible types of equivalent trichords (of which there are twelve). One form of this "all-trichord" hexachord is C C♯ D E G G♯. The trichords that it contains are distributed within the different strata to reinforce their essentially distinctive characters.

In more recent compositions such as the Third String Quartet and Symphony of Three Orchestras, the central unifying harmony is a chord of all twelve notes between which each of the eleven intervals of the octave is stated once. The central all-interval harmony of the Third String Quartet is shown in Example 12-3 together with a realization of it (lacking the highest note A♭) in measure 15. Elsewhere the intervals of this chord are parceled out between the work's two "duos" (violin 2–viola and violin 1–cello) and among its various sections.

After the completion of his opera *The Rake's Progress* (1951), a work based on the style of Mozart's Italian comic operas, Igor Stravinsky began an evolution toward a more chromatic idiom in which serialism would play an ever larger role. Between 1951 and 1957 he experimented with various approaches to serial composition which were intermingled with diatonic music of a more traditional type. His first completely twelve-tone work was *Threni* (1958), a choral piece whose texts are drawn from Lamentations. The twelve-tone method was also applied in other late works including *Movements* (for piano and orchestra, 1959), Variations (for orchestra, 1964), and *Requiem Canticles* (1966).

Stravinsky's adoption of the twelve-tone method was the last of his major changes of musical orientation. It was a transformation of compositional method also accompanied by a significant change of style, as his music became not only more chromatic but also more abstract and concise. Of many factors that contributed to this new language, probably the most decisive was Stravinsky's encounter in the early 1950s with the music of Webern. His assistant Robert Craft, who was instrumental in bringing Webern's music to Stravinsky's attention, wrote in the magazine *Score* (1957):

Example 12–3.   Carter, Third String Quartet, central all-interval harmony and realization in measure 15. © Copyright 1973 by Associated Music Publishers, Inc. All rights reserved. Reprinted by permission.

In the years between 1952 and 1955 no composer can have lived in closer contact with the music of Webern. Stravinsky was familiar with the sound of the Webern Cantatas and of the instrumental songs at a time when some of these works had not yet been performed in Europe. The challenge of Webern has been the strongest in his entire life. It has gradually brought him to the belief that serial technique is the possible means of musical composition.

At the time of the premiere of *Pierrot lunaire* in 1912, Stravinsky was favorably disposed toward the music of Schoenberg and his circle, despite its stylistic differences with his own work. But by the 1920s, a personal estrangement arose between the two composers that permanently eliminated artistic contact between them. Schoenberg's death in 1951 removed whatever personal barriers may have existed between Stravinsky and Viennese serialism, and his "musical appetite" soon led him to digest and reinterpret this idiom as he earlier had done with the languages of Glinka, Tchaikovsky, Rimski-Korsakov, Bach, Weber, and Verdi.

The ballet *Agon* is a masterpiece of Stravinsky's transition to the twelve-tone method. Since its composition (1953–57) spanned virtually this entire period of change, it is a paradigm of the composer's stages from diatonic neoclassicism to twelve-tone serialism. The ballet has no narrative scenario; it is instead an abstract "competition" (suggested by the title) among twelve dancers. The number 12 is also evident in the large structure of the work, which consists of four groups each of three dances. The groups are connected by related transitional music.

The opening movement, "Pas-de-quatre," begins with nearly diatonic motion, progressing to a chromatic passage in the middle. This music, which was composed in 1953 and which is nonserial, is also used as a coda to conclude the ballet. The music of the interludes was likewise among the first composed, and, like the Pas-de-quatre, it progresses from the diatonic to the chromatic.

Dances from the middle two groups are adaptations of seventeenth-century dance genres: a saraband in stately triple time, a lively galliard, and three branles. These and the three movements of the final group exhibit different approaches to serialism: rows containing different numbers of notes are used, and their application to lines and chords is either strict or free in order.

An example of this mixed structure is the "Bransle gay," the second movement of the third major subdivision. The *branle gay* was a popular social dance in France in the sixteenth and seventeenth centuries, given its name by the participants' swinging or shaking motions. In Stravinsky's adaptation, castanets keep a dance rhythm in triple meter, but the other parts mix duple and triple figures. The movement has a concise A B A' shape in which the B section begins at measure 321 and the reprise at measure 332. Pitches of the A section are strictly determined in order by a six-note row:

$$P_0: B \ D \ C \ F \ E\flat \ B\flat$$

The row is used in all four basic transformations and in numerous transpositions. Somewhat unusual in Stravinsky's serial music of this time is the distribution of notes from row forms into several parts rather than strict confinement in a single voice. Thus P_0 is divided among three instruments at its first entrance in measure 311 (Example 12-4).

The end of the B section (mm. 328–31), on the contrary, departs from the row and uses instead the complementary hexachord of P_0 as an unordered pitch-class set. The derivation of this set from P_0 is illustrated in Example 12-5. The row of the preceding movement, "Bransle simple," is a transposed ordering of this complement. But the order established there is not observed in these measures, which return instead to atonal harmonic principles in which order plays no systematic role.

Flutes 1-2

Bassoon

Example 12-4. Stravinsky, *Agon*, measure 311. Copyright © 1957 by Boosey & Hawkes, Inc. Reprinted by permission.

Example 12-5.   Complementary hexachords in Stravinsky's *Agon*.

One final detail should be observed. The chord in the strings and harp that concludes the B section is made up from the complementary hexachord shown in Example 12-5, with the pitch class G♯ split off as a grace note in the cello. The resulting five-note subset is shown in Example 12-6. This chord has a decidedly "Stravinskian" sound, first, because it contains the familiar dominant seventh chord, but also because it is a five-note subset of the octatonic scale (which would be completed by adding the notes A♯, C, and D♯). Throughout his early serial music, Stravinsky finds many such ways of asserting diatonic and octatonic sets, which are the common property of all his periods and styles of composition.

The orchestral Variations are among Stravinsky's late works which most reflect the style of Webern. Like Webern's Variations for Piano, op. 27, this work contains no distinct theme. It consists instead of variations upon precompositional materials, including a twelve-tone row and configurations of rhythm and instrumentation. As in Webern's music there is great abstraction, conciseness, and a texture that projects short, disjunct figures with wide leaps and frequent changes of instrumental color.

The Variations are divided into twelve sections (at mm. 1, 23, 34, 40, 47, 59, 73, 86, 95, 101, 118, and 130), and, as in *Agon*, the number 12 is also operative in other dimensions. There is virtually no motivic recurrence, development, or conventional variation, but the final sec-

(mm. 330-331)

Example 12-6.   Stravinsky, *Agon*, measures 330–331. Copyright © 1957 by Boosey & Hawkes, Inc. Reprinted by permission.

tion alludes to some of the rhythmic and textural figures of the opening. The second, fifth, and eleventh sections—which Stravinsky called "twelve-part variations" referring to their number of distinct voices—are rhythmically and metrically interrelated.

The Variations exemplify Stravinsky's techniques of twelve-tone composition in his late music. The basic series (as in works by Schoenberg) is conceived as a motivic shape, although this motive plays no further role in the piece. The series resembles those favored by Berg, since its first half is nearly diatonic:

P_0: D C A B E A♯ G♯ C♯ D♯ G F♯ F.

But, unlike the twelve-tone works of Berg and unlike most of Stravinsky's earlier serial music, the Variations contain virtually no diatonic, triadic, or octatonic sets.

Stravinsky uses the series in all of its basic forms. He emphasizes the inversion of the untransposed retrograde, which in this series is identical to the row form RI_6. The basic row forms, however, are outweighed in importance by rotational forms, both the hexachordal transposition-rotations explained in Chapter 4 and transposition-rotations made from entire series.

Milton Babbitt (1916–   ) took his point of departure as a composer from the serial works of Schoenberg and Webern. He extended the principle of order in the twelve-tone method to encompass virtually all aspects of music. Pitch, point of attack, dynamics, register, and timbre are chosen by precompositional arrangements, which are themselves interrelated since they are all derived from the basic tone row. Babbitt's development of this closed system was facilitated by his use of a mathematical model to represent elements and operations of the twelve-tone system. Through this model he made great contributions to systematic analysis of twelve-tone music and suggested avenues for the analysis of all atonal music. Aspects of Babbitt's analytic and compositional methods are discussed further in Chapter 4 and Chapter 5.

Babbitt developed his brand of integral serialism independently of related phenomena among European composers of the late 1940s and early 1950s. Unlike the Europeans, who had departed from strict serialism by the late 1950s, Babbitt has maintained its methods to the present day. His music includes works for chamber ensemble and orchestra, songs, and pieces for tape with or without live performers. These works are usually abstract and concentrated studies which do not rely upon unusual colors, motivic development, or programmatic associations for their meaning. In *All Set* (1957) he imitates sounds and rhythms of a jazz ensemble, showing the flexibility of his serial procedures. In other works, such as his three String Quartets, there is a homogeneity of rhythm that is a by-product of his method of serializing points of attack.

In several writings, Babbitt suggests that the listener must be able to perceive the intricate relationships that underlie his compositional method in order to understand his music. In his article "Who Cares If You Listen?" he points to the high degree of efficiency, determinacy, and autonomy of his music. He adds: "Compositions so rooted necessarily ask comparable knowledge and experience from the listener. Like all communication, this music presupposes a suitably equipped receptor." We shall return to works by Babbitt in the next chapter on electronic music.

Serialism in Europe: Stockhausen and Boulez

The expansion of serial composition among European composers following the Second World War is all the more remarkable since twelve-tone works by Schoenberg, Berg, and Webern had been virtually unavailable and unheard since the 1930s. European serialism after the war was catalyzed by two factors: the International Summer Courses for New Music in Darmstadt and the influence of Olivier Messiaen. The school in Darmstadt was founded in 1946 and soon became a meeting place for the emerging avant-garde. Here the music of Schoenberg and Webern was performed and studied. By the early 1950s integral serialism had become virtually synonymous with the compositional approach of its participants.

Also of importance to the onset of postwar European serialism was Olivier Messiaen, who was present in Darmstadt in 1949 and whose teaching attracted some of the outstanding younger composers of this period, including Karlheinz Stockhausen, Pierre Boulez, and Karel Goeyvaerts. Messiaen was not a serialist, but his great eclecticism and resourceful experimentation suggested procedures and styles that were then developed by his students in the serial idiom. His piano étude "Mode de valeurs et d'intensités" (1949) was especially influential. A mode for Messiaen is a preestablished, unordered set of musical elements, normally pitches. In this work he uses not only modes of pitch but also—as the title states—modes of durations and dynamics. Most important, the elements of these modes are linked together by a precompositional arrangement (see Chapter 4). A texture is produced in which traditional melody, accompanimental chords, and motivic developments are either absent or little in evidence. Instead, the music draws attention to individual notes, which burst forth in a panoply of sounds but which seem unconnected to any larger context. *Indiv.*

Karlheinz Stockhausen (1928–) used the term *punctual* (or "pointillist") to describe the texture of this piece, by which he was greatly inspired. "Pointillist—Why?," he asked. "Because we hear only single notes, which might exist for themselves alone, in a mosaic of sound." Stockhausen found an even more pronounced pointillism in music by Webern, which, unlike Messiaen's étude, used silence to aid in the disruption of linear associations and which applied strict twelve-tone order to insure unity and continuity. The combination of pointillist textures and serial organization would guide Stockhausen's early works after 1951. *pointillist & serialist*

Kreuzspiel (*Cross Play*, 1951) was his first exploitation of serial pointillism. This work is for oboe, bass clarinet, piano, and percussion; it is in three connected sections, each marked by a change of tempo. *Kreuzspiel* is opened by an introduction (mm. 1–13) which prefigures aspects of both the first section (motor rhythms in the drum-like tumbas) and second section (trichordal harmonies of the piano). The third section likewise combines features from the first two. The introduction and first section are found in Anthology no. 26.

KARLHEINZ STOCKHAUSEN
(Cologne, 1928—   )

Following the disruption of World War II, Stockhausen continued his musical and general education. In 1947 he enrolled at the Cologne Hochschule für Musik where he pursued mainly piano playing. He also attended lectures in the humanities at the University of Cologne. He studied composition briefly with Frank Martin in 1950 and earned his living as a jazz pianist. His career was furthered by the critic and composer Herbert Eimert, at whose urging Stockhausen first attended the International Summer Courses for New Music at Darmstadt in 1951. The following year he studied in Paris with Olivier Messiaen, during which time he was also an apprentice in the studio for *musique concrète* at the French Radio.

In 1953 he joined Eimert at the newly founded studio for electronic music of the North West German Radio in Cologne. He also studied phonetics with Werner Meyer-Eppler at Bonn University. He has frequently returned to Darmstadt to lecture on various subjects, and he regularly tours around the world to arrange performances of his music. He has been engaged since 1964 in a group for the performance of his own live electronic works.

Selected Works

Orchestral Music. *Spiel* (1952, rev. 1973), *Gruppen* (1955–57), *Carré* (1960, with choruses), *Momente* (1961–64, various later realizations), *Hymnen* (1969, with tape, various versions), *Fresco* (1969), *Trans* (1971), *Inori* (1974).

Chamber Music. *Kreuzspiel* (1951), *Kontra-Punkte* (1952–53), *Klavierstücke 1–11* (1952–56, some pieces later rev.), *Zeitmasze* (1955–56), *Zyklus* (1959), *Refrain* (1959), *Adieu* (1966), *Stimmung* (1968), *Amour* (1976).

Works for Tape (with or without instruments). *Gesang der Jüng-linge* (1955–56), *Kontakte* (1959–60), *Telemusik* (1966).

Live Electronic Works. *Mikrophonie* I–II (1964–65), *Mixtur* (1964), *Prozession* (1967), *Kurzwellen* (1968, various versions), *Mantra* (1970), *Ylem* (1972).

Works for Unspecified Instrumentation. *Plus-Minus* (1963), *Aus den sieben Tagen* (1968), *Sternklang* (1971).

In its rigorous application of serial procedures and elaborate preplanning, *Kreuzspiel* resembles Boulez's *Structures Ia* (see Chapters 4 and 5), which was also partly composed in 1951. Stockhausen uses simultaneous series governing the placement of attacks, dynamics, and register. A twelve-tone series controls the choice of pitches in the piano and woodwinds, but the composer does not use any of the classical transformations of the basic series associated with Schoenberg. Instead he employs forms made by shifting elements from the middle of a series progressively toward the outside. This process was inspired by Messiaen, who experimented with similar ways of permuting rows, which he called "interversion."

The "cross play" mentioned in the title refers to this method of generating row forms. It also alludes to the audible impression made by the piece, especially in its disposition of register and density. In the first section (mm. 14–91), for example, the music begins with a relatively uncluttered texture of piano, tom-toms, and tumbas (conga drums). The notes in the piano are placed in either the very high or very low registers. By the middle (mm. 50–70), the texture has become dense and busy, with the woodwind instruments playing in the middle register. Toward the end of the section, the opening texture and registral extremes gradually return, but notes from the high register at the beginning have crossed into the low register and vice-versa. Music which thus mediates between extremes soon became a preoccupation for Stockhausen.

Kreuzspiel subtly evokes the free rhythms of jazz by its irregular accents and lazy ostinato in the tumbas. The choice of tom-toms, tumbas, wood block, and suspended cymbals also suggests the timbre of African music, an exotic element that was common to works by Messiaen and his students at this time. Like Stockhausen's later music, *Kreuzspiel* makes a large gesture in sound and time that has little to do with the grammar of thematic statement, development, and return so crucial to the musical language of earlier times.

Stockhausen continued to refine this idiom of serial pointillism in other works of the early 1950s, including *Formel* (1951), *Spiel* (1952), *Schlagtrio* (1952), *Punkte* (1952), *Kontra-Punkte* (1952–53), and the early *Klavierstücke* (1952–53). But his apprenticeship at the studio for *musique concrète* at the French National Radio in Paris in 1952 led him increasingly into electronic media of composition and toward new stylistic directions. We shall return to the works of this composer in the next two chapters.

The music of Pierre Boulez (1925–   ) from the time of his Sonatina for flute and piano (1946) applies twelve-tone procedures, which he had learned from his teacher René Leibowitz. Boulez's intricate rhythmic idiom, evocations of non-Western music, and fondness for pointillist textures stem in part from Olivier Messiaen, with whom Boulez had earlier studied at the Paris Conservatory.

Boulez quickly formed a rigid attachment to integral serialism. In his article "Schoenberg is Dead" (1952), he rashly dismisses the music of Schoenberg for its formal traditionalisms. "The confusion in twelve-tone works between the theme and the series," he wrote, "shows clearly enough his inability to foresee the world of sound brought into being by the tone row." Boulez may have overlooked the extent to which the row in Schoenberg's music influences all formal elements, a phenomenon that Boulez thought limited among pre-war serialists to the works of Webern. It is also doubtful that Webern had any less allegiance to traditional forms than did Schoenberg.

Boulez's strictest essay in integral serialism was his *Structures Ia* for two pianos (1951–52). Here he achieved the elimination of traditional textures for which use he had berated Schoenberg. Aspects of the compositional technique of this work are surveyed in Chapters 4 and 5. But Boulez did not long remain a doctrinaire serialist. He soon

PIERRE BOULEZ
(Montbrison, 1925—)

Pierre Boulez began his advanced education in music in 1942 at the Paris Conservatory, where he studied with Olivier Messiaen among others. He was also tutored in twelve-tone techniques by René Leibowitz. In 1954 he collaborated in the founding of the Domaine Musical, a concert organization devoted to modern music which he subsequently conducted. His early compositions were heard at the Donaueschingen Festival and the International Summer Courses for New Music at Darmstadt. He has also been active as a writer of polemics on music and musicians. He took up residence in Germany in 1958.

Boulez became internationally renowned as an orchestral conductor in the 1960s, and he served as musical director of the New York Philharmonic Orchestra from 1971 to 1978. He now resides in Paris where he is director of the Institut de Recherche et de Coordination Acoustique/Musique.

Selected Works

Orchestral Music. *Le soleil des eaux* (with voices, 1948), *Livre pour cordes* 1968, revision of *Livre pour quatuor*, 1949), *Pli selon pli* (soprano and orchestra, 1957–62, consisting of revisions of several earlier works, including three *Improvisations sur Mallarmé*).

Chamber Music. Sonatina for flute and piano (1946), *Le visage nuptial* (with voices, 1946), *Le marteau sans maître* (1954, rev. 1957), *Domaines* (1968, rev. 1969), *Éclat* (1965, later rev.), *e. e. cummings ist der Dichter* (chorus and chamber orchestra, 1970), *. . . explosante-fixe . . .* (1971), *Messagesquisse* (for celli, 1977).

Piano Music. Three sonatas (1946, 1948, 1957), *Structures* for two pianos (two books, 1952, 1961).

evolved serial techniques in a very different direction from
either Webern or his own contemporaries. In his article
"Auprès et au loin" (1954), he suggests that the principle of
order is not essential to serialism: "The serial phenomenon," he wrote, "is not constituted of the successive
unfolding of the elements that it puts into relation. The
series is not an order of succession." Serialism became for
Boulez a private compositional approach that aided him
in choosing compositional materials and in achieving
certain stylistic goals, but that did not automate the order
in which compositional choices were made. This flexible
serialism led to music in which there was an even distribution of all chromatic pitch classes and registers, elimination of regular pulse and meter, a variety and apparent
spontaneity of color, and elimination of textures of traditional homophony and polyphony. Strict serial organization
of pitch cannot be found in his music after 1953 except in
isolated passages.

   Le marteau sans maître (*The Hammer Without Master*,
1954, rev. 1957) is Boulez's most widely imitated work in
the postserial idiom. This is a setting of three surrealist
poems by René Char (1907–) drawn from an anthology of
the same title. Boulez's setting joins an alto voice with varying combinations of alto flute, guitar, viola, vibraphone,
xylorimba, and miscellaneous percussion. The work has
nine movements of which four are vocal; the others are
instrumental glosses upon the poetry, which are intertwined in this order:

1. Before L'artisanat furieux (instrumental)
2. Commentary I to Bourreaux de solitude (instrumental)
3. L'artisanat furieux (vocal/instrumental)
4. Commentary II to Bourreaux de solitude (instrumental)
5. Bel édifice et les pressentiments (vocal/instrumental)
6. Bourreaux de solitude (vocal)
7. After L'artisanat furieux (instrumental)
8. Commentary III to Bourreaux de solitude (instrumental)
9. Bel édifice variation (vocal/instrumental)

   Each movement is uniquely orchestrated, ranging in
complexity from a simple duet for flute and voice (third
movement) to the climactic ninth movement where the
voice, all pitched instruments, and most of the percussion

are called into service. This finale dramatizes the relationship of voice and instruments that had been intimated earlier. Just as the narrator of the poem talks of being engulfed
by the ocean's waves, the vocal line is swallowed up by the
instruments and sings its last passage in a wordless
vocalization.

Char's poetry is Expressionistic in its images of violence and death and surrealistic in its absence of logical
continuity. The three short verses chosen by Boulez each
consist of disconnected, often obscure allusions, which are
juxtaposed without punctuation. Their images are interpreted by the composer in an exceedingly recondite manner. There are subtle word paintings and motivic cross references underscoring recurrences in the text: the setting of
"Le marcheur s'est tu" ("the walker is silent") in the sixth
movement, for example, recurs at the opening of the finale
at the words, "J'écoute marcher dans mes jambes" ("I hear
walking in my legs"). The vocal writing is extremely agile
and diverse, sometimes calling for the singer's mouth to be
closed or using Schoenberg's technique of speaking voice.

In fact, one important antecedent of this work is
Schoenberg's *Pierrot lunaire*, which Boulez judged Schoenberg's masterpiece. *Pierrot* shares with *Le marteau* the
medium of voice and small heterogeneous ensemble, and
the poetry of the two is related by fantastic and lurid
images. The third movement of Boulez's cycle uses the
same combination of flute and voice as the seventh movement ("Der kranke Mond") of *Pierrot*.

The orchestration of *Le marteau sans maître* is highly
virtuosic. Boulez combines in each movement instruments
with certain similarities, such as the voice and flute in the
third movement, both of which are instruments of breath
having the same general range. The commentaries to "Bourreaux de solitude" (movements 2, 4, and 8) evoke the sound
of the Balinese gamelan commonly found in Messiaen's
music, and they also allude to the syncopated pulse of African drumming.

Structures of pitch in this work are derived from a
twelve-tone row by a process which Boulez calls "multiplication." This method, which he also uses in many of his
later works, does not produce serialized music in the
Schoenbergian sense. A twelve-note series—E♭ F D C♯ B♭ B A
C G♯ E G F♯—is the source of unordered sets which are the

composer's basic materials, but the series itself does not appear.

In *Le marteau* Boulez begins by dividing the row into five segments; the notes are then placed into specific registers illustrated in Example 12-7. A segment is "multiplied" by another segment by constructing the intervals of one segment upon each pitch within the other. Duplicate pitches are then eliminated. In order to multiply the first two segments shown in Example 12-7, for example, we build the minor seventh created by the first segment upon each of the four pitches of the second segment (Example 12-8). The result is a set with seven different pitch classes.

Boulez's use of this seven-note set may be observed in the third movement, "L'artisanat furieux" (Anthology no. 15). It appears in the figure in the alto flute in the first measure (note that the alto flute sounds a fourth lower than written). In each measure of the entire movement, pitches are determined by similar multiplications.

In *Le marteau* and in several of Boulez's later works, serial preplanning governs the order in which one set follows another, but the order in which individual pitches occur is not predetermined. Beginning with the Third Piano Sonata (1957), Boulez's music admitted open forms, spontaneous choices by the performer, and other trappings of indeterminacy that will be outlined in the next chapter. It has retained the flamboyant virtuosity and abstruse refinement of *Le marteau*, and it repeatedly has returned to a literary text to provide formal models.

Numerous other European composers of the early 1950s began to write serialized music, usually allied to pointillistic textures inspired by the music of Webern. Bruno Maderna (1920–73) was associated with the Darmstadt summer courses from 1951, which provided him with a larger audience for his dodecaphonic compositions such as *Musica su due dimensioni* (1952) for flute and tape. Maderna was one of the most resourceful of the early com-

Example 12–7.   Segmentation of the series in Boulez, *Le marteau sans maître*.

Example 12-8.   Multiplication of segments.

posers of electronic music, and his later works often mix tape with live performances and theatrical gestures.

Maderna was joined at Darmstadt by his former student Luigi Nono (1924–). Nono's *Polifonica–Monodia–Ritmica* for winds, piano, and percussion (1951) is a classic example of pointillist integral serialism. In the mid-1950s his music became primarily vocal, based upon texts that expressed his political and social views. His works remained in the vein of integral serialism until the late 1950s, after which he departed from serial procedures in order to tailor his style better to the understanding of workers and the disadvantaged proletariat.

Luciano Berio (1925–) studied serial procedures with Luigi Dallapiccola in America, but he returned to Italy to compose serialized works such as his orchestral study *Nones* (1954). He was one of the first Europeans to break with serial orthodoxy, which he eliminated in favor of electronic composition, exploitation of vocal resources, and chance procedures. Henri Pousseur (1929–) was a devoted follower of Webern in the early 1950s, seeking to extend both the styles and structural principles of Webern's music. His *Quintette à la mémoire de Webern* (1955) uses the row of Webern's Quartet, op. 22, in homage to this illustrious forebear. Pousseur's music of the later 1950s and 1960s was influenced by new directions associated with Stockhausen and Boulez, which allowed open forms to govern large-scale form but which maintained Webernesque textures and sonorities on a smaller scale.

The Transformation of European Serialism: Ligeti

The vigor with which most of the leading European composers embraced serialism around 1950 was matched by the unanimity with which they eliminated these procedures after 1955. Boulez led the way as he dispensed with strict serialism almost immediately after *Structures Ia* in 1952, although he continued to defend the necessity of serialism of a more abstract kind.

Luciano Berio spoke for numerous composers of the late 1950s when he rejected the excessive emphasis on compositional method that serialism had provoked. "Even in itself," he wrote in "Poesia e musica" (1959), "serial procedure guarantees nothing. No idea is so miserable that it cannot be serialized." In its place he recommended "living and continuing contact with materials of sound." Later Berio was more outspoken in his rejection of serialism. He wrote in the *Christian Science Monitor* (1965): "Any attempt to codify musical reality into a kind of imitation grammar (I refer mainly to the efforts associated with the twelve-tone system) is a brand of fetishism which shares with Fascism and racism the tendency to reduce live processes to immobile, labelled objects, the tendency to deal with formalities rather than substance."

Henri Pousseur complained that the differentiation of elements which serialism should ensure was lost in a texture of sameness, which he termed "entropy." He wrote in "The Question of Order in New Music" (1966): "The rigorous serial procedures which determine all the detail do not seem to have a positive function. Far from establishing perceptible symmetries and periodicities, regularity in similarity and in differentiation—in other words, [in establishing] an effective and recognizable ordering of diverse figures—they seem instead to *hinder* all repetition and all symmetry or . . . all true *order*." He recommended that entropy be dispelled by combining serial preplanning with freely intuitive choice and elements of chance or mobile forms.

One of the most resourceful alternatives to strict serialism was proposed in the late 1950s by György Ligeti (1923–   ). In his article "Metamorphoses of Musical Form" (1960), he observed that serialism and the use of pointillist textures had reduced the importance of precise configurations of intervals, durations, dynamics, and other such elements. Like Pousseur, he complained that these specifics were lost to entropy, making serial composition audibly identical to chance composition. In works such as his orchestral *Atmosphères* (1961) he created an alternative to both pointillistic serialism and chance. This work is precisely notated, but it consists of such massive polyphonic structures that individual lines, intervals, and rhythms are imperceptible and contribute solely to large textures, volumes, and colors. The form of *Atmosphères* is created by the evolution of these "global" features in a way that he termed "composition with blocks of sound." In later works such as *Aventures* (1962) and *Nouvelles aventures* (1962–65), Ligeti experimented with theatrical gestures to dispel the sameness of integral serialism.

The most important device by which European serialists of the early 1950s transformed their musical language was indeterminacy. We turn in the next chapter to this important innovation in modern music.

Bibliography

An outstanding survey of postwar developments in music in Europe and America is Paul Griffiths's *Modern Music: The Avant Garde Since 1945* (New York, 1981). Reginald Smith Brindle's *The New Music* (London, 1975) is also a clear and informative account of this subject.

Elliott Carter's thoughts on music are expressed in essays and reviews that are collected in *The Writings of Elliott Carter*, ed. Else Stone and Kurt Stone (Bloomington, 1977). Also see Allen Edwards, *Flawed Words and Stubborn Sounds: A Conversation with Elliott Carter* (New York, 1971). Carter's music through 1980 is analyzed by David Schiff in *The Music of Elliott Carter* (London, 1983). The serial music of Igor Stravinsky is described in sources mentioned in the Bibliography to Chapter 8. Also see articles on his late works by Milton Babbitt and Claudio Spies in *Perspectives on Schoenberg and Stravinsky*, rev. ed., ed. Benjamin Boretz and Edward T. Cone (New York, 1972) and Pieter C. Van den Toorn, *The Music of Igor Stravinsky* (New Haven, 1983).

Pierre Boulez has not been entirely successful in expressing his views on music in his writings. The most important of these are collected and translated in *Boulez on*

Music Today (London, 1971) and *Notes of an Apprenticeship* (New York, 1968). The biography of Boulez by Joan Peyser (New York, 1976) is informative, and Paul Griffiths's *Boulez* (London, 1978) is an excellent short analytic survey of the music.

The outstanding study of music by Stockhausen is Robin Maconie's *Works of Karlheinz Stockhausen* (London, 1976). Also see Jonathan Harvey's *The Music of Stockhausen* (Berkeley and Los Angeles, 1975) and Karl H. Wörner's *Stockhausen: Life and Work*, ed. Bill Hopkins (Berkeley and Los Angeles, 1973). Stockhausen's writings are collected into the multivolume *Texte zur elektronischen und instrumentalen Musik*, which is not available in English translation. Jonathan Cott's *Stockhausen: Conversations with the Composer* (New York, 1973) is very informative.

György Ligeti's article "Metamorphoses of Musical Form" appeared in *Die Reihe,* 7 (1960; English trans., 1965); Henri Pousseur's "Question of Order in New Music" in *Perspectives of New Music,* 5 (1966); Berio's "Poesia e musica" in *Incontri musicali,* 1959; and his "The Composer and His Work" in *Christian Science Monitor,* 15 July 1965.

Milton Babbitt's article "Who Cares If You Listen?"—a title that he disavows—first appeared in 1958. It is reprinted in *Contemporary Composers on Contemporary Music,* ed. Elliott Schwartz and Barney Childs (New York, 1967).

• *13* •

INDETERMINACY

The years following World War II were marked not only by a recrudescence of serial composition, but also by an innovation of an opposite sort—indeterminacy. An element of a musical work is *indeterminate* if it is chosen by chance or if its realization by a performer is not precisely specified by notational instructions. These two situations will be called, respectively, "indeterminacy of composition" and "indeterminacy of performance." The term *aleatory* is also used to describe music of indeterminate construction, although some European writers have used this word to designate indeterminacy of a limited type which will be explained shortly.

Indeterminacy has proved to be one of the most radical innovations in musical composition of the entire twentieth century. If extensively applied, it eliminates style. It can remove all consistently distinctive features from the work of a composer and thus put his accomplishments at a distance from the listener. But few composers have achieved this effacement of style. Indeterminacy has instead served to further definite musical objectives: for John Cage it has intensified the importance of sounds and environmental noises; for Earle Brown it has increased the sensitive involvement of performers in musical decisions; for Pierre Boulez it has vivified musical materials that are otherwise subjected to complicated rational controls.

Like all important innovations in the history of

Western music, indeterminacy had a substantial history prior to its emergence as an important compositional principle. In the eighteenth century, "composition" by random selection among precomposed musical units was a popular entertainment practiced by numerous musicians. Jazz improvisation is an example of a limited indeterminacy of performance.

Indeterminate composition in the twentieth century began among experimental American composers between the world wars. In Henry Cowell's *Mosaic* Quartet (String Quartet no. 3, 1934–35), the performers are invited to choose the order in which movements are played, thus permitting the work to take on different forms. Indeterminacy among Americans after the World War II represents an unbroken continuation of the experimental spirit which had informed musical culture in this country since the turn of the century. Indeterminacy was slower in coming to Europe and was ultimately accepted there with greater caution, perhaps because there was no strong experimental movement there upon which to build.

"Action painting": Jackson Pollock, *Number 32*. (Courtesy of the Kunstsammlung Nordrhein-Westfalen, Düsseldorf.)

C'ÉTAIT
son stellaire

LE NOMBRE

EXISTÂT-IL
autrement qu'hallucination éparse d'agonie

COMMENÇÂT-IL ET CESSÂT-IL
sourdant que nié et clos quand apparu
enfin
par quelque profusion répandue en rareté

SE CHIFFRÂT-IL

évidence de la somme pour peu qu'une

ILLUMINÂT-IL

CE SERAIT
pire
non
davantage ni moins
indifféremment mais autant

LE HASARD

Choit
la plume
rythmique suspens du sinistre
s'ensevelir
aux écumes originelles
naguères d'où sursauta son délire jusqu'à une cime
flétrie
par la neutralité identique du gouffre

The mobile poetic form: a page from Mallarmé's *Un coup de dés* (Paris, 1914).

American composers were guided toward indeterminate procedures by developments among their fellow painters and sculptors. The "action paintings" of Jackson Pollock (1912–56) were made by dripping or splashing paint upon a canvas, so that the result was to an extent the product of chance. The collages of Robert Rauschenberg (1925–   ) often combine sheets of newspaper to create random and conflicting images. The mobiles of Alexander Calder (1898–1976) use colorful metallic shapes connected by wires, whose overall form is changed spontaneously by currents of wind. In Europe, on the other hand, indeterminacy was inspired by trends in modern literature. Mallarmé's free distribution of lines in his poem "Un coup de dés" ("A throw of dice") invites the reader to take different routes about the page. This labyrinthine form was imitated by Pierre Boulez in several works. Syntactical discontinuities in the writings of James Joyce were similarly an inspiration to Luciano Berio, who used indeterminacy of performance to capture Joyce's play of words and sounds.

Indeterminacy in America: Cage, Feldman, Brown, and Wolff

In Chapter 11 it was shown that the early music of John Cage, like that of his fellow American experimentalists, emphasized unusual sounds and imaginative ways of presenting them. In these early pieces colorful noise and musical sounds were strewn within systematically planned durations. Such music freely expressed the composer's tastes within the framework of preformed structures, or, to use his terms, it integrated "ideas of order" with "spontaneous actions."

By 1950 Cage's philosophy of music had changed radically. He attributed his new viewpoint to an intensified awareness of Zen, mystic philosophy, and Eastern patterns of thought. From these sources he derived the idea that art must be part of a holistic reality. Art, which is a product of mankind, must imitate nature, since humanity and nature are essentially one. The common substance of nature and the art of music is sound. Its deployment in music must reflect its reality in nature, where it occurs with ceaseless abandon, unmotivated by the human will and not produced as a metaphor for any other meaning. The composer as a creator of beautiful objects should be replaced in importance by the listener, who, sensitized to sounds, is led to an awareness of the unity of all things.

Unmotivated sound would be the primary subject of Cage's music from 1950. In his lecture "Experimental Music" (1957), he spoke of the relation of sound to humanity and nature:

> If . . . it is realized that sounds occur whether intended or not, one turns in the direction of those he does not intend. This turning is psychological and seems at first to be a giving up of everything that belongs to humanity—for a musician, the giving up of music. This psychological turning leads to the world of nature, where, gradually or suddenly, one sees that humanity and nature, not separate, are in this world together; that nothing was lost when everything was given away. In fact, everything is

gained. In musical terms, any sounds may occur in any combination and in any continuity.

Music for Cage became an activity in which the composer set in motion sonorous and visual processes whose outcome was unknown to him. Not all sounds in Cage's works are produced by performers. Random environmental noise—which Cage designated by the ironic metaphor "silence"—was also welcomed. "In this new music," he wrote, "nothing takes place but sounds: those that are notated and those that are not. Those that are not notated appear in the written music as silences, opening the doors of the music to the sounds that happen to be in the environment." His *4′ 33″* (1952) is an essay in total silence, where, for the designated period of time, environmental noise reigns as the sole material of a work of music.

Cage sought to efface his personality from his music by strategies of chance. He relied especially on tosses of coins to guide him in selecting the elements of a composition. These exercises in chance were interpreted with the aid of the *I-Ching* or Chinese *Book of Changes*, a manual originally intended to dispense divine guidance according to the fall of yarrow sticks. In other works, random imperfections in a sheet of paper were used as a compositional guide. Music which is thus indeterminate of composition was not intended to be absurd or destructive of art. Cage expressed the hope that it would move the listener by the sublimity of sound. But the indeterminate work itself was not to be an object whose contemplation affected the listener. It was, instead, solely an occasion which could not possess or lack beauty. "Value judgments," wrote Cage, "are not in the nature of this work as regards either composition, performance, or listening."

Cage's *Music of Changes* for piano (1951) was one of the first pieces to reflect his new artistic orientation. This work is partially indeterminate of composition. Most elements were selected by chance, but the larger context of sounds and textures continued to reflect his own tastes.

The structure of *Music of Changes*, as in Cage's earlier works, is articulated by a sequence of numbers, in this case 3, 5, 6¾, 6¾, 5, 3⅛. These quantities refer to durations, which are operative in large and small dimensions. On the small scale, they determine the number of measures of 4/4 time before a change of tempo can occur. A section is concluded when the numerical sequence of measures has run its course, that is, in 29⅝ measures. The total number of sections is likewise 29⅝, which are divided into four movements also corresponding to the numerical sequence: the first movement has three sections; the second, 11¾ (combining 5 and 6¾); the third, 6¾; and the finale 8⅛ (combining 5 and 3⅛).

The first section of the fourth movement (Anthology no. 9) illustrates this durational microstructure and the way in which it is animated by Cage's procedures of chance. The passage consists of 29⅝ measures of 4/4 time, divided by opportunities for new tempos into groups of 3, 5, 6¾, 6¾, 5, and 3⅛ measures. Notated sounds consist of chords, rapid figures, harmonics, and noises produced by the pianist striking the instrument in unorthodox ways. These are selected by procedures of chance, as are silences, durations, densities of texture, tempi, and dynamics. Since these procedures of chance sometimes generate unplayable configurations, Cage allowed the pianist then "to employ his own discretion."

Despite its indeterminacy of composition, *Music of Changes* still reflects the composer's musical preferences. His choices are all made from among a limited and carefully preplanned range of possibilities. He was assured, for example, that there would be an ample measure of silence in this work—it is almost Webernesque in sparseness— since the charts from which sounds were selected contained as many silences as sounds per se. The charts were also constructed so that Cage was assured that there would be a fairly even distribution of all twelve pitch classes and that the harmonic units—chords and short figures—would project primarily clusters of semitones. While Cage relinquished control over details of composition, his style is still in evidence at a higher level of construction.

In the later 1950s, Cage became dissatisfied with this apparent contradiction of his aesthetic, and he sought ways to banish his preferences more thoroughly from his music. *Music of Changes* was dismissed as "inhuman" and "a Frankenstein monster" for the strictness with which it dictated the actions of the player. Henceforth, he adopted an increasingly less specific notation. His series of Variations (1958–78) largely dispenses with precise notation and provides only a general impetus for producing sounds. In

these and other such works from the 1960s, Cage's effacement of his style is virtually complete.

Thus Cage confided to the performer a larger role in
the ultimate shape and impact of a work. In a lecture on
"Indeterminacy" given at Darmstadt in 1958, he surveyed
the roles of the performer in music of this type. The
performer, he said, might be comparable to a painter who is
asked to color a given sketch. Or he might be called upon
to give to a work its outer form or expressive content, "for
form unvitalized by spontaneity brings about the death of
all the other elements." He might be comparable to a
photographer taking one of an infinite number of pictures
of a piece, or he might be asked to react spontaneously to
other performers like a traveler who must catch an unan-
nounced departing train. Any of these roles is preferable, he
concluded, to the conventional duty of performers, who,
like laborers, do simply as they are told.

Cage eschewed this last "intolerable" circumstance by
recourse to _graphic notations._ Graphic notation communi-
cates pitches, durations, dynamics, textures, or other musical elements by symbols that usually are visually analogous
to the sounds they represent. These symbols will often be
mixed with standard notational elements. Graphic notation
is inherently imprecise, conveying only the outline of a
preconceived musical image. Since conventional notation
is specific by comparison, virtually all modern music that
is indeterminate of performance makes some use of graphic
techniques.

There has yet to develop any significant standardization among composers or performers of graphic systems, so
we shall rely for the remainder of this chapter on a few
examples from works of prominent composers to illustrate
their diversity and meaning. Cage's _Concert for Piano and
Orchestra_ (1957–58), for example, consists of a large and
fantastic repertory of graphic notations. These may be
realized in any number and in any order. Most use
conventional staffs and noteheads, but some are entirely
abstract. One of the latter is shown in Example 13-1,
regarding which the composer explains: "Any pitch area
having at least 20 chromatic tones. Space vertically =
frequency. Horizontally = time. Horizontal lines = duration
of single tones. Vertical lines = clusters or legati. Points =
short single tones."

Cage also promoted indeterminacy of performance by

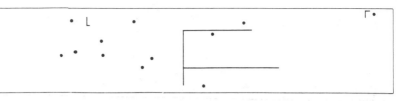

Example 13-1.   Cage, *Concert for Piano and Orchestra.* © 1960 by Henmar Press Inc. Reprinted by permission.

allowing variable forms and media. The graphs of *Concert for Piano and Orchestra*, for example, may be played in any order or quantity, either one at a time or several simultaneously by more than one pianist. The soloist(s) may be joined by any number of orchestral instruments *ad libitum*. This variable or "mobile" form was an approach to indeterminate performance that was more thoroughly explored by Cage's American contemporaries such as Earle Brown, and it was the main type of indeterminacy to be adopted by European musicians in the later 1950s and 1960s.

Cage's ideas and methods proved especially influential upon a group of musicians with whom he was associated in New York in the early 1950s, including Morton Feldman, Earle Brown, and Christian Wolff. All of these figures emphasized indeterminateness of performance rather than indeterminateness of composition, and all made important contributions to styles of graphic notation. The music of Morton Feldman, like that of Cage, relies upon spontaneous sounds. Nearly all of Feldman's music is marked by a quiet and nearly immobile interplay of sounds and textures, usually emanating from conventional instruments and voices. His methods of obtaining these pictures in sound are very different from Cage's, since they place greater emphasis on his compositional instincts rather than on routines of chance. His early music, such as the series of *Projections* (1950–51) and *Intersections* (1951–53), uses graphic scores which allow performers to choose dynamics and pitches within specific ranges, but which control duration, texture, and continuity.

Feldman's more recent compositions are conventionally notated though largely unchanged in style. *Madame Press Died Last Week at Ninety* (1970), for example, is characteristically slow, repetitive, and inarticulate. It is more conventional in form than the graphic scores, as it uses motivic recurrences and is framed by the same six-note chord in the celesta at the beginning and end.

The music of Earle Brown (1926–   ) prior to 1952 was conventional in notation, reflecting partially serial or freely atonal structures. In 1952 his notational practices changed drastically. In a series of works collectively designated *Folio* (1952–53), he experimented with ways of notating relative durations by noteheads of various elongations. This "time-notation," as it was called by the composer, was in certain variations adopted by many composers later in the 1950s and 1960s. Brown's *1953* for piano uses time notation together with other elements of indeterminacy, as the pages can be read with either side up and with any combination of treble and bass clefs. An excerpt is illustrated in Example 13-2.

Other works from this collection are almost totally indeterminate in both composition and performance. *December 1952*, for example, consists of a matrix of horizontal and vertical lines and blocks shown in Example 13-3. These visual symbols are intended solely to be a stimulus to spontaneous decisions by the player(s), as their design does not necessarily represent any preconceived interpretation. "The composition may be performed," the composer notes

Example 13-2.   Brown, "1953" from *Folio*. Copyright 1961 by Associated Music Publishers Inc. Reprinted by permission.

Example 13-3.   Brown, *December 1952.* Copyright © 1961 by Associated Music Publishers, Inc. All rights reserved. Reprinted by permission.

in the Preface, "in any direction from any point in the defined space for any length of time and may be performed from any of the four rotational positions in any sequence." Its appearance also reveals Brown's interest in modern art, especially in the geometrical studies of Pieter Mondriaan (1872–1944) and his Dutch contemporaries.

In later music, however, Brown retreated from the "conceptual mobility" of *December 1952.* He sought instead a middle ground of determinacy and indeterminacy, which would result in what he called "open" or "mobile" forms. Works such as the String Quartet (1965) consist of pre-composed sections of varying degrees of notational specificity. These are selected and placed into order by the instrumentalists, either freely or under guidelines by the composer. The performers are admonished in the preface to the score to make rational and sensitive choices and to respond to the decisions of their fellow players:

> What I am trying to imply is not only a great responsibility on the part of the performers to perform the work "as written" but also an intense

Models for graphic musical notation. Pieter Mondriaan, *Composition with Lines*. (Courtesy of the Rijksmuseum Kröller-Müller, Otterlo, The Netherlands.)

awareness of ensemble and individual flexibility, the material as written and within this concept of performance relativity.

I would like to think that an intensified sense of human and sonic presence and intuitive performance contact can be extended beyond the "normal" precision-goal of most chamber music performing, into an area of immediacy of action, reaction, and flexibility, while maintaining the basic shape and character of the work.

By telling the performers to maintain "the basic shape and character of the work," Brown reveals his intention to establish a style—a distinctive compositional profile. Brown's music seeks to vivify this style by engaging the performers in a more intense and spontaneous participation. His concept of mobile forms, more than the chance procedures of Cage, would prove analogous to formal developments among European composers of the late 1950s and 1960s.

Christian Wolff (1934–   ) came under the influence of Cage from the beginning of his work as a serious composer. His music is highly indeterminate of performance, intended primarily to allow the performers "freedom and dignity." By the late 1950s he developed a notation that not only guided the players in their choice of pitch and texture, but also provoked a rhythmically diverse interaction between them by their cueing one another.

Cage's experiments in indeterminacy of the 1950s were carried into new areas in the 1960s by figures such as La Monte Young, George Brecht, and the Englishman Cornelius Cardew. The first two were part of a group in New York called Fluxus, which in the early 1960s sponsored "events" or "happenings" mingling theater, comedy, and random sounds. We shall pick up the thread of these developments again in Chapter 16.

The spirit of Fluxus was also present in the work of Cornelius Cardew (1936–81). Cardew's group for free improvisation called AMM gave way in 1969 to his Scratch Orchestra, in which untutored musical and improvisational activities were substituted for the traditional values and background of an orchestra of trained musicians.

Indeterminacy in Europe: Boulez, Stockhausen, Berio, and Lutosławski

Although composition by chance, mobile forms, and graphic notation played a substantial role in works by major European composers of the 1960s and beyond, the influence of indeterminacy there was moderated by a strong commitment to serialism and a more traditional view of the composer's role. Indeterminacy offered European serialists a way to overcome a major drawback of their idiom: its sameness. The maximal differentiation of pitch, duration, register, and color that was insured by integral serialism ironically produced not the effect of variety, but one of homogeneity and statistical uniformity. Even the most devoted of Europe's serialists recognized that this "entropy," as the phenomenon was often called, tended to produce monotony and a style different from what was intended.

Indeterminacy began to make inroads among European composers by the late 1950s, largely through the influence of John Cage, who lectured at Darmstadt in 1958, and Karlheinz Stockhausen, whose inexhaustible experimentation touched upon numerous indeterminate methods. Among the major European composers, indeterminacy never became an end in itself. It was instead an instrument by which distinctive and relatively traditional styles could be realized. Graphic notation was used by György Ligeti in the organ piece *Volumina*, for example, to accomplish the interplay of textures that was basic to his style. In works by Mauricio Kagel, improvisation by performers served to uncover new sounds and theatrical modes of expression. Luciano Berio's indeterminate notation in his cycle of *Sequenzas* liberated the instrumentalist's virtuosity.

This limited application of indeterminacy has been called "aleatory" by European writers such as Boulez and Lutosławski, to distinguish it from the more extensive applications of chance among American composers. The term aleatory is defined in this restrictive sense by Werner Meyer-Eppler in his article "Statistic and Psychologic Problems of Sound": "A process is said to be aleatoric if its course is determined in general but depends on chance in detail."

We shall now survey some of the aleatoric aspects of music by four major European composers of the postwar decades: Pierre Boulez, Karlheinz Stockhausen, Luciano Berio, and Witold Lutosławski. The first three began their compositional careers as serialists; Lutosławski turned to serialism in the late 1950s. By the 1960s all four composers had devised musical languages in which indeterminate techniques played a role.

Of these four figures, Pierre Boulez maintained the strongest allegiance to serial composition. But after his most doctrinaire essay in integral serialism—the first book of *Structures* for two pianos (1952)—he gradually shifted toward freer modes of expression. By the time of his Third Piano Sonata (1957) and second book of *Structures* (1961), he had incorporated some cautious opportunities for mobile forms.

Boulez explained his apparent volte-face in several polemics written in the late 1950s. In the article "Alea" (1958), he condemns composers of music by chance, referring no doubt to Cage and his circle:

> Chance . . . masks a basic weakness in compositional technique, it [is] a protection against the asphyxia of invention, the resort to a more subtle poison that destroys every last embryo of craftsmanship. I would willingly call this experiment—if experiment it be, since the individual does not feel responsible for his work, but merely throws himself by unadmitted weakness, by confusion, and for temporary assuagement into puerile magic.

But Boulez also attacks an excessive attachment to serial preplanning: "Schematization, quite simply, takes the place of invention; imagination—an auxiliary—limits itself to giving birth to a complex mechanism. . . . As for the imagination, it is careful not to intervene after things are under way. . . . We plunge into statistical lists that have no more value than other lists."

He proposes to eliminate both extremes of aleatory and serialism, replacing them with a style that admits limited elements of chance in a context also mixing serial procedures and intuitive choices. The form of a work should thus resemble a labyrinth: "The work must provide a certain number of possible routes," Boulez wrote in the article "Sonate, que me veux-tu?," "with chance playing a shunting role at the last moment." By the use of mobile forms and optional passages, he created works that were analogous to a "moving, expanding universe" in which the outer form would be renewed upon each performance. "We have respected the 'finished' aspect of the occidental work, its closed cycle," he wrote in "Alea," "but we have introduced the 'chance' of the oriental work, its open development."

These features are much in evidence in the Third Piano Sonata. In this work Boulez took his departure from language and literature, which not only provided a model for variable form but also suggested ways in which the instrumental sonata could be expressive and intelligible. In the literary works of James Joyce and in some of the poetry of Stéphane Mallarmé, he found a spontaneous variability of syntax and order that opened new dimensions of meaning. He imitated these free structures by allowing the performer to choose the order in which some elements of the composition could be played.

The work is made from building blocks that are put into a syntax at the moment of performance. These formal elements are themselves based upon models from verbal expression. The sections of the Sonata are given titles drawn in part from phonetics, rhetoric, and literature. The entire work consists of five movements, each of which the composer calls a "formant"—a term from phonetics referring to a primary acoustical element of spoken sound. The formants carry titles such as "Trope" and "Strophe." Boulez uses all of his powers of artifice in this work to make the instrumental sonata intelligible by analogy to primitive verbal expression.

The second formant, "Trope," illustrates Boulez's idea of the formal labyrinth. The movement has four sections— Text, Parenthesis, Commentary, and Gloss—whose titles develop the rhetorical metaphor. The player can begin with any of the four sections, continuing in order through the cycle. He can also elect to place the Commentary after the Gloss rather than before. In Parenthesis and Commentary, he may freely elect to perform or omit optional passages enclosed in brackets, and some pitches are indeterminate of duration. Otherwise, the sonata uses a freely serialized method.

Its style is consistent with most of Boulez's music. The surface is adorned with a busy, virtuosic filigree. Traditional lines and chords are entirely absent, replaced by an ornate counterpoint of attacks, registers, and densities. There is no consistent pulse, rhythmic pattern, or meter; instead, the passage of time is marked by an interplay of freely developing motions and colors.

Until the early 1960s, Karlheinz Stockhausen's music followed the same general evolution as that of Boulez. Both composers moved from strictly serial composition to an idiom where serial procedures were mingled with limited indeterminacy of performance and mobile forms. But Stockhausen has since proved to be of a more experimental temperament than the other postwar serialists. He has moved with startling swiftness through many developments in contemporary music including surrealistic theatrical music (e.g., *Originale*, 1961), verbal scores of "intuitive music" (*Aus den sieben Tagen*, 1968), minimalist pieces (*Stimmung*, 1968), and innovative uses of electronic media. We focus now upon several works characteristic of his music of the later 1950s and early 1960s which use indeterminate features of performance.

Piano Piece XI (1956) is Stockhausen's earliest example of a composition in mobile form, and it immediately provoked Boulez to compose the closely related "Constellation" movement of his Third Piano Sonata. Stockhausen's piece consists of nineteen brief passages in conventional notation. The player begins with any one of these "groups" and moves randomly to any others. Each group is played with a unique combination of tempo, dynamics, and style of attack, which is determined by indications attached to the end of the previous passage. When a group is played for the second time, certain changes are made (primarily transpositions at the octave), and the piece ends when the player lights upon a group for the third time.

Piano Piece XI exemplifies what the composer referred to as "group" composition, which several years before had replaced the "punctual" style of early works such as *Kreuzspiel*. In punctual music, the listener is confronted by relatively undifferentiated arrays of single notes, short figures, and silences—constellations, that is, of individual points of sound, each with its own pitch, loudness, register, and duration specified by interrelated series. Group composition, on the other hand, introduces differentiation into these otherwise static and homogeneous works. A group consists of a passage of short duration which is made distinctive by some musical characteristics such as a particular tempo, interval, contour, or timbre. Longer groups are called "moments."

In Piano Piece XI the structure of pitches in each group

is fairly similar, but the distinctiveness of the group is insured by the unique combination of tempo, attack, and dynamics that the player must observe. There is no logic to the overall form nor sense of direction in the succession of groups, which causes the listener to focus all the more upon present time—represented by the musical process of a group or moment—rather than upon linearly connected musical arguments. This emphasis upon the present is underscored by the composer in his article "Moment Form" (1960):

> Musical forms have been composed in recent years which are far removed from the schema of dramatic form. These new forms neither drive toward a single climax nor toward several such planned and antici- pated climaxes. In them the customary stages of introduction, transition, tension, and relaxation are not represented by a developmental curve encom- passing the entire work. . . . In these new forms every "now" is not simply the result of what has gone before nor an upbeat to what follows or to what is expected, but instead a personal, indepen- dent, centralized entity existing for itself. These are forms in which a moment is not a point on a time line, not a particle of a measured duration, but rather forms in which the concentration on the now—on every now—makes vertical slices which penetrate across the horizontal presentation of time into a timelessness which I call eternity.

A work closely related to the mobile form of Piano Piece XI but larger and more dramatic in conception is *Momente* (*Moments*, 1961–64, several later versions). Here the brief groups of the Piano Piece are expanded to larger units or "moments." The large and diverse medium, which includes soprano solo, four choruses, brass, percussion, and two organs, creates visual effects suggesting a symbolic drama.

Its form consists of a succession of moments that can be rearranged and reconstituted at each new performance. Each moment is distinguished by an emphasis upon melody (synonymous with monodic or heterophonic textures), tim- bre (or homophonic textures), or rhythm (or polyphonic textures). Some moments are tinted by allusions to other moments, and some transitions between moments also make allusions to moments already heard or yet to come.

The timbral resources of *Momente* are broad and imaginative. The chorus not only sings but makes other sounds by clapping hands, talking, and stamping feet. These noises serve both to mediate between instrumental and vocal sounds—a type of homogenization of sources of sounds that occupied Stockhausen in many compositions—and also mediate between noisy audience reactions which greeted many of his works and sounds normally produced by the performing artists.

Zyklus (*Cycle*, 1959), for solo percussionist, differs from both Piano Piece XI and *Momente* in that its sections are organized into a definite succession. It is nevertheless mobile in form since the player can begin with any of the seventeen sections of the work and proceed through the remainder of the cycle.

As is often the case in works by Stockhausen, the title designates a form or procedure that is operative on several levels. Cyclical form is reinforced visually by the circular disposition of instruments, which requires that the percussionist move steadily around the circle as he proceeds through the formal cycle. *Zyklus* in fact consists of an intricate web of simultaneous cycles, each governing some musical element or process and each subjected to the rational control and coordination characteristic of Stockhausen's earlier serial compositions. One such cycle controls the number of attacks of nine of the thirteen instruments as the player progresses through the various sections. Another cycle determines the degree of determinacy or indeterminacy of events in a section, and so forth.

Example 13-4 shows two of these sections, divided by the double horizontal line, and it also illustrates Stockhausen's techniques of graphic notation. The music can be read as shown or turned upside down. The section at the top is maximal in indeterminacy. Notes in the part for tom-toms, for example, are freely and densely sprinkled into its measure-like divisions. The section at the bottom, on the contrary, is maximal in determinacy in that it establishes relatively simple, discrete rhythmic figures and sonorities. Its notation is still approximate, but much less so than the random configurations at the top.

Example 13-4. Stockhausen, *Zyklus.* Copyright © Universal Edition (London) Ltd., London 1961. Used by permission of European American Music Distributors Corp., sole U.S. agent for Universal Edition.

LUCIANO BERIO
(Oneglia, 1925—   )

Berio received his musical education at the Conservatory in Milan, and he subsequently studied with Luigi Dallapiccola at Tanglewood. Beginning in 1954 he attended the Summer Music Courses at Darmstadt. In 1955 he collaborated with Bruno Maderna to found the Studio di Fonologia in Milan, where both composers later realized electronic compositions. With Maderna he also established a series of concerts and a periodical devoted to modern music, both called *Incontri musicali.*

In the 1960s he lived primarily in the Unites States, where he taught at Mills College, Harvard University, and The Juilliard School. Since 1972 he has resided mainly in Italy. He was married to the soprano Cathy Berberian, with whom he collaborated on numerous compositions.

Selected Works

Orchestra. *Nones* (1954), *Sinfonia* (1968, fifth movement added in 1969).

Chamber Music. *Sequenzas* for various solo instruments and voice (1957–75), revisions of some *Sequenzas* for different media entitled *Chemins, Tempi concertati* (1959), *Sincronie* (for string quartet, 1964).

Works for Tape (with or without instruments). *Thema (Omaggio a Joyce)* (1958), *Différences* (1959), *Visage* (1961), *Laborintus II* (1965), *Questo vuol dire que* (1969).

Works for Voice(s) and Instruments. *Epifanie* (1961), *Circles* (1962), *Coro* (1976), *Recital I (for Cathy)* (1972).

Arrangements. *Folk songs* (1964, orchestral version 1973).

By the late 1950s the music of Luciano Berio, like that of Stockhausen and Boulez, had departed from strict serialism to a more distinctive style which admitted limited mobility of form and indeterminacy of performance and which relied upon graphic notation. Berio had a deep interest in the human voice and its ability to convey emotions in addition to a wide spectrum of musical colors. His methods of manipulating the voice were much influenced by Stockhausen, especially by *Gesang der Jünglinge* (see Chapter 14), in which Stockhausen attempts to mediate between vocal and synthetic sounds and to obliterate any absolute distinctions between them.

Berio responded with a series of works that combined the voice with diverse media and that exploited its sonorous capacity and ability to convey emotions on a primitive and abstract plane. His *Thema (Omaggio a Joyce)* (1958) used readings from Joyce's *Ulysses*, which were taped, modified electronically, and reconstituted into a montage of recognizable words and senseless vocal sounds. In an article "Music and Poetry: An Experiment" (1959), Berio told of his intention to create in this work a new relationship of word and tone: "My real goal was neither the juxtaposition nor jumble of two diverse systems of expression, rather, it was intended to establish a relationship of continuity between them, enabling the transition from one to another to be unnoticeable."

In *Circles* for voice, harp, and percussion (1962), Berio transplanted the techniques of *Thema* to a nonelectronic medium. This work is a setting of three poems by e. e. cummings, the first two of which are recapitulated in varied shapes to create an A B C B' A' form. This layout of materials is strongly directed toward the climactic middle section. In this focal passage the parts are graphically indeterminate, as the voice explodes into fragmented noises that approximate the timbres of the instruments. To reinforce this similarity of vocal and instrumental sounds, the percussionists blurt out nonsense syllables and the singer— in a theatrical gesture reminiscent of many works by Stockhausen—moves to a new position closer to the instruments and begins to play upon wood chimes. Example 13-5 shows this climactic passage and Berio's freely suggestive notation.

Berio's idiom owes much to the electronic and instrumental works of Stockhausen of the 1950s, but it is based

Example 13-5. Berio, *Circles.* © copyright 1961 by Universal Edition (London) Ltd., London. Used by permission of European American Music Distributors Corp., sole U.S. agents for Universal Edition.

on a much more intuitive groundwork. While Stockhausen's music often is inspired by a scientific or philosophical model, Berio's is informed by direct contact with his sources of sound. His music goes beyond Stockhausen's in its immediacy of impact and resourceful handling of the voice.

Works such as *Circles* opened the way for many related works of the 1960s and 1970s, especially by composers in America where Berio resided during much of this time. Several of the works of George Crumb—*Ancient Voices of Children* (1970), for example—are a continuation of Berio's liberation of vocal technique.

The music of Witold Lutosławski (1913–   ) prior to 1958—including his First Symphony (1941–47), Overture for string orchestra (1949), and Concerto for Orchestra (1954)—is reminiscent of the style of Béla Bartók. It makes a colorfully dissonant use of the orchestra, its themes reflect the physiognomy of Eastern European folk song, and its textures create a rhythmically vivacious, asymmetrical polyphony. Lutosławski's Funeral Music for string orchestra (1958) was his first work to apply a highly novel version of the twelve-tone method, through which his music was more thoroughly irradiated by the chromatic scale and made even more severely linear and contrapuntal.

In 1961, beginning with his orchestral *Jeux vénitiens* (*Venetian Games*), Lutosławski turned to controlled aleatory to free both the rhythmic and textural dimensions of his music. The composer has attributed this change of style and compositional method to his encounter in 1960 with John Cage's *Concert for Piano and Orchestra:* "While listening to it, I suddenly realized that I could compose music differently from that of my past. That I could progress toward the whole not from the little detail but the other way round—I could start out from the chaos and create order in it gradually" (from Steven Stucky, *Lutosławski and his Music* [Cambridge, 1981], p. 84).

Lutosławski devised a music that he termed "aleatoric counterpoint," in which pitches in all instrumental and vocal parts are precisely notated and rhythms are improvised by the player within certain guidelines. The effect is usually a vivacious and busy polyphony in which the particular notes, intervals, and lines are subsumed into a texture. Passages of aleatoric counterpoint normally alternate with conventionally notated passages, and each block-like section projects a distinct texture that is linked to its neighbors in subtle ways. Lutosławski refined the style of *Jeux vénitiens* in music composed later in the 1960s and 1970s, including Three Poems by Henri Michaux for orchestra and twenty-part chorus (1963), String Quartet (1964), Symphony no. 2 (1967), and *Livre pour orchestre* (1968).

Bibliography

A history of indeterminacy in the twentieth century is recounted by Michael Nyman in *Experimental Music* (New York, 1974). Reginald Smith Brindle's *New Music* (London, 1975); Paul Griffiths's *Modern Music* (New York, 1981); and David Cope's *New Directions in Music*, 4th ed. (Dubuque, 1984) are also recommended.

Graphic notations by contemporary composers are illustrated in the anthology *Notations*, ed. John Cage and Alison Knowles (New York, 1969), in Brindle's *New Music* (cited above), and in Erhard Karkoschka's *Notation in New Music*, trans. Ruth Koenig (London, 1972). There have been several noteworthy attempts to collect, categorize, and standardize modern notational practices. Kurt Stone's *Music Notation in the Twentieth Century* (New York and London, 1980) is especially authoritative, and the reader is also referred to the Proceedings of the International Conference on New Music Notation in *Interface*, 4 (1975) and to Gerald Warfield's *Writings on Contemporary Music Notation: An Annotated Bibliography*, Music Library Association Index and Bibliography Series, no. 16 (Ann Arbor, 1976).

John Cage has been an eloquent spokesman for his ideas on music. His most important lectures and articles are reprinted in *Silence* (Middletown, Conn. 1961), which was the first of several anthologies of his writings. Other statements by Cage are found in Richard Kostelanetz, ed., *John Cage* (New York, 1970); a brief analytic survey of his music is provided by Paul Griffiths in *Cage* (London, 1981).

Earle Brown discusses his ideas on mobile forms in

"Form in New Music" (1965), reprinted in *Source*, 1 (1967). Morton Feldman reveals his impatience with European composers of indeterminate music in "Pre-determinate/Indeterminate," *Composer*, 19 (1966).

Writings by and about Pierre Boulez and Karlheinz Stockhausen were surveyed in the Bibliography to Chapter 12. Boulez's attitudes toward indeterminacy are discussed in "Alea" (1958), English translation in *Perspectives of New Music*, 3 (1964), and in "Sonate, que me veux-tu?" (which deals specifically with his Third Piano Sonata), *Perspectives of New Music*, 1 (1963). Stockhausen's article "Moment-form" appears in German in his *Texte zur elektronischen und instrumentalen Musik*, vol. 1 (Cologne, 1963).

Luciano Berio's ideas on the relationship of verbal and musical expression are sketched in his articles "Poesia e musica: un'esperienza," *Incontri musicali*, 3 (1959); "Form" in *The Modern Composer and His World*, ed. John Beckwith and Udo Kasemets (Toronto, 1961); and "The Composer and His Work," *Christian Science Monitor*, July 15, 1965. The last of these is a diatribe against serialism. There is still no comprehensive study of Berio's music.

Lutosławski's life and works are traced by Steven Stucky in his *Lutosławski and his Music* (Cambridge, 1981). Also see Lutosławski's "About the Element of Chance in Music" in *Three Aspects of New Music* (Stockholm, 1968). Werner Meyer-Eppler's article "Statistic and Psychologic Problems of Sound" is found in *Die Reihe*, 1 (1955; English trans., 1958).

•14•

ELECTRONIC
MUSIC

The climate for renewed experimentation in music after the Second World War was intensified by a revolution in technology. Of several new avenues opened to the composer by postwar scientific research, none was more enticing than the prospect of using tape recorders and electronic equipment for the production and manipulation of sound. By approximately 1950 these new devices had given birth to *electronic music,* a medium in which the generation of musical sounds and their modification, storage, and reproduction are due, at least in part, to electronic means. We shall limit our definition of electronic music to those compositions in which the *original* conception is for these electronic media.

Electronic music was built upon technical and aesthetic foundations of earlier twentieth-century music. A direct precedent was the increased emphasis on diverse sounds. A fondness for unusual sound is especially evident in the experimental idiom of Americans such as Cowell, Varèse, and Cage. Their application of noise to music was also prefigured by experimental compositions of Italian Futurists such as Luigi Russolo, Russian Constructivists such as Alexander Mosolov, and French and German Dadaists during the years following the First World War.

Experimental use of noise and microtonal scales led to the invention of primitive electronic musical instruments, some of which attracted the attention of major composers. One of the earliest such devices was the "Telharmonium," invented by the Massachusetts technician Thaddeus Cahill around 1906. This electronic keyboard instrument transmitted sounds over telephone lines. It was mentioned by Ferruccio Busoni in his *Sketch of a New Esthetic of Music* as a means by which Busoni's theory of microtonal scales could be easily realized.

Among many electronic instruments that followed, the *ondes Martenot* ("Martenot's waves") proved to be the most important. This monophonic keyboard instrument, named after its inventor Maurice Martenot (1898–1980), produces a glassy tone that can be varied in dynamics and vibrato. It is tuned to the pitches of the chromatic scale, but it can also slide between notes. It was used by numerous French composers including Varèse, Messiaen, and Boulez.

Most types of electronic music depend not only on electronic devices for the production of sounds, but also on electronic means for their storage and reproduction. Disc recordings and film soundtracks were used experimentally as compositional media by several composers in the 1920s and 1930s. A typical experiment by artists at the Bauhaus school of design in Dessau involved drawing on a film soundtrack, which was then played by cinematic audio equipment. But the development of the magnetic tape recorder around 1950 was the decisive technological advance that made electronic music a practical reality.

Shortly after electronic music came into its own in the late 1940s, it branched into five basic media:

1. *musique concrète:* recorded music whose sounds are produced naturally or by conventional instruments;
2. pure electronic music: recorded works whose sounds are produced by electronic devices;
3. recorded music combining electronic and *concrète* sounds;
4. live performance plus recorded sounds;
5. live electronic music: live performances whose sounds are immediately modified by electronic means.

These media did not unfold as a chronologically ordered development. Each was in existence by the early

1950s or before. By 1970 there had occurred a decisive shift away from recorded electronic music toward those types involving live performance, as the traditional spontaneity and theatricality of the concert proved desirable to most composers and listeners.

We shall now survey each of these five media and trace within each the musical styles, compositional or structural features, and studio equipment which they have produced.

Musique Concrète

"Concrete" music was the invention of Pierre Schaeffer (1910–   ), a broadcaster and engineer at the Radiodiffusion-Télévision Françaises in Paris in the 1940s. In 1948 he composed a series of five études in which recorded sounds of everyday objects or musical instruments were manipulated, edited, and reassembled on phonograph discs for radio broadcast. He later termed such music "*concrète*" because he worked directly with sources of sounds rather than abstractly through the medium of musical notation.

The first of these studies, "Étude aux chemins de fer" ("Railroad Study"), is made, as the title suggests, from the sounds of a locomotive. The sounds are not modified, but are juxtaposed and reassembled in an attempt to imbue them with musical structure. The ascending and descending interval of the fourth of the locomotive's whistle recurs as a formal element, and the clatter of train tracks creates rhythm and meter. In other studies Schaeffer obscured his sources of sound by manipulating phonograph equipment. Timbre and pitch, for example, were altered by changes in the speed of playback, hybrid sounds were created by abutting different parts of different sounds, and entirely new contours of sound were obtained by playing a recording backward. The final version of a work was made by superimposing, mixing, splicing, and otherwise editing these prerecorded elements. With the introduction of tape recording equipment (at first opposed by Schaeffer), these manipulations and techniques of reassembly were greatly expanded and facilitated.

Schaeffer's music was normally referential: the origins of its sounds were usually recognizable. This realism was dissipated in 1949 when he began a collaboration with Pierre Henry (1927–   ). Henry possessed the musical training which Schaeffer lacked, and the works that they composed jointly—beginning with *Symphonie pour un homme seul* (1949–50, later rev.)—reveal greater possibilities inherent in this medium. *Le voile d'Orphée* (*The Veil of Orpheus*, 1953) was extracted and revised by Henry from the opera *Orphée* (1953). The former is called a "cantata," and it combines vocal sounds with unidentifiable noises. The voice becomes intelligible at the climactic reading of a Greek Orphic hymn. Its dramatic and energetic use of sound—reminiscent of the instrumental works of Edgard Varèse—goes far beyond the referentialism of Schaeffer in its powerful abstraction.

The original studio for *musique concrète* at the French Radio run by Schaeffer and Henry was expanded in 1951, when it became known as the Groupe de Recherches de Musique Concrète; it was again reorganized in 1958 as the Groupe de Recherches Musicales. Varèse, Messiaen, Boulez, and Stockhausen worked there briefly. The most successful collaborator was Iannis Xenakis (1922–   ), who composed a series of works which he called "electroacoustic" music between 1955 and 1962. Xenakis was trained as an architect and mathematician, and he used his knowledge of statistics to develop a type of music in conventional media which he termed *stochastic*. In composing such works, Xenakis first makes decisions regarding the medium and basic musical materials and processess. The details of composition are then worked out automatically by mathematical formulas or computer programs which guarantee a random or "stochastic" distribution of events. In his *musique concrète*, however, Xenakis found that natural sounds were already random, thus allowing him to bypass the recondite methods that underlie his instrumental compositions. *Concret P-H* (1958), for example, uses the highly amplified sounds of burning charcoal, which emits a sparkling gossamer of noise. Other works such as *Bohor* (1962) (using the startlingly rich sounds of oriental jewelry and musical instruments) derive their shape from slowly evolving densities, which are manipulated by editorial techniques into dramatic soundscapes.

Pure *musique concrète* did not produce masterpieces beyond the essays of Henry and Xenakis. It was superseded by the flexible resources of synthetically generated sound, which was more compatible with serial organization demanded by many of the younger composers of the 1950s. *Musique concrète*, nevertheless, was the earliest important medium of electronic music. It demonstrated the usefulness of recorded sounds—especially those of the human voice—and it initiated technical processes and studio techniques that were adopted and developed by composers in other media.

In the early 1950s in New York City, Vladimir Ussachevsky (1911–) and Otto Luening (1900–) used early tape recorders to produce works related to French *musique concrète*. Their medium—sometimes called "tape music"—differs from *musique concrète* since it takes its departure from a notated instrumental composition. This composition is recorded on tape and then manipulated by simple techniques such as change of speed, addition of reverberation, and the "feedback effect." Feedback is obtained and stored by dubbing the sounds on a tape as it crosses the playback head onto the same tape at the recording head a small distance away. The effect is a shimmering network of echoes. Ussachevsky's *Sonic Contours* (1952) uses a composition for piano in a tuneful and diatonic style, which is recorded and manipulated primarily by feedback. The works of Ussachevsky and Luening were the first important essays in electronic music in America. But like the idiom of their French contemporaries, tape music soon gave way to more sophisticated styles and apparatuses.

Pure Electronic Music

The distinguishing feature of this medium is the source of its sounds, which are synthesized by electronic devices rather than recorded from live sources as in *musique concrète*. The term "elektronische Musik" was coined around 1950 by German pioneers of such music in order to distinguish it from works of their French counterparts. While our modern notion of electronic music has become considerably broader than this one medium, we shall now use the term "electronic" music in the more restrictive sense of recorded works whose sounds are electronically produced.

The technology for creating electronic signals which are convertible to sounds of fixed or variable pitch had been known since the early twentieth century. Research into the nature of musical sounds and the ways in which they can be simulated electronically was carried on in the early 1950s by the German scientist Werner Meyer-Eppler (1913–60) and musicians Robert Beyer and Herbert Eimert (1897–1972). These three figures were instrumental in founding the first studio for "elektronische Musik" at the North West German Radio in Cologne in 1951. Their studio was brought to great prominence beginning in 1953 by the work there of Karlheinz Stockhausen, which culminated in his electronic masterpieces *Gesang der Jünglinge* (1955–56) and *Kontakte* (1959–60). The studio was used later by Ernst Křenek, Henri Pousseur, Gottfried Michael König, György Ligeti, and other prominent composers. Stockhausen's first works at the studio in Cologne were two *Electronic Studies* (1953 and 1954). These were built entirely from electronic sounds devoid of overtones, and their construction reflects the serialized procedures of composition that were embraced by Stockhausen at this time. The composer also developed a notation for these works giving sufficient technical information for the music to be independently realized.

The compositional procedure of musicians at Cologne or at any of a number of other studios that were founded in Europe and America in the 1950s was divided into three broad phases. Composition began by generating electronic signals that could be converted by loudspeakers into musical sounds. These signals were then modified to obtain more varied characteristics; finally, they were reassembled on tape in a musically satisfying order or mixture. There are several electronic devices that produce signals corresponding to sounds with different colors. The "sine-wave" generator produces pitches of glassy sound without overtones. It was this most basic signal that was preferred by Stockhausen in his early *Electronic Studies*. The "sawtooth-wave" generator produces a nasal pitch with all overtones, and the "rectangular-" or "square-wave" generator, a hollow tone with only odd-numbered harmonics. A "white-noise" generator produces a sound without definite pitch, suggesting the rush of a waterfall, and an "inharmonic" generator can produce bell-like sounds with irregular overtone patterns.

Devices that modify these basic sound elements include "modulators," by which two incoming signals interact to produce a new signal. The *ring modulator* is the most common of these instruments; it produces sums and differences of the incoming frequencies, which can create a sound of wild distortion. "Filters" change the color of a tone by reducing the audibility of some of its overtones, and "reverberators" are devices that introduce echoes. Ostinatos and other such periodic repetitions are easily obtained by placing a musical phrase on a loop of tape. The electronic composition is then assembled by combining these modified signals in the desired order, relative prominence, and texture.

Composition of electronic music in the 1950s was often a tedious exercise in splicing and mixing tape. But studio procedures were greatly simplified in the 1960s by the invention of *synthesizers*, which allowed the composer to generate a sequence of sounds and to combine several manipulations of these source signals in a rapid and facile manner. The first important such tool was the RCA Electronic Music Synthesizer, developed by Dr. Harry F. Olson in the mid-1950s and turned over to the Columbia-Princeton Electronic Music Center in New York in 1959. With this machine the composer encodes on paper tape the succession of sounds he desires, each of which may be given a specific pitch, volume, color, articulation, and duration. The device then realizes the sounds and records them on tape in as many as four channels.

The RCA Synthesizer was of the greatest use to a composer such as Milton Babbitt, since it allowed complete precision in realizing the numerical relationships that underlay serial structures. Babbitt's *Composition for Synthesizer* (1961) and *Ensembles for Synthesizer* (1964) consist entirely of synthesized sound on tape. Both works are serialized and limited to the tonal resources of the traditional twelve-tone scale. A filigree of brief motives, massive chords, and rapid-fire bursts of sound alternate to create a great sense of space and motion. Babbitt's more recent electronic music reflects the general trend of the 1970s toward works combining tape with live performance.

Although Babbitt has been the major composer to use the RCA Synthesizer, the device has helped to produce many other works by numerous musicians. *Time's Encomium* (1968-69) by Charles Wuorinen was realized in part by this machine. The work, over a half hour in duration, uses the twelve tempered pitch classes and serialized structures favored by Babbitt. But it relies more heavily upon sonorous effects. Synthesized sounds, for example, alternate with the same passages electronically modified, most obviously by the addition of reverberation.

Electronic composition was made widely available in the 1960s by the introduction of modular, voltage controlled synthesizers, which have been marketed under such trade names as Moog, Buchla, and ARP. These devices have little in common with the RCA Synthesizer. They consist of several electronic components or "modules," each of which produces an electronic signal. These signals can take on different functions: they can be converted by a loudspeaker to audible sound or they can act upon ("control") the performance of other modules. This latter capability was revolutionary in the ease with which it allowed electronic sounds to be altered. For example, a module producing a pitch can be made to change its frequency simply by applying a "control voltage" to it. The initial pitch can take on a vibrato, tremolo, or other such modifications by the application of other types of voltage signals. Indeed, the possibilities for interaction among modular components provide the composer with a greatly expanded repertory of sounds and greater ease with which they can be obtained.

Music composed with such synthesizers has been both abstract and representational. A series of works by Morton Subotnick (1933–   ) realized on the Buchla synthesizer is of the more abstract type. The composer seeks to express in them some image contained in their title. *Silver Apples of the Moon* (1967), *The Wild Bull* (1968), *Touch* (1968), *Four Butterflies* (1974), and *Sky of Cloudless Sulphur* (1978) are examples. Subotnick's music is very direct, as it uses splashy sounds, spatial gyrations, and elements of conventional music such as rhythms of jazz.

The modular synthesizer is perhaps most widely known for its use in recreating works of the classical masters, such as Walter (Wendy) Carlos's adaptations of music by Bach on the Moog Synthesizer in a recording entitled

"Switched-On Bach." Such electronic transcriptions of pre-existent works are also found in a recording of 1955 made by the engineers of the RCA Synthesizer (RCA Victor LM 1922), in which electronic music was interpreted not as a distinctive idiom but as a means by which preexistent works could be performed.

Computer technology has had several applications to electronic music. In the early 1960s computer programs for sound generation were devised that allowed composers to bypass traditional electronic studios and rely instead on increasingly widespread and sophisticated computer hardware. The style of music first realized by computer programs, such as *Quartets in Pairs* by J. K. Randall and *Changes* by Charles Dodge, was virtually indistinguishable from the type of music that could be realized in the classic studio. But by the early 1970s the dramatic advances in computerized simulation of speech led to computer music of a more distinctive type. Charles Dodge's *Speech Songs* (1973) and *The Story of Our Lives* (1974) use such programs to create works which imaginatively evoke simulated readings of modern poetry.

Recorded Music with Electronic and Concrete Sounds

Electronic music since 1950 has increasingly mixed its styles and media. In the early 1950s, composers both in the Parisian studio for *musique concrète* and at the studio for electronic music in Cologne were generally devoted to a single medium. Stockhausen and his colleagues at Cologne, for example, at first avoided the use of sounds recorded acoustically and even rejected all electronic sounds except the elemental sine-wave tone.

But the earliest masterpieces of electronic music and, indeed, the true maturity of the genre resulted from a freer combination of methods and philosophies. Music made from both concrete and electronic sounds allowed composers to combine the dramatic power of the style of Pierre Henry with the fastidious refinement and structure of the early *Electronic Studies* of Stockhausen. By the later 1950s this mixed medium was exploited by several composers in major works. The concrete sound that was most desired was the human voice. It was a sound with unparalleled power to fix a listener's attention and unique in its ability to express meaning precisely.

The medium of taped music combining vocal and electronic sounds was popularized by a single work, Stockhausen's *Gesang der Jünglinge*. This was perhaps the first masterpiece of electronic music, and it was soon followed by several other works of a similar type. In the following discussion, we shall deal with Stockhausen's *Gesang* and two related pieces: Varèse's *Poème électronique* (1958) and Berio's *Visage* (1961). The three are in very different styles, each reflecting the different artistic personalities of these composers. Stockhausen's *Gesang* is refined and philosophical; Varèse's *Poème*, direct and dramatic; and Berio's *Visage*, human and emotional.

Stockhausen's *Gesang der Jünglinge* is a thirteen-minute work using recorded sounds of a boy soprano singing and speaking texts from the apocryphal "Song of the Three," the hymn of praise to God sung by Shadrach, Meshach, and Abed-nego upon being cast into the blazing furnace of King Nebuchadnezzar. To these vocal sounds, the composer adds a virtuosic array of electronic sounds of the sine-wave type, filtered white noise, and sounds of an impulse generator. These materials are used in a construction that mixes aleatoric elements with highly abstracted serial procedures. The piece is divided into six sections or "textures," but the distinctions between them are scarcely perceptible except in the quiet and sparse third texture, from 2' 52" to 5' 15.5".

It was Stockhausen's intention in *Gesang der Jünglinge* to "mediate" between the vocal and electronic sounds: words of the voice are sometimes broken into noises that seem to merge with the electronic sounds; at other times, distinct German words appear, especially the phrases "lobet den Herrn" and "preiset den Herrn," both meaning "praise the Lord," which recur as formal and programmatic elements. The voice is often compounded into choral effects, and the impact of the work is greatly enhanced by the skillful manipulation of spatial contrasts.

Edgard Varèse's lifelong interest in technology, new musical instruments, and sound as the primary element of music came to fruition late in his career in the electronic medium. His first work involving tape was *Déserts* (1954), in which an ensemble of winds, brass, and percussion alternates with taped sounds. The electronic portions of this piece were begun in the manner of the "tape music" of Luening and Ussachevsky, in which an instrumental ensemble was recorded and enhanced by electronic means. The tape was completed at the studio of the Groupe de Recherches de Musique Concrète in Paris in 1954.

Varèse's only work entirely in the medium of tape is *Poème électronique*. It was commissioned by the Philips Corporation for use at the World's Fair in Brussels in 1958 in a tent-like pavilion designed by the architect Le Corbusier (1887–1965). Varèse's music, composed on three channels, was played continuously over 400 loudspeakers in the pavilion to accompany abstract visual projections.

The work is highly eclectic in its sources of sound. Purely electronic sounds were synthesized at the Philips Laboratories in Holland in 1957; these were subsequently combined with recorded sounds of bells, organ, excerpts of percussion music from his own earlier works, and, of great dramatic significance, an eerie wail of a human voice. As in most of Varèse's music, *Poème électronique* is tied together by recurrences of a short motive, in this case a high-pitched figure sliding upward between three chromatic tones. The work is slowly paced, which increases its dramatic impact in a way that has the opposite effect of Milton Babbitt's later high-speed studies on the RCA Synthesizer. Varèse's dramatic use of sound reaches its climax with the entrance of the voice in an unearthly moan. Despite the absence of a text, the voice vividly conveys dramatic meaning by its tortured sound and by the serene vocalization at the end. "I wanted it to express tragedy—an inquisition," the composer later remarked.

Most works in the electronic medium by Luciano Berio were composed during the years 1955 to 1961, when he collaborated with Bruno Maderna at the Studio di Fonologia Musicale in Milan. His *Thema (Omaggio a Joyce)*, a taped work assembled from readings in James Joyce's *Ulysses*, was a turning point in his style as a composer. Most of his compositions from this time, whether performed or taped, employ the voice in a dramatic and unorthodox fashion.

Visage combines electronic sounds with those of a solo

soprano. Its dramatic treatment of the voice surpasses Varèse's *Poème* by thrusting the voice into a position of greater prominence and by allowing it to rush headlong through a whole gamut of emotions. The form of *Visage* is shaped by a gradual disintegration in the voice and in the vivid personality or "visage" that it represents. At the beginning the singer utters sounds of fear, satisfaction, joy, and sadness in a dizzying soliloquy accompanied by electronic commentary. By the end of the piece, however, the voice has been completely obliterated and swallowed up by electronic noise. The work is unified by recurrences of the word *paroles* ("words"), which is the single intelligible vocal utterance.

Many other composers have been attracted to the medium of taped music which combines electronic and recorded sounds. *Events* (1963) by Mel Powell (1923–   ) uses three different readings of Hart Crane's poem "Legend," which are manipulated with the addition of electronic sounds. The vivid imagery and dislocated syntax of the poem invite the highly dramatic and collage-like realization. *Sonic Seasonings* by Walter Carlos is a sort of *Pastoral Symphony* of electronic effects. It mixes sounds recorded in nature, instrumental passages, and electronic noises into a vivid depiction of the four seasons.

Live Performance with Taped Sounds

Music in media that we have now surveyed—electronic works, that is, which are entirely contained on tape—either eliminates the performer or relegates him to the role of an unseen maker of sounds. Such music has had no precedent in history. The performer had earlier been the indispensable medium by which the composer's thoughts were conveyed to the audience, and since the nineteenth century the performer had in fact rivaled the composer as the central figure in musical creation.

Some composers at first relished the opportunity to repossess this creative territory and bypass the performer altogether. Taped music allowed them direct contact with the audience and helped to eliminate the inevitable imper fections of live performances and interpretations that were not faithful to the composer's intent. But it soon became plain that these advantages were outweighed by the loss of spontaneity and of the drama of live performance. By 1970 music entirely on tape had lost favor, as composers of electronic works sought to revive the concert as a relevant musical event.

Live performance with coordinated taped sounds offered a straightforward compromise. This type of music had been composed since the early 1950s. Bruno Maderna's *Musica su due dimensioni* (1952, rev. 1958) combined solo flute with sounds on tape, and Varèse's *Déserts* called for an alternation of wind and percussion ensemble and recorded sounds. Vladimir Ussachevsky and Otto Luening collaborated on several works of the mid-1950s for tape and orchestra, including *A Poem in Cycles and Bells* (1954). Their *Concerted Piece for Tape Recorder and Orchestra* (1960) places taped sounds in the role of soloist in a traditional concerto.

By the 1960s this hybrid medium had branched into several styles. Milton Babbitt combined live music for soprano with taped sounds in three works, *Vision and Prayer* (1961), *Philomel* (1963), and *Phonemena* (1969–70). The first of these is a setting of poetry of the same title by Dylan Thomas. The electronic sounds were realized on the RCA Synthesizer and are organized serially. The voice is treated in a restrained fashion, alternating between recitation and conventional singing.

Berio's *Questo vuol dire che* (1969), on the other hand, merges tape with chorus and uses vocal techniques that are much more unconventional. This work combines folk texts in three languages and nonsensical vocal noise. Electronic music by Luigi Nono also combines tape and voice, but in his works the voices are vividly intelligible and serve to emphasize the message of socialism and struggle against economic and political tyranny, which is the purpose of his music. *La fabbrica illuminata* (1964), for example, combines a tape (made from vocal sounds and noises from a factory) with a soprano protesting against the degrading existence of laborers.

Electronic compositions of Mario Davidovsky (1934–) and Jacob Druckman (1928–) include series of works for instrumental performers and tape. Davidovsky has com-

posed eight such pieces which he calls *Synchronisms*
(1963–74). The taped sounds are derived in part from the
instruments that they accompany. The related series *Animus* (1966–69) by Jacob Druckman includes three pieces,
combining tape with trombone, voice and percussion, and
clarinet. His *Synapse→Valentine* (1970) uses double bass
and tape in a similar way.

Druckman's *Animus III* (1969) for tape and clarinet
enhances the performing situation by an amusing theatrical encounter between player and tape. In a note to the
score, the composer outlines the story: "The clarinetist
enters in the person of an arch-virtuoso, self-confident
almost to the point of arrogance. During the sixteen min-
utes of the work, there is a gradual dissolution of the personality of the player. The person who leaves the stage at
the end of the work is dissociated and hysterical to the
point of insanity." The taped sounds suggest both a rival
musician—whose abstract "virtuosity" plants seeds of self-
doubt within the clarinetist—and the audience, who
respond to his playing by laughter and rude gestures.

Live Electronic Music

This medium, in which sounds produced in live concert situations are immediately manipulated by electronic
devices, has been the primary area of concentration and
innovation in electronic music since 1970. It has brought
about close contact between "serious" composers and performers and rock musicians, a development that will be
traced in Chapter 16. The medium has also been essential
to a group of American composers often designated as
"minimalists": Philip Glass, La Monte Young, Terry Riley,
and Steve Reich. Their music will also be considered in
Chapter 16.

Live electronic music harkens back to experimental
compositions by John Cage in the 1930s. His series of five
Imaginary Landscapes (1939–52) calls for diverse electronic
instruments, including phonograph recordings, radios, phonograph cartridges, and oscillators. Cage's *Cartridge Music*
(1960) was the first important piece in which sounds were

modified electronically on the spot. Like Cage's other works in electronic media after 1952, this piece is indeterminate of composition and performance. Any number of players attach phonograph cartridges and contact microphones to any sound-producing materials, and the noises that result are varied by amplifiers and reproduced on loudspeakers.

Cage's experiments were developed with remarkable diversity in a series of compositions by Karlheinz Stockhausen beginning with *Mikrophonie I* (1964). This is a work in "moment form" (see Chapter 13) in which the sonorous events of each moment are precisely notated. Two performers produce sounds on a large tamtam, two other players position microphones, and two players control filters and amplifiers.

Stockhausen's *Mixtur* (1964) for orchestra and *Mikrophonie II* (1965) for chorus and Hammond organ use ring modulation to modify performed sounds, a technique to which he returned in *Mantra* (1970) for two pianos and percussion. *Solo* (1965–66) is for one instrumentalist whose music is recorded on a tape loop as it is performed. The recorded sounds and newly performed sounds are progressively added to the tape, building up ostinatos of increasing complexity.

Stockhausen was active from 1964 as a performer, touring with an ensemble devoted to realizations of his own music. *Prozession* (1967) was written for this group. It is a lengthy work improvised by players on keyboard, string, and percussion instruments from excerpts drawn from Stockhausen's own earlier compositions. The music is then modified by on-the-spot filtering and amplification. *Kurzwellen* (1968) is similar except that the players improvise upon music they hear on radios.

Other composers who have worked in the medium of live electronic music include Max Neuhaus and Morton Subotnick. Neuhaus's recording entitled "Electronics and Percussion" (Columbia MS 7139) includes realizations of music by Earle Brown, Sylvano Bussotti, and John Cage; his interpretations apply techniques of amplification and feedback. Recent compositions by Morton Subotnick such as *The Wild Beasts* (1978), *After the Butterfly* (1980), and *Axolotl* (1980) combine live instrumental performance with an imaginative application of the voltage controlled synthesizer. While Subotnick and others had earlier used the synthesizer to produce manipulations of electronic sounds on tape, in these words he uses a tape of sounds to control the synthesizer, which in turn modifies the sounds of the performer. Subotnick first composes music for the performer using standard notation. This music is played and picked up by a microphone by which it is relayed to the synthesizer for modification and reproduction through loudspeakers. The modification of sounds is guided by a "gesture sketch" made by the composer in the form of a tape of sounds of varying pitch and loudness. This tape is not audible at the performance, but instead serves to trigger the synthesizer to modify the performed music. These "ghost electronics," to use Subotnick's term, are an extension of the traditional modulators found in the classic electronic music studio and used widely in the live electronic idiom. But they are capable of a much wider range of manipulation of the incoming signal, as they can produce changes in its volume, direction, pitch, rhythm and attack, and timbre.

Bibliography

Two excellent surveys of electronic music are Elliott Schwartz's *Electronic Music: A Listener's Guide* (New York, 1973) and Paul Griffiths's *Guide to Electronic Music* (New York, 1979). An exhaustive bibliography of literature on this subject to 1967 is found in Lowell Cross, *A Bibliography of Electronic Music* (Toronto, 1968). Current developments in computer applications to music are found in the *Computer Music Journal* (1977–); also see Wayne Bateman's *Introduction to Computer Music* (New York, 1980). Hubert Howe's *Electronic Music Synthesis* (New York, 1975) is a detailed introduction to studio techniques and use of the synthesizer. A history of the early days of electronic music is given by Lowell Cross in "Electronic Music, 1948–1953," *Perspectives of New Music,* 7 (1968), 32–65.

Stockhausen's "Origins of Electronic Music," *Musical Times,* 112 (1971), 649–50, seeks to assert the priority of

European developments in this medium over American initiatives. Stockhausen's article "Actualia," *Die Reihe,* 1 (1955; English trans., 1958) deals with aspects of *Gesang der Jünglinge.* Otto Luening gives a lively account of his introduction to electronic media in his memoirs *The Odyssey of an American Composer* (New York, 1980). Studies of works by other composers of electronic music are surveyed in the Bibliographies to Chapters 12 and 13. Recorded examples of sounds and their modification by control voltage are found on "The Nonesuch Guide to Electronic Music," Nonesuch HC 73018.

A discography of works cited in this chapter follows:

Babbitt	*Composition for Synthesizer,* Columbia MS 6566
	Ensembles for Synthesizer, Columbia MS 7051
	Phonemena, New World NW 209
	Philomel, Acoustic Research AR 0654
	Vision and Prayer, CRI SD 268
Berio	*Visage,* Candide CE 31027
Cage	*Cartridge Music,* Time 58009
Carlos	*Sonic Seasonings,* Columbia PG 31234
	Switched-On Bach, Columbia MS 7194
Davidovsky	*Synchronisms nos. 1–3,* CRI SD 204
	Synchronisms no. 5, CRI SD 268
	Synchronisms no. 6, Turnabout TV 34487S
	Synchronisms no. 8, Vox SVBX 5307
Dodge	*Changes,* Nonesuch H 71245
	Speech Songs CRI SD 348
	The Story of Our Lives, CRI SD 348
Druckman	*Animus III,* Nonesuch H 71253
Henry	*Orphée,* Philips 839 484 LY (with Pierre Schaeffer)
	Le voile d'Orphée, Ducretet-Thomson DUC 8 LDG 1497
Maderna	*Musica su due dimensioni,* Compagnia generale del disco ESZ 3
Nono	*La fabbrica illuminata,* Wergo 60038
Powell	*Events,* CRI 227 USD

Randall	*Quartets in Pairs*, Nonesuch H 71245
RCA Electronic Music Synthesizer	*Sounds and Music of the RCA Electronic Music Synthesizer*, RCA Victor LM 1922
Schaeffer	*Étude aux chemins de fer*, Ducretet-Thomson DUC 8 LDG 1497
	(with Pierre Henry): *Symphonie pour un homme seul*, London DTL 93121
Stockhausen	*Gesang der Jünglinge*, DGG 138811
	Kontakte, DGG 138811
	Kurzwellen, DGG 139 461
	Mantra, DGG 2530 208
	Mikrophonie I and II, Columbia MS 7355
	Prozession, Candide CE 31001
	Solo, DGG 137 005
	Studie I, II, DGG LP 16133
Subotnick	*After the Butterfly*, Nonesuch N 78001
	Axolotl, Nonesuch N 78012
	Four Butterflies, Columbia M 32741
	Silver Apples of the Moon, Nonesuch H 71174
	Sky of Cloudless Sulphur, Nonesuch N 78001
	Touch, Columbia MS 7316
	The Wild Beast, Nonesuch N 78012
	The Wild Bull, Nonesuch, H 71208
Ussachevsky	*Sonic Contours*, Desto DC 6466
	(with Otto Luening): *Concerted Piece for Tape Recorder and Orchestra*, CRI 227 USD
	(with Otto Luening): *Poem in Cycles and Bells*, CRI 112
Varèse	*Déserts*, CRI SD 268
	Poème électronique, Columbia MS 6146
Wuorinen	*Time's Encomium*, Nonesuch, H 71225
Xenakis	*Bohor*, Nonesuch H 71246
	Concret P-H, Nonesuch H 71246

• 15 •

ECLECTICISM

Composers throughout the twentieth century have discovered sources for their own musical speech in the works of others. Despite the pronounced originality of much of the music of this century, there has been nonetheless a broad reliance upon preexistent styles and upon frequent borrowings from earlier music. We shall call composition of this type *eclectic.*

Eclecticism has been a significant element of the art of music since its early history. Certain repertories of medieval chant were assembled by singers and composers from preexistent melodic formulas, and early polyphony used preexistent lines as a basis for contrapuntal elaboration. Among the great composers of the common-practice era, Johann Sebastian Bach was notably eclectic. Most of his compositions for the church incorporate traditional Lutheran hymns, and he drew freely upon established styles such as the language of the French clavecinists and the instrumental idiom of Vivaldi. Eclecticism was less prominent among composers of the classical and early romantic periods because of the widespread acceptance of a common stylistic language. But it was revived in the twentieth century as the prospects for a new common practice grew increasingly dim. Eclecticism offers the modern composer a link with his cultural forebears and a ready way to make his music accessible and to imbue it with meaning.

In the twentieth century eclecticism has appeared in

three principal guises: the assimilation and use of established styles, quotations of preexistent music, and artistic arrangements. Each of these has been in evidence both before and after the Second World War. The adoption of elements from an earlier style of Western music is the basis of neoclassicism, a dominant trend in music between the world wars. The styles imitated by the neoclassicists were varied, but their reinterpretations gave rise to music with much in common, including allegiance to the triad, diatonic scales, traditional forms, and regularity of rhythm and meter. As we shall see shortly, the eclecticism of postwar composers such as Messiaen, Berio, and Penderecki did not manifest such common traits.

While the neoclassicists looked for antecedents in Western art for points of departure, other composers found usable styles in the more remote areas of popular music or music of the Orient. The percussive, metallic sonorities of the Balinese gamelan were imitated by Debussy and many of his French contemporaries and successors. Music of the East was also evoked in works by American composers such as Cowell, Cage, Harrison, and Alan Hovhaness (1911–). Charles Ives, on the other hand, assimilated the styles of American vernacular music and musicians—the gospel singer, the country band, the ragtime pianist, and the patriotic march among others.

Quotations from preexistent musical works have occurred repeatedly in this century. Richard Wagner was no doubt the composer most often cited by earlier twentieth-century composers. Wagner's monumentality of manner invited caricature: thus Debussy quotes the opening of *Tristan und Isolde* in his piano piece "Golliwogg's Cake Walk," parodying Wagner's hyperemotional rhetoric. Hindemith quotes from King Mark's music in *Tristan* in his opera *Das Nusch-Nuschi* (1920) as an ironic reference to the plight of a character who is to be castrated for indiscretions with an emperor's wives. *Tristan* was quoted with programmatic meaning by Alban Berg in his string quartet *Lyric* Suite as a secretive reference to his love for Hanna Fuchs-Robettin.

Quotation served many other purposes among composers of the first half of the century. Charles Ives quoted popular American tunes in order to educe his artistic roots. His use of music by his contemporaries such as Debussy or

Tchaikovsky conveys his disdain for their lack of substance. The symphonies of Mahler frequently quote from among this composer's own earlier works in order to document their autobiographical or self-reflective content.

In the postwar era, quotation has often gone beyond its earlier ironic or referential function to take on an abstract and often enigmatic quality, where sources are quoted in such profusion and variety that no single point is made. The quotation-collages of Bernd Zimmermann (1918–70), which include his opera *Die Soldaten* (1964), *Monologe* for two pianos (1964), and *Photoptosis* for orchestra (1968), pile quotations from all eras of musical history into an olio of provocative but ununified sounds. Mauricio Kagel's *Ludwig van* (1969) is a mad hodgepodge of themes from the music of Beethoven. Michael Tippett's *Songs for Dov* for tenor and chamber orchestra (1969–70) quotes from music by Beethoven, Wagner, Musorgski, and Tippett's earlier music. We shall return shortly to the quotation-collage in reference to Luciano Berio's *Sinfonia.*

An especially fruitful product of twentieth-century eclecticism has been the *artistic arrangement:* a transcription of a preexistent work that reflects the artistic personality of the arranger. Such works were common in the first half of the century, especially in the superb folk-song arrangements of Falla, Bartók, Ravel, Ives, and others. Stravinsky's ballet *Pulcinella*—an arrangement of music by Pergolesi and other eighteenth-century composers—and Webern's setting of the six-part ricercar from Bach's *Musical Offering* are imposing examples of the artistic arrangement which go far beyond the aphoristic folk song.

Eclecticism became an ever stronger element in music after World War II. But it differed from the pre-war phenomenon in the greater diversity of styles that it produced and the greater variety of sources that it appropriated. In works of composers whom we shall now discuss—Olivier Messiaen, Peter Maxwell Davies, George Rochberg, George Crumb, Luciano Berio, Krzysztof Penderecki, and Hans Werner Henze—we shall see little of the stylistic consistency that marked the work of pre-war eclectics. Instead, eclecticism became an abstract and varied means of artistic orientation from which the most diverse musical utterances could emanate.

Olivier Messiaen

Among all major composers of the postwar era, Olivier Messiaen (1908–   ) best exemplifies the spirit of eclecticism. His music is largely assembled from preexistent sources, some of which he enumerates in the Preface to his *Technique of My Musical Language*: "birds, Russian music, Debussy's *Pelléas et Mélisande*, plainchant, Hindu rhythmics, the mountains of Dauphiné, and, finally, all that evokes stain-glass window and rainbow." But these borrowed elements are rarely presented in a straightforward manner: instead, they are transformed and reconstituted as an entirely original idiom. In his *Technique* Messiaen refers to this process of transformation as the "deforming prism" through which all of his materials must pass.

The varied and often exotic sources of Messiaen's works are chosen both for their musical values and for their contribution to an elaborate symbolism that all of his music embodies. Three broad and interrelated subjects inform his work: premises of the Catholic faith, human love, and nature. Messiaen has stated that the last two are symbols of divine love, which underlies his understanding of Christianity.

Messiaen's music is in many respects a continuation of the modern school of French and Russian composition of the late nineteenth and early twentieth centuries. Like Scriabin and Rimski-Korsakov, Messiaen vividly associates colors with certain chords and tonalities. Like Stravinsky, Scriabin, Rimski-Korsakov, Debussy, and Ravel, he often exploits the harmonic resources of the octatonic scale. This is one of seven symmetric sets that he calls "modes of limited transposition" and uses in most of his works. Like Debussy and Ravel, he frequently evokes the percussive sonorities of the oriental gamelan.

Messiaen's music is relatively consistent in style, except for a period in the early 1950s when he experimented with pseudo-serial techniques and pointillist textures (see Chapter 12). His treatment of rhythm and meter—one of the most distinctive aspects of his music—is discussed in Chapter 5. In general, the element of time in

OLIVIER MESSIAEN
(Avignon, 1908—)

Messiaen has attributed his artistic sensitivity to his parents. His father was a scholar of English literature; his mother, a poet. His desire to pursue the career of a musician stemmed from a childhood hearing of *Pelléas et Mélisande.* Messiaen attended the Conservatory in Paris from 1919 to 1930, during which time he studied composition with Paul Dukas and became a celebrated organist. He collaborated with André Jolivet, Daniel Lesur, and Yves Baudrier in the group "Young France," which from 1936 called for a music of renewed depth as an alternative to the superficial wit of French neoclassicism.

During the Second World War Messiaen spent two years in Silesia as a prisoner of war, during which he composed his *Quartet for the End of Time.* Since 1942 he has taught various subjects at the Conservatory in Paris and held private composition classes. He long served as organist at the Church of the Holy Trinity in Paris.

Selected Works

Orchestral Music. *Turangalîla-Symphonie* (1946–48), *Réveil des oiseaux* (1953), *Oiseaux exotiques* (1956), *Chronochromie* (1960), *Sept Haïkaï* (1962), *Couleurs de la cité céleste* (1963), *Et exspecto resurrectionem mortuorum* (1964), *Des canyons aux étoiles* (1974).

Chamber Music. *Quatuor pour la fin du temps* (1940), *Le merle noir* (flute and piano, 1951).

Piano Music. Preludes (1929), *Visions de l'amen* (two pianos, 1943), *Vingt regards sur l'enfant Jésus* (1944), *Cantéyodjayâ* (1948), "Mode de valeurs et d'intensités" (1949), *Ile de feu I* and II (1949), *Catalogue d'oiseaux* (1956–58), *La fauvette des jardins* (1972).

Organ Music. *L'ascension* (1934), *La nativité du seigneur* (1935), *Les corps glorieux* (1939), *Messe de la pentecôte* (1950), *Livre d'orgue* (1951), *Méditations sur le mystère de la sainte trinité* (1969).

Songs. *Poèmes pour Mi* (1936), *Chants de terre et de ciel* (1938), *Harawi* (1945).

Choral Music. *O sacrum convivium!* (1937), *Choeurs pour une Jeanne d'Arc* (1941), *Trois petites liturgies de la présence divine* (1944), *Cinq rechants* (1949), *La transfiguration de notre seigneur Jésus-Christ* (1963–69).

his work is not organized by subdividing a steady beat or regular metric group. Rhythms are instead spun from small values into freely varied larger shapes.

Harmonies are generally derived from Messiaen's modes of limited transposition, which are sets of between six and ten pitch classes dividing the octave symmetrically. These modes are atonal sets: they do not necessarily relate to a keynote, and they are subject to free reordering and transposition.

Mode 1: C D E F♯ G♯ A♯ (C)
Mode 2: C C♯ D♯ E F♯ G A A♯ (C)
Mode 3: C C♯ D E F F♯ G♯ A A♯ (C)
Mode 4: C C♯ D D♯ F♯ G G♯ A (C)
Mode 5: C C♯ D F♯ G G♯ (C)
Mode 6: C C♯ D E F♯ G G♯ A♯ (C)
Mode 7: C C♯ D D♯ E F♯ G G♯ A A♯ (C)

The first mode is a whole-tone scale, which Messiaen uses infrequently, and the second mode—his most characteristic large harmony—is the octatonic scale. His harmonies sometimes emphasize dissonant chords with triadic components, which he attributes to the "addition" of dissonant notes to familiar chords. Messiaen also states that his music typically asserts a keynote perceptible over spans of varying length, but his work makes no significant use of common-practice tonality.

In the rhythmic dimension, Messiaen has frequent recourse to preexistent sources. He was especially fond of the 120 rhythmic patterns or "talas" that had been assembled in a treatise by the ancient Hindu theorist Sharngadeva. Other rhythms are derived from the metric feet of Greek poetry. In his orchestral work *Chronochromie*, Messiaen uses rhythms derived from permutations of the numbers 1 to 32. Each integer represents a duration of the same number of thirty-second-note values. He refers to these permutations as "interversions" and uses the rhythmic patterns that resulted in several later pieces.

Messiaen asserts in his *Technique* that melody is the primary factor in his music. "Supremacy to melody," he writes, "the noblest element of music." The most striking of his melodic borrowings are his imitations of bird song. From his youth, he had studied and transcribed the songs of birds, which were applied in his music from 1941. The bird songs are first passed through his deforming prism, as their calls must be reinterpreted in the twelve traditional pitch classes and approximated in register, color, and rhythm. Bird song offered Messiaen not only a "found object" of great musical interest, but it also symbolized for him the music of God as He is revealed in nature. Messiaen also appropriates plainchant, motivic fragments from traditional Indian music, and paraphrases of motives from works by which he was inspired, especially from Musorgski's *Boris Godunov* and Debussy's *Pelléas et Mélisande*.

Couleurs de la cité céleste (*Colors of the Celestial City*, 1963) synthesizes most of Messiaen's earlier eclectic procedures. This work, written for clarinets, brass, piano, and percussion, is based upon five passages from the Revelation of John, the last book of the New Testament. These passages emphasize the colors that John so vividly describes in his vision of Jerusalem—colors that Messiaen seeks to evoke by combining his instrumental forces into blocks of sound.

The composer describes his manipulation of sound and color in the Preface to the score:

> The form of this work relies entirely on colors. Melodic or rhythmic themes and masses of sounds and timbres are transformed like colors. Within their constantly changing shapes can be found (by analogy) warm and cold colors, complementary colors influencing their neighbors, colors washed out toward white or compressed toward black. These transformations can be compared to characters acting on several superimposed stages, who simultaneously unfold their different stories.

The form of this one-movement piece consists in an alternation of five types of music: bird songs, quotations from Gregorian alleluias, slow-moving chords evoking colors, music depicting the abyss, and passages based on Indian and serial-derived rhythms. These sections are distinctly separated by changes of tempo, by intervening silence, and by their own harmonic and melodic character. The total effect is of a mosaic that is put together arbitrarily, or, as Messiaen writes in the Preface, "The work does not end, never having truly begun. It turns on itself, interlacing its temporal blocks as in a cathedral's rose window, made from flamboyant and invisible colors."

The harmonic language of *Colors* does not rely primarily upon the modes of limited transposition. Although these sets occur in passing, the composer dwells more upon chords and constellations of pitches embracing the entire chromatic set, reflecting his experiments with integral serialism of a decade earlier. The three "color chords" at rehearsal 11 (Example 15-1) will illustrate this emphasis on the aggregate. All twelve pitch classes are found in the verticalities of each measure. These chords are labeled in the score "yellow topaz, clear green chrysoprase, and crystal," after the colored gems mentioned in Revelation. It may be observed also that the chord heard on the downbeat of the second measure of rehearsal 11 (see Example 15-2) is a form of Messiaen's mode 4.

Messiaen quotes four plainchant Alleluias, each chosen because of the appropriateness of its text to images from

Example 15-1.   Messiaen, *Couleurs de la cité céleste,* non-transposing score. Copyright by Alphonse Leduc, Paris. Owners and publishers for all countries. Reprinted by permission.

Revelation. These chants illustrate different ways in which Messiaen uses preexistent sources. The Alleluias for the Feast of Corpus Christi and Dedication of a Church are quoted intact, although they are harmonized in an atonal manner. The Alleluia for the Eighth Sunday after Pentecost, on the other hand, is quoted in contour, but with intervallic

Clars.

Mode 4 (transposed)

Tpts.,
Tbns.

Example 15-2. Messiaen, *Couleurs de la cité céleste*. Copyright by Alphonse Leduc, Paris. Owners and publishers for all countries. Reprinted by permission.

distortions (Example 15-3). The Alleluia for the Fourth Sunday after Easter is entirely distorted and used as a *Klangfarbenmelodie* divided between bells, horn, clarinets, and piano (Example 15-4).

The quotations from chant and color chords alternate with quotations of bird songs, the latter dispensing with brass and using hard and bright sounds evocative of the oriental gamelan. A middle section (rehearsal 42 to 62) applies five rhythmic patterns derived from the talas of Sharngadeva, and this passage also interlaces rhythms based on interversions of the numerical series used by Messiaen in *Chronochromie*.

Peter Maxwell Davies

While Messiaen's musical sources are unparalleled in their diversity, the various means of application of preexistent materials are more exhaustively explored by Peter

a) Alleluia Magnus dominus

Al   -   le - lu   -   -   -   -   ia

b) Piccolo Trumpet

Example 15-3. Messiaen, *Couleurs de la cité céleste*. Copyright by Alphonse Leduc, Paris. Owners and publishers for all countries. Reprinted by permission.

a) Alleluia Christus resurgens

Example 15-4. Messiaen, *Couleurs de la cité céleste.* Copyright by Alphonse Leduc, Paris. Owners and publishers for all countries. Reprinted by permission.

Maxwell Davies (1934–   ). Davies has focused largely upon Gregorian chant and works of medieval and Renaissance composers who have themselves adapted preexistent material. *Alma redemptoris mater,* composed in the year of his graduation from the Royal Manchester College of Music (1957), sets the tone for most of his later works in its adaptation of a work of Renaissance polyphony. This chamber piece is dependent on John Dunstable's motet of the same title, which is based on the Marian antiphon "Alma redemptoris mater." Davies's use of his model is highly abstract, mirroring structural principles of Dunstable's motet rather than quoting or paraphrasing.

Davies's assimilation of early music has produced artistic arrangements of works by Buxtehude, Dunstable, Purcell, and others as well as pieces in which the model is only dimly perceived. He often reinterprets ways in which early composers used preexistent material, such as cantus firmus or parody techniques, or he imitates other structural principles of medieval and Renaissance music such as isorhythm, metric prolations or proportions, and varied canonic devices. His *Antechrist* (1967) for instrumental ensemble includes a complete quotation of an anonymous medieval motet, "Deo confitemini—Domino," which is surrounded by music abstractly derived from this motet. *Psalm 124* weaves three Renaissance works into a freely dissonant counterpoint.

Ave maris stella (1975) for instrumental sextet takes its title from plainchant. This source is heard only at the very end of Davies's lengthy piece, and most of the music is drawn from a matrix of numbers and pitch classes recalling the procedures of integral serialism. This "magic square" determines nondodecaphonic series of pitches and series of numbers dictating durations. Davies returned to the same matrix in his Symphony no. 1 (1973–76).

Regardless of its sources or preplanned compositional structures, the music of Davies is highly varied in style. Most works are freely chromatic and atonal with a considerable use of triadic sonorities and tonality by assertion. Other works (such as the carols from *O Magnum Mysterium*) are pseudo-modal, imitating the texture of Renaissance polyphony but much freer in treatment of dissonance. A series of compositions written around 1969 evoke foxtrots and other popular music. One such work is the orchestral *St. Thomas Wake* (1969). Three separate styles interact in this piece: a pavane by John Bull (played on harp) from which Davies borrowed his title; foxtrots played by a dance band; and "serious" symphonic music played by orchestra. Material from the pavane is developed by both orchestra and dance band.

Also around 1969 Davies worked in "multimedia" or theatric music—an important development in the postwar era to be discussed further in Chapter 16. His pieces of this type include *Eight Songs for a Mad King* (1969), to be discussed presently, *Vesalii icones* (1969) for dancer and instrumental ensemble, and *Missa super l'homme armé* (1968, rev. 1971) for speaker and instrumental ensemble.

Eight Songs for a Mad King dramatizes the insanity of the English monarch George III (1738–1820) during the last decade of his life. George was an amateur player of harpsichord and flute and a great devotee of the music of Handel. During this period of mental incompetency, he is known to have sought diversion by teaching birds to sing. The work consists of eight texts written by Randolph Stow (which

incorporate lines thought to have been spoken by the king).
These are sung or declaimed by a character acting the part
of the monarch, and they depict his interests, obsessions,
and reflections upon his plight. Four of the six instrumentalists sit in bird cages, representing the birds that the king
coaches to sing.

The seventh song, "Country Dance" (Anthology no. 17),
finds the king regaling the people of Windsor by a mad
rendition of the tenor recitative "Comfort Ye, My People"
from Handel's *Messiah*. His mood suddenly turns grim, as
he grabs a violin from one of the caged performers and rails
on the evils of the world. Toward the end he smashes the
violin—representing his soul—and dissolves into a wrench-
ing, disconnected monologue. Davies treats the Handelian
recitative in the style of a cocktail pianist, which gives way
to a foxtrot as the king encourages the merrymakers of
Windsor. As the king's momentary lucidity gives way to
tortured ravings, the music descends into a cacophonous
din.

In the eighth and final song ("The Review: A Spanish
March") King George solemnly pronounces his obituary. He
leaves the stage howling, and, as a final recollection of
beatings which he had received, he is followed offstage by a
bass drum played with leather whips.

George Rochberg

"I think borrowing is one of the essential traditions of
music, an ancient one. And if you are a borrower, as I am,
then I see nothing to prevent borrowing from oneself." This
excerpt from an interview in *Soundpieces* (1982) underscores the conversion to eclecticism of George Rochberg
(1918–   ). His works of the 1950s and early 1960s, including
Twelve Bagatelles (1952), Symphony no. 2 (1956), and Piano
Trio (1963), combine serialism with the grandiloquent styles
of Mahler and early Schoenberg. By the mid-1960s he had rejected serialism. He writes:

> I had become completely dissatisfied with [serial-
> ism's] narrow terms. I found the palette of constant

chromaticism increasingly constricting, nor could I accept any longer the limited range of gestures that always seemed to channel the music into some form or other of expressionism. The over-intense manner of serialism and its tendency to inhibit physical pulse and rhythm led me to question a style which made it virtually impossible to express serenity, tranquillity, grace, wit, energy. [From liner notes to Nonesuch Records, H 71283.]

Rochberg's flight from serialism had an aftermath different from the general collapse of European serialism of the late 1950s. The Europeans moved from serialism into other avant-garde areas—indeterminacy, theater, and composition with textures among others—but Rochberg looked to the nineteenth century for usable alternatives.

The music of Charles Ives pointed his way. In the Second String Quartet (1961), Rochberg adapted Ives's multilayered polyphony in which strata are partially distinguished by different tempi. Ives's music also had a far-reaching effect on Rochberg in its eclectic combination of diverse styles and preexistent music. These features were refined by Rochberg in the quotation-collages *Contra mortem et tempus* (1965) and *Music for the Magic Theater* (1965, rev. 1969), in which music by Ives, Varèse, Webern, Mahler, Beethoven, and Mozart mingle in order "to project an almost cinematic series of shifting ideas and levels."

By the time of the Third String Quartet (1971–72), another new idiom—which he termed "multi-gestural"—was in place. Here the composer adopts a different preexistent style in each movement. These styles may evoke the language of a single earlier composer, as in the third movement, which recalls the quartets of Beethoven in its expansion into the very high and low registers. Other movements represent a conflation of several styles, including those of the earlier twentieth century.

Such multigestural music, writes Rochberg, "makes possible the combination and juxtaposition of a variety of means which denies neither the past nor the present." His basic language, nevertheless, became common-practice tonality, which he embraced wholeheartedly as a flexible means to a unified and comprehensible musical speech. Accordingly, Rochberg makes little attempt to reinterpret tonality as did many neoclassicists between the world wars. He does not seek such expressions of originality: "I have had to abandon the notion of 'originality,'" he writes, "in which the personal style of the artist and his ego are the supreme values."

The Sixth String Quartet (1978) is one of Rochberg's most successful eclectic works. Its first and fourth movements (Fantasia and Serenade) are atonal, each touching briefly upon familiar styles of the early twentieth century (including those of Webern and Bartók). The second and fifth movements (Scherzo and Introduction/Finale) are in the keys of B♭ and G, and the finale is especially indebted to the finales of Beethoven's quartets. The central third movement (Anthology no. 29) is in the form of variations upon material from a canon by Johann Pachelbel (1653–1706). The borrowed material consists of a basso ostinato of four measures length and the head motive of the leading canonic voice (Example 15-5).

This subject is elaborated not as a canon but as a chaconne, that is, by continuous variations upon either or both lines. The variations move stylistically from the idiom of the baroque (mm. 1–12), through the elegant tunefulness of the classical period (mm. 13–24), into the early romantic period (mm. 25–45), finally coming to an emotional climax with the language of Mahler and his post-Wagnerian contemporaries (mm. 45–72). The final variations are reflective upon all of the preceding, ending with fragments of the primary material.

George Crumb

George Crumb (1929–) has developed a distinctive approach to composition that brings together quotations of Western music and elements from music of the Orient.

Example 15-5.   Pachelbel, Canon in D.

Most of his works contain an intricate symbolism, and all are informed by the liberation of sound stemming from electronic music.

Beginning with *Night Music I* (1963), Crumb repeatedly uses the surrealistic poetry of Federico García Lorca (1899–1936) in words for solo voice and diverse instruments. These vocal pieces owe much to the style and innovative treatment of voice of Luciano Berio, as was seen in Chapter 13, for example, in Berio's *Circles*. But while Berio's pictures in sound symbolize the flux of human emotions, Crumb's tend to dwell upon dark subjects and the stark elemental images evoked by Lorca's poetry.

Crumb's *Black Angels* (1970) is for a string quartet in which each instrument is amplified and reverberated to produce a surrealistic aura. The four instrumentalists also play on a variety of percussion instruments, crystal glasses, and other implements. *Black Angels* was written during the years of the Vietnam War, and it expresses Crumb's belief that deviltry was then much afoot and locked in battle with godly forces. His musical treatment also suggests that these opposing elements are often combined inextricably in the same substance, epitomized by the satanic figure of the black angel. Numbers are the primary symbols of these inseparable opposites: 7 and 3 represent elements of good; 13, evil. The durational patterns that express these quantities frequently illustrate that 13 can be constituted by groups of 7s and 3s. Symbols of evil also include quotations of the chant "Dies irae," use of the tritone (the "devil in music"), and imitations of the "devil's trill" occurring in Tartini's violin sonata of the same title. Forces of good are represented by natural sounds of insects, triadic harmonies, and the ethereal tones of crystal glasses.

The quartet is divided into thirteen sections that are grouped in three parts, numbers that again show the interpenetration of good and evil. Part 1 ("Departure," sections 1 through 5) represents the descent of the soul from a state of divine grace; part 2 ("Absence," sections 6 through 9), the spiritual vacuum of the godless; and part 3 ("Return," sections 10 through 13), redemption. This arch-like shape is articulated by three sections of special importance—the first, seventh, and thirteenth—each of which is called a Threnody. Some of the sections recapitulate or "echo" earlier music.

In this work, as in Crumb's music in general, an aura of mystery is created by unusual sounds and an exotic mixture of styles and quotations. The sixth section, "Pavana lachrymae" (Anthology no. 27), quotes the theme of the slow movement of Schubert's String Quartet in D minor, which was taken by Schubert from the introduction to his song "Death and the Maiden." The music is converted into a dirge-like pavane in which the strings imitate a consort of viols. A solo violin inserts sounds of insects, thus creating a composite image of life and death.

The next section is the central Threnody, the diabolical "Black Angels!" Here evil reigns: the strings begin with superimposed tritones, and they continue with inventions upon Tartini's devil's trill. Yet the spiritual void is not entirely without hope, as the symbols of God are also in evidence. The movement occurs as the seventh in the cycle of thirteen, and the basic harmonic element—the trichord D♯–A–E—represents a conflation of thirteen semitones (D♯ to E) and seven semitones (A to E).

Berio, Penderecki, and Henze

The works of Luciano Berio are of such diversity that they fall into several major styles of postwar music. Among them is eclecticism. Berio's *Folk Songs* (1964) are in the genre of the artistic folk-song arrangement so favored earlier in the century. This collection of songs in several different languages is arranged for voice and chamber ensemble. "Black Is the Color of My True Love's Hair" (Anthology no. 16), a song in folk style written by John Jacob Niles (1892–1980), is set for voice, viola, harp, and cello. The melody is repeated virtually unchanged in its three stanzas. It is in Aeolian mode on D, and Berio imitates the irregular rhythms of a free vocal rendition of the well-known tune. The harp adds a modal accompaniment. Its first two stanzas move through a descending diatonic scale; the third stanza (rehearsal 5) finds the descending scale in the upper staff of the harp part, supported by chords drawn from the mode. The viola imitates "a wistful 'country dance fiddler.'" Its introduction to the first verse is free in rhythm and meter and plays upon the prevailing mode with twangy double stops and pungent dissonances. It accompanies the vocal stanzas without rhythmic coordination.

Berio's most important eclectic work is the third movement of his *Sinfonia* (1968, rev. 1969). The symphony, originally in four movements with a final fifth movement added in 1969, is for large orchestra and eight solo voices. Its texts consist of disconnected phrases from various sources, primarily *Le cru et le cuit* by Claude Lévi-Strauss in the first movement and Samuel Beckett's *The Unnamable* in the third movement. The second movement, "O King," is a tribute to Martin Luther King in which the words consist solely of sounds from King's name, which gradually become perceptible as such.

The third movement is assembled from diverse quotations. As a musical backdrop the orchestra plays a version of the entire third movement (scherzo) of Mahler's Second Symphony. Into this continuum the composer floats quotations from music that relates in different ways to the Mahler work. "The whole point of this section of *Sinfonia*," Berio writes, "[is as] a documentary on an *objet trouvé* recorded in the mind of the listener." Berio mentions eighteen different composers whom he quotes, but the most prominent are Ravel (*La Valse, Daphnis et Chloé*), Debussy (*La Mer*), Richard Strauss (waltzes from *Der Rosenkavalier*), and Stravinsky (*Rite of Spring*). The movement by Mahler chosen by Berio is of significance. This scherzo was adapted by Mahler from his own earlier song "Des Antonius von Padua Fischpredigt" for use in the Second Symphony. Berio thus carries the process of quotation into a more abstract cycle, gaining a corresponding richness of allusion.

The music of Krzysztof Penderecki (1933–   ) in the 1950s was mainly serial, but by 1960 he had followed the general European development in which serialism was replaced by other avant-garde directions. His alternative to serialism was analogous to that of Ligeti and Lutosławski in its manipulation of masses of sounds, each characterized more by its texture and volume than by particular collections of pitches or intervals. Penderecki focused with great resourcefulness upon innovations in sound, including expanded sonorities of voices and conventional instruments.

New playing techniques were often notated by a combination of conventional and graphic means.

The *St. Luke Passion* (1965) marked a turning point in Penderecki's work toward an idiom that combined in an eclectic manner composition with masses of sound and various stylistic ideas from earlier music. This lengthy and slowly paced work utilizes three mixed choruses, boys' chorus, soloists, speaker, and large orchestra. It combines free twelve-tone serialism, triadic textures, and slowly evolving masses of sound. These elements are sprinkled with quotations from chant and references to the BACH motive, the latter in homage to the passion music of J. S. Bach.

Hans Werner Henze (1926–   ) was one of the large number of European composers associated with the Darmstadt Summer Courses in the 1950s who helped to revive serial composition. Like virtually all of these musicians, he subsequently dispensed with strict serialism and developed his own distinctive language. Henze's music has maintained close stylistic contacts with the atonal idiom of the Viennese modernists—especially with Berg, whose lyrical treatment of the voice, wide and expressionistic range of emotion, and rich, triadically based dissonant harmony characterize Henze's musical language.

By the mid-1960s Henze's use of Bergian atonality was modified by a pronounced eclecticism. By this means he sought to increase the accessibility of his music in order to convey its political and social message. Most of Henze's vocal works from this time deal with the oppression of workers by political and economic establishments. An example is *Voices* (1973), a collection of twenty-two songs in various languages for soprano or tenor, orchestra, and electronics. Some of the songs ("Heimkehr" and "Gracia") adopt the styles of Schoenberg, Berg, and Webern; others parody popular music such as the cabaret song ("Recht und Billig"), the spiritual ("The Worker"), marches, and Italian serenades.

Bibliography

Olivier Messiaen surveys aspects of his early compositional style in *The Technique of My Musical Language*, trans. John Satterfield, 2 vols. (Paris, ca. 1956). Robert Sherlaw Johnson studies the music in *Messiaen* (London, 1975), and volumes of interviews with Messiaen by Antoine Goléa and Claude Samuel are recommended for the reader of French.

Paul Griffiths's *Peter Maxwell Davies* (London, 1982) surveys music by this composer through 1981, and the volume also contains interviews with Davies and Davies's own notes on selected pieces. *Peter Maxwell Davies: Studies from Two Decades* (London, 1979), ed. Stephen Pruslin, is a collection of essays on various works.

The writings of George Rochberg usually focus upon twentieth-century compositional materials and styles rather than upon his own music. "The New Image of Music," *Perspectives of New Music*, 2 (1963), for example, surveys the liberation of sound and texture in modern music in general. His liner notes to recordings of his works are good sources of information on specific pieces. Also see the interview with Rochberg in Cole Gagne and Tracy Caras, *Soundpieces* (Metuchen, N.J., and London, 1982).

George Crumb is also interviewed for *Soundpieces*. An analytic assessment of harmony in selected works by Crumb is made in Thomas R. de Dobay's "The Evolution of Harmonic Style in the Lorca Works of Crumb," *Journal of Music Theory*, 28 (1984). Writings by and about Luciano Berio are surveyed in the Bibliography to Chapter 13. Penderecki's music is studied in literature in Polish, but there are no substantial discussions in English.

·16·

RECENT MUSIC IN EUROPE AND AMERICA

The patterns of growth in music during the two decades following World War II are now relatively clear. These were years when innovation and experiment were dominant forces. Serialism was rekindled into a bright but short-lived flame, and from its ashes grew many styles planted by the avant-garde earlier in the century—among them atonality, indeterminacy, electronic music, and eclecticism. But since the mid-1960s the development of music has been neither consistent nor uniform. This period has witnessed a sporadic continuation of earlier approaches, with little consolidation into a mainstream and even less prospect for the emergence of a common practice.

In the last decade, however, a new conservativism has appeared—mainly in the United States—as an identifiable stylistic direction. It is characterized by simplified and conventional materials and intensified contact with popular music (especially rock) and with earlier styles of art music. These features are perhaps inevitable reactions against the complexities of the postwar avant-garde, and they signal the efforts of some contemporary musicians to win a larger audience. The composer Philip Glass is a proponent of this new accessibility: he dismisses Boulez and other postwar modernists as "these maniacs, these creeps, who were trying to make everyone write this crazy creepy music." Glass continues:

> There was a time when there wasn't this tremendous distance between the popular audience and concert music, and I think we're approaching that stage again. For a long while we had this very small band of practitioners of modern music who described themselves as mathematicians, doing theoretical work that would someday be understood. I don't think anyone takes that very seriously anymore. [From Robert Palmer's liner notes to *Einstein on the Beach*, CBS records, M4 38875.]

But it is still premature to judge whether Glass's assessment reflects the beginnings of a significant movement. Some further thoughts upon the future course of musical style will be found in the epilogue to this chapter.

We shall now conclude our survey of music in the twentieth century by considering four important developments in works of the last twenty years, all of which represent a measure of the new conservativism. These are minimalism, neoromanticism, theatric or multimedia music, and the interactions of serious composition with rock music. As with all of the important developments in music of this century, they are the outcome of earlier styles and of basic shaping forces that have guided the direction of music throughout the century.

Minimalism: Young, Riley, Glass, and Reich

The American tradition of experiment in music fostered a new and distinctive style in the 1960s in the works of four composers: La Monte Young (1935–), Terry Riley (1935–), Philip Glass (1937–), and Steve Reich (1936–). Their idiom, which has been widely influential since that time, is often called *minimalism*, despite the inadequacy of any single term to describe their diverse styles. The unifying features of their music include repetition and ostinato (hence "minimal" in compositional materials), diatonic melody and harmony, controlled improvisation, and extended lengths. Minimalism has proved a distinctively American phenomenon by its emphasis on sound per se, by its relationship to non-Western music and to modern visual arts, and by its links with earlier American experimentalists such as John Cage.

Minimalism was prefigured by La Monte Young in the early 1960s. Young at first wrote twelve-tone music, but his direction as a composer changed after he met Cage at Darmstadt. He followed Cage to the New School for Social Research in New York, where he produced Cage-like happenings with the multimedia group Fluxus. His works with Fluxus include fifteen *Compositions 1960*. Each consists of a verbal score: a brief written statement instructing the performer in some activity or musical gesture. Number 7 of this series, for example, shows the notes B and F♯, which are "to be held for a long time." Number 2 instructs the performer to build a fire in front of the audience; number 10, to "draw a straight line and follow it."

Young found his mature style in 1964 in *The Tortoise: His Dreams and Journeys*. This work is an open-ended situation for improvisation within certain boundaries. Prior to the performance of part of the piece (Young has given subtitles to many partial realizations), the players and singers decide which upper partials of a given fundamental pitch will be sounded. The fundamental is begun as a drone, usually played on electronic equipment, and the instrumentalists and singers then add and sustain the harmonics. With the aid of amplification, a certain resonance or color is obtained, which is the objective of the music. Rhythm is freely created as the performers enter and drop out, but melody in the traditional sense is entirely absent.

Like all of the minimalists, Young is involved with the performance of his own music. In the mid-1960s he created a group called the Theater of Eternal Music to perform his works. Ideally, this group should perform in what Young has called a Dream House—a permanent environment in which his harmonies would be ever present.

Although the music of La Monte Young is little accessible outside of live performances by his own ensemble, its concept has been influential both on his American colleagues and on certain Europeans. Karlheinz Stockhausen's *Stimmung* (1968) uses pitch resources in a similar way. This lengthy work calls for six voices to sing exclusively the fundamental B♭ and five of its upper partials. Young's music was especially influential on Terry Riley among younger American composers. Riley, who performed with Young in the 1960s, discovered in Young's music the refreshing attractiveness of consonant sonorities and a way of extending simple materials into lengthy works.

Riley at first devoted himself to long solo concerts in which he improvised on saxophone and keyboard instruments with the support of live electronic and tape equipment. His first success as a composer was *In C* (1964). This piece consists of fifty-three short figures, each having a precise rhythm and a contour based on notes of a C mode (with occasional F♯'s and B♭'s). An eighth-note pulse on the note C is established by one player, which runs throughout the composition as a point of reference for rhythm and pitch. Any number of instruments in the soprano register begin with repetitions of the first figure, moving gradually and in general coordination with the other players through the entire set of fifty-three. The listener's impression is of a mesmerizing regularity, but with subtle interactions of figures and a gradual evolution of rhythm, harmony, and color.

In later works such as *Rainbow in Curved Air* (1969) and *Poppy Nogood and the Phantom Band* (1968), Riley returns to his improvisations on saxophone and keyboard, enhanced by live electronic techniques and tape delay. These soliloquies share with *In C* the use of regular rhythmic pulse and diatonic or modal melody and harmony. The live electronic medium helps to enrich their texture and reinforce their repetitiveness, all of which ally them to the atmosphere of rock. Riley is indeed more an improvisor in a semipopular style than a composer: "I put my music down on a tiny sheet of paper," he writes, "and spend all of my time playing."

His more recent compositions, however, dispense with the aura of rock and evoke traditional Indian music instead. "Embroidery"—one of three *Songs for the Ten Voices of the Two Prophets* (1982)—is improvised on an electronic music synthesizer that imitates the sounds of the tabla and sitar. Riley adds a nasal cantillation with traditional Indian ornaments and slides between tones. The words refer to Eastern art and, obliquely, to drugs.

Indian music was an inspiration to all of the minimalists. Its customary use of drones has a clear parallel in the music of Young; its continuous repetitions of rhythmic figures or talas and improvisation within scalar types or ragas is echoed in music by Riley, Reich, and Glass.

The additive rhythmic process of Indian music was the point of departure for all of the music of Philip Glass composed after the mid-1960s. Glass's music relies upon repetition of a limited number of musical elements which are spun out in the manner of an Indian tabla player improvising upon a tala. His early works in this vein are monophonic exercises in improvised rhythms and lines. In *1+1* (1968) the player is instructed to tap on an amplified table top, improvising upon combinations of two rhythms shown in Example 16-1. These two figures are to be put together into gradually evolving patterns that Glass calls "arithmetic progressions." In Example 16-2 we see one such pattern, where five of the eighth-note values are separated by a steadily increasing number of the figure containing two sixteenths and an eighth.

Glass's more recent music is written to be performed solely by his own ensemble of amplified keyboards and woodwinds, which is sometimes expanded to include voices and strings. It is accordingly richer in texture. The opera *Satyagraha* (1979) calls for a conventional orchestra.

The six pieces in his recording "Glassworks" (CBS 37265, 1982) are exemplary in their comfortable and consonant sonorities, simple harmonic changes, and regular pacing, which banish complexities of structure or meaning. Regular rhythms, standard harmonic progressions, and high levels of amplification link his music to rock, which may in part account for the immense popularity of his concerts with a public not otherwise involved with serious music. We shall return shortly to Glass's *Einstein on the Beach*, in which his musical style is applied to modern theater.

♫♩ and ♪

Example 16-1.   Rhythmic elements in Glass's *1+1*.

Example 16-2.   Rhythmic elaborations in Glass's *1+1*.

The music of Steve Reich has undergone a more pronounced evolution than has that of Young, Riley, or Glass. His career as a composer was launched in 1964 by his experiments in *musique concrète* made from taped words and phrases. Reich at first intended to enhance the melodious nature of certain speaking voices by creating ostinatos and other such manipulations of their words, while preserving their comprehensibility. One such experiment led to his discovery of a *phase process,* which can be observed in his early tape piece *Come Out* (1966). From the words of a youth arrested in riots in Harlem, Reich selected the phrase "come out to show them," which is played repeatedly on a tape loop in two channels. One channel gradually moves ahead of the other—it comes out of "phase"—which ultimately distorts the words beyond comprehension but creates slowly changing rhythms and new melodic fragments by the interplay between channels.

Beginning with *Piano Phase* (1967), Reich transferred the phase process from the medium of tape to live instrumental music. Two pianists play a short repeated figure in unison; one player then gradually increases tempo, moving out of phase with the other pianist. Eventually the two return to a unison. A series of instrumental phase pieces followed: *Violin Phase* (1967), *Four Organs* (1970), *Phase Patterns* (1970), and *Drumming* (1971). The last of these is Reich's longest and most elaborate essay to explore the phase process.

Phase music is entirely the result of allying the initial material to a process which, when set in motion, automatically generates the form and substance of the work. It is closely analogous to a contemporary movement in the visual arts in America sometimes called "conceptual" art. "Arcs from Corners and Sides" by Sol LeWitt (1928–) is made from a minimum of materials—semicircular arcs—and a plan by which the arcs radiate from the four sides of a square. The design that results is enriched by other symmetrical patterns created by areas of varying densities of lines. These additional patterns are the unexpected result of the artist's concept.

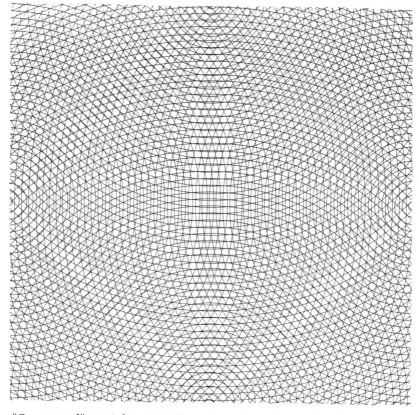

"Conceptual" art: Sol LeWitt, "Arcs from Corners and Sides." (Courtesy of the artist.)

Phase pieces by Reich contain similar "secondary" rhythms and melodic fragments. The composer refers to these as the "mysteries" of an otherwise automated idiom. "These mysteries," he writes in "Music as a Gradual Process" (1968), "are the impersonal, unintended, psycho-acoustic by-products of the intended process. These might include sub-melodies heard within repeated melodic patterns, stereophonic effects due to listener location, [or] slight irregularities in performance, harmonics, or difference tones." For these secondary patterns to be audible, the instruments or sounds must be of the same timbre, which lends Reich's music of this period a sameness of sound that he would avoid in later pieces.

Reich has reinforced the secondary rhythms and melodies in some works by instructing other players to double them—underlining them, as it were, for the audience. An example is found in a passage from *Violin Phase* illustrated in Example 16-3. In this work violins 1–3 repeatedly play the same phrase. But by the point illustrated in Example 16-3 the second violin has moved two beats ahead of violin 1; violin 3 is four beats ahead of violin 1. Among several secondary rhythms or melodic fragments that are created by this phasing differential is the recurrence of low C♯ in the rhythm shown in the lowest staff. The fourth violin may play this resultant pattern in order to reinforce its audibility.

Clapping Music (1972, Anthology no. 28) is based on the phase principle. The first performer repeats the pattern shown in measure 1 throughout the piece. The second performer begins in unison, but, while maintaining the same pattern, leaps ahead by an eighth-note value in coordination with the upper part. The second player continues to increase his lead over the first player until he has completed an entire cycle and returned to unison, whereupon the piece ends. In each measure save the first and last, different secondary rhythmic patterns will be heard.

After 1973 Reich's music took several different directions, but he has not returned to the phase processes of his earlier works. *Music for Mallet Instruments, Voices and Organ* (1973) uses other processes together with a richer texture. This piece consists of three strata: voices and organ, bells, and marimbas. The first group plays sustained chords and the last two set up rhythmically active, repeti-

m. 7

Violin 1

Violin 2

Violin 3

Violin 4
(reinforcing
secondary
rhythm)

Example 16-3.   Reich, *Violin Phase.* © 1979 by Universal Edition (London) Ltd., London. Used by permission of European American Music Distributors Corp., sole U.S. agent for Universal Edition.

tive patterns. The texture of *Music for Mallet Instruments* is further elaborated in *Tehillim* (*Psalms,* 1981). This work, a setting of four passages from Hebrew Psalms for four sopranos and orchestra, has little in common with the repetitiveness of minimalism. Its first and fourth sections use canon and repetition of larger musical units. The slow third section is less repetitive and more chromatic than diatonic. But the texture of the work is reminiscent of Reich's earlier music in its overlay of slow-moving chords and animated lines. Its continual division of beats into metric groups of twos and threes is reminiscent of the music of Stravinsky from the time of *Les noces.*

Minimalism has proved enormously influential among other American and European composers of the 1980s. In England, Gavin Bryars and Michael Nyman have allied minimalist elements to a continuation of the improvisational spirit of Cage and Cardew. Music by the Dutch composer Louis Andriessen (including *De Staat, De Tijd,* and *Hoketus*) uses minimalistic ostinatos, and Glenn Branca and Paul Dresher have fused minimalistic styles to the media of rock.

The music of John Adams (1947–   ) calls upon conventional media—orchestra, chamber ensembles, and solo piano—to realize his adaptation of minimalism. His *China Gates* for piano (1977) consists of a succession of "gates" or changes of mode, each of which punctuates a static ostinato. Each section is divided into three strata—a bass pedal point and two lines in the upper register made from repetitions of short figures. The pitch content of each gate is strictly confined to one "mode" or diatonic set.

Neoromanticism

Neoclassical composers who dominated music in Europe and America between the world wars delved into all major styles of Western music except romanticism. The nineteenth century was then still too immediate a presence in music to be imitated, especially since neoclassicism was at first a reaction against romantic illusion and rhetoric.

Furthermore, music in nineteenth-century styles was written continually until the 1940s by several outstanding composers trained in the nineteenth century, among them Richard Strauss, Alexander von Zemlinsky, and Hans Pfitzner.

But by the 1970s the romantic era had taken its place among other stylistic periods that had no continually living tradition. It thus offered the contemporary composer a new source of inspiration. Figures such as Krzysztof Penderecki and George Rochberg known for their eclectic combination of styles have increasingly focused on the romantic period. Penderecki's *Te deum laudamus* (1980), composed to honor the election of his countryman John Paul II as Pope, not only uses the harmonic and tonal vocabulary of romanticism, but it also has the breadth and massive affirmation of music of the late nineteenth century.

Neoromanticism has been an especially important trend in American music since the later 1970s. The works of David Del Tredici (1937–   ) are widely acclaimed examples. Del Tredici was trained as a concert pianist, and his early music is for the medium of keyboard. His compositions between 1959 and 1966 consist mainly of settings of the poetry of James Joyce. Since 1968 he has dwelled almost exclusively on music for soprano and orchestra inspired by Lewis Carroll's *Alice's Adventures in Wonderland* (1865) and its sequel *Through the Looking Glass* (1872). To date, these include *Pop-Pourri* (1968), *An Alice Symphony* (1969), *Adventures Underground* (1971), *Vintage Alice* (1972), *Final Alice* (1976), and *Child Alice* (1981).

The later *Alice* pieces are wholeheartedly romantic. Although they are not based on the idiom of any single nineteenth-century forebear, they reflect Mahler's diverse world of sound and sudden alternations of the mundane and the ecstatic. They also incorporate some of the sonorities of late-nineteenth- and early-twentieth-century Russian orchestral music. Del Tredici's idiom has much in common with Wagner, including a fairy-tale subject symbolizing realms of human emotion, slow pacing and substantial length, and the use of themes and motives with dramatic associations. Like Schumann, Del Tredici avails himself of musical figures or mottos with autobiographical significance, and he unifies his works by a technique of transformation of themes reminiscent of Liszt. His application of harmony and tonality is based on late-nineteenth-century techniques.

Final Alice tells of Alice's trial from the concluding chapters of *Alice's Adventures in Wonderland*, with the interpolation of related verses. The libretto is laid out as a narrative in which orchestral music, recitations, and arias alternate. The melody of the first aria recurs in Lisztian transformations, and other musical figures return as leit-motives with specific dramatic meaning. At the very end, Del Tredici adds his own musical signature; thirteen repetitions of a motto are counted by the soloist in Italian from *uno* to *tredici* (thirteen), the last number making explicit the identity of the composer.

The first part of the cycle *Child Alice* (completed in 1981) is entitled *In Memory of a Summer Day* (1980), a work for which Del Tredici won the Pulitzer Prize. Its three connected movements create a ternary shape. The first part consists of an orchestral introduction and the song "Simple Alice," the latter a strophic setting of Carroll's poem that prefaces *Through the Looking Glass.* An orchestral march and trio, "Triumphant Alice," follow as the middle part, which programmatically depict some untold fable. The concluding aria "Ecstatic Alice" recapitulates much of "Simple Alice," but in a more ebullient mood.

It was the composer's intention in this work to focus not upon the adventures of Alice, but, instead, to capture the bittersweet nostalgia of Carroll as he reflected upon the happy hours spent with the child Alice Liddell and her sisters, during which his fantastic tales were first spun. In the song "Simple Alice" we encounter Alice in the innocence with which she is recalled by Carroll. The aria "Ecstatic Alice," on the other hand, portrays Carroll's passionate love for the child Alice. Del Tredici indulges here in the hypothesis that Carroll had formed an erotic attachment to Alice Liddell. This idea—the substance of which is historically unlikely—is the composer's typically romantic statement that things are not what they seem.

Theatric Music

Musical genres that were allied to theatric arts prior to the twentieth century were limited primarily to opera and ballet. In this century there has been a great expansion in the ways that music has been combined with other dramatic forms of expression, and we shall refer to these innovative hybrid genres as *theatric* or *multimedia* music.

Traditional opera has not had the importance in this century that it experienced in earlier times. Most opera companies have chosen to base their repertories upon the more popular works of the eighteenth and nineteenth centuries rather than to risk large sums to mount untried pieces. Furthermore, the alliance of dramatic narratives to avant-garde musical styles has not been notably successful outside of atonal Expressionist opera.

The most important operatic composers after the Second World War have conservatively maintained traditional lyric textures and sonorities. The three outstanding figures of this era are Benjamin Britten, whose opera *Peter Grimes* was discussed in Chapter 10, Hans Werner Henze (see Chapter 15), and Gian Carlo Menotti (1911–). Menotti was born in Italy but has lived primarily in the United States since the 1920s. He has composed in many genres, including works for chorus, songs, ballet scores, and other instrumental music, but he is best known as a specialist in operatic composition. Menotti writes his own libretti, which usually make a direct appeal to the emotions of the audience. His themes have included social satire (*The Unicorn, the Gorgon and the Manticore*, 1956), comedy (*The Telephone*, 1947), verismo tragedy (*The Consul*, 1950), biblical stories (*Amahl and the Night Visitors*, 1951), and political criticism (*Tamu-Tamu*, 1973). These texts are set to music in a tuneful fashion. Menotti has not aimed at an innovative musical language, but, in his best works, he achieves a direct and effective dramatic style.

New modes of musical theater were evident early in the twentieth century, at least in part as reactions against the giganticism of Wagnerian music drama. Stravinsky's *L'histoire du soldat* is a fable acted out by a few players, a dancer, and a narrator with incidental music. Manuel de

Falla's *El retablo de Maese Pedro* uses puppets to present a story from Cervantes's novel *Don Quixote*. Schoenberg's *Pierrot lunaire* imitates the ambience of the German artistic cabaret: an actress in costume projects the fantasies of the clown Pierrot by recitation in the eerie "speaking voice."

Multimedia music played an especially large role after the Second World War in the experimental arts in America, where the genre took on greater abstraction than in Europe. The forefather of multimedia music in America was the resourceful Harry Partch (see Chapter 11). Beginning in the 1940s Partch composed what he termed "corporeal" works—pieces combining instrumental music, mime, costume, and recited poetry—which deal with subjects ranging from Greek mythology to human dramas of the Great Depression.

The abstract multimedia event or "happening" became fundamental to the work of John Cage after 1952. In his lecture "Composition as Process" (1958), Cage referred to the importance of visible actions in the experience that his music was intended to frame: "[My recent compositions] are occasions for experience, and this experience is not only received by the ears but by the eyes too. An ear alone is not a being. I have noticed listening to a record that my attention moves to a moving object or a play of light."

The content of Cage's theatric music of the 1950s and 1960s is largely indeterminate: *Theater Piece* (1960), for example, instructs up to eight performers to devise their own independent program of activities based upon general guidelines. *4' 33" no. 2* (1962) consists similarly of a verbal score which guides the performers in meaningless exercises in sight and sound. Cage's purpose in these works is to mirror the indeterminate appearance of a natural event, or, in his words, "produce a kind of chaos characteristic of nature."

His verbal scores were models for the Fluxus group in New York in the early 1960s. Among composers active in this movement such as La Monte Young, Takehisa Kosugi, and Nam June Paik, Cage's celebrations of nature dissolved into a comedy of the absurd. Kosugi's "Music for a Revolution"—one of a number of works of "danger music"—instructs the performer to "scoop out one of your eyes five years from now and do the same with the other eye five years later." Young's "Piano Piece for David Tudor no. 1" has the player "bring a bale of hay and a bucket of water onto the stage for the piano to eat and drink. The performer may then feed the piano or leave it to eat by itself. If the former, the piece is over after the piano has been fed. If the latter, it is over after the piano eats or decides not to."

The theater pieces of Philip Glass—*Einstein on the Beach* (1976), *Satyagraha* (1979), *Music/Theater no. 1: A Madrigal Opera* (1980), *Akhnaten* (1983), and *CIVIL warS* (1984)—represent more monumental and artistic contributions to American theatric music. These works approach the genre of opera except for their lack of dramatic narrative and traditional singing. *Einstein on the Beach* and *CIVIL warS* are collaborations with Robert Wilson, who devised their scenarios and staging. Wilson's theater is non-literary; it derives from modern dance and visual arts. His themes are often based upon the lives of great figures from the past—Einstein, Freud, Stalin, Albert Speer, Queen Victoria, Lincoln, and others who significantly reshaped the course of history. His works are not created by dialogue or narrative; they rely instead on a collage of disjunct and symbolic images.

In *Einstein on the Beach*, Wilson manipulates three images that have cryptic relevance to the life of the physicist Albert Einstein (1879–1955): a train, trial, and spaceship. Each recurs several times during the work's nine scenes, and each is supplemented by subsidiary images—a bed in the trial scene, a field connected with the spaceship, a prison associated with the trial, and a figure representing Einstein himself, who plays the violin and observes the other activities on stage. The actors also dance in two scenes and recite incongruous or illogical speeches.

Glass's music is highly structured. It consists of figures derived from a few simple harmonic progressions, which are distributed through the nine scenes in varied recurrences. Continuity is promoted by a so-called Knee Play, which connects each act and functions as a prologue and epilogue. The Knee Plays consist of related stage activities by two actors and recurrent music that derives from themes heard within the different acts.

Glass's ensemble of electric keyboard instruments and woodwinds is augmented by a solo violinist and by a choir that counts rhythmically and sings in solfège (perhaps

reflecting Glass's years of training with Nadia Boulanger).
The music is minimalistic, as it consists of repetitive ostinatos made from relatively few pitches, spun out by a
steady rhythmic motion gathered into asymmetrical meters.
The ostinato figures are entirely diatonic, and they generally outline simple harmonic progressions. They undergo
gradual changes—such as rhythmic extensions and con-
tractions—that give the music a sense of organic life. The
music does not express the poetic content of the images on
stage; in fact, it could be allied to any scenario. It is a
further abstract image which contributes to the totality of
Wilson's "living theater."

The European development of new genres of theatric
music has been more orderly and structured than the
American. Peter Maxwell Davies has been one of the most
active composers of multimedia music. His *Eight Songs for
a Mad King*—discussed in Chapter 15—dramatizes the
insanity of George III by a series of straightforward musical
and visual symbols. *Vesalii icones* is a set of fourteen
dances in which the dancer portrays images from both the
Christian stations of the cross and the anatomical drawings
of Andreas Vesalius. *Miss Donnithorne's Maggot* (1974)
returns to the spirit of the *Eight songs* in its portrayal of
the ravings of the jilted Miss Donnithorne.

Most of the works of Stockhausen since 1970 have
incorporated theatricalities. His earliest such work was
Originale (1961), his answer to Cage's *Theater Piece* of the
previous year. *Originale* is an elaboration upon Stockhausen's *Kontakte* (for tape, pianist, and percussionist),
which is performed amid the incongruous activities of a
film crew, recording technician, child playing with blocks,
newspaper salesman, and other actors. His later works of a
theatrical type include *Ylem* (1972), in which instruments
act out the movements of interstellar bodies by exploding
at the big bang of a gong and taking their places throughout
the cosmos of the auditorium. *Inori* (1974), for orchestra
and mime, is a musical and gestural realization of thirteen
attitudes of prayer from various cultures.

The Argentine composer Mauricio Kagel (1931–) has
specialized in theatrics since 1960. His *Sur scène* (1960)
places music itself—played by pianists and percussionists—
into a dramatic role. It interacts thus with a lecturer, mime,
and the commentary of a singer. The spirit of Fluxus is evi-

dent in Kagel's *Pas de cinq* (1965), which consists solely of five performers walking about the stage. *Variationen ohne Fuge* (1971–72) dramatizes borrowings among composers, perhaps as a satire upon the contemporary trend toward eclecticism. The work consists of an orchestration of passages from Brahms's Variations and Fugue on a Theme by Handel, op. 24. During the thirteenth variation, an actor impersonating Brahms enters the auditorium and sits on the conductor's podium. He subsequently delivers a monologue on Hamburg, Brahms's place of birth. As the orchestra continues with another variation, an actor representing Handel enters and sits by Brahms. The orchestra then plays Handel's theme upon which Brahms made his variations, and the two actors depart arm in arm.

Interactions with Rock

After the First World War, jazz idioms were eagerly adopted by composers of serious music in order to vivify their work. Assimilations of jazz waned in the 1930s and 1940s, but they were revived in music by the American composer Gunther Schuller (1925–   ) in the 1950s. Schuller coined the term "third stream" to designate an idiom in which jazz and concert music were combined. In works such as his *Concertino* (1959), *Conversations* (1959), and *Variants* (1960), jazz ensembles interact with orchestra or string quartet; other pieces such as his *Seven Studies on Themes of Paul Klee* (1959), Concerto for Orchestra (1965–66), or the opera *The Visitation* (1966) contain passages in which the classical orchestra plays in the style of jazz.

Popular musicians of the twentieth century have also incorporated aspects of art music. George Gershwin (1898–1937) was a pioneer in attempts to synthesize the realms of popular and serious composition, and contemporary performers such as Peter Nero and the group Emerson, Lake, and Palmer have availed themselves of the classics.

Since the mid-1960s, music of the avant-garde has been increasingly reflected in rock music. Unquestionably, the Beatles led the way to a varied style of rock that admitted musical elements from many sources. Their songs "Good Day Sunshine" and "Being for the Benefit of Mr. Kite" applied changing, asymmetrical meters, which made such pieces unsuitable to accompany dancing. The Beatles' music demanded to be heard primarily as artistic expression. They were especially resourceful in applying modern techniques of electronic and taped music. High levels of amplification and feedback produce a backdrop of noise in works such as "Tomorrow Never Knows," which helps to express a recurrent theme in their songs: the seemingly new realms opened by drugs or hallucinatory experiences. "Revolution 9" is a milestone in rock, as it merges diverse elements of speech, electronically manipulated noise and music, and spatial effects into a lengthy collage. This piece has no sung text and little that would identify it as rock rather than as serious avant-garde composition. The recurrent words "number nine" lend it a cryptic focus and meaning.

The Beatles were the first great eclectics of rock. Not only did they use styles from the avant-garde, but they also incorporated elements of earlier classical and non-Western music. Songs such as "Penny Lane" and "For No One" use obbligato solos by orchestral instruments—the piccolo trumpet and French horn, respectively—lending to these numbers a flavor of the baroque. Tunes such as "Love to You" and "Within You Without You" use media of traditional Indian music.

Since the retirement of the Beatles, no rock group has matched their innovative appropriations from the avant-garde. But the use of electronic media is still much alive in rock, ranging from predictably deafening levels of amplification to more imaginative techniques of tape delay and application of the synthesizer. Extensive electronic manipulations underlie music of Brian Eno, David Bowie, and the German group Tangerine Dream.

An increasingly widespread area in which rock musicians have benefited from serious avant-garde composition is their adoption of minimalist styles. Minimalism has a natural alliance to rock in its diatonic or modal melody, sustained pulse, and ostinato-like repetition of brief melodic fragments and harmonic progressions. The minimalists did not borrow from rock; theirs was instead an original development within the experimental tradition of

American serious music. Philip Glass has emphasized this relationship: "When you talk about concert musicians, you're talking about people who actually invent language. They create values, a value being a unit of meaning that is new and different. Pop musicians package language" (from Robert Palmer's liner notes to *Einstein on the Beach*, CBS Records, M4 38875).

Echoes of minimalism may be heard in music by many contemporary rock groups—Tangerine Dream, Talking Heads, Pink Floyd, and The Police among them. "Synchronicity" (1983) by The Police is an example. At the beginning of this song, the percussion establish a repetitive figure recalling a work by Riley or Glass. This line is then elaborated by a rock rhythm and vocal overlay.

The Talking Heads are the contemporary rock group who perhaps best represent a continuation of the eclectic spirit of the Beatles. Their work is fructified by contacts with ethnic music and the avant-garde. "I Zimbra" from the album *Fear of Music* (1979) uses African drumming and a colorful pseudo-African dialect, which is elaborated by a minimalistic ostinato. "Memories Can't Wait" from the same recording uses discordant streams of sounds to accompany its hallucinatory words.

A novel combination of rock and serious music is achieved by Laurie Anderson (1947–). Her album *Big Science* (1982) contains music from a multimedia work *United States I–IV*, in which music, recitation, and visual projections depict aspects of life in this country. The music is essentially enhanced narration, often using a device called a Vocoder by which speech sounds are modulated by other signals. Anderson has an engaging way of delivering her texts, which are accompanied by diverse types of music. Her album *Mister Heartbreak* (1984) is more abstract in its verbal message, and it relies upon sounds of the jungle in its accompaniment.

Epilogue

In his book *Music, the Arts, and Ideas* (1967), Leonard Meyer advances the hypothesis that music of the later twentieth century will remain in a "dynamic steady state" in which relatively small variations in style will be observed, but from which no strongly unified practice will emerge. The nearly twenty years that have elapsed since his prediction have apparently borne out Meyer's thesis. We seem to live in a time of pluralism of musical styles, each with its own adherents.

But will the perception of this era be altered in the future? Will coming generations see the unstable multiplicity of styles that seem now so apparent? There is a great likelihood that they will not. Contemporary music will by then have experienced a most powerful catharsis: the test of time. Works of new music may now attract attention for various reasons: an ingenious construction, a novel or engaging style, or the forceful personality and promotional work of the composer. But music endures for other reasons, even though these are intractably difficult to define. Among them no doubt are a quality of sound that captures the imagination of the sensitive listener, the composer's mastery of his language, and the substance of what he wishes to communicate.

Now in the last decades of the twentieth century, we have reached a point when we can begin to see the effects of time at work in music composed earlier in the century. Some composers who were well known in their own era are now forgotten; others endure by repeated performances of their work. Musicians today continue to study and perform, for example, the music of Arnold Schoenberg. There is a mastery and substance to it that goes deeper than a thorny surface that continues to baffle many listeners. Schoenberg's music has nonetheless endured, and it now makes a living and lasting contribution to our culture.

But regardless of what judgments will eventually be made upon the music of our own century, our task of understanding the culture in which we live is no less vital and challenging. It demands of us a broad-minded perspective, a conscientious study of its major works, a sensitivity to its shaping forces, and a curiosity about art that refuses to be quenched.

Bibliography

A survey of minimalism and of the earlier works of Riley, Reich, Young, and Glass is given by Michael Nyman in *Experimental Music: Cage and Beyond* (New York, 1974). A more up-to-date account is in Wim Mertens's *American Minimal Music*, trans. J. Hautekiet (New York, 1983). Also see the interviews with Reich and Glass in Cole Gagne and Tracy Caras, *Soundpieces: Interviews with American Composers* (Metuchen, N.J., and London, 1982), which also contains valuable lists of works by these figures. Articles on English and European minimalists are found in *Contact*, 21–23 (1980–81). Steve Reich's ideas behind his music are expressed in articles collected in his *Writings About Music* (Halifax and New York, 1974).

John Rockwell's *All-American Music: Composition in the Late Twentieth Century* (New York, 1983) contains chapters on Philip Glass, Laurie Anderson, the Talking Heads, David Del Tredici and other serious and popular American musicians. It also contains a useful bibliography. Regarding theatric music, see Richard Kostelanetz's anthology *Theatre of Mixed Means* (New York, 1968). Chapter 18 ("Beyond Modern Music") of Eric Salzman's *Twentieth-Century Music: An Introduction*, 2nd ed. (Englewood Cliffs, 1974) surveys minimalism, contemporary popular music, and musical theater.

Leonard Meyer's *Music, the Arts, and Ideas* (Chicago and London, 1967) is a collection of essays dealing with various aspects of contemporary music, including a broad discussion on the processes by which musical styles evolve and on the purpose and understanding of experimental music.

INDEX

Pages numbered in *italic* type contain musical examples; those numbered in **bold face** contain sketches of a composer's life and works.